SEVENTH EDITION

The Other World

Issues and Politics
of the Developing World

Joseph N. Weatherby

Craig Arceneaux

Emmit B. Evans, Jr.

Dianne Long
California Polytechnic State University, San Luis Obispo

Ira Reed
Trinity University, Washington, D.C.

Olga D. Novikova-Carter
Howard Payne University, Brownwood, Texas

D0027659

PEARSON
Longman

New York Boston San Francisco
London Toronto Sydney Tokyo Singapore Madrid
Mexico City Munich Paris Cape Town Hong Kong Montreal

Editor-in-Chief: Eric Stano
Senior Marketing Manager: Elizabeth Fogarty
Production Manager: Bob Ginsberg
Project Coordination, Text Design, and Electronic Page Makeup: Nesbitt Graphics, Inc.
Cover Design Manager: Wendy Ann Fredericks
Cover Designer: Base Art Co.
Cover Photos: Clockwise from top left: © Jeff Greenberg/PhotoEdit Inc.; © AP Photo/Karim
    Kadim; © Patricio Crooker/Fotosbolivia/The Image Works; and © Zheng
    Xianzhang/Panorama/The Image Works
Visual Researcher: Rona Tuccillo
Senior Manufacturing Buyer: Dennis J. Para
Printer and Binder: RR Donnelley & Sons Company/Crawfordsville
Cover Printer: Phoenix Color Corporation

Library of Congress Cataloging-in-Publication Data

The other world : issues and politics of the developing world / Joseph N.
Weatherby . . . [et al.].—7th ed.
    p. cm.
  Includes bibliographical references and index.
  ISBN 0-321-39154-3
  1. Developing countries. I. Weatherby, Joseph. II. Title.
D883.O87 2006
909′.09724—dc22
2006010208

Visit us at www.ablongman.com

ISBN 0-321-39154-3

4 5 6 7 8 9 10—DOC—09 08 07

Contents

PART II

Other World Regions

9 CENTRAL ASIA AND THE SOUTHERN
   NEAR ABROAD

CONCLUSION

Preface

*Washing one's hands of the conflict between the powerful and the
powerless means to side with the powerful.*

—PAULO FREIRE

Much of our perception of the world is from an American perspective. We tend
to focus on events in our country, those in other Western nations, and, until recently, on U.S.–Soviet relations. Yet, despite the military, political, and economic
power of the United States, we account for only 5 percent of the world's population. Clearly, most of the world exists outside of our country. Indeed, this Other
World has become crucial in understanding the larger world in which we live.

This book aims to help students grasp some of the main dimensions of contemporary global issues in the Third World, which we term the "Other World." It
is intended to present that part of our world that is considered non-Western in its
orientation. To appreciate the Other World in today's international climate, we
need to know more about its geography, culture, traditions, and political and historical development.

The Other World, Seventh Edition, is a primer on Third World issues, with an
interdisciplinary focus. We make no apology that this book is what it appears to
be: a descriptive introduction to selected world issues. It is descriptive because we
emphasize basic information on geography, culture, and political tensions in the
Other World. The book targets general education students rather than the special-
ist. Our position is that these students are better served by a book that emphasizes
specific issues, events, and places in a clear, jargon-free way, rather than by one
written for political science majors and graduate specialists.

We also hope that our analysis will be welcomed by readers who are looking
for a supplementary textbook to use in international relations, comparative government, and geography courses in which coverage of the Third World is needed.
Our point of view is that at the beginning of the twenty-first century, the focus of
world politics has shifted away from an East-West dimension to a North-South
dimension.

Two traditional approaches dominate the study of global politics: the comparative approach and the area studies approach. The former addresses the political
situation in selected countries with an emphasis on their values, institutions, levels of modernization, and types of governments. A deficiency of this method is
that it often fails to provide an overview of the geographical areas in which the
separate states are located. However, comparative studies are dominant in the social sciences because of their ability to account for similarities and differences
among political communities.

The second approach, area studies, centers on the study of geographic regions. This perspective focuses on a region's general characteristics, including geography, climate, economics, political and social structures, culture, religion, and history. Instead of contrasting the differences among states with dissimilar backgrounds, this method promotes an understanding of the peoples and countries in geographical proximity to one another.

This book combines both perspectives. First, it gives an overview of issues relevant to the understanding of contemporary problems common to the Other World. Second, it provides regional coverage of Latin America, Africa, Asia, the Southern Near Abroad, and the Middle East and then describes the similarities and differences within these regions. Third, it traces events and issues in selected countries in each region.

All of the chapters have been rewritten to take into account the effects of changing conditions as the people of the Other World enter the twenty-first century. We have attempted to keep the topics as relevant and up-to-date as possible. Time does not stand still, so we apologize in advance for any illustrations that may have become dated because of the rush of events.

NEW TO THE SEVENTH EDITION

- ◆ New Chapter 5, Latin America, written by Craig Arceneaux brings a new perspective to the study of this important region.
- ◆ Completely updated Chapter 9, Central Asia and the Southern Near Abroad, written by Olga Novikova-Carter. A native Russian, Olga brings a unique perspective about this little-known part of the world.
- ◆ Differing views on the War on Terror and the invasion of Iraq are covered in Chapters 2, 3, and 9.
- ◆ A pertinent discussion on the role of women in Central Asia appears in Chapter 9.
- ◆ Chapter 6, Sub-Saharan Africa, has been thoroughly revised by Ira Reed to include a detailed discussion of the relationship between Sub-Saharan Africa and the United States.
- ◆ The chapter on the Middle East and North Africa contains new material on the War in Iraq and the conflict between Israel and Palestine.
- ◆ Review questions, key terms, and useful Web site listings have been updated at the end of each chapter.

It is our hope that the readers of the new edition of *The Other World* will gain an understanding of the major issues that affect much of the world's population. If we are to comprehend the political turmoil in the Middle East or the food crisis in Africa, we need to be aware of the dynamics of life in those regions. Finally, we believe that issues in the Other World do not respect borders and that global interdependence will be a fact of life in the future.

All involved in this book benefited from comments made by the following reviewers:

Ahmed El-Afandi, Winona State University
Charles Blake, James Madison University
David H. Carwell, Eastern Illinois University
Robert C. Dash, Willamette University
Dorith Grant-Wisdom, University of Maryland
Obika Gray, University of Wisconsin-Eau Claire
Lyman Heine, California State University, Fresno
Waltraud Morales, University of Central Florida
Quintan Wiktorowicz, Rhodes College

We believe that this text is stronger because of the help of others:
Jane Weatherby provided aid in overcoming the technical difficulties of this project. Chelsea Lawrence and Ashley Swallow worked long hours to generate information found in many of the tables. Bobbie Jo Sims helped with proofreading and editing early drafts of the manuscript.

A special thanks to the staff at Nesbitt Graphics, Inc. for their guidance throughout the editorial and production stages. We would also like to acknowledge the help of Eric Stano and Sarah Orzalli at Longman who were indispensable in getting this text into print.

Randal Cruikshanks, Earl Huff, Reg Gooden, and Richard Kranzdorf made important contributions to the success of the fifth and the sixth editions of this text. Their earlier work provided the basis for the current chapters on Africa and Asia and the Conclusion. Without their research and support in the first four editions, the later editions of *The Other World* would have been extremely difficult, if not impossible, to write.

Our friends Earl Huff and Forrest generously loaned photographs to us from their personal collections. Because of the number of coauthors, we each have the luxury of blaming the others for whatever errors may have gone unnoticed.

JOSEPH N. WEATHERBY
CRAIG ARCENEAUX
EMMIT B. EVANS, JR.
DIANNE LONG
IRA REED
OLGA D. NOVIKOVA-CARTER

About the Authors

Joseph N. Weatherby has been a professor of political science at California Polytechnic State University since 1968. He is currently the Sandefer scholar-in-residence at the General Douglas MacArthur Academy of Howard Payne University, Texas. In 1977 he was an invited visiting scholar at Wolfson College, the University of Cambridge, England. He has been awarded a summer Fulbright to the Middle East, an NEH Fellowship in Middle East Studies at the University of Michigan, and a Joseph P. Malone Fellowship in Arab and Islamic Studies. He is the author of *The Middle East and North Africa: A Political Primer* published by Longman in 2002. At Cal Poly, he has chaired the academic senate and received the university's outstanding teaching award. He holds B.A. and M.A. degrees from Baylor University, Texas, a foreign trade degree from the American Graduate School for International Management, Arizona, and a Ph.D. in political science and Middle East studies from the University of Utah.

Craig Arceneaux is associate professor of Political Science at California Polytechnic State University, San Luis Obispo. He has been a member of the faculty since 2001. Dr. Arceneaux's teaching and research interests focus on Latin America and issues of democracy, political economy, and civil-military relations. He is the author of *Bounded Missions: Military Regimes and Democratization in the Southern Cone and Brazil* (Penn State Press, 2001), and *Transforming Latin America: International and Domestic Origins of Change* (University of Pittsburgh Press, 2005). He has published articles in *Armed Forces and Society, Bulletin of Latin American Research, Comparative Political Studies, Latin American Politics and Society,* and *Journal of Political and Military Sociology.* Dr. Arceneaux holds an M.A. in Political Science from the Ohio State University and a Ph.D. in Political Science from the University of California, Riverside.

Emmit B. Evans, Jr., has been a faculty member in the political science department at California Polytechnic State University since 1990. He has conducted research in Kenya, Mexico, and at the Scripps Institution of Oceanography, and was the executive director of a rural community development organization in the southwestern United States for 10 years. His teaching and research interests are in the areas of comparative development administration, world food politics, and contemporary global issues. He is a former Peace Corps volunteer, having served in East Africa. He earned a Ph.D. in political science from the University of California, Berkeley.

Dianne Long teaches political science and public policy at California Polytechnic State University in San Luis Obispo, California, where she has been a member of the faculty since 1982. Her teaching and research interests center on comparative public policy and administration, particularly poverty and development. A former Peace Corps volunteer in Central Africa, Dr. Long continues her writings on the nature of Third World peoples and politics. As a contributor to several chapters in *The Other World*, she brings to the text a perspective on issues affecting women and the changing nature of world governmental institutions. She holds a Ph.D. in political science from Michigan State University.

Ira Reed is Professor Emeritus at Trinity University, Washington, D.C., where he joined the political science faculty in 1983; he previously taught at Mount Vernon College and Georgetown University. He teaches primarily comparative politics courses, including introductory classes and those focusing on Africa, developing areas, Russia and East Europe, and Western Europe, as well as courses on American politics, U.S. public policy, weapons and peace, political courage, democratization, and political futures. He now serves as adjunct professor for Virginia Tech, where he teaches online graduate courses on the politics of developing areas and U.S. public policy. He has published in *The Journal of Third World Studies* and has frequently presented papers at the annual meetings of the American Political Science Association, the Third World Studies Association, the World Future Society, and other national and regional associations. He holds a B.A. in political science from Virginia Tech and a Ph.D. in government from Georgetown University.

Olga D. Novikova-Carter is a native of Odessa, Ukraine. She became a professor of political economy at Odessa State Economic University, Ukraine, USSR in 1979. Her teaching and research interests centered on socioeconomic analysis of migration, minority-related issues, and market development in countries of the former Soviet Union. Since 1991 she has combined her teaching responsibilities at Howard Payne University, in Brownwood, Texas, with responsibilities of an international business coordinator and consultant for companies and nonprofit organizations. Her responsibilities have included facilitating communication between different ethnic groups in the countries of the former Soviet Union during crisis situations and conducting training workshops for local government officials on institution building, poverty reduction, and social services. She has frequently presented papers at academic conferences and meetings. As a contributor to a chapter in *The Other World*, she brings to the text a firsthand knowledge of problems related to the transitional stage of the development of new economic and social structures in the countries of the former Soviet Union. She holds a Master of Economics degree and a Ph.D. in political economy from Odessa State Economic University, Ukraine, USSR. She serves as a coordinator of social programs for international students at Howard Payne University.

The Other World

Dianne Long

I am a citizen, not of Athens or Greece, but of the world.

SOCRATES

Socrates was a man of wide vision and understanding, a "citizen of the world" who knew about the great Babylonian, Assyrian, and Egyptian empires that had dominated "the world" long before his time. But his world included only the Mediterranean regions and the area we now call the Middle East. He would have had little awareness or knowledge of the Far East and the complex civilization of the Zhou dynasty that was in existence during his lifetime. Even if he had some fragments of information about China, it is certain that the Mayan civilization, flourishing on the other side of the world, was totally unknown to him.

Like Socrates, we have all seen the maps and globes that represent our world. But we tend to have limited perspectives based on our small knowledge of much of the world and its peoples. Many of us are not aware that the United States makes up less then 5 percent of the world's population. One-fifth of the human race is Chinese, 17 percent live in India, and hundreds of millions of others live in states that have only recently gained their independence. Almost all of the 312 million people added to the world's population since 2000 live in the developing world.[1] The developing world comprises more than two-thirds of the world's states, the vast majority of which are economically less developed and less industrialized than the Western economies.

The world of ancient Greece consisted of a small portion of what we now call Europe, Africa, and Asia, and included less than one million people. Today we know that over 6 billion people inhabit five massive continents. Sophisticated communications and complex social, economic, and political interactions increasingly link them into a "global village." These linkages bring Americans into increasing contact with those parts of the Earth about which we have little knowledge or awareness—the "Other World."

This chapter looks at Other World definitions and characteristics. The following chapters consider colonial domination, economic development, and conflict resolution. The final chapters consider the major regions and suggest important issues.

DEFINING THE OTHER WORLD

The Other World is often described as the have-not, underdeveloped, developing, less-developed, South, nonindustrialized, or Third World countries. Although political scientists, economists, and geographers do not always agree about which specific countries make up this area, the term *Other World* refers to most of the countries in Latin America, Africa, Asia, and the Middle East. These countries include more than three-quarters of the world's population, yet our daily references to them tend to include little more than sparse observations about a cultural orientation or a few generalizations about national politics.

The term *Third World* arose in the Western industrialized community, during the years when it referred to itself as the *First World* and to the Soviet republics and satellites as the *Second World*. These were the nonaligned states, neither siding with the West nor with the Soviet bloc. The term *Third World* had historically been used in reference to those states that were late to develop industry or to adopt modern economic structures. Outside of major cities, the peoples in these areas continued to have persistent and overwhelming socioeconomic problems. For the most part, the Third World countries often lacked stable political structures and had characteristically been dominated by First or Second World countries. Their currencies were unstable and not easily convertible into American dollars, British pounds, or Japanese yen. However, over the last two decades, many countries—especially China and India—have made significant progress in modernization, development of industries and international markets, and advancement in information technology. It is not uncommon to place a telephone call in the United State or Europe and find that the customer representative is sited in India or another part of this developing world.

The discussion in this text includes some developed countries that, because of location, history, or culture, are distinct. For example, Kuwait, South Africa, and Israel attract special attention because of their regional importance and relationships with powerful sponsors outside their areas.

THE CHANGING WORLD

The world today is rapidly changing. Western concepts and traditions of political systems based on competing parties dependent on popular support have been arrayed against the centralized systems of radical socialism in the Soviet sphere.

In the 1990s, however, the Soviet Union fell apart, and many of its constituent and satellite countries are remodeling themselves to fit into the Western system. At the same time, many states of Western Europe are moving even more closely together into an economic entity called the European Union. Germany reunified into a single state that includes both the Western element and the formerly Communist element and is clearly included within the European Union. Some of the countries of Eastern Europe are undergoing changes as well; however, old ethnic rivalries have emerged, resulting in conflict and bloodshed, as in the Croatia-Serb-Bosnia political crisis.[2]

Terrorism rooted in ethnic and religious beliefs has grown exponentially. The tragedy of the destruction of the World Trade Center in New York on September 11, 2001, brought home the realities of the have-not world that is unhappy about U.S. involvement in Middle East affairs. American military action in Afghanistan and Iraq in response to terrorist threats has escalated anti-Western sentiments at the same time that the U.S. seeks democratization of institutions and privatization of economies of the Middle East. Support for some nations and regimes such as Israel, and economic embargoes on others, such as Iran, have fostered hatred toward the United States and other Western powers. That hatred finds its expression in hostile acts of terrorism. The growth of Islamist terrorism revealed itself in bombing attacks of commuter trains in Madrid, Spain (2004), and London, England (2005). Hundreds of people were killed or wounded. Terrorism continues to threaten those seen as the enemy. Continued military engagement of U.S. and allied forces agitates terrorist cells worldwide.

Natural disasters, such the Tsunami in Asia in 2004, with its massive tidal wave flooding coastal communities, remind us of the fragility of the manmade environment and the challenges governments face with destruction and reconstruction. Deadly hurricanes struck the Caribbean and the U.S. Gulf of Mexico in 2004 and 2005. In Haiti alone, the death toll climbed to over 3,000. Similar statistics are expected for the hurricanes of 2005 in the gulf coastal communities. Poverty, homelessness, disease, and destruction caused by natural disasters are not isolated to one area of the world alone.

Increasingly developing states are moving toward democratization and free markets. Countries in today's world that claim to follow a democratic and capitalist model acknowledge the importance of individual rights and free markets. *Democratic* assumptions include a belief in the equality of political and economic rights possessed by all people in the society. *Capitalism* assumes private ownership of production and trade combined with a largely unrestricted marketplace based on the belief that the market is self-regulating and should be free of government intervention unless it fails. The individual is assumed to maximize self-interest, to privately own property, and to compete with others to achieve efficient production, distribution, and consumption of goods and services. The individual is important—both economically and politically. People are free to own property, start businesses, trade, and make profits with minimal government intervention.

In reality, however, markets sometimes fail. When they do, the people demand government intervention and regulation to ensure that suitable products are available at tolerable prices. In most economies that appear to be capitalist, socialist elements are present to a considerable degree.

Socialist values may also be present in both the developed and developing worlds. These values include the belief that society and markets need to be controlled by government to minimize abuses by the powerful and greedy. The society, or *collective*, holds property for "the common good," and individuals are encouraged to cooperate with one another rather than to compete against each other. In some societies, both sets of values coexist. Government may regulate the mail system, the phone system, roads and waterways, railroads and other transportation systems, health care, the education system, and other elements important to the economic life of a society. At the same time, private ownership of homes and businesses is tolerated but regulated according to community interests.

The radical form of socialism, called *Marxism*, is based on the writings of Karl Marx and Friedrich Engels, who saw human history as a struggle between the exploiting and the exploited classes. In Marxist states, the government plays a dominant role in controlling economic affairs, which produces the political system called *Communism.* Today, however, the dismantling of the Russian version of Marxism has coincided with widespread abandonment of traditional Marxism in the developing world. Communism, modified in various ways with segments of capitalist markets, still exists in North Korea, China, Cuba, and Marxist-led Eastern European states.

In reality, neither the socialist nor the capitalist model seems to produce optimal results. As a result, no economy is purely capitalist or socialist. Today, mixed economies prevail. In such economies, there are places where government intervention is appropriate. For example, government is often responsible for national defense and providing services to victims of poverty, but private firms provide consumer goods and services. Mixed economic systems require political frameworks that not only encourage markets to develop but also allow regulation when markets fail. They provide opportunities for, as well as safeguards against, private individuals and groups that control communications, transportation, banking, and other vital parts of the political economy.

As ideologies blur and international agreements bring industrial states closer, it is difficult to predict the political and economic changes that will occur. The evolution into a global economy causes changes in the power relationships. These changes may lead to increasing international conflict as nations form regional trading blocs driven by the pursuit of profit rather than by political ideology. Control of labor and raw materials may become the principal source of conflict in the post–cold war era as First World nations and trading blocs compete with one another, and as developing nations and masses attempt to resist increasing domination. The 1991 Persian Gulf War indicated the kind of conflict that may characterize the New World order. The Iraqi attempt to establish strong leadership of the Arab world by its invasion of Kuwait threatened the supply of oil to, and therefore the economic stability of, the United States, the European Union, and Japan. It appears that the Soviet Union acted to protect Iraqi interests in the cold war.

In response, the United States was able to persuade the Soviet Union, and most members of the United Nations (UN), to accept using massive military force to end Iraq's occupation of Kuwait.[3] In 2002, the U.S. initiated military action in Afghanistan, and in 2003, the U.S initiated military action in Iraq. The U.S. saw itself as an international cop using a preemptive strike foreign policy to crack down on terrorist activity and rumored weapons production. Many powerful nations, including France and Germany, opposed such action, noting that the United Nations should police states for international law infractions, not the U.S. In the aftermath of toppling the leaderships in both Afghanistan and Iraq, the task of rebuilding continues to be challenged by terrorists, ethnic rivalries, failing infrastructures, and staggering socioeconomic inequalities.

UNDERSTANDING THE OTHER WORLD

Consideration of economics, technology, and political structures is important when trying to understand the world's peoples. Geography is also a significant factor. The view of the earth from the first *Apollo* spacecraft revealed it as a small marble of three colors: the blue of oceans, the brown of continents, and the changing swirls of white clouds that envelope its climates. The earth's topographical and geographical features, in continuous dynamic balance with its climates, have influenced much of the destiny of the peoples occupying these fragile lands and traversing its seas. What the *Apollo* photos do not show is the proliferation of national divisions and boundaries. They do not show sharp economic or cultural differences between areas, nor do they indicate quality of life.

This discussion of the developing Other World is descriptive and explanatory. We observe the social, political, and economic conditions in various geographic locations, and we attempt to explain events and untangle relationships among factions within states and conflicts between states. The developing world looks to the West for modernization, but seeks its own brand of political, social, and economic framework.

Modern social systems are specialized and interdependent. Much of this specialization occurred in the modern world as a result of the Industrial Revolution at the turn of the nineteenth century, when the factory and the workplace away from home became characteristic and symbolic of modern life. More complex and intricate machinery and processes were invented, driving us into a world where computers urge us to act at a faster pace. Today, the spread of technology, especially in communications and transportation, is accelerating the pace of change.

In 1945, when the UN was founded, 31 of its 51 members, or 61 percent, could have been described as developing states. Since then the UN has grown to include 191 members;[4] most new members are developing states. Their entry into the UN has shifted the balance of influence and voting power in the General Assembly from Western to non-Western dominance. For many new states, the

move from colonial status to independence was gained through political and social upheaval. However, as discussed in later chapters, ethnic and regional loyalties are still strong and impede the development of national unity in many of
these states.

Today, violent conflict prevails in 21 different locales in the world and involves millions of people. Because of these conflicts, there are almost 12 million
refugees displaced from their homelands. More than two decades after the U.S.
military withdrawal from Southeast Asia, battles still occur in the Vietnam-
Kampuchea-Laos area. Tensions also continue between India and Pakistan. The
war between Iran and Iraq during the 1980s was one of the more bitter conflicts in
recent years, taking more than 1 million lives. The Iraqi occupation and annexation of Kuwait became a global crisis. Sporadic fighting is endemic among other
countries in the Middle East, as well as in the former states of the Soviet Union. In
addition, the Afghanistan conflict has pushed people across the borders into
Pakistan where they live in holding camps in cold temperatures at near starvation.
Former Palestine and Afghanistan are principal sources of refugees (about 3 million in each country in 2003). Another principal source is Sudan (about 2.5 million
refugees).[5]

Africa is also a troubled continent, where civil strife exists in almost every
country. Diverse ethnic groups divided by language, culture, and ancient rivalries
vie for power and wealth. The crossroads of Africa, the Congo, is beset by such
chaos and bloodshed that trade routes and economies are being severely disrupted. Military conflict between Ethiopia and Somalia has continued for years,
as has the military and economic disruption in Uganda, Angola, Mozambique,
South Africa, Sudan, Somalia, and their respective neighbors. In Latin America,
struggles continue in Guatemala, El Salvador, Honduras, Peru, Chile, and
Ecuador. UNICEF, the UN agency dedicated to helping the world's young people,
held a World Summit for Children in 1990. Leaders of 70 countries addressed the
problems of children as both victims of and fighters in war, as well as the brutal
exploitation of child labor. The summit's participants reflected on the millions of
starving or undernourished children, the millions who receive no formal education, and the many forced to scratch out a living on city streets.[6]

The current situation in Afghanistan highlights the troubling circumstances of
the population. Afghanistan has occupied a favored invasion route since ancient
times. Foreign empires ruled over tribal peoples until the mid-eighteenth century.
Although the country achieved statehood since that time, Afghanistan has remained a tool of her more powerful neighbors. As an example of this, most of the
turmoil and human suffering that currently exists is the result of more than 25
years of outside interference that has totally destroyed any political legitimacy
within the country. The Afghanistan of regional warlords, each backed by a rival
neighbor, created a situation of instability in central Asia. Terrorist camps
prompted the U.S. with British assistance to bomb the country. Whether the weak
regime that has emerged in Afghanistan can eventually take its place as a contributing member of the new states in this part of the world is an unanswered
question.

CHARACTERIZING THE OTHER WORLD

The great diversity of the peoples and cultures of the Other World means that it is impossible to speak of any significant uniformity among them. The generalizations below, however, describe common features of many of these countries.

1. Dependence on Western powers
2. Delayed modernization
3. Population explosion
4. Unequal distribution of wealth

In general, the Other World faces a wide variety of significant problems. Our task in this book is to outline the major themes and give specific examples.

Dependence on Western Powers

Most Other World countries have historically been colonies of major Western powers. Their economic, educational, religious, and political systems are now heavily influenced or dominated by their histories and resulting patterns of *neo-colonialism* or indirect control over one country by another. Although nominally independent, emerging countries usually maintain economic and political ties with their former colonial masters, preserving many of the established patterns of commerce, politics, and daily life. Such patterns, however, tend to perpetuate the dependence of the new nation on its former rulers. Political and economic institutions designed to extract resources from the colonies are slightly modified and carried into the post-independence era. These institutions, now occupied by indigenous politicians and business leaders, still primarily serve the interests of the industrial powers. These political and economic elites depend on First World governments and corporations for power and position. Dependency exists in varying degrees. Some are still almost completely dependent on other powers, whereas others are moving away from dependency. In the 1990s, private capital from the West flowed into emerging markets of the Other World. Western capital rose from $44 billion in 1990 to $265.7 billion in 1997.[7] Asia and Latin America, participating heavily in the ups and downs of investment, brought about upheavals in global economies, which affected the financial markets of the United States and Western nations. At the same time, massive financial flows from the West have outgrown regulatory frameworks and have caused such negative effects as increased ecological damage and threats to local cultures as their traditional values and strengths become displaced by Western consumerism.

Inflation (rising prices without corresponding increases in goods and services) creates additional hardships. Many peoples not only have low incomes but also find that inflation decreases the value of what little they have. In attempting to support and stabilize economic development, Other World governments have borrowed heavily from First World banking institutions. Latin American nations alone owe more than $500 billion to banks in the United States, Western Europe, and Japan.[8] Large debt levels constitute a risk of general economic instability for the entire world.

Delayed Modernization

Sanitation of food, water, and environment is a crucial factor in human health, but only one-third of the Other World has access to adequate sanitation. Facilities for adequate disposal of human wastes are especially inadequate in rural areas, where 2.3 billion people live. In India, for example, less than 10 percent of the population has toilets. Poor sanitation in urban areas is a serious threat to public health because bacteria, viruses, and parasites in human wastes contaminate public drinking water.[9]

Although communication linkages are growing, Other World peoples have little access to telephones, newspapers and magazines, television, and the Internet. In China, for example, only 4.5 telephone lines exist for every 100 people in comparison to 60 lines per 100 people in the United States. Cellular phones are quickly catching on worldwide as a flexible resource to a community, even with those who are illiterate. In Cambodia, over 60 percent of phone users subscribe to cellular phones. The Internet is primarily a tool in industrial countries—home to 90 percent of subscribers.[10] Internet use, however, is catching on, particularly in China and India. Some use it for telecommuting and educational services, and others for protesting human rights and environmental violations and maintaining cultural ties.

Although developing countries have been slow to industrialize, auto production in the 1990s set new records. Latin America and Asia are areas sited for new car factories, and General Motors is investing $2.2 billion in new car plants in Poland, China, Argentina, and Thailand.

Most developing states have high rates of illiteracy and a shortage of experienced and skilled teachers, technicians, managers, scientists, and engineers. Moreover, the limited number of technologists is usually isolated in a few population centers in each country. Industrialized nations have four times as many managers and technicians per capita. Some countries, such as South Korea, now have intensive training programs to assist in the development of exports and industrialization. Many other countries, however, are unable to mount such training programs. Sometimes they are unable to pay wages appropriate to certain levels of training (e.g., to physicians), so that the danger of a "brain drain" to the higher-paying rich countries always exists.

Management and technological know-how are critical to industrialization and modernization. Because of a lack of capital and appropriate technology, developing countries have difficulty installing and maintaining sanitation systems, energy systems, transportation and communication networks, national security, and government services. The potential for agricultural and industrial progress is also curtailed. Even when financial and technical aid is imported to these areas, there is often little capability to maintain systems and provide inventories of replacement parts and equipment. Technological projects depend on efficiency, punctuality, organization, centralization, and productivity, but often these values conflict with those that are culturally dominant in the developing areas of the world. Local autonomy and interdependence, individual community status, decision by consensus and traditional tribal authority, and personal cooperation are usually more highly regarded than industrialized, organizational values. This situation produces conflict within a larger traditional developing society. Also, erosion and displacement of values may bring chaos to previously stable and self-sufficient Asian, African, Middle Eastern, and Latin cultures, leading to serious social and psychological disruptions. Development raises very fundamental ethical questions about meddling in peoples' lives. One thing is certain: Once change has been introduced to a developing country, there is no going back.

Population Explosion

It took 2 million years for the world's population to reach 1 billion, but it took only 100 years to reach the second billion. Today, the world's population is exceeding 6 billion and is growing still. Each year, 90 to 100 million people are added. If the present rate continues, over 9 billion people will populate the earth by the year 2050. The greatest majority will live in the Other World, where the

Population Control: Two young girls enjoy a holiday goat cart ride in China where the population growth rate is controlled by the state. SOURCE: FORREST

population is growing at two to three times the rate of the population in the industrialized world. Some of the dramatic increases are due to better sanitary conditions and medical technology in some areas, which have led to increased infant survival and increased longevity.[11]

Birthrates and poverty are closely linked. In poverty-level cultures, families face the dilemma of needing workers but also having too many mouths to feed. In larger families, each person's share of the family resources is small. The poorer the family, the more likely the adults will find it desirable to add new family members as future caretakers and workers. Poor societies are dependent on children, adolescents, and young adults to care for the elderly and to support family unit economies. In addition, in poor families, inadequate nutrition and medical care may lead to low birth weights and infant deaths. The higher the likelihood of early death or disability, the more likely new workers must be born into families to ensure that the work gets done and there are providers for the elderly. When the fittest survive to learn traditional skills and values, and when those survivors stay in the clan and village to provide for all, including the very young and very old, the pattern of life continues. However, if young workers find it desirable to move from farms to cities, or if drought or war diminishes food supplies, life hangs on a thread for the children and the elderly left behind in rural areas. In many nations, food production has increased with improvements in farm management and crop techniques. Without an adequate infrastructure to allocate and distribute these increased supplies, more food does not necessarily mean more food on the tables for the bulk of the population.

Disease continues to reduce populations. The number of people living with human immunodeficiency virus (HIV) and acquired immune deficiency syndrome (AIDS) worldwide is estimated to be almost 40 million, with the largest number living in sub-Saharan Africa and Asia. Over 2 million are children who are believed to acquire the disease from mothers before birth or after birth through breastfeeding. As this disease continues to spread, primarily through sexual contact, governments and pharmaceutical industries argue over who will pay for costly medications.

Unequal Distribution of Wealth

The most compelling similarity among developing states is the severe poverty of most of their people, who generally live at a subsistence level. Over half of the world's population survives on an annual per capita income of $800 (U.S.) or less. Haiti, for example, is one of the most impoverished countries in the Western Hemisphere. Its per capita gross domestic product (GDP) is approximately $1,600 (U.S.). Poverty has important impacts on quality of life as well. In Haiti, almost 40 percent of the population is under 15 years of age, about 53 percent is illiterate, and life expectancy is only 50 years. By contrast, the per capita annual income in the United States is more than $37,800, 97 percent of the population is literate, and life expectancy is 75 years for men and 80 for women.[12]

The World Bank continues to study the world's poor. The World Bank's *World Development Report 2005* indicates that progress is being made toward overall economic growth in the developing world. Fewer people are falling be-low the poverty line in countries like China and Indonesia, and increases in life expectancy have occurred in the Middle East, Asia, and Latin America. These gains can be attributed to foreign aid and productive use of labor, as well as in-creased basic social services in education, health care, and family planning for the poor. Still, nearly half the world's people live on less than $2 a day, and 1.2 billion people live on $1 a day.[13] People at these levels are deemed unable to have access to adequate food, shelter, and other necessities of life. The World Bank study shows a decline by nearly one-third in the number of world poor in the last decade. Conditions in Africa, however, continue to run contrary to the worldwide decline in poverty. Africa's share of the world's poor has doubled from 16 percent to 32 percent in the last decade.[14] That continent faces intractable problems such as high population growth; weak basic economic infrastructure; and wars that have devastated Liberia, Angola, Namibia, Mozambique, Ethiopia, Somalia, and the Sudan. Over 43 percent of the population south of the Sahara lived in poverty in 2000.

THE DILEMMA OF THE OTHER WORLD

Everywhere national, cultural, and political systems are shifting in response to complex internal and external pressures and conditions. In the Other World, how-ever, change is occurring at a speed never before seen and in a context of inade-quate structures and resources, while leaders express uncertainty about develop-ment goals and management strategies for handling chaos.

When the United States became independent in 1776, the world was chang-ing, but it was changing slowly. Events happened and news spread at the speed of sailing ships and a foot's pace. As things changed, the fundamental patterns of ru-ral and city life evolved slowly. However, in the developing world, centuries of change have occurred in only 30 years or less. A person whose grandparents had never traveled more than 10 miles from their birthplace may now be on a flight to London or New York. While the father plows with oxen, a brother may be operat-ing a diesel tractor, and a sister may be learning the intricacies of world economies. Countries are being pulled rapidly in one direction or another by con-tending political, social, and economic forces over which they have little control. Deeply felt religious values and beliefs that gave stability to people's lives in the past are crumbling, to be replaced by new and alien philosophies.

During recent years, there have been attempts by the world's major financial agencies, particularly the World Bank, to help developing nations relieve persist-ent poverty and participate in world markets. Large loans have been made to such countries. These loans do not always accomplish their purposes. In some coun-tries, the money is diverted and stolen by corrupt rulers or governments. Other countries continue to be severely handicapped by their lack of technology, educa-tion, and effective leadership, or by their particular geographic circumstances. Whenever large loans have been made, economic improvement did not result.

Countries were unable to repay loans, and were further crushed by high interest costs. This dilemma is now being addressed by an increasingly concerted international action by which loans are forgiven. Help for developing nations can succeed, but there needs to be good diagnosis of the circumstances that face each nation. When a major obstacle is corrupt leadership or government, that problem must be addressed. If a nation is landlocked and mountainous, such as Bolivia, development will be difficult and transportation systems will need to be designed.

As we continue into this century, witnessing regional wars and military threats within various regions, it is difficult for the world to ignore the need for development and the impact the lack of it has on stability, world security, and international trade. New patterns of cooperation and conflict originate from the human experience and interplay with politics, geography, culture, history, economics, and human behavior.

The international community has an unprecedented agreement on the goals for reducing poverty, the eight Millennium Development goals. Created in 1990, each goal is to be reached by 2015. They are:

1. Eradicate extreme poverty and hunger
2. Achieve universal primary education
3. Promote gender equality and empowerment of women
4. Reduce child mortality
5. Improve maternal health
6. Combat HIV/AIDS, malaria, and other diseases
7. Ensure environmental sustainability
8. Develop a Global Partnerships for development

These goals are paving the way for significant action in the years to come to combat poverty and make real progress in human development.

SUMMARY

The Other World is marked by dependence on Western powers, delayed modernization, population explosion, and unequal distribution of wealth. The rapid social and economic changes have been hard on some populations. Women, minorities, and the poor suffer more than others in the sea of change as social and economic structures change. Democratization has had many promises for developing peoples, but struggles remain as old social, governmental, and economic systems change. Although improvements have been made, war, human rights violations, disease, and poverty act to disrupt the lives of many. The prevailing violence across the globe involves millions of people and displaces many from their homelands. Lack of a stable currency and extensive borrowing for creating and building infrastructure contributes further to the struggles of peoples of the developing world.

 **ISSUES FOR DISCUSSION**

1. Will the world population explosion crush us all?

Predictions about population growth have been alarming. Demographers have projected astounding growth rates for the world—particularly for the Other World. Recently, however, they lowered their estimates by 4 billion. New trends show a global stabilization with a target population of 9.4 billion people by 2050 instead of the 11.9 billion originally anticipated. What accounts for this lowered projection?

One answer is global conflict, in which thousands die annually across the troubled nations of the world. Yet another is the increased number of AIDS/HIV deaths, which are growing dramatically. Human casualties also result from changes in the earth's climate, causing natural disasters and effecting food supplies. Another answer is social change, such as family planning practices that significantly contribute to slow population growth. For example, China in the early 1970s had one of the highest population growth rates in the world. At almost 1 billion people, making up one-fifth of the world's population, China introduced stringent family-planning policies. The "later, longer, fewer" campaign of 1972, for example, focused on lowering the birthrate from six children for each woman to one. By 1979, fertility had fallen to 2.7 children, and the one-child policy led to even further reductions, especially in cities.

Social change causes disruption in other areas of life. In China, the pattern of one child in cities and two children in rural areas has caused shortages in services for the aged, because fewer young adults are available to care for their parents. In addition, preference for male children, increased longevity of the elderly population, and fragmentation of the extended family have fractured the society. Are these family-planning policies desirable?

2. Should the West intervene when abuses occur in the Other World?

It is not easy to generalize about ethnic and religious differences among peoples. Geographic and historic diversity divides people into separate and conflicting ethnic and religious groups, each with its own customs and traditions.

In some areas of the world such groups are mixed together and have managed to coexist. But some contemporary national boundaries include populations that are in long-standing conflict with each other. Also, some ethnic/religious populations live on both sides of national boundaries. Examples are seen in the Middle East. Turkey, Iraq, and Iran are contiguous, but in Turkey there is a dominant population of moderately religious

Moslems and a minority population of Kurds. The Kurds live on both sides of the border with Iraq. Kurds are Sunni Moslems, but in Iraq they are a minority in a country dominated by Arabic Shia Moslems. The Sunni Moslems have been in conflict with the Shia Moslems since the seventh century. At the other end of Iraq is Iran, which has a Persian, not Arabic, culture with a very conservative government dominated by Shia Moslems. However, in the area where Iran has a boundary with Afghanistan and Pakistan there are many Sunni Moslems. Some of these countries also contain populations of Armenians, Jews, Assyrians, and Zoroastrians straddling national borders. Each country has its own traditions and laws affecting religious belief and practice. They range from tolerant to aggressively intolerant.

Different examples are observable in India and Pakistan, which have high proportions of females. Women have little value and are regarded as financial burdens on families, who must provide wedding gifts (dowries) to shift the financial responsibility elsewhere. The murder of female babies and young wives by poisoning, burning, and neglect is frequent but officially hidden. In contrast, many Chinese villages have alarmingly few females of marriageable age because of abortions and infant deaths. In some geographic areas of India and China, ethnic cleansing of religious and ethnic minorities is systematically practiced, though rarely reported.

Among the Bedouin people of Saudi Arabia, family honor is esteemed and cultural codes are very important. The father is central to the family and society, and both young men and women are expected to obey family wishes. Marriages are arranged to protect desert wells and to cement relationships between families. Although Bedouins have moved to cities in large numbers, rather than following the nomad life of the desert as they have for centuries, traditional values have changed little. Family honor is valued, and women are excluded from modern production. This exclusion has served to trivialize women's decision-making role and minimize their influence within the society.

Since the creation of the United Nations in 1945, over 100 major international or ethnic conflicts have left 20 million dead. The United Nations was powerless to intervene because proposed interventions were vetoed in the Security Council—300 such vetoes occurred. During recent years, following the cold war, such vetoes have ceased, and demands for United Nations action have accelerated dramatically. Thus, it seems when conflicts arise, nations depend on others to intervene.

As some parts of the world clamor for global governance, there are also increasing expressions of nationalism. Other World peoples are establishing sovereignty under ethnic, religious, social, or linguistic identities. This fragmentation of the previous nation-state system causes a vacuum of international power and effectiveness, thus threatening economic and social well-being in various geographic areas. How can we protect human rights and preserve national autonomy?

3. Can poor people prosper when a wage economy is introduced?

Over one-half of the world's people exist in subsistence economies. To many, the coming of a wage economy and the elimination of subsistence are positive features of modernization. With wages, it is argued, greater possibilities exist for improving family conditions and for trade with other peoples.

As men in previously subsistent societies begin to earn cash wages, however, they do not always spend them in ways that benefit the family. They may buy alcohol or attractive merchandise. At the same time, women continue to have little access to resources. Women often are prevented from owning land, entering into contracts, or engaging in business enterprises. Over time, women's traditional contributions to family survival are discounted. Activities such as planting and harvesting crops, gathering forest products, husbanding of food supplies, crafting clothing and household products, and caring for children and elderly family members, seem to have less value than cash wages. These activities are not only discounted by wage-earning men in the family but also by government statisticians and economic experts unaccustomed to costing out women's work.

World Bank studies show deterioration in children's nutrition even though wages and purchasing power have increased through development projects. When cash crops such as coffee, bananas, tobacco, cotton, cocoa, or specialized foods are introduced, the disparity between wages and child nutrition worsens. Both men and women tend to focus on earning cash. Women work on family cash crop lands instead of in family gardens, which provide food for the table and food to sell at market. As families seek to maximize acquiring cash, the best lands are used for that purpose and only deteriorated soils are used for family gardens. Thus, women work harder, but families do not always benefit. What should be done to relieve this situation?

Review Questions

1. What are the characteristics of the Other World?
2. How have social structures changed in the Other World?
3. How has modernization changed people's lives in the Other World?

Key Terms

- **First World**—Western states, primarily the U.S. and Europe.
- **Second World**—Former states of the Soviet Union.
- **Third World**—States with limited development, primarily in the Southern Hemisphere.

* **Capitalism**—A system of private ownership of property, with little or no government intervention, with emphasis on the individual.
* **Socialism**—A system of collective ownership of property with considerable government intervention, with emphasis on the common good of all.
* **Communism**—A system with extreme government control, the most radical of which is called Marxism.
* **United Nations**—International governing body established with 51 countries in 1945 has increased to 191 countries today. Members are dedicated to reducing global conflict.
* **Modernization**—Introduction of systems for sanitation, communication, industry, transportation, management, and technology.

Useful Web Sites

World Bank site: www.worldbank.org
United Nations site: www.un.org
United Nations Development Programme site: www.undp.org
United Nations Fund for Women site: www.unifem.org
Center for Third World Organizing site: www.ctwo.org

Notes

1. *The World Almanac and Book of Facts 2005* (New York: World Almanac Books, 2005), p. 848.
2. Ibid., 525.
3. Ibid., 747–847 for descriptions of important events by country.
4. Ibid., 854-857 for a brief sketch of the UN.
5. Ibid., 850.
6. United Nations. *Human Development Report 1998* (New York: Oxford University Press, 1998), presents data on the haves and have-nots with special attention to women and children.
7. World Bank. *World Development Report 1999/2000* (Washington, D.C.: World Bank, 2000), p. 72.
8. Ibid., 81–82.
9. Ibid., 220.
10. Ibid., 266–267.
11. *World Almanac 2005* (New York: World Almanac Books, 2005), p. 458.
12. World Bank. *World Development Report 1997* (Washington, D.C.: World Bank, 1997), pp. 843–845 and *World Development Report 1999/2000* (Washington, D.C.: World Bank, 2000), pp. 250–257.
13. World Bank. *World Development Report 2005* (Washington, D.C.: World Bank, 2005), p. 31.
14. World Bank. *World Development Report 1999/2000*, pp. 236–237.

A Student Guide to Useful Reference Materials on the Other World

Most college and university libraries maintain government documents with reports on countries and the issues that concern them. Documents are available in paper form, and they are available on the World Wide Web, where governmental agencies have Web sites and newspapers have ongoing news briefs and articles covering global issues. The many reports published by the UN are invaluable, particularly the *Statistical Yearbook* and *Demographic Yearbook.* Some autonomous UN agencies that maintain data on specific issues include the World Health Organization (WHO), the Food and Agriculture Organization (FAO), the International Monetary Fund (IMF), and the International Fund for Agricultural Development (IFAD).

The *U.S. Statistical Abstract* has data on U.S. aid to foreign states, trade statistics, and other information. The State Department also publishes annually a *Status of the World's Nations.*

Several other useful sources include the *Political Handbook of the World,* Arthur S. Banks, ed. (New York: McGraw-Hill, 2005); *New State of the World Atlas,* Michael Kidron and Ronald Segal, eds. (New York: Simon & Schuster, 2005); Charles L. Lewis and Michael C. Hudson, *World Handbook of Political and Social Indicators* (New Haven, Conn.: Yale University Press, 2004); and *Student Atlas of the World Politics,* 7th edition (New York: McGraw Hill, 2005).

Also, many countries publish their own statistical abstracts on a regular basis. General information can be obtained in any quality almanac, such as *The World Almanac,* published annually by the Newspaper Enterprise Association (New York).

The Old and the New: Colonialism, Neocolonialism, and Nationalism

Joseph N. Weatherby

We the English seem, as it were, to have conquered and peopled
half the world in a fit of absence of mind.

JOHN ROBERT SEELEY, NINETEENTH-CENTURY HISTORIAN

It is easier to conquer an empire than it is to keep it.

JOSEPH CHAMBERLAIN, BRITISH COLONIAL SECRETARY

The West has been involved in colonial activity for almost six centuries. No area of the world has managed to avoid being affected completely by this experience. Places as diverse as Gibraltar and the Falkland Islands are still areas of contention.[1] The dismantling of the major colonial empires held by the Western powers has been one of the key political developments since World War II. The postwar period has witnessed the rise of both neocolonialism and nationalism as major features of the Other World. This chapter discusses Western colonialism, neocolonialism, and the Other World's reaction to those events, that is, nationalism.

COLONIALISM

Few subjects in international politics evoke as much emotional reaction as colonialism. Most people have a general idea of what the term means, but attempts to establish a definition agreeable to all are frustrating. It is unnecessary to trace its inconsistent use to determine that its meaning is in the eye of the beholder. To avoid confusion, however, some of the more important aspects of colonialism need to be described.

In earlier times, the term *colonialism* simply described a country's foreign settlements, or colonies. Writers in the complex world of the later twentieth century used *colonialism* interchangeably with the word *imperialism* to describe the extension of control by one state over another. Used in today's context, both of these terms have an anti-Western bias.

Colonialism and imperialism have slightly different meanings. Colonialism is a relationship in which a group of people located in one country is subject to the authority of the people of another country. This authority can be exercised through direct control by the dominant country, as in the most typical form of colonialism, or through indirect influence, as in neocolonialism. *Neocolonialism* is the process by which rich, powerful, developed states use economic, political, or other informal means to exert pressure on poor, less powerful, underdeveloped states. In both direct colonialism and indirect neocolonialism, the dependent community can be made up of an indigenous people, immigrants, or a combination of the two. Imperialism, however, is the act of acquiring or holding colonies or dependencies. Thus, whereas colonialism describes a relationship between the dominant and the dependent, imperialism is the process of establishing that relationship.

Fifty years ago political scientist Fredrich Schuman described imperialism this way, "In the loose usage of historians, the term often refers to any instance of a state acquiring colonies or building an empire, particularly when the lands involved are overseas and/or the peoples affected are alien in culture and race."[2]

Through the years, the terms *imperialism* and *colonialism* have evoked a wide array of emotional responses. Western countries in the last generation of the Victorian period rationalized that colonialism was a beneficial process that would help to bring a "backward" Other World into the light of the modern age. Their leaders often argued that the highest calling of society was to extend the benefits of Western civilization to its "black, brown, and yellow brothers" in the rest of the world. Bryan Moynahan states, "The essence of empire—a prodigious self confidence, and the nerve to treat other people's houses as one's own—...".[3] Sir Winston Churchill put it this way, "The act is virtuous, the exercise invigorating, and the result often extremely profitable."[4]

In addition, Westerners were certain that they were destined by history to act as the trustee for a less fortunate colonial world. It was in this spirit that President William McKinley justified the annexation of the Philippines on the grounds that the United States would bring Christianity to the islands. For many westerners, the expression *white man's burden* was both a challenge and an honor.[5]

Today, colonialism no longer implies honor. There is little doubt that the Other World considers it a disparaging word. Using this contemporary tone when speaking of the American and French experience in Vietnam, General Vo Nguyen Giap said, "The Americans were on the side of the colonialist—the American generals are not very good students of history. Dien Bien Phu paved the way for us to defeat not only the French but later the Americans and now to defend our country against the Chinese."[6]

HISTORY OF COLONIALISM

Many critics charge that colonialism is both a recent development and a result of the expansion of exclusively Western power into the less technically advanced areas of the world. If judged by its definition, it is apparent that colonialism is neither new nor exclusively Western in origin. History is full of examples of one people exercising control over another. Even the history of Western Europe has been colored by the invasions of Huns, Mongols, and Turks. Most of the world's peoples have been guilty of practicing some form of domination at some time in history.

For almost all of the last 600 years, the West has played the leading role in the colonial drama. In Western colonialism's early stages, Portugal and Spain were the major European participants. They were so powerful that in 1494 a papal settlement, the Treaty of Tordesillas, divided the colonial world between them. Under the terms of this agreement, the Portuguese had largely a free hand in Africa, Brazil, and parts of Asia, and the Spanish were free to conquer the rest of the Americas and the Pacific. Soon the colonial fever had spread to the Netherlands, England, and France, each of which carved out great empires of their own in the sixteenth and seventeenth centuries. All of these European actors converged in the Americas, in general, and the Caribbean basin in particular.[7]

Speaking romantically of this period of Christians, conquistadors, and buccaneers, William Lyle Schurz wrote,

> The conquest was a thing of superlatives and the men who took part in it were supermen. For never has sheer human will and force of personality accomplished so much through the efforts of so few on so vast a stage. The conquerors not only gave a new world to Castile, their discoveries and conquests resulted in a worldwide social and economic revolution that radically changed the whole pattern of life in Europe and its overseas dependencies.[8]

The first phase of Western colonialism ended in 1781 at Yorktown, Virginia, when American rebels won their independence from the British. At that time, many people in England and other parts of Europe believed that colonies were no longer worth the effort required to hold them. This view was confirmed by the early nineteenth-century withdrawal of the Spanish and French from many areas in Latin America.

Because of perceived needs created by the industrial revolution, colonialism evolved into a new phase during the second half of the nineteenth century.

Markets and minerals became the driving forces that led Europeans to establish new colonies throughout the Other World. During this period, many states attempted to acquire colonies. Although the old imperial powers were in the forefront of the new colonizing activities, they were soon joined by Italy, Germany, Japan, and eventually the United States.

Maps at the end of the nineteenth century showed Britain with an empire that included Hong Kong (1841) in the east, India (1661) in South Asia, and African holdings almost too vast to contemplate. France's empire included Algeria (1830), Tunisia (1881), and Indochina (1884). In the twentieth century, France would acquire Syria (1920), Lebanon (1920), and part of Morocco (1912). Although Spain lost its American empire by 1898, it still maintained modest colonial enclaves in North Africa (1470–1580), West Africa (1860), Fernando Po (1778), and Guinea (1844). Portugal's empire included the ancient enclaves of Macao (1557) and Goa (1510) along with the more profitable colonies of Angola (1484) and Mozambique (1498).

Lesser colonial powers included the Netherlands, Belgium, Germany, Italy, and the United States. The Netherlands controlled the Dutch East Indies (1610–1641). Belgium's king owned the Congo (1884) until 1908, when he ceded the territory to the people of Belgium as a colony. The Italians were established in the horn of Africa (1889) and in this century they carved out an empire in Libya (1911). The Germans held major colonies in Southwest Africa (1884), New Guinea (1884), and Tanganyika (1885) now called Tanzania. The United States acquired the Philippines, Cuba, and Puerto Rico through its victory over Spain in the Spanish-American War of 1898. In the twentieth century, the United States leased the Panama Canal Zone (1903), purchased the Virgin Islands (1916), and gained control over the Pacific Trust Territories (1947).

Although few people realized it at the time, traditional colonialism was a dying movement when the twentieth century began. Spain's day in the imperial sun was already over, and the decline of the other powers was soon to follow. As if by apology, even those colonies acquired by Western states in the early years of the century were called *protectorates,* a legal fiction, rather than *colonies.*

When the end finally came to traditional colonialism, it occurred with swift finality. Germany lost its African possessions with its defeat in World War I. Italy and Japan were forced to follow the German example at the end of World War II. In the aftermath of World War II, most of the former possessions of England, France, Belgium, the Netherlands, and the United States won their independence. The impact of independence on the Other World can best be understood if one considers that these territories included, among others, India and Pakistan (1947), the Dutch East Indies (1949), French North Africa (1956–1962), the Belgian Congo (1960), and the Philippines (1952). Today, only a few quaint anachronisms remain to remind the world of almost 600 years of Western colonial rule. Examples of these out-of-the-way places include St. Pierre and Miquelon, Madeira, St. Helena, and Aruba, which are still closely associated with France, the United Kingdom, Portugal, and the Netherlands, respectively.

As an epitaph to this period, it should be noted that the peoples subjected to colonial rule in the nineteenth century were both non-Western and nonwhite—

characteristics that were not important at the time, but have been used by contemporary critics in the Other World to present their grievances with the West in racial terms. It is interesting to note that the former Soviet Union largely escaped criticisms of this type. Even though it contained vast amounts of territory and encompassed millions of people, the Soviet empire was masked by a Marxist ideology to which many in the Other World were sympathetic. To them, the stigma of colonial racism was to be applied only to Western powers.

Since 1994, the Russian government has been involved in a "dirty war" with Islamic separatists in the breakaway republic of Chechnya. This conflict, combined with new knowledge of how the Soviet Union treated non-Russians in the past, makes it clear that the earlier Other World views of the Soviet Union and colonialism were incorrect.

MOTIVES FOR COLONIALISM

In view of the long period and large number of Western nations involved, it should not be surprising to learn that colonies were established for a variety of reasons. Many of the stated reasons for establishing colonies were only cover-ups for the real motives. Still, there must have been powerful incentives to induce nations and generations of adventurers to risk hardship and death to establish and hold colonies.

If we look back in history, we can identify at least five purpose motives that led the Western states to establish colonial empires. The participants neither simultaneously nor universally subscribed to these motives. Their importance varied depending on the Western country involved and the land selected for occupation. Any list, however, should include the following motives.

1. The crusading ideal
2. Economic incentive
3. Military motives
4. Outlets for surplus population
5. Prestige

Religious and Cultural Motives

Certainly, the desire to spread the Christian faith induced the nations of Western Europe to establish colonies in the Other World. This movement had its birth in the successful reconquest of Spain and Portugal from the Moors in 1492. It was a natural extension of this proselytizing zeal to follow the footsteps of the retreating Moors into Africa and from there to conquer a new world in the Americas. For these Iberians, the introduction of Catholicism was as important as the accumulation of resources in their early colonies. At the time when a continent's wealth was to be had in the Americas, the religious crusade was also vigorously pursued. Today, centuries after both the gold and the colonies have disappeared, Latin

America's Roman Catholic population, second in size only to Europe's, stands as a legacy to the serious purpose of the religious crusades of Spain and Portugal.

The cultural motivation was also important, affecting both the colonizers and the colonized. One has only to visit former colonies along the North African coast to see the cultural impact of the English, French, Italians, and Spanish, which has survived long after their departure. The Spanish, Portuguese, and French each believed that the highest gifts they could bestow were their language, their culture, and their religion. This cultural "gift" was part of their colonial policy until almost the end of their overseas adventure.

The special emphasis on the importation of culture meant that the indigenous culture of the colony was not considered worthy enough to be maintained. In many places, the native culture virtually died out. Modern Egyptians, referring to the French contact with their country in 1798, say with cynicism that the French were in Egypt for only three years, but if they had been allowed to stay for 15, Egyptians would "say their prayers in French." Similarly, Muammar al-Qaddafi, the leader of Libya, has ruefully remarked, "Any personal action on our part springing from our personality or from our values is cast into doubt, and we ourselves have begun to doubt. That precisely is how colonialism has affected us."[9]

Economic Motives

Religious and cultural colonialism often went hand in hand with economic colonialism. From the very beginning of the Western colonial experience, colonies were seen as a business and the aim of the colonizers was to produce a profit. The desire to become rich was certainly in the mind of almost everyone who dared to tempt fate by joining in any colonial enterprise. Colonies were always used for the profitable import and export of goods by the mother country. In the nineteenth century, economics became the spur that led to the redrawn maps of the Other World.

One might wonder if colonies were actually profitable. The answer depends on the time in history, the location, and the conditions in the colony. For example, in the latter part of the eighteenth century, the French colony of Saint Domingue, whose economy was based on a slave-powered sugar monopoly, was so lucrative that British claims to vast territories in Canada were considered for possible exchange. Today, almost 200 years after independence, the French have gone; the great plantations are no more; there is a worldwide surplus of sugar; and part of the territory—now known as Haiti—is the poorest country in the Western Hemisphere. The boom and bust of this plantation legacy was repeated in Brazil with natural rubber and in other parts of the world with cotton, tobacco, and coffee. At times, colonies held by Belgium in the Congo, the Netherlands in Indonesia; France in Indochina; and Britain in Africa, China, and India were very profitable.

It is easy to summarize some of the reasons colonies were economically desirable for their mother countries. They furnished food, minerals, and even human labor. In return, the mother country supplied the dependent territory with finished products. This arrangement, often monopolistic, gave the mother country's industries preferential trading opportunities unavailable to others. It should be remembered that economic colonialism was not exclusively a one-way street. The countries most successful with their colonies were able to strike a balance between their own desire for economic advantage and the needs of their subject peoples.

Strategic Motives

Following in the footsteps of those who carried the flag for gold and gospel were others who saw the need to protect the mother country's investments. These colonies were established to support more valuable possessions, such as the Spanish occupation of the Caribbean Islands to protect and support the mineral-rich

Nassau, Bahamas: Independent since 1973, this strategic colony was established by the British in 1729 to threaten Spanish colonies in the Caribbean. British Nassau was also used as a base for Confederate blockade-runners during the American Civil War. Lord Dunmore built Fort Fincastle in 1763 to protect Nassau from attack. SOURCE: JOE WEATHERBY

Ceuta: In Christian hands as early as 1415, this fortress town has been a Spanish possession on the coast of Morocco since 1578. The mountain above Ceuta and the Rock of Gibraltar are called the Pillars of Hercules. SOURCE: JOE WEATHERBY

colony of New Spain (Mexico). In the nineteenth century, Britain adopted a foreign policy based on the establishment of a world empire dependent on control of the seas. To be successful, the British had to establish a string of strategic colonies—including such diverse outposts as Hong Kong, Aden, Malta, Gibraltar, and the Falkland Islands—for the defense of major colonies and for refueling and repairing the fleet. The importance of strategic colonies to the survival of the British Empire was reaffirmed at the beginning of World War II, when Winston Churchill said that if the Spanish had attempted to neutralize Gibraltar he would have been forced to seize the Canary Islands to keep the sea lanes to Australia free from German U-boats.[10]

Another type of strategic colony was established to serve as a defense for the mother country itself. The British Crown's 1000-year association with the Channel Islands, located just off the French coast, has provided a first line of defense against a second Norman conquest of the home islands. In the same way, much of Spain's North African enclave empire was established to guard against a repeat of the Moorish invasion of the Spanish mainland.

Finally, some strategic colonies were established by nations pursuing a world balance of power. The value of these colonies is understandable only when analyzed in the context of the great-power politics that existed at the time they were established. For example, the nineteenth-century German occupation of the Marshall Islands and Nauru was probably motivated more by international politics than by hopes for economic gain. Certainly, the visit of the German gunboat *Panther* to Agadir in 1911 provoked Allied fears of German power that led to the Franco-Spanish partition of Morocco in 1912. In that incident, France and Britain invited Spain to occupy northern Morocco to prevent the possible establishment of a German military presence in North Africa, which might upset the balance of power in Europe. It should be clear that the importance of strategic colonies cannot be evaluated by normal standards for other colonies. They may have been costly to hold, as in the case of the Falklands, and their importance lay primarily in their ability to help maintain or safeguard other interests of the mother country.

Strategic colonies have been the most difficult to deal with in the age of decolonization. Many of them had little or no economic worth. Often they were established and settled by the mother country as territories carved out of another land. In Gibraltar, Ceuta, and the Falklands, establishing military bases also involved the expulsion of the indigenous population and resettlement by immigrants considered loyal to the imperial authorities. Today, in the face of Other World pressures for independence, it is questionable which party has the right to make the decision that determines a colony's future. Should it be determined by the territory's current residents or by the descendants of the original inhabitants? The question is more complex than it appears.

Spaniards have lived in Ceuta since the fifteenth century, Italian immigrants have inhabited Gibraltar since the beginning of the eighteenth century, and Scots have resided in the Falklands since the early nineteenth century.[11] If one accepts the notion that ancient claims to colonial lands may be pursued in opposition to the present inhabitants, it raises the specter of calls for resettlement in many areas of the world. Yet this is precisely the argument advanced by those who wish to see colonial territorial fates based on historic ties rather than current reality.

Before ending this discussion, we should not overlook those strategic enclaves where the people have no wish for separation from the mother country. One example of this type of colony is Gibraltar, which has been in British hands since it was taken from Spain almost 300 years ago. Originally maintained to protect the trade routes to British East Africa and South Asia, Gibraltar has lost its strategic purpose. With the 1997 British withdrawal from Hong Kong, the Spanish government renewed the call for a return of the 1,396-foot-high rock to Spanish rule.

As José Rodriguez-Spiteri of the Spanish foreign ministry stated in June 1997, "There are lessons to be learned from Hong Kong that could be applied to Gibraltar."[12] The Spanish then suggested a co-sovereignty agreement with the Gibraltarians retaining British ways in an autonomous Spanish state. The 27,000 Gibraltarians however, have repeatedly opposed any efforts to join Gibraltar with Spain. The British problem is that the two issues are not comparable. On the one hand, the British held 90 percent of Hong Kong on a 99-year lease. Legally, that land reverted back to China when the lease expired in 1997. Britain was forced to hand over Hong Kong at the end of the lease regardless of the views of the residents.

The case for a British Gibraltar is different: The Treaty of Utrecht in 1713 awarded Britain sovereignty over Gibraltar in perpetuity. Should territories such as Gibraltar be returned against the will of the inhabitants merely because the land is contiguous to a larger state?

The issue is complex, and postwar solutions to similar disputes are inconsistent. Usually the colonial power has attempted to arrange the best deal possible for the inhabitants before agreeing to abandon the colony. This was the case with the British withdrawal from Hong Kong. They negotiated a promise from China to let Hong Kong maintain internal autonomy for 50 years in a policy called "one China, two systems." Portugal and China then agreed to a similar arrangement regarding Macao. However, the British were willing to fight a war with Argentina in 1982 to maintain their control over the Falkland Islands. Each time the British and Spanish have attempted to reach an agreement on co-sovereignty that effort has failed because of opposition coming from Gibraltar's residents. In November 2002, Gibraltar again expressed its opposition to any union involving Spain when they voted 98.97 percent against any sovereign-sharing scheme.[13]

This dispute argued before the United Nations Special Committee on decolonization in 2005 centered around two opposing positions. Spain argued that the governing principle for Gibraltar should be historic territorial integrity of Spain. Gibraltarians countered that the most fundamental right of people in the decolonization process must be self-determination not territorial integrity. The United Nations' position established in 2004 is that, "Where there is no dispute over sovereignty, the principle of self-determination is a fundamental human right."[14]

The future is still unclear for places like Gibraltar, where the residents are not Spanish and do not wish to become Spanish. Whether Britain would go to war to defend Gibraltar as they did in the Falkland Islands is an unanswered question. It is clear that the British are prepared to do anything short of war to protect the stated interests of the residents of Gibraltar.

Finally, it should be noted that over the years many strategic colonies have developed artificial economies and large populations. If suddenly granted independence or absorbed by surrounding territories, these enclaves and their inhabitants would not be able to survive. The mother countries are often forced to maintain and support them long after the empires they were designed to protect have disappeared. Some of the Pacific and Caribbean islands are examples of this type of misfortune, and many of the flashpoints featured throughout this book illustrate the disputes that occur over their fates.

Surplus Population Motive

At different times, the argument that colonies would serve as outlets for a mother country's surplus population has been advanced to justify colonial enterprises. In the past, Britain and France sent convicts, debtors, and other undesirables to Australia and the Americas; and as late as the 1930s, the Japanese talked about relieving their population problem by sending surplus people to Manchuria. Although immigration has often been used as an argument for expansion, it is difficult to find cases in which the exportation of a surplus population was the primary motivation for establishing a colony.

It is easier to find cases in which immigration was used to justify territorial expansion—for example, the nineteenth-century territorial expansion of the United States and Russia. Some critics of Israel's past settlement policy have charged that Jewish immigration into Jerusalem and the West Bank of the

Jordan was encouraged by the government to justify the expansion of Israel's borders.

In 2005 the *Jerusalem Post* reported that the Jerusalem municipality intended to destroy a number of "illegally" constructed Arab homes in a neighborhood near old Arab east Jerusalem. The *Post* quoted Meir Margalit of the Israeli Committee Against House Demolitions as saying, "Arabs in east Jerusalem can't get building permits and especially in that area." The implication was that without permits all Arab construction in the area was considered illegal and subject to removal. At the same time, Jews apply for permits and build legally. Margalit charged that the aim of this "clearance" was to establish a band of Jewish settlements around Jerusalem, making the establishment of a future Palestinian capital in the city impossible.[15]

Prestige Motive

Probably the most enigmatic motivation for colonization was the establishment and maintenance of colonies as symbols of greatness. If one looks at the world's remaining colonies, it is evident that many are still held for the purpose of prestige. Spain continues to hold the North African enclaves of Ceuta and Melilla long after the justification for them has ended. These colonies have little economic value, and their existence weakens Spain's claims to the British-held enclave of Gibraltar. However, to Spain, these small possessions form a link to a glorious overseas tradition. For modern Spaniards, the crusading ideal, the empire, the civil war, and the tradition of military service in Africa far outweigh any political and economic liabilities that these colonies may bring.

In July 2002, a dozen Moroccan policemen were expelled from the uninhabited Mediterranean islet of Perejil located off the Moroccan coast by members of the Spanish Foreign Legion based in the enclaves. As the *Irish Times* put it, "Madrid's annoyance with the 'invasion' undermines its position on a land issue closer to home. Such a forthright response left Spain with this tricky job of justifying its presence in Morocco while at the same time insisting Britain quits Gibraltar."[16] Because of the rise of anticolonial feelings throughout the Other World, few other powers continue to maintain colonies purely for prestige, although it may partially explain the French role in Martinique and Guadeloupe and the British hold on the Falkland Islands.

THE LEGACY OF COLONIALISM

Sir Winston Churchill expressed a justification for traditional colonialism when he wrote:

> To give peace to the warring tribes, to administer justice where all was violence, to strike the chains from the slaves, to draw the richness from the soil, to plant the earliest seeds of commerce and learning, to increase in whole peoples their capacities for pleasure and diminish their chances of pain—what more beautiful or valuable reward can inspire human effort.[17]

Most of the Other World has achieved independence during the last 50 years. Because the colonizers inevitably justified their empires with the claim that they were bringing the benefits of Western civilization to a backward world, it is appropriate to assess the results of their efforts.

Government

The primary interest of the colonial powers was economic, and the quality of preparation for independence varied. In many places, the British left a class of native civil servants who were prepared to keep the machinery of government running after the British had gone. However, where the evacuation was not amicable or where the mother country's own civil servants had governed, little native expertise existed after independence. This sad state prevailed in many of the colonies of France, Belgium, and Portugal. When Belgium recognized the independence of the Congo in 1960, there were fewer than a dozen university graduates in the country. The highest position held by Patrice Lumumba, the Congolese leader, had been postmaster general.[18] Even under the best of conditions, the bureaucratic transfer from colony to independence was not easy. More often than not, coups, corruption, and dictatorships—not Western-style democracy—were the legacy of colonialism.

Education

One of the claimed benefits of colonialism was access to modern education. Since the beginning of the nineteenth century, Other World students have studied in Europe and the United States, and Western schools teaching modern science and mathematics have been established throughout the Other World. Unfortunately, the results of Western education have not met initial hopes and expectations. There have been generations of Western-trained elites who are not accepted in the West and who are viewed with suspicion in their own countries. It was said in the nineteenth century that the Ottomans sent their best young people to Paris to learn to become soldiers and engineers. Once they learned French, they read the writings of Hobbs, Locke, and Rousseau instead of artillery manuals. These young people then returned home as "Young Turk" revolutionaries dedicated to the overthrow of the Ottoman Empire. This destabilizing process has been repeated thousands of times in many countries in the last 150 years. For example, many members of the first cabinet established in Iran after the Shah was deposed in 1979 were Western-trained and held Western passports. For years, these leaders had been working from exile in Europe and America for the downfall of the Shah. Many other Western-trained elites have become anti-Western as their education has given them the perspective to see the hypocrisy of Western policies when applied to their own countries. These elites become disenchanted when they realize they would have better spent their time studying the foreign policies of Britain, France, and the United States than utopian Western philosophers. Their disillusionment with the motives of the West has been matched only by their dissatisfaction with conditions at home. Overeducated for the economy, unable to adjust to their own country, and resentful of the West, many of these educated elites have become a major source of instability in the Other World.

Economics

The economies of the Other World are invariably tied to the needs of the developed world. Agriculture in the former colonies is oriented to crops like coffee, tea, and sugar, and industry is oriented to the export of raw materials. For example, after independence from France, the Algerians found that one of their major industries was the cultivation of grapes for wine, a beverage that they were forbidden by their Moslem religion to drink. To compound the problem, the postcolonial French had developed new sources for grapes so there was little market for Algerian wine. The Algerians were forced to destroy many of their vineyards and replant with crops more suited for domestic consumption. The Algerian experience has been repeated as a sad economic fact of postcolonial life throughout much of the Other World.

Health

One of the undeniable legacies of colonialism has been the extension of modern health practices to areas in which they had not been available. Even where the healthcare needs of the impoverished still overwhelm the available clinics, the situation has improved during the past three decades. Western-initiated improvements in medical care, hygiene, and clean water have dramatically increased life expectancy everywhere in the Other World. The result is that adults are living longer and fewer infants are dying. Unfortunately, these advances have outstripped social practices geared to a more brutal age. The result is a population explosion in the Other World that threatens to destroy any chance for people to enjoy the material gains of the twenty-first century. Egypt, which only 100 years ago had no population problem, now has a growth rate that requires an increase in water storage capacity equal to the construction of a new Aswan High Dam every 10 years, just to irrigate enough land to feed its people. With no change in social policy, Other World countries, such as Egypt, are leaking lifeboats, the inhabitants bailing water but doomed ultimately to sink in a sea of humanity. In one way or another, the population explosion, brought on in part by modern health practices, threatens the future of almost every government in the Other World.

Stability

Unlike nations in the West, many states of the Other World have failed to achieve internal unity. The boundaries of most are the result of balance-of-power decisions rather than any desire by Westerners to create states containing the seeds of geographic or cultural unity. The result is a postcolonial world that has few of the economic, social, or political elements generally thought necessary to establish stable governments.

The colonial experience must be judged to have had a generally negative impact on the peoples of the Other World. Although significant material benefits have been inherited from the West, they are offset by the economic, social, and political problems that are the legacy of colonialism.

NEOCOLONIALISM

Today, the great colonial powers of the past no longer occupy the center stage of world affairs. The fate of the world is not determined by traditional colonial powers like Spain, Portugal, Holland, or Belgium. Because colonialism was a primary force in the affairs of nations for nearly six centuries, this question can now be asked: Is colonialism dead or is it merely reappearing in a new form? If traditional colonialism is the only type to be considered, it must be concluded that this era of history has probably come to a close.

The second half of the twentieth century was characterized by the arrival of almost 100 Other World states on the international scene. This rapid evolution of colonies into sovereign states led to a situation in which many former colonies fell under the influence of "new" imperial powers.

The old imperial powers laid the foundations for the Other World as it exists today. They drew the arbitrary boundaries that continue to be a source of conflict. They developed an economic system geared to the provision of needed products for the developed world. They created a leadership caste, which now perpetuates an unfair economic system that exploits the majority for the benefit of the few. The result was the creation of a new colonial system that allows one-fourth of the world to acquire the major portion of the world's resources.

Fifty years after formal independence, much of the Other World is characterized by hunger, poverty, overpopulation, political instability, and economic dependence. Most of these problems are the legacy of a colonial world that emphasized economic return to the mother country with little regard for the needs of the indigenous inhabitants. Much of the economic, cultural, political, and social institutions of the Other World still serve the interests of the developed world, which is the successor to colonial rule. The economic imbalance between rich and poor, the production of crops for export while children go hungry, and the exportation of bulk raw materials while luxury consumer items are imported are only some of the many problems of the new dependent relationships that have evolved between the developed world and the Other World. As previously stated, the leading colonial powers during the great period of Western expansion were also leaders in world politics. Since World War II, the major neocolonial states have shaped most political events. Today, the United States, Germany, and Japan play dominant roles in the economic affairs of many Other World states. These neocolonial powers and their older allies, Britain and France, are now the developed world's political leaders. In this context, traditional colonialism is dead, but neocolonialism is very much alive.

What Is Neocolonialism?

Neocolonialism differs from traditional colonialism in at least two respects. First, there is no official acknowledgment of colonial ties because the subordinate government has established legal independence. Unlike traditional colonialism, the control exerted here is indirect. Second, this influence is exercised through the interaction of the dominant nation's banking, business, cultural, and military leaders with the Other World's elites. This process results in relationships that are dependent on the wishes of the dominant power. The political, military, and economic requirements of the controlling state drive the relationship between the two entities, whereas the needs of the subordinate country are secondary. Today, the Other World has become a dumping ground for consumer goods and military hardware exported from the developed world. Often these imports must be paid for with borrowed funds, which mortgage the future for people in the Other World.

The influence exercised by a dominant power over a dependent state ranges from the activities of multinational corporations to the approval of international bank loans. In an independent world market, it is not unusual for the value of an American corporation's sales to exceed the gross domestic product (GDP) of a medium-sized state. Many Other World states are particularly vulnerable to multinational economic pressure (see Table 2.1). In this environment, externally provoked domestic economic problems lead to political instability. Other World leaders go along with a neocolonial relationship to survive.

In most cases neocolonialism is not driven by malice but by the marketplace. It is not a matter of illegal exploitation, but rather a case of the rich, through superior

Little America: Two typical street scenes in the walled American compound at Dhahran, Saudi Arabia. SOURCE: JOE WEATHERBY

TABLE 2.1   A 2005 Comparison of the Gross Sales of Seven Major American Corporations with the GDP of Selected Other World States

Corporation	Sales in $ Billions	Equals Approximate GDP
Wal-Mart	258	Morocco, Nigeria
General Motors	195	Algeria
Ford Motor Co.	164	Israel, Angola, and Jordan
IBM	89	Kenya, Kuwait, and Lebanon
American International Group (AIG)	81	Tunisia
American Electric Power	67	Sudan
Home Depot	64	Iraq

SOURCE: Adapted from *The World Almanac and Book of Facts 2005 Edition, The 21st Century World Atlas; Millennium Edition.* Gross domestic product (GDP) is defined as the market value of all goods and services that have been bought for final use during a year. The GDP covers all workers and goods employed within a nation's borders.

purchasing power, being able to influence Other World economics. This process occurs because the wealthy can outbid the poor for goods and services. The neocolonial relationship is manifested in at least four unequal associations: cultural, political, economic, and military dominance. Taken together, they constitute a degree of control exercised by the developed world that exceeds anything thought possible during the original fight for independence. For instance, it has been estimated that the nations of sub-Saharan Africa could owe as much as 68 billion dollars to international bodies including the World Bank, the International Monetary Fund, and the African Development Bank.

The developed states are just now beginning to recognize the problem. They understand that debt repayment burdens prevent the poorest of Other World countries from building hospitals, schools, and other needed infrastructure projects. The fundamental issue for donor nations is how to relieve debt while insuring new money is effectively spent without engaging in economic colonialism. In 2005, the G-8, G-7 plus Russia, donor states took steps to resolve this issue by agreeing to forgive 100 percent of the debts owed to eighteen of the world's poorest states. This relief was done using a case-by-case method based on the debtor states' efforts to make economic and social progress.[19]

Cultural Domination

Traditional imperial powers established colonies based on the assumption that their cultures were superior. The Spanish, Portuguese, and French took steps to destroy the indigenous cultures of the colonies and to replace them with a culture imported from the mother country. This policy resulted in the total destruction of many societies in the Other World. Although they took a more benign view, even the British spoke of "the lesser breeds." Colonial policies created a westernized upper class throughout the Other World. Two hundred years after independence, Latin American culture is still dominated by Spanish and Portuguese tradition. Thirty years after the French withdrawal from Tunisia, Tunisian elites still speak French. In 2002, the upper-class children of the Egyptian revolution talk of London while they play polo and croquet at the British-founded Gezira Club. These Western-oriented elites have become the transmission lines for foreign cultural domination in the Other World.

Radio, television, advertising, newspapers, magazines, books, and the Internet present a seductive message of Western cultural superiority. From Mexico City to Rabat, from Manila to Lima, young people have been conditioned to want jeans and rock music. Schools that are often patterned after systems from abroad further reinforce this cultural dominance.

In a society of scarcity, such as exists in much of the Other World, the obsession of the elites to create a native version of Western society has caused scarce resources to be diverted from the country's real needs to serve the interests of the few at the top. This practice leaves the developing nations vulnerable to other forms of neocolonial domination.

Political Domination

Much of the Other World is made up of unstable systems of artificially created states, each of which is fearful of its neighbors and therefore continually preparing for war. Thus many developing states seek the aid of other states to achieve political goals that otherwise would be impossible, making them prime candidates for outside influence.

Other World leaders need financial, technological, and military support from the developed world. To get this help, many are willing to submit to varying degrees of outside political influence. In a recent example of this kind of political pressure, in 2005, the *Hindustan Times* reported that the United States had decided to release Lockheed F-16 fighters to Pakistan as a reward for its support of the War on Terror, but, at the same time, it offered India the opportunity to replace its MIG-21 aircraft with U.S. fighters. In offering arms to both sides in a conflict, the U.S. gains influence over the leadership by making both sides dependent on American suppliers.[20] Over time, this unequal relationship undermines the popular legitimacy of the government in question, and as a consequence, it forces authorities to continue the arrangement to remain in power.

During the cold war, Western intervention in the political affairs of Other World states was rationalized as a necessity to "contain communism." In the aftermath of this struggle, foreign interventions will be more difficult to justify. In recent years there has been less emphasis on maintaining the balance of power and more concern about securing access to Other World markets, resources, and cheap labor. In the twenty-first century, these goals may be uncomfortably similar to those of the imperial powers of an earlier age.

Economic Domination

Economic neocolonialism may be pursued as the dominant country's formal policy, or it may occur subtly as the result of informal private activities. For example, whereas Western economic aid is clearly policy-driven, the activities of such great multinational powers as Ford, Standard Oil, and General Electric operate largely outside of the control of both the dominant and dependent countries. On occasion, the dominant government and private corporate policies may coincide, but this is not always the case. Such ambiguity makes the Other World charge that there is always a link between the policies of the neocolonial power and the multinational corporation, but this charge is difficult to prove. Some American corporations have used their foreign operations to frustrate their own government's policies on trade. The bottom-line strategy for multinationals is profit, not foreign policy.

The multinationals advocate free-trade policies that enable them to buy as cheaply as possible and sell for the highest price, regardless of where the market is located. They maintain that a policy of free trade will eventually result in the establishment of a system that will provide the greatest good for the greatest number of people.

No matter the intentions, people in the Other World believe that the economic impact of neocolonialism has a negative effect on their independence. In their eyes, the history of foreign trade has been the promotion of activities that work almost entirely to the advantage of the developed world. Its policy of keeping markets open to free enterprise virtually guarantees that it will continue to maintain a stranglehold on the wealth of the Other World. The rules of the game of trade have been made by the developed world and benefit the developed world. Economic neocolonialism is a legacy of this modern system of trade.

Military Domination

Much of the Other World is politically unstable. To survive in this hostile environment, the weak have had to pursue a policy of nonalignment or seek the protection of a powerful ally. After World War II, the United States and the Soviet Union courted these countries in an effort to structure a favorable balance of power. The result was the creation of military client-state relationships that involved most of the Other World. Since that time, the neocolonial powers have supplied massive amounts of sophisticated weapons to Other World countries. Weapon availability, parts, and training are all indirect methods for major powers to affect the behavior of their clients. The final outcome of the Falklands War (1982) was influenced by the U.S. spare parts embargo, which denied service to equipment supplied earlier to the Argentine Air Force. Without spare parts, the Argentineans were severely handicapped in both the size and the number of air strikes that they could mount against the British. This deficiency was one factor that ultimately helped to turn the tide of battle in favor of the British forces.

The militaries of the Other World form the life-support system for the arms business in the developed world. Arms sales have been significant sources of income and influence for the United States, the former Soviet Union, South Africa, and a number of states in Europe. Years ago, former U.S. president, Jimmy Carter expressed concerns about U.S. arms policy when he stated, "We also need to change our weapons production and weapons sales overseas as a basic foundation for jobs in this country."[21]

In the guise of offering a helping hand to friendly nations, developed states are able to tie clients to their arms industry. During the cold war, this policy allowed sophisticated military hardware to fall into the hands of Other World leaders. In many cases, balance-of-power issues took precedence over the consideration of local issues when decisions on arms sales were made. On more than one occasion, leaders of selling countries were shocked to find that client states were fighting each other in local conflicts with the weapons that were intended for use in the cold war—for example, the hostilities between India and Pakistan, and between Iran and Iraq.

The 1990 Iraqi invasion of Kuwait demonstrated the folly of indiscriminate sales of advanced military technology to the Other World. To the surprise and horror of leaders in the developed world, the Iraqis showed that their acquisition of military technology had a level of sophistication that made a military response from the developed world difficult. In the end it took a half-million troops and a war to force the modern Iraqi army to leave Kuwait.

Developed nations have found that once their most advanced military technology is in the hands of a foreign leader, they can no longer control its use in the low-intensity conflicts that occur in the Other World. The development of sophisticated arms industries geared to exports by China, Brazil, South Africa, Turkey, Israel, North Korea, and South Korea has introduced a new dimension to this problem. The end of the cold war and the "build down" of the military forces in the United States and the former Soviet Union threatens to cause a "fire sale" of surplus military hardware, further complicating the issue.

In the wake of the 1991 U.S. victory over Iraq in the Persian Gulf, American arms sales to the Other World exploded. The U.S. government was placed in the embarrassing position of condemning Russian arms sales while, at the same time, increasing sales of its own.

The Hindusian Times called attention to the hypocrisy of the American position on arms sales stating, "The United States has more weapons and military services than any other country in the world. Between 1992 and 2003, the United States sold 177.5 billion dollars in arms to foreign nations. In 2003 the Pentagon and State Department delivered or licensed the delivery of 5.7 billion dollars of weaponry.[22] It should be noted that the 2003 U.S. arms sales almost doubled the GDP of Liberia. If the proliferation of exported weapons continues, the developed world's ability to influence low-intensity conflicts will be greatly reduced.

In summary, neocolonialism, like traditional colonialism, describes a process in which one people exerts power over another people. In the case of neocolonialism, the subject people are legally independent, so the dominant power's influence is indirect. Because the practice of neocolonialism is now so widespread, it must be considered one of the two major influences on contemporary politics of the Other World. The second is nationalism.

NATIONALISM

Like modern colonialism, nationalism is largely a Western invention. With the rise of the nation-state in Europe during the eighteenth century, Europeans abandoned their traditional loyalties to clan, church, and crown.[23] No longer were political leaders successfully able to command large followings purely on the basis of divine right, family ties, or papal decrees. For the first time, Europeans started to confer legitimacy on what was to be called the nation-state. This entity would have authority over a group of people, called a nation, who believed that they had a common cultural identity. Leaders who emphasized this linkage to reinforce the legitimacy of their rule strengthened the sense of identity between the nation and state. Commonly proclaimed symbols of nationhood included racial, linguistic, religious, and historical ties that separated one people from another. In time, the nation's flag, anthem, special days, and other traditions assumed a quasi-religious character that was almost unquestioned. Like the mystics of ancient times, the modern leader who successfully captured these images was able to rule. Today, leaders wrap themselves in the national colors at every opportunity to establish legitimacy in the minds of the people. Modern nationalism represents the idea that the merger of the nation and the state creates an entity that is more than the sum of its parts. The individual's personal interests are subordinate to the interests of the nation-state. What makes the nation-state different from states of the past is the transference of the people's loyalties to the state instead of to the crown, religion, city, or clan, establishing the desired legitimacy.

Nationalism is based on the notion of exclusivity and, therefore, the superiority of one nation over another. Conversely, one of the features of nationalism is the use of fear of others to encourage unity. The "foreign devil" is one of the primary motivations for modern nationalism; that is, leaders in both the East and the West portray other leaders as foreign devils to secure popular support for their own policies. The perception of an Osama bin Laden, Abu Musab al-Zaqawi, George Bush, or Fidel Castro as a foreign devil depends on one's location.

Nationalism in the Other World is part of the legacy of colonialism. As colonial administrators, teachers, soldiers, and missionaries sought to replicate the culture of Europe, they inadvertently planted the seeds of nationalism. Students learning about Magna Carta rights, the French Revolution, and American independence could not avoid drawing parallels between their own situations and the struggles of young Westerners of another age. Nationalism appeared in the hearts and minds of Western-trained elites long before it became the mass movement that it is today. For example, Western-educated intellectuals formulated the beginning of a theory that all Arabs form a single nation. At the time, their purpose was to create unity for a common Arab struggle for independence. Similar nationalists led movements in many Other World locations during the nineteenth and twentieth centuries.

For many years the Marxist-Leninist model was seen by nationalists as an alternative to the Western approach to development, with its neocolonial implications. However, the collapse of the economy in the former Soviet Union has discredited much of this effort in the eyes of many in the Other World. There is doubt about whether the Marxist-Leninist approach will continue to have much influence.

Some nationalists sought to chart a new course between the push-pull approaches of the East and the West. For them, nonalignment was the only way for the individually weak but collectively strong states to avoid the reimposition of colonialism in a new form. During the 1950s, Nkrumah in Ghana, Sukarno in Indonesia, and Nasser in Egypt effectively used the East-West rivalry to play one side against the other. With the end of the cold war, Other World nationalists had little to bargain with when they were forced to deal with the developed nations. It is questionable whether nonalignment will be a viable policy for them to pursue in the future.

SUMMARY

After nearly 600 years, Western colonialism has come to an end, and more than 100 new nations have gained their independence. Born out of the colonial struggle for independence, these new states are engaged in the uneven process of nation building. The traditional symbols of nationalism may not be universally present. Many countries have yet to meet the criteria necessary for a state as it is recognized in the West. Admittedly, these states have artificial and often illogical boundaries and are divided by political ideology and religion. However, they have a common legacy of colonialism, which unites them. This unity is based on the development of a militant nationalism that is anticolonial, antineocolonial, and anti-Western.

If the hostility to the West is to be reduced, the Western policymakers must strive for a new fairness in dealing with the Other World. Fairness needs to be applied to policies on arms sales, trade, and banking. The present neocolonial practices carried out by the West ensure that extreme poverty will be the fate for millions of Other World people. The poor will continue to pay high prices for what they purchase from the West while being paid low wages for what they produce. The perpetuation of this unfair relationship is simply a license for the West to "strip-mine" the Other World for anything that is of value. As long as this situation persists, the West should not be surprised at the hostility, social unrest, and ethnic rivalry coming from the Other World.

ISSUES FOR DISCUSSION

1. Should the Other World be held to the same labor standards advocated in the developed world? The case for hand-tied oriental carpets and the issue of child labor are considered.

For every person living in the United States there are approximately 21 people living elsewhere. The majority of these people live at a subsistence level in the Other World. The circumstances of their existence dictate conditions

Break Time: Child rug weavers taking a break in a North African carpet factory.
SOURCE: JOE WEATHERBY

of work that often seem harsh and immoral to Westerners. Is it possible or even fair to hold the Other World states to the same labor standards that have taken 200 years to evolve in the industrialized West?

There is a saying that the wealth of a society can be measured by the age at which the young must go to work. The International Labor Organization (ILO) has estimated that, "There are 250 million economically active children world wide."[24] Their jobs include working for debt bondage, armed conflict, drug trafficking, prostitution, and slavery. Child labor also includes work involving the production of readily accepted commercial goods in the West such as the production of oriental carpets.

In oriental carpet factories stretching from Morocco across North Africa and South Asia to India and Nepal, the age of children working at the looms is young indeed. Ranging in age from four to midteens, thousands of young girls work for up to 14 hours a day in the carpet factories. Fine, hand-tied oriental carpets are produced by children because their hands are considered to be faster and they are more patient in their work than adults are.

Oriental carpets are highly praised and find a ready market in the homes and offices of the United States and Europe. Almost all of these carpets are manufactured for export. Few Westerners understand or care to hear about the pain and suffering that is involved in the production of these beautiful, expensive works of art.

The defenders of child labor in the Other World point out that carpet factories and other industries are not unlike the nineteenth-century textile mills and mines that helped to create the wealth of modern Europe and the United States. To them, these harsh conditions are a temporary but necessary part of the development process. Other World businesspeople are outraged when they hear reformers in the West calling for boycotts of their goods simply because they were produced with the help of child labor. They are quick to point out that labor reform is simply another way for the West to restrict competition in a free-market economy. Other World states compete with the only advantage that they have—the willing backs of their young. To them, the old colonial metaphor still applies: After 200 years of playing industrial poker, the West has acquired enough of the economic chips to pronounce the game immoral and demand that the Other World join in a game of contract bridge.

The dilemma for the Other World is clear. The West is attempting to impose its own moral standards on a world that has very different values. In much of the Other World, a child who helps to support a poor family by working at the wheel or the loom is considered to be a good child. In places where the only advantage that industries have over the West is low labor costs, there is no alternative to child labor if the family is to live.

This same story can be repeated in industries that manufacture products destined for Western markets, including sporting goods, textiles, and shoes. Labor organizations in the West have asserted that as many as 100 million children must work in the factories of the Other World for their families to survive.

The developed world may have seen the elimination of the worst excesses of the nineteenth-century England of Charles Dickens. Cripplers may no longer haunt the slums of Cairo looking for children to turn into the beggars described in the stories of Naquib Mahfouz. Nevertheless, harsh working conditions for children remain throughout the Other World.

Under the circumstances, should the reader boycott the carpets, textiles, sporting equipment, and shoes manufactured in the Other World because of these labor excesses? To do so could deprive millions of poor people of their only hope for a livelihood. Or should the reader assume that, as has occurred with industrialization in the West, labor conditions will improve in Other World industries as manufacturing gradually improves the standard of living?

2. Can a terrorist be a freedom fighter?

*There cannot be good and bad terrorists, our terrorists
and others . . . All those who have resorted to arms in
order to resolve political disputes, all those
organizations, all those structures and individuals who
carry out these policies should not be tolerated.*
RUSSIAN PRESIDENT VLADIMIR PUTIN[25]

*The international community cannot tolerate states
which assist and harbor terrorists and use terrorism as
an instrument of their state policy.*
FORMER INDIAN PRIME MINISTER ATAL BEHARI VAJPAYEE[26]

The United States government, in presidential Executive Order number
13224, defines terrorism as an activity that:

   a. Involves a violent act or an act dangerous to human life, property, or
      infrastructure, and
   b. Appears to be intended,
   c. Intimidates or coerces a civilian population,
   d. Influences the policy of a government by intimidation or coercion, or
   e. Affects the conduct of a government by mass destruction, assassina-
      tion, kidnapping, or hostage taking.[27]

*A terrorist group is a structured organization . . . of
more than two persons, acting in concert to commit
terrorist offenses. . . . These offenses are committed with
the aim of intimidating and seriously altering or
destroying the political, economic, or social structures
of countries.*
EUROPEAN UNION DEFINITION OF TERRORISM[28]

*We will direct every resource at our command, every
means of diplomacy, every tool of intelligence, every
instrument of war, to the destruction of the global
terror network.*
U.S. PRESIDENT GEORGE W. BUSH[29]

*Wrong a man, deny him all redress, exile him if he
complains, gag him if he cries out, strike him in the face
if he struggles, and at the last he will stab and throw
his bombs.*[30]
GEORGE KENNAN, POLITICAL ANALYST AND DIPLOMAT

Who Is the Terrorist? The Traditional View

The subject of who is a terrorist is as confusing as the preceding statements
are contradictory. Were the French, Dutch, Danish, and Norwegian resistance fighters who sought to end the World War II Nazi occupation of their
countries terrorists? Were the supporters of the Russian, Yugoslav, and
Greek partisan movements also terrorists? What about the members of the

Irish Republican Army and their opponents, the various protestant paramilitaries: Are they also terrorists?

Two old clichés still apply when labeling who is a terrorist.
One person's terrorist is another person's freedom fighter.
History tends to get written by the winners.

In the past, it could be said that terrorism was a strategy, not a movement. It was and is a strategy used by the weak against the strong. Terrorism involves the use or threat of violence against innocent people to influence political behavior. It is a strategy of conflict that involves a low risk to the perpetrators. It is inexpensive and it works. Terrorists rely on the intimidating effects of assassinations, random bombings, or airplane hijackings to accomplish their goals.

Individuals, groups, and some states use terrorism. The decision to do so is mostly the result of having no other realistic chance to affect political outcomes. In the case of the September 11 attack on the World Trade Center, an airplane hijacking became an option because the terrorists knew that after the American military victories over Iraq and Serbia they could not hope to confront the military power of the United States directly. What the terrorists hoped to do was demonstrate to the Other World the vulnerability of the United States to this kind of strategy. If one looks at the loss of life, the loss of jobs, the general economic damage, including the collapse of the travel industry, one would have to conclude that the terrorists' attack was successful.

A New Definition of Terrorism

After the September 11, 2001, terrorist attacks on the United States, President George W. Bush broadened the fight against terrorism. In a State of the Union address, he declared that as part of the war on terror, the United States was opposed to an "axis of evil" made up of Iraq, Iran, and North Korea. He drew a linkage between this axis of evil and the American effort already being waged against nonstate terror groups in the Other World. He made good on his threat to oppose these states by leading a "coalition of the willing" in a war that toppled the government of Iraq.

While the evil of the Iraqi regime cannot be denied, many people have difficulty finding a link between the axis of evil states and a more traditional view of the use of terrorism as a strategy.

In an address delivered at the National War College by James Woolsey in November 2002, he made clear what the linkage was. He stated that he agreed with Professor Eliot Cohen of Johns Hopkins in arguing that America was now fighting World War IV. If World Wars I and II were conventional wars and World War III was a cold war lasting 40 years, then World War IV was the war on terror. "What is different after September 11th is not that these . . . groups came to be at war with us. They've been at war with us for some time. It's that we finally may have noticed and have decided, in part, that we are at war with them."[31]

By viewing the war on terror as a world war, the axis of evil statement comes into clear focus. This war may have been going on since the Iranian hostage crisis of 30 years ago. It will not simply end with a short military victory over Iraq. To be successful, the war against terror will have to be fought with the same dedication, vigor, and courage that we displayed in World Wars I, II, and III.

Because the conflict is different, World War IV will not require "the collection of pots and pans, the planting of victory gardens, or even the creation of fallout shelters." However, it will require a commitment that lasts years after the red, white, and blue ribbons have faded and have been removed from houses. The new terrorists with a global reach, whether part of the axis of evil or nonstate organizations, such as Al Qaeda, can only win if Americans lose heart or grow disinterested in the effort. In many ways World War IV will be more difficult to sustain than earlier conflicts. There will be few Normandy landings or Berlin airlifts to mobilize support. This continues to be a frustrating, dirty, low-intensity conflict that may go on for years.

How Has Global Terrorism Changed Since the Fall of Baghdad?

Military defeats in Afghanistan and Iraq have combined with policy shifts in Libya to deprive global terrorist organizations of many former safe havens and have left them without the ability to maintain a centralized command structure. In response to these events, the terrorists have decentralized their movements, which exist in disaffected communities throughout the world. Using modern communications and weapons, these organizations present new threats. While using western technology, these terrorists oppose western society and values. It has been said that any spot in the Other World becomes important if the United States says it is important.

The United States and its allies have chosen to fight a major battle in the war on terror in post-invasion Iraq. This battlefield becomes a magnet attracting like-minded terrorists from all over the Moslem world. For their view of the world to prevail, they must prevent Iraq from becoming a modern, liberal, tolerant democracy.

America has chosen to fight this battle in the heart of the Arab world. If America and its allies are successful, it will cause profound change in the Middle East and North Africa, which will, in turn, have a major impact on terrorists everywhere whether they are independent or under centralized direction. It is for this reason that Iraq is a battle in the War on Terror that the United States and its allies cannot afford to lose.

Terrorism as a strategy cannot be ended. However, global terror organizations can! Other terrorist groups can be limited and, in time, contained at an acceptable level. The answer is for the established powers to actively engage the grievants in a way that will offer other opportunities for resolving conflict.

In the case of the Other World, the grievances that lead to the use of terrorism as an option lie in the colonial past, the unresponsive governments, the festering Arab/Israeli dispute, the massive ignorance, the grueling poverty, and the total lack of hope among the masses. Many of these grievances are legitimate. They produce a frustration and a seething anger among willing recruits to terrorism. A solution may be found in the developed world's serious willingness to work to resolve the injustices that cause the anger expressed by the peoples of the Other World.

Review Questions

1. Describe the differences between colonialism and neocolonialism.
2. What were some of the motivations for traditional colonialism?
3. Were there benefits to the Other World gained from Western colonialism?
4. Define imperialism.
5. Define nationalism.

Key Terms

- **Artificial states**—Former colonies whose borders provide no internal unity because they are the result of balance-of-power decisions made in Berlin, London, and Paris.
- **Colonialism**—The relationship between a group of people in one country who are subject to the authority of the people in another country.
- **Neocolonialism**—The process by which developed states use informal, indirect means to exert pressure on politically independent, less developed states.
- **Other World nationalism**—It is different from traditional nationalism because it is also anticolonial.
- **Population growth**—Caused by a combination of social practices geared to a more brutal age and modern health practices.
- **Prestige colonies**—Colonies that are created to glorify the mother country.
- **Strategic colonies**—They are used to support major colonies.
- **White man's burden**—An expression glorifying colonialism taken from an 1899 poem by Rudyard Kipling.

Useful Web Sites

The Commonwealth: www.commonwealth.org.uk
UNICEF, USA: www.unicefusa.org
United Nations Association, USA: www.unausa.org
International Court of Justice: www.icj-cij.org

Notes

1. For over 100 years, Argentina has claimed the Falkland Islands under the Spanish name Malvinas. In 1982, it fought a war with Britain for control of the island, which Britain won. Since most maps use the English name, that practice will be followed in this chapter.
2. Schuman, Frederick, *International Politics: The Western State System and the World and the World Community* (New York: McGraw-Hill Book Co., Inc., 1958), p. 307.
3. Brian Moynahan, *The British Century: A Photographic History of the Last Hundred Years* (London: Endeavor Group UK, 1997), p. 16.
4. Valerie Pakenham, *Out in the Noonday Sun: Edwardians in the Tropics* (New York: Random House, 1985), p. 10.
5. The expression "white man's burden" comes from the Rudyard Kipling poem of the same name. A verse is quoted here:

   > Take up the white man's burden
   > And reap his old reward:
   > The blame of those ye better
   > The hate of those ye guard.

   Quoted from *Who Said What When: The Chronological Dictionary of Quotations* (London: Bloomsbury Publishing Ltd., 1988), p. 200.
6. William Tuohy, "Viet Nam, A Key Battle Reverberates: Dien Bien Phu Recalled," *Los Angeles Times*, 5 May, 1984, p. 18.
7. See W. M. Will, "Power, Dependency, and Misperceptions in the Caribbean Basin," Chap. 2 in *Crescents of Conflict*, ed. W. M. Will and R. Millett (New York: Praeger, 1985).
8. William Lyle Schurz, *This New World* (New York: Dutton, 1957), p. 112.
9. See Muammar al-Qaddafi, "Third Way," in *Islam in Transition: Muslim Perspectives*, ed. John Donohue and John Esposito (New York: Oxford University Press, 1982), p. 103.
10. Winston S. Churchill, *Their Finest Hour: The Second World War* (Boston: Houghton Mifflin, 1949), p. 519.
11. Lewis M. Alexander, ed. *World Political Patterns* (Chicago: Rand McNally, 1963), p. 262.
12. Edward Owen, "Give Us Hong Kong Over Gibraltar," *The Express*, Sunday, 22 June 1997, p. 83.
13. "Rock Around the Clock: A Gibraltar Settlement Can Be Put Off, But Not Forever," *The Financial Times Ltd.*, London, 10 June 2003, Edition 2, p. 30.
14. "Petitioners Tell Decolonization Committee Sovereignty Dispute Between Spain, UK Should Not Displace the Right to Self-Determination." H. T. Media Ltd., June 7, 2005, accessed from Lexis-Nexis Academic Database.
15. Stuart Winer, "Shaky Foundations," *Jerusalem Post*, June 17, 2005, Features, p. 4.
16. Frank Sholdice, "Spain Keeps Firm Grip On Its Outpost in North Africa," *The Irish Times* (Ireland) 28 January 2003, p. 9.
17. Pakenham, p. 10
18. Daniel Papp, *Contemporary International Relations* (New York: Macmillan, 1984), p. 112.
19. "G-8 Leaders Pledge Action on Africa, Mideast," taken from the *Washington Post*, *The Dallas Morning News*, Dallas, Texas, July 9, 2005, p. 18A.
    Note: Since 1975 the heads of state or government of the major industrial powers have been meeting annually to deal with economic and political issues dealing with the international community as a whole. Today they are collectively called the G 8.

20. "U.S. Congress clears F-16 Sale to Pakistan," *The Hindustan Times*, H. T. Media, Ltd., June 10, 2005, taken from Lexis-Nexis, the Academic Universe.
21. See Jimmy Carter, *New Age Journal* (March/April 1990): 52–54, 132–134.
22. "U. S. Congress Clears F-16 Sale to Pakistan," *The Hindustan Times*, H. T. Media, Ltd., June 12, 2005, taken from Lexis-Nexis, the Academic Universe.
23. The Treaty of Westphalia (1648), which ended the Thirty Years' War in Europe, is the acknowledged beginning of the modern nation-state.
24. Roncevailles, Carina, "Weekender: Labor and Management; Campaign to Curb Child Labor," *Business World*, Business World Publishing, Manila, 7 February 2003, p. 27.
25. Clara Ferreira-Marques, "Putin Warns Against 'Double Standards' on Terrorism," Reuters Release (Moscow) 6 November 2001.
26. Ibid.
27. Executive Order 13224: Blocking property with persons who commit, threaten to commit, or support terrorism. Issued by President George W. Bush on 24 September 2001.
28. "EU Gears Up to Fight Terrorism," BBC news release (U. K.) 20 September 2001.
29. "War on Terrorism Two Months Later: The War on Six Fronts," *The Dallas Morning News*, 11 November 2001, p. 31A.
30. Lloyd Pettiford and David Harding, *Terrorism: The Undeclared War* (Wiltshire, U.K.: Selectbook Ltd., Davizes, 2004), p. 13.
31. James Woolsey, "The War on Terrorism; The Pitcairn Trust Lecture on World Affairs, Foreign Policy Research Institute, Philadelphia, 1 October 2002.

For Further Reading

Barnett, Thomas P. M. *The Pentagon's New Map: War and Peace in the Twenty-First Century.* New York: Berkley Books, 2004.
Berthon, Simon, and Robinson, Andrew. *The Shape of the World: The Mapping and Discovery of the Earth.* New York: Rand McNally, 1991.
Danzinger, James. "The Developing Countries in the Post-Cold War World." Chap. 17 in *Understanding the World: A Comparative Introduction to Political Science.* New York: Longman, 1996.
Gellner, Ernest. *Nations and Nationalism.* Ithaca, N.Y.: Cornell University Press, 1983.
Ghaliand, Gerard, and Rageau, Jean-Pierre. *Strategic Atlas: A Comparative Geopolitics of the World's Powers.* New York: Harper & Row, 1990.
Lapping, Brian. *The End of Empire.* New York: St. Martin's Press, 1985.
Payne, Richard, and Nassar, Jamal. *The Politics and Culture in the Developing World: The Impact of Globalization,* New York: Longman, 2003.
Pettiford, Lloyd and David Harding. *Terrorism: The Undeclared War.* Wiltshire, U.K.: Selectbook Ltd., Devizes, 2004.
Porch, Douglas. *The Conquest of Morocco.* New York: Alfred A. Knopf, Inc., 1982.
Poulsen, Thomas. *Nations and States: A Geographic Background to World Affairs.* Englewood Cliffs, N.J.: Prentice Hall, 1995.
Snow, Donald. *Cases in International Relations: Portraits of the Future,* New York: Longman, 2003.

Political Economy

Emmit B. Evans, Jr.

*Creating an economy that is both socially and ecologically
sustainable [is] the central challenge facing humanity as the new
millennium begins.*

CHRISTOPHER FLAVIN[1]

We whirl headlong into the twenty-first century at a pivotal time in human affairs. On the one hand, we are fast approaching global limits of social and environmental sustainability. A group of 1,670 leading world scientists recently issued a "warning to humanity" urging that we have no more than a few decades to reverse trends that are carrying us toward "spirals of environmental decline, poverty and unrest leading to social, economic and environmental collapse."[2] On the other hand, global changes eroding the power of the centralized political and economic structures that have long controlled human affairs are creating opportunities to build a new, more democratic, and sustainable world.

As described in Chapter 2, the global systems of production and distribution that have determined the contrasting lifestyles of the citizens of the industrialized West and the Other World were initiated 500 years ago. The first voyage of Columbus in 1492 marked the beginning of patterns of Western domination that have evolved through a series of stages to the globalization of today.

This chapter traces the evolution of the global political economy from mercantilism to capitalism to globalization, and explores the challenges and opportunities before us as we realize our common future with the peoples of the Other World in a rapidly evolving global society.

POLITICS, ECONOMICS, AND POLITICAL ECONOMY

Politics is commonly defined as the authoritative allocation of scarce values, or who gets what, when, and how. The political process, in other words, determines how those things people value most (such as survival, material goods, wealth, and status) are distributed among a society's, or the world's, peoples. Analysts of the political process have long noted that *power* is the primary factor that determines who gets what and when; an even more concise definition of politics is that it is simply the exercise of power. Power, in turn, is defined as the capacity to control other people's behavior.

There are three types of power: violence, knowledge, and authority. In conflict over the allocation of those things people value, violence is the most fundamental type. Most people place a high premium on avoiding pain and on survival. As Thomas Hobbes observed, when nothing else is turned up, clubs are trumps; the only appeal to violence is violence itself. However, there are limits on the use of violence to maintain political control: Coercion is expensive, violence tends to escalate, and people will not tolerate rule by violence indefinitely. To maintain their regimes over time, political elites must base their rule more on knowledge and authority.

Most political elites attempt to rule through authority, an institutionalized form of power based on the claim that government has the legitimate right to rule. However, the authority of government ultimately derives from its ability to control the forces of violence in society. *Government* is defined as the institution that has the *enforceable* right to control people's behavior. In determining the allocation of scarce values, laws are actually a form of sublimated violence through which the decisions of government are backed by the ability to enforce dictates with a court system and police and military forces.

Governments that last over time also derive much of their power from the control of knowledge. Elites use knowledge power both to control what people know and to create and manipulate images and ideologies they want people to believe. As noted by Niccolò Machiavelli, with time, the rule of lions must give way to the rule of foxes.

Analysts of the political process have long noted that self-interest is the driving force, or the engine, of government. Those with political power strive to advance their personal interests, serving broader community interests only to the extent necessary to maintain their positions of control. Closely related is the observation that power corrupts, or compels those with the power to determine who gets what to use public resources for private benefit. And absolute power corrupts absolutely.

The logic of the preceding definitions and observations carries one directly to the conclusion that all governments are *oligarchies*, or political systems controlled by a few to further their self-interests. Governments serve political elites either directly, as in communism and fascism, or indirectly through payoffs derived from serving the interests of economic elites, as in socialism and capitalism. If power determines who gets what and if power corrupts, then there is a natural human tendency for those in control of government to use its institutions and processes for personal gain.

In analyzing political and economic affairs, it is useful to think of politics and economics as closely related, interconnected processes. Before the emergence of classical liberalism from the eighteenth-century writings of John Locke and Adam Smith, politics and economics were in fact studied under the single discipline of *political economy*. The artificial separation of that study into fields of political science and economics has been in large part driven by the assertion that there is no necessary connection between politics and economics. The position is that, under a free-market system, government need only be involved in economic affairs to the extent necessary to provide for defense, protect private property rights, and supply some of the infrastructure for the economy.

Wealth and political power are inseparably linked, however. Governments are integrally involved in the economic affairs of most countries, usually serving the interests of the dominant economic group in society. In communist and fascist systems, governmental and economic institutions are formally fused, and political and economic elites are one and the same. In socialist and capitalist systems, nominal separations between governmental and economic institutions are bridged by informal networks of mutual interests between elites and by "revolving door" mechanisms through which individuals circulate back and forth between institutions. The role of political elites in free-market economies is to maintain conditions within which economic elites have the freedom to pursue their interests with a minimum of interference from other interests in society. Freedom here is the freedom to maximize profit through manipulating supply and demand and the psychology of consumer need and preference.

Pause and reflect for a moment on the fundamental connections between political and economic processes apparent in the following definitions.

POLITICS: Who gets what, when, and how
ECONOMICS: The production, distribution, and use of wealth

The perspective of political economy, which views politics and markets as "in a constant state of mutual interaction,"[3] therefore provides a useful analytical tool.

STAGES OF GLOBAL POLITICAL ECONOMY

Mercantilism

Mercantilism was based on the belief that the power and glory of a government was a direct function of the wealth of its monarchy. The goal of a mercantilist political economy was the accumulation of as much wealth in precious metals as possible. The initial voyages of global exploration financed by Spain and Portugal were essentially quests to locate new sources of gold and silver, and the conquests of Other World territories that followed created colonies to implement and maintain the mercantilist system.

Mercantilist political economy was simple and direct. The colonial powers posted governors, military forces, and administrators in the colonies of the Other World to manage and enforce the mining and transfer of precious metals from the Other World to the monarchies of the West. The first global political economy incorporated the peoples of the Other World into a global order as forced labor to produce wealth allocated to the coffers of the royal families of Europe.[4]

Capitalism

The process of industrialization brought two fundamental changes in global political economy. First, it created a new economic elite of industrial capitalists and financiers whose wealth and power grew to outstrip that of monarchs. As a new economic class of capitalists emerged with increasing power, the control of Western governments shifted from royal families to new oligarchies controlled by those with industrial and financial wealth. Second, the economic value of the colonies shifted from precious metals to the raw materials of industrial production and capitalist trade. The colonial military and administrative structures established as a part of mercantilism now served to transfer industrial raw materials and trade goods to benefit a new capitalist Western elite.

FROM COLONIALISM TO NEOCOLONIALISM AND "DEVELOPMENT"

The exploitation of Other World peoples and resources under mercantilism in the initial stages of capitalism was explicit. The Western colonial powers wanted the wealth of the Other World, and used the force of colonial control and administration to extract it. The transition from colonialism to neocolonialism described in the preceding chapter was accompanied by a seemingly new approach to Other World political economy that appeared to change an emphasis on exploitation to a new emphasis on the development of Other World countries. *Development* appeared on the international agenda with the winding down of the colonial era and the explosion of newly independent states in the late 1940s.

For many, economic development was part of the logic of political independence. Industrial economies were an integral feature of the Western states that formed the model for most of the new political entities. And for the masses caught up in the torrent of rising expectations released by the promises of independence, a higher standard of living seemed a right that had been won through the struggle for political freedom. For others, building the economies of the new states presented opportunities to establish more effective forms of domination and control through new and more subtle forms of colonialism.

Development has been a dominant feature of Other World economic, political, and social affairs for the past 60 years. Disagreements over how it should be pursued and, indeed, how the concept should even be defined have been the source of ongoing conflicts that have ranged from discussion and debate to terrorism

The Global Marketplace: Fried chicken in China, Pepsi in Qatar, and McDonald's in Saudi Arabia. SOURCE: JOE WEATHERBY

and war. It is consequently difficult to understand the contemporary Other World without an understanding of development. Toward that end, in the following pages we consider various definitions based on competing systems of values and beliefs, survey the history of development efforts, evaluate the successes and failures of those efforts, and consider the prospects for development as we proceed in the twenty-first century.

Values, Ideologies, and Development

Attempts to define development in social, economic, or political terms begin on shaky conceptual grounds. Most people think of the concept as an unfolding of events through a succession of states or changes, each of which is preparatory for the next and all of which contribute to some final end. Such efforts are thus exercises in *teleology,* or attempts to explain natural phenomena as being directed toward some final cause or purpose. The assumptions that such ultimate purposes exist and, if they do, that we are intellectually capable of discerning them may be presumptuous from the start.

Human beings are, however, a precocious lot, and doubts about the limits and validity of our knowledge have seldom stopped us from designing grand theories that explain current events in terms of where we are headed. Karl Marx's communist utopia and John Maynard Keynes's capitalist utopia were both built on teleological theories. What people usually do when defining "where we are headed" is describe that future state in terms of their personal values, or where they would *prefer* for us to go. It is at this point that political values and ideologies (or belief systems) become important in defining development.

Development and Conservative Values   A fundamental element in conservative value systems is the belief that one of the keys to human development lies in providing those with special strengths and abilities the freedom to pursue their individual interests without constraint. In a dialogue with Socrates reported over 2,300 years ago by Plato in *The Republic,* a Greek sophist named Thrasymachus argued that it is the natural right of the strong to take more than their equal share of what the world has to offer. The strong are morally justified in designing and operating the institutions of government to pursue their interests; "might makes right." Over the intervening years, these ideas, which have become known as the Doctrine of Thrasymachus, have provided the rationale for a variety of conservative ideologies that often argue—in social Darwinist, survival-of-the-fittest terms—that protecting the special positions and abilities of those who have risen above the common masses is necessary for the evolution of the human species and the grandeur of humanity.

Capitalism is a contemporary version of the Doctrine of Thrasymachus. One of its basic tenets is that the most secure avenue to development is provided by supply-side economic strategies that encourage and facilitate the accumulation of capital by the able and adept. According to Keynes, in order to develop, societies must pass through a transnational phase in which human greed and avarice are unleashed by the drive for personal profit to propel us through the "tunnel of economic necessity," wherein a concentration of capital in the hands of a few will create an industrial system capable of producing material abundance.

In the Other World, capitalist ideas and ideals have taken the form of "takeoff"—or modernization—theories, which hold that the surest way to achieve development is to maximize the opportunities for investment by private firms, most of which are located in the industrialized world. The goal is to create a critical mass of concentrated capital that will support the takeoff of Other World economies into sustained economic growth. A more liberal interpretation of this theory adds that the investment of public funds in physical and human infrastructure is a necessary complement to the private market.

In capitalist economic systems, the primary measure of economic progress used throughout the world is the rate of increase in gross domestic product (GDP, formerly gross national product [GNP]), a quantitative measure that represents the total of all goods and services produced by an economy in a year. In Other World countries pursuing takeoff development strategies, increases in GDP indicate that economic output is expanding and economic development is taking place.

From a conservative perspective, substantial inequality in the distribution of the wealth created by expanding economic output is viewed as natural, necessary, and just. Human beings are viewed as unequal in essence: The poor are poor because of shortcomings *within themselves,* often considered to stem from race, gender, or class. Efforts to substantially improve their lot are not only futile but unjust in that they take from those at the top of society, who have earned their position through their special talents and virtues, and whose unencumbered progress is necessary for human evolution. Although life is unavoidably harsh for the poor, the capitalist utopia does promise eventual material abundance for all. In the short run, relative economic prosperity for the weaker members of society can best be achieved by the creation of jobs through the concentration of capital into large-scale industries.

Development and Liberal and Radical Values   Those who hold liberal and radical belief systems take a very different view of the nature and degree of differences among people, which lead to very different definitions of the goals of development and how those goals should be pursued. From this perspective, human beings are considered to be equal in essence: Although a certain level of inequality is natural in any society because of relatively minor differences in health, intelligence, and emotional balance, the tremendous inequalities that exist within societies and among countries are viewed as primarily the result of shortcomings *within political and economic processes and institutions.* Julius Nyerere, a former president of Tanzania, captures this idea when he writes that

> even when you have an exceptionally intelligent and hard-working millionaire, the difference between his intelligence, his enterprise, his hard work, and those of other members of society cannot possibly be proportionate to the difference between their "rewards." There must be something wrong in a society where one man, however hard-working or clever he may be, can acquire as great a "reward" as a thousand of his fellows can acquire between them.[5]

Whereas liberals and radicals agree on the essential equality of human beings, they differ in their solutions to inequality. Liberals advocate peaceful, step-by-step reforms, often based on programs to redistribute wealth from the rich to the poor and to create more equal opportunities for the poor to compete. Radicals believe that, given the resources commanded by world political and economic elites and the manner in which they control existing political and economic institutions, established powers will always be able to keep ahead of and nullify any reform efforts. They argue that justice and equality for all can be achieved only through the overthrow of established political and economic institutions and the rebuilding of individual societies and the international order.

Whether achieved through evolutionary or revolutionary means, definitions of development put forth by liberals and radicals consistently target egalitarian values as the end toward which development should be directed, emphasizing freedom from poverty and exploitation. Measures of progress include the degree to which nutrition, health, housing, education, and economic security are available equally to all. Here, *equally* is not defined in absolute terms, but as "free of extremes": Because of differences in abilities that are free of extremes, some have more than others, proportionate to differences in abilities. Such definitions often include the ideal that society should encourage and facilitate the self-fulfillment and self-realization of all. This ideal is central to the utopia envisioned by Marx, where all would share equally in the resources of society and be free to develop their full potential as human beings. More recent examples carry the same theme: A contemporary writer hopes that "development will become a means to serve people";[6] another argues that "development should be a *struggle* to create criteria, goals, and means for self-liberation from misery, inequity, and dependency of all forms."[7]

As the world is becoming increasingly aware of the devastating and threatening global effects of pollution and resource depletion, environmental goals have been merged with egalitarian values to create concepts such as *eco-development,* or balanced social and environmental development. *Sustainable development* is defined as living within the limits of natural systems while ensuring an adequate standard of living for all, meeting the needs of the present without compromising the ability of future generations to meet their own needs.[8]

Such definitions make a sharp distinction between growth and development. *Growth* is defined as things simply getting bigger, or quantitative increases in economic output. In contrast, *development* is defined as things getting better through qualitative changes, which result in improvements in life for all in harmony and balance with nature. Strategies proposed to pursue such change generally emphasize decentralized efforts controlled by local populations to improve life and habitats at the local level. Supporters are encouraged to "think globally and act locally." *Appropriate technology,* or technology suitable to particular applications and needs even when more sophisticated technologies are available, is often a part of such strategies.[9] An example would be the use of 10,000 workers with picks and shovels instead of 10 Caterpillar tractors to build a system of levees to control the flooding of small, family agricultural plots, thus supporting small farmers and workers who might otherwise be unemployed and preserving topsoil that would otherwise be washed away.

A History of Development Efforts

Competing conservative and liberal or radical value systems gave rise to two different approaches to development after World War II. Some countries, including Cuba, Algeria, Libya, Angola, North Korea, Vietnam, and Cambodia, broke out of the world political and economic order that had been established by the colonial powers and joined the states of the Soviet empire and China to establish development programs ostensibly designed to pursue egalitarian values. With assistance from the major Second World powers, they adopted the ideas and ideals of Marx, Lenin, and Mao to create centralized command economies in which property was communally owned and economic activities were closely orchestrated by socialist and communist party elites.

Most Other World countries remained within the orbit of the old colonial order. With assistance from the Western industrial nations, they adopted development programs grounded in takeoff theory to establish free-market economies guided by capitalist economic policies and practices.

Free-market approaches are now coming to dominate most of the world, including the former states of the Soviet bloc and China. To understand the history of development efforts, it is important to explore the ascendancy of the free-market system of international capitalism.

Immanuel Wallerstein employs the concept of political economy in his study of the system of international capitalism, which he terms the *capitalist world-economy*, that has expanded from its genesis in sixteenth-century Europe to drive much of the politics and economics of the globe today.[10] Tracing that expansion, Wallerstein describes how the pattern of international relations among great world powers ranges on a fluid continuum: At one end, there is an almost even balance among powers of roughly equal strength (a rare and unstable condition); in the middle the powers group into two or more camps, with no side being able to impose its will (the usual state of international affairs); at the other end, a single great power is able to dominate (also a rare and unstable condition). He defines the latter end of the continuum as *hegemony*, or a situation in which one single world power is so dominant that it "can largely impose its rules and its wishes . . . in the economic, political, military, diplomatic, and even cultural arenas."[11] Such a condition of hegemony existed when the United Kingdom dominated world affairs from roughly 1815 to 1873, when the United States came to occupy a similar position of world dominance from 1945 until the early 1970s, and with the end of the Cold War and the emergence of the United States as the world's sole hyper-power.

U.S. Hegemony and a New Postwar World Order The establishment of hegemony by the United States at the very same time that programs to develop the Other World were launched had a profound effect on the nature of development efforts and the role and position of Other World states in the international political economy. The United States emerged from World War II as the unchallenged dominant power in the world. It was able to use its power to implement a new world order that was carefully designed to serve its interests and the interests of the other former colonial powers in the capitalist world economy. The foundation for this new order was laid through the Bretton Woods agreements, signed by the Allied powers in 1944.

The Bretton Woods system erected three pillars around which the new order was built. The International Monetary Fund (IMF) was established to further cooperation on monetary matters among the countries of the world. Under IMF guidance, the U.S. dollar became the standard against which the value of other currencies was set, and the United States became the banker for the world. The General Agreement on Tariffs and Trade (GATT) was designed to promote world trade. Periodic trade conferences were scheduled to facilitate negotiations among world trading partners with the goal of maintaining "free" trade through low tariffs on internationally traded goods and services. The International Bank for Reconstruction and Development—or World Bank—which was originally created to facilitate investment in Europe after World War II, turned toward stimulating investment in the Other World.

The United Nations was chartered in San Francisco in 1945 as an international governmental organization designed to resolve political and economic conflicts between and among countries and promote world peace and development (see Figure 3.1). Two quasi-legislative bodies comprise the core of the UN: the General Assembly, to which most states (now about 190) belong, and the Security Council.

Only the Security Council can take direct military action to enforce its decisions. The Council is composed of five permanent members—the United States, Britain, France, Russia, and China (each of which has the power to veto any proposal of the

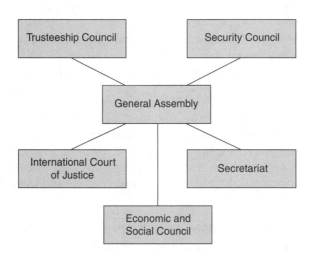

FIGURE 3.1 Core of the United Nations

Council)—and 10 temporary, rotating members (none of which has veto power). Lacking the power to enforce its decisions, the General Assembly serves basically as a forum for expressing the opinions of member states.

Early Development Efforts With the success of efforts to rebuild the economies of Europe and Japan fresh at hand, the Western industrial nations launched a flurry of bilateral and multilateral efforts in the 1960s, which was dubbed the "development decade." The stated intent was to propel Other World economies to a point from which they could take off and achieve self-sustaining growth. John Kenneth Galbraith, a Harvard economics professor who had served as U.S. ambassador to India, published a book in 1964 that aptly described these early development efforts as attempts to copy the institutions and processes of the modern industrial powers. "Development," he observed, "is the faithful imitation of the developed."[12] Galbraith noted three characteristics of these attempts: symbolic modernization, maximized economic growth, and selective growth.

Symbolic modernization gave a developing country the appearance of modernity. Airports and four-lane highways were built, tall buildings were erected, and impressive government offices were constructed. Efforts to maximize economic growth were directed at increasing economic output as measured by GNP. Growth strategies emphasized large initial capital investments from the World Bank, from private firms located primarily in the industrial nations, and from First World governments, with the goal of establishing industrial bases that could then be expanded. Domestic rates of taxation and savings were set to promote the fastest rate of growth possible.

Some efforts were targeted at building the infrastructure for an industrial society through the strategy of selective growth. A variety of foreign aid programs, many organized under the umbrella of the Development Assistance Committee of the Organization for Economic Cooperation and Development (OECD), were created to address this need. Electric, water, sewer, and communications systems were installed; loans were made to farmers and small businesspersons; and agricultural education and community development activities were initiated. The "green revolution" of the 1960s and 1970s is a good example of a selective growth strategy. Increases in agricultural production were sought to generate funds for industrial expansion through earnings from export crops and to increase the supply of food in Other World countries. Programs were undertaken to encourage the replacement of family-scale farms, which used native seeds, composting, traditional pest-control methods, and hand implements, with large-scale agribusinesses employing hybrid seed strains, fertilizers, pesticides, herbicides, irrigation, and mechanized farm machinery.

Those who conceived of and measured development in terms of increases in economic output were pleased with the results of these early efforts: With some exceptions, development programs were generating dramatic increases in GNP. However, it did not take long for those who had hoped that the development decade would result in a better standard of living for the masses of Other World peoples to realize that the strategies described above were not contributing significantly to that goal. Benefits were accruing primarily to a few, while living conditions for most were not markedly improving; in fact, for some they were actually declining. Along with Galbraith's book, others with titles such as *False Start in Africa*[13] pointed out that the hollow imitation of Western symbols and an emphasis on supply-side economic policies, industrial development, and Western technologies would not result in the kind of economic and social change that would significantly benefit the many. The almost singular emphasis on building an industrial infrastructure and raising GNP meant that basic essentials such as food, housing, and health services were often neglected in favor of exporting minerals and cash crops to earn foreign exchange, much of which was sent back overseas in the form of profits for foreign corporations or spent on importing luxury goods for indigenous political and economic elites.

A Balance Sheet of Development   We are now in a position to evaluate the accomplishments of more than 50 years of sustained development efforts guided by takeoff theory. Advocates of this approach point with satisfaction to statistics that show that Other World GDP per capita has been growing at higher rates than were achieved by the industrial nations in comparable periods of their history, that life expectancy is increasing faster in decades than it did in an entire century in the industrialized world, and that substantial gains have been made in literacy and access to education. Critics point out that while these statistics accurately reflect the fact that conditions have improved in some ways for many and in many ways for some, they hide the true nature of economic processes that have resulted in tremendous disparities within Other World societies and among Other World countries: More than one-third are now so poor and economically underdeveloped that they are placed in a special "Fourth World" category in which development seems impossible.

Statistics compiled and updated annually in the United Nations *Human Development Report* provide a useful balance sheet of the status of human development.[14] Whereas the estimated share of the world's population living in extreme poverty fell from 28 percent in 1990 to 21 percent in 2000, some 2.5 billion people (roughly 40 percent of the world's population) survive on less than $2 per day, and some 15 percent survive on less than $1 per day. In the Other World, 1 billion people do not have safe water, 2.6 billion do not have adequate sanitation, 800 million suffer from malnutrition, and 11 million children die each year before reaching their fifth birthdays. Whereas average income per household is growing worldwide, more than 1.3 billion people live in extreme poverty. Over the past decade, poverty rates have increased in Sub-Saharan Africa; Latin America and the Middle East have registered no progress; and gains in South Asia have been negated by a growing population, creating an increase in the absolute number of people living in poverty.

After completing a similar evaluation in which he noted there were more people living in absolute poverty in 1987 than in 1960, Paul Harrison concluded

> this balance sheet can only be read as progress if one abstracts from the
> human realities. In terms of concrete individual experience, there is a
> greater absolute quantity of human suffering in the world today than

ever before, and all the indications are that it will increase as we approach the millennium. For all the talk and all the action about development, *virtually no progress has been made in the task of eliminating absolute poverty; indeed, there has been gradual regress.*[15]

Harrison's comments parallel those of an Egyptian who once commented that the overall effect of development efforts in Egypt was that more people now lived longer in greater misery. Such is the state of human development throughout much of the Other World today as progress falters in reaching the Millennium Development Goals set by the United Nations General Assembly in 2000.

The links among poverty, security, and population growth are important in understanding this increase in absolute poverty. Poverty and fertility rates are directly related: The higher the degree of poverty in a society, the higher the rate of population increase. The instinct to survive dictates that poor families have more children than wealthier families for practical economic reasons: Children are a source of security for those living at the margins of survival. More children mean more hands to help with the difficult tasks of eking a living out of a subsistence environment; a working child can contribute to household resources by age 6 and produce more than she or he consumes by age 12. More children increase the probability that one of them might be fortunate enough to secure an education, a rare job, and cash earnings to contribute to the family. More children mean a greater likelihood that someone will be around to help when old age makes it impossible to survive on one's own. High infant and childhood mortality rates mean that the odds of accomplishing all of these objectives are improved by having enough children to replace those who die young.

In transferring much of the wealth of the Other World to the industrialized nations, the forces of colonialism and neocolonialism have substantially contributed to the poverty that is fueling population increases in the Other World. These global shifts in wealth and family security have also contributed to declining fertility rates in the First World. Population policies that address fundamental issues of family security, rather than simply encouraging or enforcing birth control, are the surest way to reduce rates of population growth.

The manner in which the international political economy produces and distributes wealth is well illustrated by the production and distribution of world food resources. If the wheat, rice, and other grains produced throughout the world were distributed equally to all the world's peoples, each individual would receive 3,600 calories per day, well above the average U.S.-recommended daily allowances of 2,700 calories for adult males, 2,000 for adult females, and 1,300–3,000 for teenagers. Yet 9 million children die every year from starvation, and 4 billion people do not have enough to eat. The typical Western family of four consumes more grain (directly and indirectly in the form of meat) than a poor Indian family of 20.[16]

India, where more than one-third of the world's hungry people live, is one of the top cash crop exporters in the Other World. The "green revolution" was instrumental in boosting India and a number of other countries to the status of agricultural exporters. However, the benefits of increased agricultural production in those countries have often accrued to those wealthy farmers who could obtain bank loans to purchase the large irrigated farms, mechanized equipment, and expensive seeds, fertilizers, pesticides, and herbicides required for green revolution agriculture. Many poor farmers in these countries have in the process been displaced, driven to marginal dryland plots or the cities where they are unable to afford the food now produced through expensive farming methods on the lands they once tilled.

Brazil provides an especially illustrative example of the balance sheet generated by an economic development process driven by the singular pursuit of increased economic production. In 1964, a military coup established a new government that opened the country to foreign investment by providing an array of attractive incentives and freedoms. In the following 10 years, which became known as "the Brazilian economic miracle," the country's GNP tripled, and Brazilian executives became for a time the highest paid in the world. Meanwhile, the real income of 80 percent of the population declined; the production of basic necessities such as food, clothing, and housing remained stagnant; and Brazil's infant mortality rate became the second highest in Latin America. Foreign-owned corporations gained control of 100 percent of Brazil's tire and rubber production, 95 percent of its automobile production, and 80 percent of its television and radio industry (while 60 Brazilian electronics firms were driven out of business or taken over by foreign firms). Foreign-owned companies, some with holdings in the millions of acres, displaced Brazilian farmers and shifted the emphasis from agricultural production to export products such as soybeans and beef for fast-food restaurants in the First World. These shifts created a shortage of black beans, the staple in the diet of Brazil's poor, with a resulting increase in malnutrition.[17] Surveying these statistics, a group of Catholic bishops and clerics issued a statement on the condition of the Brazilian people in 1975, concluding that

> the Brazilian miracle has resulted in privileges for the wealthy. It has come as a curse upon those who have not asked for it. The rich become always richer and the poor always poorer in this process of economic concentration. Far from being the inevitable result of natural deficiencies, this tragedy is the consequence of international capitalism. Development came to be defined not in terms of the interests of Brazilian society, but in terms of the profits made by foreign corporations and their associates in our country.[18]

Mexico's more recent "economic miracle" repeated the same pattern. By the early 1990s, strong economic growth had resulted in a dramatic concentration of wealth and a widening gap between the rich and the poor: While 92.4 percent of the population earned less than $5,700 U.S. per year, the top of Mexico's socioeconomic hierarchy was occupied by seven Mexican billionaires, more than in Britain or Saudi Arabia. And the Mexican government signed a free-trade agreement with the United States and Canada—the North American Free Trade Agreement (NAFTA)—that encouraged a flood of foreign investment and ownership in the country. In 2005, the United States government approved the Central American Free Trade Agreement (CAFTA) in an effort to establish a similar relationship with Guatemala, El Salvador, Honduras, Costa Rica, Nicaragua, and the Dominican

Republic. The pattern of increasing growth and increasing inequality has also characterized the political economies of the Asian Tigers of China, Taiwan, South Korea, Thailand, Indonesia, Malaysia, and India in recent years.

Understanding the Balance Sheet   The preceding balance sheet is not difficult to understand if one considers that the roots of capitalism lie in conservative value systems. Development based on takeoff theory has primarily benefited the strong because it is intended to; the accounting system of the capitalist world economy prioritizes individual gain, not egalitarian values. The history of Other World development is consistent with the 400-year trend of capitalism—an ever-increasing concentration of wealth in the hands of a few, much of which is spent on luxury consumption and speculation rather than being reinvested in any industrial infrastructure that might significantly benefit the many in either the short or the long run.

Through an analysis known as *dependency theory*, liberals and radicals in fact argue that, given the position of the Other World in the international political economy, development that would substantially improve the lives of a majority of the Other World's peoples is unlikely to occur at all. They point out that the designation "Third World" is an accurate description of that position: Although there is really only *one* world of political economy, with all the world's states linked in various fashions to the whole, most of the countries of Africa, Asia, and Latin America occupy tertiary positions on the periphery of the dominant political and economic order. Their primary function, as it was under formal colonialism, is to provide raw materials and cheap labor for the industrialized powers. Other World countries are now dominated by structures of neocolonialism that differ little in substance from the colonialism of the past.

From the perspective of dependency theorists, Other World political systems are particularly dependent on the Western industrial powers. Neocolonialism operates through the collusion of Other World political elites, who have been co-opted into serving foreign interests. Independence means only that political institutions originally established to facilitate and enforce the extraction of wealth from the Other World are now occupied by African, Asian, and Latin American politicians and bureaucrats instead of by expatriate colonial officials. These new elites serve as "brokers," managing the flow of resources from their countries in return for brokerage fees (or commissions) in the form of foreign aid and other payoffs, which they use to maintain their positions of political control and to build their personal fortunes.

The rule of many Other World political elites in the neocolonial era constitutes a contemporary mercantilism in which national political economies are operated to increase the wealth of the rulers.[19] The widespread corruption, or the use of public office for private gain, that pervades Other World politics is a key factor in explaining why the development programs of many countries have done little to improve the lot of the masses. Much of the political instability endemic to Other World political systems stems from the fact that governments operated openly for private gain (or *kleptocracies*) have little legitimacy among, or acceptance by, a significant proportion of the population, in neocolonial times as in the past. The Al Qaeda movement of Osama bin Laden is one example of an attempt to free a country (in this case, Saudi Arabia) from a corrupt and repressive regime propped up by a neocolonial power (in this case, the United States).

Power vacuums resulting from the end of the cold war are contributing to spiraling levels of violence in many parts of the Other World. In the decades before the fall of the Soviet empire, both the United States and the Soviet Union delivered a substantial portion of their foreign aid in the form of military assistance. Other World dictators who were willing to wave one flag or another as clients in the ideological contest between capitalism and communism, sometimes adroitly playing one side off against the other, amassed enormous military capabilities. With the cold war balance of power now ended, stockpiles of weapons are fueling disastrous conflicts between and within Other World states. This factor played prominently in the rise of the Taliban in Afghanistan following the defeat of the Soviet Union in 1990, the 1990 invasion of Kuwait by Iraq, and in bloody civil wars and anarchy in Somalia in 1992, in Rwanda beginning in 1994,[20] and in Liberia in 2003.[21]

Perhaps more difficult to understand than the balance sheet of development is the fact that those countries that followed communist and socialist development strategies have been only a little more successful in accomplishing egalitarian goals and probably less successful in preserving the natural environment. The inequalities that have developed in these states, although less dramatic than those in the capitalist world, indicate that the tendency of the powerful to serve their self-interests is not unique to capitalism. Economic growth and social inequality is a common pattern, with increases in economic output accompanied by increasing inequality throughout history.[22] The 400-year history of capitalism is an extension of a trend that began 6,000 years ago when humankind first established urban-based civilizations capable of creating wealth in surplus of the resources needed for human survival, a trend accelerated 2,000 years ago when Western civilization emerged in the Greek city-states and legitimized the value of individualistic materialism. While an appreciation of capitalist ideology helps one understand the particular details of the process through which development has come to benefit primarily a few in the capitalist world economy, one must go beyond the level of ideology to the underlying realities of politics, power, and self-interest to understand the universal links between increased economic output and greater inequality.

Increases in economic output, in Mesopotamia or ancient Greece or the Other World of the post–World War II era, go primarily to those groups within a society, and to those states within the international political economy, that are able to control the forces of violence and the institutions and policies that determine the distribution of that output. At this level of analysis, ideologies primarily represent efforts by political elites to use knowledge power to convince the public that the government is being operated in the public interest. While ideologies are useful in defining the goals and values that people of various persuasions believe *should* be served by development, they are relatively insignificant in determining political realities. The actual outputs of governments operating with "competing" ideologies are only marginally different; in this context, one can appreciate the observation that while under capitalism man exploits man, under communism it's the other way around.

GLOBALIZATION

The 1970s marked the emergence of globalization as the latest stage in the evolution of the global political economy. *Globalization* is an international regime in which the economic interests of multinational corporations and other nonstate actors (such as the International Money Fund and the World Trade Organization) are coming to supersede the interests and powers of individual states. In the preceding chapter, colonialism was defined as a relationship in which a group of people located in one country is subject to the authority of people in another country. The logic and the drive of the capitalist world economy is now creating a fundamentally different global regime in which all the world's people are increasingly subject to the power of multinational institutions.

National boundaries and loyalties are of little significance in a global economy driven by the exclusive and ceaseless pursuit of profit. In the evolving age of postindustrial production, the demand (and compensation) for labor is predicted to decline as a transnational elite seeks custom, designer goods made by specialized producers hired at the lowest wages possible from a global labor pool, rather than the standardized products of the mass assembly lines that have provided employment to many in the past.

Riccardo Petrella, a futurist for the European Union, describes how the forces of globalization are separating all the world's peoples into two classes that cut across national boundaries, divided into the "fast" and the "slow" on the basis of access to computer-based information and communications technologies. In this evolving structure, a global upper class of the affluent and privileged living in a high-tech archipelago of hyperdeveloped, walled, and gated city-regions and consisting of less than one-eighth of the world's population is emerging among a global underclass consisting of seven-eighths of the world's population left to fend for itself in a disintegrating social and environmental wasteland.[23]

Colin Leys defines this new international regime as a world

1. Dominated by multinational corporations
2. Regulated by the International Monetary Fund
3. Enforced by the military might of the United States[24]

In an era characterized by the privatization of government functions, private mercenary armies are also being formed to enforce this new global system. Private companies such as Vinnell Corp of McLean, Virginia, MPRI of Alexandria, Virginia, Booz Allen Hamilton, Inc. of McLean, Virginia, DynCorp of Reston, Virginia, and Executive Outcomes, a South African corporation formed by ex-members of the notorious apartheid-era 32nd Battalion of the South African special forces, offer states and corporations able to afford multimillion-dollar fees a full spectrum of military services and products.[25] Revenues from the private security market are expected to rise from 55 billion dollars in 1990 to 202 billion by 2010. Private mercenary armies have been active over the past decade on every continent but Antarctica.[26] Every post–cold war U.S. military operation from the Persian Gulf to Somalia, Zaire, Haiti, Bosnia, Kosovo, Croatia, Afghanistan, and Iraq has involved significant involvement from private military corporations.

The development programs that characterized much of the history of the Other World beginning in the 1940s are being rapidly abandoned under globalization. Since the 1970s, foreign aid programs have been steadily and significantly reduced as Other World countries are directed to pursue their economic development through integrating their economies into the global marketplace. As part of globalization, the functions of the GATT have been assumed by the World Trade Organization (WTO). Established in 1995 and headquartered in Geneva, Switzerland, the WTO has become a powerful multinational force working to set the rules of trade between and among the countries of the world.

The forces of globalization are driving down the standard of living of many in the Other World. The internal affairs of many Other World countries are coming increasingly under the direct control of IMF officials, who are imposing *structural adjustment programs* that change domestic spending patterns to make possible repayments on enormous debts owed to First World financial institutions. These changes often include cuts in health, education, and other social service programs. Much of this debt was incurred during oil shortages in the 1970s and grew with a rise in interest rates in the 1980s. In African countries, this debt typically amounts to five times annual export income.[27] Many Latin American countries now pay out one-fourth of their export receipts in debt payments on long-term loans, some of which do not even cover interest due. *Privatization programs,* which transfer the control of government services to private, for-profit firms, are further loosening the thin ties that link public resources to public needs. Globalized corporate agriculture is destroying jobs and small farms that have sustained Other World populations for millennia.[28]

The social, economic, and environmental costs of globalization have sparked backlashes in both the Other World and industrialized countries. The massive popular protest against the WTO in Seattle in 1999 brought together a coalition of trade unionists, environmentalists, farmers, students, religious activists, women, and indigenous peoples that now shadow meetings of the WTO, IMF, World Bank, and other multinational economic organizations around the planet.[29] The infusion of Western economic and cultural forms has sparked resistance throughout the world that Benjamin Barber aptly characterizes as driving a conflict between "Jihad" (or reactionary fundamentalism) and the "McWorld" of global capitalism.[30]

The U.S.-led War on Terror following the September 11, 2001, attacks on the World Trade Center and the U.S. Pentagon, U.S. policies emphasizing unilateralism over multilateralism, and the U.S. invasion of Iraq in 2003 present additional challenges to globalization. Restrictions on foreign travel and international trade stemming from heightened security measures, foreign policy disputes, rising worldwide anti-Americanism, and mounting violence against U.S. military forces, diplomatic offices, and commercial interests around the world are all working to severely restrict the openness required for a global economy.

CONCLUSIONS

The Politics of Change

Globalization and reactions against globalization both work to undermine the evolution of more democratic forms of government and society that could lead to more egalitarian and environmentally sustainable development processes. Globalization heralds a global class apartheid in which the strong are free to pursue their interests unencumbered by any sense of connection with or responsibility to the social commonwealth or the environmental commons. Fundamentalist reactions against globalization are driven by a parochial exclusiveness and hostility toward others at odds with the essence of democratic values and culture.

In contrast, those who prefer a different future face tremendous challenges. The qualitative changes in societies and in the international political economy necessary to achieve change that would serve egalitarian and environmental values are vast in range and scale. The range of change would have to include political, economic, and social processes and institutions, for all of these aspects of human organization are inseparably linked. Within this web of interconnections, it is impossible to separate economic development from political development or social development; improvements in the economic conditions of the less powerful could be achieved only through parallel improvements in political and social conditions. The scale of change would have to be fundamental, for the processes and institutions that currently determine the use and allocation of the world's resources are deeply and firmly entrenched. Changes of this extent would require radical transformations in the power relationships that hold these systems together.

However, as we proceed into the twenty-first century, there are signs that the centralized Western power structures that have long dominated our affairs are beginning to crumble under the pressure of converging crises of overpopulation, environmental destruction, resource scarcity, economic discontinuity, and sociopolitical decay. These crises may create opportunities for change in chaos not present in more stable times. As the Chinese have long noted, when there is great disorder under the heavens, the opportunities for change are excellent.

E. F. Schumacher observes that whereas some have challenged the ethic of materialism and argued for different priorities throughout history, "Today, however, this message reaches us not solely from the sages and saints but from the actual course of physical events. It speaks to us in the language of terrorism, genocide, breakdown, pollution, exhaustion."[31] Samuel Huntington hypothesizes a resurgence of Confucian, Japanese, Islamic, Hindu, Slavic-Orthodox, Latin American, and African civilizations against a Western civilization now at the peak of its power and global intrusiveness.[32] Benjamin Barber describes forces working to diminish the power of the nation-state.[33] And Alvin Toffler argues that we are at one of the greatest turning points in history as breakdown and exhaustion in health, education, transportation, welfare, urban, and ecological systems converge to challenge the centralized power structures that control our societies.[34]

The peaceful revolutions against authoritarian rule that swept the Soviet Union and Eastern Europe at the end of the 1980s and early 1990s provide tantalizing support for these theses, as do mounting signs of institutional collapse, widespread public disenchantment in the Western industrial nations, and the recent rise of left-center governments as a reaction to the free market policies of globalization in Brazil, Argentina, Uruguay, and Venezuela. Democratization and local autonomy movements that are erupting across the Other World, fueled by the irrepressible force of global mass communications support these theses as well. A proliferation of globally based nongovernmental organizations (NGOs) is working to build a global civic culture and new global institutions working to control the excesses of globalization and directing the forces of global integration toward the common good.[35]

Changing power relations could provide those who envision development as a way to serve people and to create the means for self-liberation with opportunities in the coming years that seemed impossible in the past.[36] If the information technologies that are elevating knowledge to a position as the dominant source of power were dispersed among the world's masses, the resulting diffusion of power could result in the first true democracies the world has ever known. On the other hand, if the new technologies are controlled by a few, we could be plunged into a new Dark Age of Orwellian proportions. In the coming decades it is likely that those who control knowledge and the technologies of knowledge will also control wealth, violence, and the institutions of government.

As we proceed through a time of pivotal change in human affairs, the individual actions of each of us will count more than at any time in previous years, for we are all participants—whether as consumers, investors, or political activists—in the international political economy that we share with the peoples of the Other World. Our common future depends on our common efforts to build a more socially and ecologically sustainable world.

SUMMARY

The first global political economy of mercantilism was created as part of the colonial era that began with the first voyage of Columbus in 1492. Mercantilism evolved into capitalism as industrial and financial elites came to control Western governments. Beginning in the 1940s, Other World international relations and domestic affairs were dominated by a concern with development. Driven primarily by the capitalist world economy, development programs guided by takeoff theory resulted in significant increases in GNP/GDP and improvements in the lives of some Other World peoples; they also contributed to increasing inequality and growing numbers of people living in absolute poverty. Whereas takeoff theorists attribute these problems to the necessities of progress, dependency theorists view them as the result of the exploitation of the Other World by the industrial powers and Other World political elites through structures of neocolonialism. Advocates of both schools ground their positions in political ideologies that express fundamental beliefs and values about the way the world should be.

Globalization and fundamentalist reactions against globalization are now interacting to undermine the possibility of a more democratic future, with direct implications for increasing inequality, poverty, and environmental decline and increasing levels of political, economic, and social instability. Other trends indicate the possibility of changes in power relations that could make possible development designed to promote egalitarian and environmental values. We are living at a pivotal time of convergence in human affairs that will have fundamental consequences for the future of the global community we inhabit with the peoples of the Other World.

ISSUES FOR DISCUSSION

1. Can you refute the Doctrine of Thrasymachus?

The Doctrine of Thrasymachus consists of two reinforcing parts. Part I states that it is the natural right of the strong to take more than their equal share of what the world has to offer. This is a philosophical statement, or one that addresses what is considered to be right and wrong, good and bad. Here Thrasymachus asserts the unbridled right of the strong to take from the weak, drawing on their physical strength, intelligence, or any other attribute that would enable them to overpower others. Any means imaginable, including violence and fraud, is morally justified. Part II states that might makes right. Here Thrasymachus addresses how the strong use government to serve their interests by writing and enforcing laws that work to their advantage. The idea that whatever the mighty say is right is right underlies the concept of relative justice—whatever the strong say is just is just, with some laws legitimately applied unequally to different citizens and some laws legitimately applied only to certain groups. For Thrasymachus, justice is whatever is in the interests of the strong.

Liberty, or the freedom to pursue one's interests without constraint, and equality, or freedom from relative poverty and exploitation, are conflicting values; a society cannot encourage one without sacrificing the other. On the one hand, if citizens are free to pursue private interests without constraint, some will invariably take advantage of others, creating greater inequality in society; on the other hand, efforts to build more egalitarian social orders can only be pursued by restraining personal liberty. The ideas expressed in the Doctrine of Thrasymachus are thus among the most significant in the history of political thinking in that they so unequivocally proclaim the value of liberty. They take us to the core of one of the central dilemmas of political organization: Government policies that restrain liberty stifle initiative, whereas policies that encourage liberty result in exploitation. As the basis for the conservative ideas and ideals that provide the foundations of capitalism, takeoff theory, and the ethic of globalization, they also take us to the heart of what development should be and can be about.

If Thrasymachus is right, it follows that all governments are oligarchies, or political systems operated by a few to serve their interests. While most governments claim to have been created by God to serve the people, such claims are part of the fraud perpetuated by elites to hide the fact that government is in fact designed to serve the interests of the strong. If the political institutions that control peoples' behavior to allocate societies' scarce values are operated by a few to serve their interests, it further follows that what we call "civilized" life rests on the exploitation of the weak.

Attempts to refute or support the ideas expressed by Thrasymachus are central to political philosophy. Can you refute the Doctrine of Thrasymachus? If so, how? If not, why not? Consider your response from both normative and empirical perspectives: normative analysis is concerned with what should be, or with moral judgments of right and wrong; empirical analysis is concerned with what is, or the way things are in actual fact.

2. Internationally, how can you best protect yourself in an era of globalization and increasing inequality and conflict?

With 4.6 percent of the world's population, the United States presently consumes 40 percent of the world's resources. With 15.4 percent of the world's population, the other industrialized countries consume another 40 percent. The 80 percent of the world's population living in the Other World is left to live from the remaining 20 percent of world resources.

These inequalities have been cited as one of the sources of the conflict resulting in the attacks on the World Trade Center on September 11, 2001. In his book *Blowback: The Costs and Consequences of American Empire,* Chalmers Johnson posits that in the decade following the end of the cold war, the United States used military force and financial manipulation to help maintain and increase the inequalities described above, and that the twenty-first century may be a time of reckoning for the United States.[37] Specifically addressing the events of September 11 in a *Los Angles Times* Opinion article titled,

Money, Sun, and Sand: Since the 1970s Georgetown, capital of the Cayman Islands, has provided a tax-free refuge for the funds of the rich and famous from around the world. The branches of many foreign banks have been opened here to serve these customers. SOURCE: JOE WEATHERBY

"The Lessons of Blowback," Johnson argues that in response to the attacks, the United States should

- Recognize that the terrorism of September 11 was not directed against America but against American foreign policy
- Listen to the grievances of the Islamic peoples
- Stop propping up repressive regimes in the area
- Protect Israel's security but denounce its apartheid practices in Palestinian areas
- Reform its "globalization" policies so that they no longer mean that the rich are getting richer and the poor poorer.

Johnson concludes that if the United States' only response to the September 11 attack is military reprisal, "the end result will not be 'victory' in a 'war on terrorism' but a further cycle of terrorist attacks, American casualties and escalation."[38]

Considering the implications of the preceding for your own safety and security, what do you feel you can do to most effectively address the increasing level of international violence characteristic of today's world?

3. Do you owe posterity a sustainable world?

It is estimated that the human species has been on the planet for some 4.5 million years. For the bulk of that time, we had little effect on the natural environment, as our hunting and gathering activities caused only slight disturbances in the self-regulating natural ecologies we inhabited. We began concerted and determined efforts to dominate and control the environment to serve human ends 6,000 years ago with the first urban-based civilizations, and have since been so successful that our technologies are now overwhelming the natural systems we evolved with and upon which we depend for our survival. Our impact has become so substantial that we have damaged many of the self-regulating and self-balancing mechanisms that controlled the natural world, creating disturbed ecosystems that can be kept from chaos and collapse only through constant human intervention and manipulation.

Many in the scientific community are now questioning our ability to maintain the necessary balances and equilibriums. The cumulative and long-term effects of pollution, resource depletion, and species and habitat losses seem to be so significantly altering the living world that doubts are being raised about our ability to sustain life as we know it. Unless we dramatically change our stewardship of the earth, our environment will probably become so irretrievably mutilated over the coming decades that future generations could suffer vast misery and eventual extinction.

In response, some ask, "So what? Why should we care? What has posterity ever done for me?" At its extreme, the ethic of globalization in fact includes a nihilistic view that the planet is already so overburdened with population and pollution problems that it is beyond saving and that we should therefore live life to the hilt in the time we have remaining. This view provides another rationalization for the short-term greed that is driving the contemporary global economy.

Do you owe posterity a sustainable world? If not, why not? If so, on what is this obligation based? Exactly what are you willing to give up in your current lifestyle and levels of consumption to make life tolerable and possible for future generations? In pursuit of the goal, are you willing to become more actively involved in the political process? How?

4. What are the challenges to and costs of attempting to maintain colonial rule in the twenty-first century?

While Iraq was not involved in the September 11, 2001, attacks on the World Trade Center and the U.S. Pentagon, it appears to many that a group known as the Neoconservatives in the White House used the event along with unsubstantiated claims that Iraq possessed Weapons of Mass Destruction that posed an imminent threat to the world to justify the 2003 U.S. invasion and occupation of Iraq.

In an article titled "Beyond Regime Change," Sandy Tolan describes current U.S. policy in the Middle East as a neo-imperial vision to redraw the map of the Middle East as ambitious as the 1916 Sykes-Picot Agreement through which the British and the French carved up the Ottoman Empire.[39] Tolan documents a blueprint to:

1. Control the flow of Middle Eastern oil
2. Ensure Israel's continued regional military superiority

Much of this "neo-imperial vision" is not in fact new, but a throwback to direct colonial rule. As the world's sole hyper-power, U.S. officials seem to believe they have the military might to reestablish the kind of direct rule exercised by the U.S. during the colonial era in the Philippines, Cuba, and Puerto Rico and by the British and French in their colonial empires. The initial administration of an occupied Iraq by U.S. officials and no-bid contracts to insider U.S. firms to "rebuild" the country met the basic criteria of colonial occupation defined in international law: territorial annexation, rule by foreign nationals, and control of natural resources.[40] Since the transfer of limited power and sovereignty to Iraqis with the disbanding of the Coalition Provisional Authority in 2004, the United States has worked to establish a neocolonial Iraqi government sympathetic to American interests.

What are the challenges to and costs of attempting to maintain colonial rule in the twenty-first century? What forces help make such control possible? What forces are working against it? Will the United States government be able to successfully transition to neocolonial control in Iraq, installing a broker government to serve its interests? Why or why not?

Review Questions

1. Define *politics* and *economics*. How are politics and economics related? What is the role of government in the process of economic production and distribution?
2. Describe and explain the difference between colonialism and neocolonialism.
3. Explain the difference between *growth* and *development*. Describe and explain the results of more than five decades of programs to achieve development in the Other World.
4. Describe the links between poverty and population increase.
5. Define and describe the nature of globalization. What are the implications of current global trends for our natural environment and for social and political stability?

Key Terms

+ **Politics**—Who gets what, when, and how; the authoritative allocation of scarce values.
+ **Power**—The use of violence, knowledge, and authority to control the behavior of others.
+ **Oligarchy**—Government by the few, in the interest of the few.
+ **Economics**—The production, distribution, and use of wealth.
+ **The Doctrine of Thrasymachus**—(a) It is the natural right of the strong to take more than their equal share of what the world has to offer, and (b) might makes right.
+ **Neocolonialism**—Indirect control of Other World countries by First World countries and multinational interests.
+ **Brokers**—Other World political leaders who act in the interest of First World countries and multinational interests.
+ **Sustainable development**—Living within the limits of natural systems while ensuring an adequate standard of living for all; meeting the needs of the present without compromising the ability of future generations to meet their own needs.
+ **Structural adjustment programs**—Domestic spending plans to make possible repayments on loans; often include cuts in health, education, and other social service programs.
+ **Globalization**—Emerging international regime in which the economic interests of multinational corporations and other nonstate actors supersede the interests and power of nations.

Useful Web Sites

OneWorld.net: www.oneworld.net
Oxfam: www.oxfam.org.uk
Reshaping World Politics: NGOs, the Internet, and Global Civil Society:
www.oswego.edu/reshaping
United Nations Development Programme: www.undp.org
World Trade Organization: www.wto.org

Notes

1. Christopher Flavin, "Rich Planet, Poor Planet," in *State of the World 2001*, ed. Linda Starke (New York: W.W. Norton & Company, 2001), p. 5.
2. Union of Concerned Scientists, *World Scientists' Warning Briefing Book* (Cambridge, MA: Union of Concerned Scientists, 1993), p. 4. More recently, see J.F. Rischard, *High Noon: Twenty Global Problems, Twenty Years to Solve Them* (New York: Basic Books, 2002).
3. Jeffrey A. Freiden and David A. Lake, *International Political Economy: Perspectives on Global Power and Wealth* (New York: St. Martin's Press, 1987), p. 1.
4. Howard Zinn, *A People's History of the United States 1492–Present* (New York: HarperPerennial, 1995), pp. 1–8.

5. Julius K. Nyerere, *Ujamaa: Essays on Socialism* (Nairobi: Oxford University Press, 1968), pp. 2–3.
6. Charles K. Wilber, ed. *The Political Economy of Development and Underdevelopment* (New York: Random House, 1988), p. 25.
7. James J. Lamb, "The Third World and the Development Debate," *IDOC-North America* (January–February 1973): 20.
8. See "The Cocoyoc Declaration," adopted by participants in the UNEP/UNCTAD Symposium on Patterns of Resource Use, Environment and Development Strategies, Cocoyoc, Mexico, October 8–12, 1974. Reprinted in *International Organization* 29, no. 3 (summer 1975): 893–901; Lester Brown, et al., *State of the World 1991: A Worldwatch Institute Report on Progress toward a Sustainable Society* (New York: Norton, 1991); Jim MacNeill, Pieter Winsemius, and Taizo Yakushiji, *Beyond Interdependence: The Meshing of the World's Economy and the Earth's Ecology* (New York: Oxford University Press, 1991); and World Commission on Environment and Development, *Our Common Future* (New York: Oxford University Press, 1987).
9. See E. F. Schumacher, *Small Is Beautiful: Economics as if People Mattered* (New York: Harper & Row, 1973).
10. Immanuel Wallerstein, "The Three Instances of Hegemony in the History of the Capitalist World-Economy," in *International Political Economy: A Reader,* ed. Kendall W. Stiles and Tsuneo Akaha (New York: HarperCollins, 1991), pp. 427–435.
11. Ibid., p. 428.
12. John Kenneth Galbraith, *Economic Development* (New York: Houghton Mifflin, 1964), p. 3.
13. Rene Dumont, *False Start in Africa* (New York: Praeger, 1969).
14. *United Nations Development Programme, Human Development Report 2005* (United Nations Development Programme, 2005).
15. Paul Harrison, *Inside the Third World: The Anatomy of Poverty* (London: Penguin Books, 1990), pp. 465–466 (emphasis in the original).
16. Ibid., p. 276.
17. *Controlling Interest: The World of the Multinational Corporation* (San Francisco: California Newsreel, 1978).
18. Ibid.
19. Robert H. Jackson and Carl G. Rosberg, "The Political Economy of African Personal Rule," in *Political Development and the New Realism in Sub-Saharan Africa,* ed. David E. Apter and Carl G. Rosberg (Charlottesville: University Press of Virginia, 1994), p. 292.
20. See Robert D. Kaplan, "The Coming Anarchy," *This World,* (13 March 1994), pp. 5–10.
21. Roger Morris, "Hurtful Hand on Liberia: U.S. Policy Bears Much of the Blame for That Nation's Calamity," *Los Angeles Times,* 31 August 2003, p. M5.
22. Gerhard E. Lenksi, *Power and Privilege: A Theory of Social Stratification* (New York: McGraw-Hill, 1966).
23. Riccardo Petrella, "Techno-apartheid for a Global Underclass," *Los Angeles Times,* 6 August 1992, p. D6.
24. Colin Leys, "Learning from the Kenya Debate," in *Political Development and the New Realism in Sub-Saharan Africa,* ed. David E. Apter and Carl G. Rosberg (Charlottesville: University Press of Virginia, 1994), p. 227.
25. Elizabeth Rubin, "An Army of One's Own," *Harper's Magazine,* February 1997, pp. 44–55.
26. P.W. Singer, *Corporate Warriors: The Rise of the Privatized Military Industry* (Ithaca: Cornell University Press, 2003), p. 9.

27. Debt relief to African countries totaling $40 billion in 2005 cancelled less than one-sixth of Africa's $295 billion debt, and left out crucial countries such as Nigeria. The "relief" was more for image than for substance. See Abraham McLaughlin, "What debt relief means for Africa," *The Christian Science Monitor,* 13 June 2005, p. 1.
28. See Vandana Shiva, *Stolen Harvest: The Hijacking of the Global Food Supply* (Cambridge, MA: South End Press, 2000).
29. See Robin Broad, ed., *Global Backlash: Citizen Initiatives for a Just World Economy* (Rowman & Littlefield Publishers, Inc., 2002).
30. Benjamin Barber, *Jihad vs. McWorld: Terrorism's Challenge to Democracy* (New York: Ballantine Books, 2001).
31. E. F. Schumacher, *Small Is Beautiful: Economics as if People Mattered* (New York: Harper & Row, 1973), pp. 293–294.
32. Samuel P. Huntington, "The Clash of Civilizations?" *Foreign Affairs* 72, no. 3 (summer 1993): 22–49.
33. Benjamin R. Barber, *op. cit.*
34. Alvin Toffler, *Powershift: Knowledge, Wealth, and Violence at the Edge of the 21st Century* (New York: Bantam Books, 1990).
35. See George Soros, *Open Society: Reforming Global Capitalism* (New York: Public Affairs, 2000); and Craig Warkentin, *Reshaping World Politics: NGOs, the Internet, and Global Civil Society* (New York: Rowman & Littlefield Publishers, Inc., 2001).
36. See Sheila L. Croucher, *Globalization and Belonging: The Politics of Identity in a Changing World* (New York: Rowman & Littlefield Publishers, Inc., 2004).
37. Chalmers Johnson, *Blowback: The Costs and Consequences of American Empire* (New York: Owl/Metropolitan Books, 2001).
38. Chalmers Johnson, "The Lessons of Blowback," *Los Angeles Times,* 30 September 2001, p. M1.
39. Sandy Tolan, "Beyond Regime Change," *Los Angeles Times* (December 1, 2002), p. M1. Tolan's sources include Richard Perle (Pentagon Defense Policy Board), David Wurmser (Special Assistant to the State Department), Donald Rumsfeld (Secretary of Defense), Paul Wolfowitz (Department of Defense), Elliot Abrams (Senior National Security Council Director), Dick Cheney (Vice-President), Patrick Clawson (Institute for Near East Policy), Michael Ledeen (American Enterprise Institute), and Ariel Sharon (Prime Minister of Israel). See also Emmit B. Evans, Jr., "Iraq and the New American Colonialism," *Moebius* (Volume 1, Number 2, Spring 2003).
40. See Helena Cobban, "Military occupations—the good, bad, and ugly," *The Christian Science Monitor* (March 27, 2003), p. 11.

For Further Reading

Apter, David E., and Rosberg, Carl G., eds. *Political Development and the New Realism in Sub-Saharan Africa.* Charlottesville: University Press of Virginia, 1994.
Barber, Benjamin R. *Jihad vs. McWorld: Terrorism's Challenge to Democracy.* New York: Ballantine Books, 2001.
Barber, Benjamin R. *Fear's Empire: War, Terrorism, and Democracy.* New York: W.W. Norton & Company, Inc., 2003.
Barfield, Claude E. *Free Trade, Sovereignty, Democracy: The Future of the World Trade Organization.* Washington, D.C.: The AEI Press, 2001.

Broad, Robin, ed. *Global Backlash: Citizen Initiatives for a Just World Economy.* Rowman & Littlefield Publishers, Inc., 2002.

Clapham, Christopher. *Third World Politics: An Introduction.* Madison: University of Wisconsin Press, 1985. *Foreign Policy* 107 (summer 1997), Globalization: The Debate.

Croucher, Sheila L. *Globalization and Belonging: The Politics of Identity in a Changing World.* New York: Rowman & Littlefield Publishers, Inc., 2004.

Grieder, William. *One World Ready or Not: The Manic Logic of Global Capitalism.* New York: Simon & Schuster, 1997.

Harrison, Paul. *Inside the Third World: The Anatomy of Poverty.* London: Penguin Books, 1990.

Johnson, Chalmers. *Blowback: The Costs and Consequences of American Empire.* New York: Owl/Metropolitan Books, 2001.

Lenksi, Gerhard E. *Power and Privilege: A Theory of Social Stratification.* New York: McGraw-Hill, 1966.

Perkins, John. *Confessions of an Economic Hit Man.* San Francisco: Berrett-KJoehler Publishers, Inc., 2004.

Rischard, J.F. *High Noon: Twenty Global Problems, Twenty Years to Solve Them.* New York: Basic Books, 2002.

Schumacher, E. F. *Small Is Beautiful: Economics as if People Mattered.* New York: Harper & Row, 1973.

Singer, P.W. *Corporate Warriors: The Rise of the Privatized Military Industry.* Ithaca: Cornell University Press, 2003.

Soros, George. *Open Society: Reforming Global Capitalism.* New York: Public Affairs, 2000.

Tinder, Glenn. *Political Thinking: The Perennial Questions.* 6th ed. New York: HarperCollins, 1995.

Toffler, Alvin. *Powershift: Knowledge, Wealth, and Violence at the Edge of the 21st Century.* New York: Bantam Books, 1990.

Union of Concerned Scientists. *World Scientists' Warning Briefing Book.* Cambridge, Mass.: Union of Concerned Scientists, 1993.

Warkentin, Craig. *Reshaping World Politics: NGOs, the Internet, and Global Civil Society.* New York: Rowman & Littlefield Publishers, Inc., 2001.

Women and Development

Dianne Long

*Talking about man without talking about woman is like clapping
with one hand.*

ANONYMOUS

Visual glimpses of the developing world in Western media often capture the faces, figures, and activities of women. Photos depict the tall Masai women of East Africa with their colorful garb, the Indian women in saris carrying children and water, the formless Afghan women veiled in blue burkas from head to toe scurrying through the marketplace. The developing world cannot truly be understood without discussing women. Yet these images and the stories accompanying them do not fully tell us about the lives of women in the Other World.

Women play a crucial role in development. Surprisingly little attention has been paid to their important involvement until very recently. The primary reason for this lack of attention is the fact that most attempts at development activities had been carried out by male-dominated institutions and reported from the perspective of international bureaucracies that did not recognize women's roles. However, women are an essential link to population control. They carry heavy responsibility for food production, not only for their own families, but also for community marketplaces. They contribute significantly to wage labor, even though wages tend to be very meager. Because they bear responsibility for family health and nutrition, they are aware of how pollution, desertification, and deforestation affect community health and prosperity. In the developing world, women face many obstacles—political, economic, and social. In various areas of the world, female children are less valued. This leads to high infanticide and child mortality rates. Neglect, violence, multiple pregnancy, poor nutrition, and hard physical labor take their toll on women's well being. In many areas of the developing world, school enrollments of females and literacy rates are lower than those for males. Individual and economic opportunities for females are diminished throughout life.

This chapter takes note of four major factors that affect women in developing countries. They are:

1. The legacy of colonialism
2. The push for modernization
3. The evolution of nationalism
4. The pervasiveness of globalization

Examining these factors as they affect women adds to our understanding of women's past, present, and future in the Other World.

WOMEN AND THE LEGACY OF COLONIALISM

Colonialism was not a new concept to either the European powers or to the colonies. It was the foundation of the Roman and Ottoman empires. What was new about colonialism in the eighteenth and nineteenth centuries was the scale of exploitation. This exploitation was largely fueled by the Industrial Revolution that arose in Britain. The period from 1750 to 1850 was one of rapid and profound social and economic change. Britain changed from a traditional agricultural society to a modern industrial one. The invention of the steam engine in 1769 and the development of steam for power resulted in the building of roads, railroads, and canals and started cotton textile manufacturing in England. By 1830, it had been established in France, and soon thereafter, industry was a dominant factor in Germany and other countries of Europe. The United States and Russia entered the industrial age. Industrialization produced and required expanded markets, cheap labor, and raw materials, for which the industrial nations turned to the less developed areas of the world, primarily Africa and Asia. *Imperialism,* the extension of rule of one society over another, was a natural consequence.

The pre-colonial world had a variety of cultural arrangements. Living in clans and extended families, women's lives had been shaped by centuries of local custom and necessary adaptation to change. There is no doubt that they shared power and responsibilities in order to survive. Certainly their human experiences are reflected in every historical and geographic context. Western colonization, however, pushed aside the traditional patterns and introduced new concepts and requirements for gender both in private and in public, placing primary emphasis on the reproductive function of women and their role in the rearing and nurturing of children. Women's lives were considered to be limited to this "private" or internal sphere of home and children, while men were considered to operate in the "public" or external sphere, managing matters outside the home. Men were seen as having roles that included economic planning and building, settling conflicts, waging war, and bonding with other males for political and economic strength.[1]

Oriental Carpets: Carpet weaving is a common occupation for women in Central Asia, Pakistan, India, and China.
SOURCE: JOE WEATHERBY

European values shaped women's lives. In the sixteenth and seventeenth centuries, Spanish and Portuguese colonizing efforts brought Catholicism and "macho" attitudes that diminished the roles of indigenous women. In the nineteenth century, a pattern of patriarchy spread throughout industrialized Europe and was introduced into the developing world. In the new industrial world, both politics and economics were considered to be male concerns, and female power over any part of the sector declined. European cultures put decision making and property into the hands of male heads of household. Women were part of that property. Thus, a patriarchal pattern replaced other customary patterns. England, especially, became a world power. During the rule of Queen Victoria (1837–1901), England was transformed from an island at the edge of Europe to an empire where the sun never set, and where the monarch was crowned the Empress of India and ruler of vast areas of Africa and the Pacific. Although the monarch was a woman, power was in the hands of political and industrial men.

Colonial administrators, taking charge of the developing world from a Victorian perspective, ignored the importance of women to community life and to local economies. The few female rulers like Queen Victoria ruled in order to maintain the elite family royal line. Men made decisions, held property, and restricted women to subservient roles. In Africa and Asia, women had been primarily agricultural workers. New developments introduced into these areas required that men be trained to work for wages on plantations and large-scale farms. The men often resisted and ignored the training, and Colonial administrators often failed to comprehend the weakness of their agricultural programs. Nevertheless, development established ownership and dominance, men were forced to comply with new conditions, and women were shut out of their traditional subsistence farming. Even where women had strong political and economic roles—as they did in West Africa—their positions in traditional societies were eliminated. They could no longer hold any positions of importance, such as clan chiefs, judges, or managers of resources.[2]

Traditional societies usually held their land in common, not as individuals. Land reform was introduced with colonialism. European powers granted land titles to European entrepreneurs, government officials, and important "native" leaders. The government redefinition of ownership, and land grants, dispossessed women in the private economy, and empowered male leaders in the public economy. Families were forced to abandon the subsistence farming that had always met family needs. Their land was taken for commercial agriculture. Women, who had always done at least half of the agricultural work, were deprived of their lands and were pushed into smaller and less fertile areas to continue their struggle to feed their families and neighbors. Food supply, distribution, nutrition, and health of women and children suffered. The land that had been community property, farmed for the common good, had become commercial, used for the profit of others.[3]

Even today, women in the developing world face challenges as farmers and homemakers. Vandana Shiva, one of India's leading physicists and environmental activists, documents the impact of corporate agriculture on small farmers, the majority of whom are women. In *Stolen Harvest*, Shiva chronicles the resistance movement of women organized to protest new commercial shrimp industries in India where 15 jobs are lost for every new job created. The shrimp industry competes for water, and tankers need to import small quantities for household drinking and other needs. Contaminated water is often used for cattle causing cattle to die. Milk and beef become scarce.[4] The intrusion of companies such as Monsanto, with its genetically engineered seed and its herbicides, destroy hundreds of weed species of plants that poor women depend upon for food, fodder, and medicine.[5]

In the developing world, women continue to be deprived of educational opportunities. They are less likely to be chosen by families to attend school, and they are the first to be taken out of school to help at home and bring needed monies to families. School fees are a burden on poor families and scarce funds translate to fewer school opportunities for girls and young women. Literacy rates for women in many countries are unacceptable. In Niger, not even 10 percent of women are literate; most have completed less than three years of formal schooling. The statistics alone do not tell the whole story.

In Guatemala and other Latin American countries, *machismo* dominates as an aggressive assertion of male dominance over women. Likewise the idea of *"marianismo"* exists in some cultures where women are considered morally superior to men. These scripted roles are expected to hold families together. Such self-images contribute to political conservatism that is easily exploited by political parties and military regimes. In Saudi Arabia and Qatar more women then men are attending university, yet they are barred from many occupations. When women break traditional gender roles, governmental and religious leaders complain. Also, dual education is often very expensive. The refusal to let women drive is inefficient as fathers work only part-time and must run errands part-time. Thus, in Saudi Arabia and elsewhere, companies prefer to hire foreigners and unemployment increases especially with young family men. Productivity, too, suffers when women who represent half of the potential work force cannot participate.

Today, women's work is largely unpaid. We can assume that the persons here are fully engaged in the workplace. Although they work longer days in support of families and bring funds into the family, 70 percent of women's time is unpaid work. The remainder centers on market activities, including raising crops and animals for sale, home crafts, manufacturing and related assembly, and prostitution. Women work on average 60–90 hours a week in developing areas. International organizations are continuing to work to get countries to report data related to work time and to indicate the statistics for men and women. With better data, the UN and nonprofit organizations can address women's work and equity issues by developing policies and programs to help women. Even today, women's work is not valued in the marketplace, and it is not compensated in the home.

THE EVOLUTION OF NATIONALISM

The colonial era was disrupted by the economic and political events of the twentieth century: the Great Depression and World War II. Major realignments of power occurred, and many areas of the world experienced an explosion of newly independent states. The spirit of *nationalism*—a political philosophy that holds that the welfare of the nation-state is paramount—spread. Nationalism, however, necessarily treats individual rights and group rights within the society as secondary. Women, in particular, have had to take a back seat to nationalism.

In 1945, 51 nations formed the United Nations. Since then, many new nations have formed: 191 nations are now UN members—most are from the Other World. The original 51 nations of the UN had been in existence for many years and had long-standing political and economic structures, clear geographic boundaries, and an established national identity. In contrast, the new nations created after World War II were created out of the colonial lands with arbitrary boundaries and a legacy of dependence upon colonial powers. Nation building required citizens to take on a national identity to serve as an empowering ideology. This proved difficult in some places where governments attempted to oversee a coalition of various

Processing Silk: This woman is operating a machine that unrolls the cocoons of silkworms to make thread. SOURCE: JOE WEATHERBY

competing cultures. In other places, religious beliefs and cultural patterns initially helped to forge a new identity. In the North African nation of Algeria, for example, the nationalist effort was imbued with strong family values and Arab-Islamic codes prescribing women's roles. However, in Algeria, women worked for independence as they have done in Palestine and elsewhere, only to be asked to go back to the kitchen when independence was won. Women protested. Nevertheless, upon independence from France in 1962, the new rulers of Algeria committed themselves to socialist modernization while attempting to set aside gender concerns in deference to national development. In 1992, however, civil war caused further disruptions. Terrorists and extreme political groups harassed women and created a general uneasiness in the population. A successful union of Islam with culture helped create a national identity for other nations in the Middle East, notably Iran, Iraq, and Lebanon. Palestinians, even without a homeland, also forged a national identity out of a merger of religious and cultural values.

A nation-state comprises many power relations within its boundaries: economic, political, legal, and cultural. The creation of legitimacy is a prime consideration. New nations have reduced and simplified social codes to give them legal force. Modern African nations, for example, used the "rule of law" to gain legitimacy. By law, women gained legal rights to schooling, property, and divorce.

In practice, applications of law were sometimes arbitrary and women were denied rights. Many codes continued to emphasize the public-private divide. Modern legal processes emerged as a form of imperialist intervention. Although women worked with men in the struggle for independence, economic opportunity, basic human rights, and the right to vote, women's voices were ignored as new states worked to design new governing institutions. As nations evolved, the battle for human rights—including those of women—was viewed with the suspicion that champions for such causes were collaborating with an imperialist Western enemy.

The case of Afghanistan illustrates this point. The Taliban leadership dominated other tribes, establishing a very conservative religious policy that disallowed the education of women and relegated women to wearing the *burka*—the blue covering transforming a woman into a shapeless, faceless identity. Women teachers and professionals lost their jobs and were punished for appearing in public without a male protector. Women were confined to their homes. Before the fall of the Taliban regime, protest was regarded as treason and could be met with harassment or death. Women have returned to school and to market, and many women removed the burka, following the fall of this Afghan government. Others have taken up government posts and organized campaigns for elected positions in legislatures and in executive offices in local governments.

In general, new nations have adopted bureaucratic forms of government. In these large formal organizations, decisions are made at the top of the organization and those below follow orders. These decision structures have served male interests. New governments pushed women aside and intruded in both private and public lives. Although patterns of opposition from women were different from one geographic space and one historical time to another, any resistance caused new social conflicts. In the end, women and the state viewed each other with suspicion.

The lack of a middle class necessary for running a democracy made governing difficult. Thus, it is not surprising that in some nations, only women from the upper classes have been able to represent women's issues. In China, India, Pakistan, and the Philippines for example, political women came from the upper economic educated stratum of society. They knew little of the struggle of poor women. Their individual successes were dependent upon pragmatic male support in political parties and state government. Gender-specific issues, such as prenatal care, contraception, and women's property rights were discouraged.

During the last two decades, women have begun to enter local politics and legal disputes to represent their interests. Beginning in the mid-1960s, women have entered politics in greater numbers and a few women were even elected to the office of head of state. Sinmavo Bandaranaike of Sri Lanka held office from 1959 to 1970 after her husband's assassination, and again from 1970 to 1977. Her daughter Chandrika Bandaranaike Kumaratunga became prime minister in 1994 and president later in the year when she named her mother as prime minister. Indira Ghandi of India held power from 1966 to 1977 and again from 1980 to 1984. Her son Rajiv followed as prime minister. Likewise, Benazir Bhutto of Pakistan followed her father into the post of prime minister from 1988 to 1990. This pattern illustrates the dominance of ruling elites.

Until very recently, women historically had been left out of political leadership. In 1980, women held fewer than 10 percent of parliamentary seats in advanced democracies of Europe and the U.S. By 2005, seats increased to 15 percent, and now seats held by women reach over 20 percent in many countries. Thirty-six percent of Cuba's parliamentary seats are held by women, Costa Rica has 35.1 percent, and Argentina has 34 percent in the lower house and 33 percent in the upper house. In comparison, the United States has 15 percent in the lower house and 14 percent in the Senate, Niger 12 percent, Ethiopia 8 percent in each house, and 6 percent of Chad's parliamentary seats are held by women.[6]

With democracy and multiple-party governments giving women the opportunity to run for elected office, they willingly take to the campaign trail. Dr. Massounda Jalal was forced to stop teaching in Kabul University in Afghanistan when the Taliban took power. She signed up to head a United Nations program and started bakeries in Kabal to allow war widows to feed their families. When the Taliban fell, she ran for president, getting 1 percent of the vote. She hopes to run again. In Afghanistan, about 44 percent of all registered voters are women. In Iraq, more than 55 percent of the voters are female and represent a third of the delegates elected to design a constitution. Despite obstacles, women want to be integrated in society. In Afghanistan, the plan is for women to have 25 percent of the seats in the lower house and 17 percent in the upper house reserved for women representatives. In Iraq, women are lobbying for 40 percent of the seats.

In November 2005, Ellen Johnson-Sirleaf became the victor in Liberia's first presidential elections since the end of fourteen years of civil war. Named the "Iron Lady" by supporters, she will become the first elected female head of state in all of Africa. She has a political career spanning over thirty years beginning with criticizing Liberia's military regime in the 1980s, and later going into exile. Educated in the United States, she held a number of banking positions, including Africa director at the United Nations Development Programme. Many think her banking experience and her Harvard education will help steer the Liberian economy as President of Liberia.[7]

However, political leaders manipulate the traditional family concept to reinforce their own authority. Just as the father makes decisions in a family, in new states the leader makes decisions for "the children." As women make educational gains and move into work roles outside the home, there are big impacts. Families enjoy the added income and social status. Their children can compete for better marital partners. Women gain self worth and can begin to negotiate power within the family and community. And they can begin to challenge socially approved norms of dress and behavior.

In new nations, government corruption has often developed as the way of doing business. Legal and illegal uses of power operate with little public accountability. Even with clear laws, rulers are often above the law and corruption is a part of everyday living. Some politicians, bureaucrats, and citizens give the law itself a low status. Capacity to enforce law is overshadowed by other interests, and the rule of law is undermined. Protest then replaces petition. Although their visibility makes them open to punishment, women in many parts of the world have come to organize to confront the nation's rulers, its rules, and its pattern of corruption. They have come to address two main issues of our time: nationalism and the oppression of women.

WOMEN AND THE PUSH FOR MODERNIZATION

There is a widespread belief that modernization, along with democratization, urbanization, and industrialization, will improve women's lives, offering opportunities and rising economic and social status. This belief has not always proved true. Modernization was introduced to agricultural communities to improve production of cash crops. Foreigners developed large-scale plantations and other agricultural businesses. Men—and some women and children—found that they could survive only by going to work for the new owners, usually for low wages and long hours to buy food and other necessities. Commercial agriculture created powerful new requirements. It required advanced technology and training, modern equipment, synthetic fertilizers and herbicides, and the money to buy them. Commercial agriculture provided colonial people with technical training in agricultural methods. Modernization did not trickle down to everyone. Women continued to have smaller garden areas to grow crops for the table. Soils and water supply were at times marginal, and harvests could be disappointing. In some countries, women also went to work on plantations for small wages, while still carrying the responsibilities for house, family, and garden. Caught up in both the deteriorating family economy and modernization requirements, their lives were not improved.[8]

New financing mechanisms were introduced along with changes in agricultural production, distribution, and consumption. Local farmers were required to adapt to the new agricultural industries introduced into the Other World or they were displaced from the land. Trying to maintain themselves, they acquired debt. The World Bank, the UN, and nongovernmental organizations (NGOs) extended loans to farmers to buy seed, equipment, and fertilizer. Credit was not extended to women. Having no access either to economic resources or to technical training, they were marginalized and excluded. Even in North Africa and Asia, where women farmers first cultivated cotton and rice, women became irrelevant to commercial agriculture.

Forests, along with other natural resources, were placed under new ownership. Extracting timber became a commercial enterprise. Forests had traditionally been the source of firewood for heating and cooking; for fruits, plant products, clothing, and important herbs in medicinal preparations; and for small and large animals for food and other necessities. Now women were excluded from forestlands that had always been crucial to their way of life.

Like other natural resources, mines were claimed for commercial use. Minerals and ores were important materials for shaping farming and household

Broken Stereotype: Western dressed Moslem women wait outside a school in Baku, Azerbaijan for the posting of their children's grades. SOURCE: OLGA CARTER

implements. In the new system, tools could only be purchased with hard currency. Without currency, women did without. In many areas of the world, women had traditionally managed fisheries and brought home the catch to feed the family and sell at market. With colonialism and modernization, commercial companies took the place of women.

Urbanization (the rise of cities) developed from the economic needs of the Industrial Revolution. Factories for production, banks for finance, and offices for government and commercial operations were built. Industrialization required urbanization; urbanization brought with it modernization. Villages developed into cities with electricity, telephone and telegraph communications, water and sanitation systems, contemporary buildings, roads and railroads, and other essentials of modern life. Jobs were centered in cities, and both men and women migrated to them out of economic necessity. Men took jobs in industry and in low-waged building projects. Women worked in industry too, primarily in textiles and parts assembly for manufactured goods. Where women could not find jobs, they turned to earning wages by domestic labor or prostitution to survive. Apart from traditional families and clan protection, women became even more vulnerable to violence, disease, and isolation.

Gender equality is an important component of modernization. Colonialism set the values for inequity, and modernization needs to address this issue. Indeed colonialism can be considered an obstacle to modernization today. If gender discrimination is a source of endemic poverty, then efforts are required to diminish the discrepancies between men and women. The two dominant approaches to achieving equity are *mainstreaming* and *empowerment*. The goal of mainstreaming is to bring women into the regular economic, political, and social life enjoyed by men. The goal of empowerment calls for the design of special opportunities for women to have choices in their lives. Progress is slow even though some gains have been made.

The United Nations Development Program (UNDP) has six practice areas for mainstreaming.[9] The first of these is full participation of women in democratic governance. In Pakistan, 30 percent of local government seats are reserved for women. The second is poverty reduction. Two-thirds of the one billion adults who cannot read are women. They are the first to leave school and the last to get medical care. Third is crisis prevention and recovery. More than 80 percent of refugees from war and internal crisis are women and children. Fourth, energy and environment programs are needed to bring access to modern energy services and to reduce pollution. Fifth, information and communication technologies are

Style Show: Chinese women modeling western dresses near Shanghai.
SOURCE: JOE WEATHERBY

important to increasing women's skills and abilities to network for their own safety, welfare, and ability to engage in the society at large. Lastly, HIV/AIDS is pandemic, spreading quickly in Africa and other areas of the world. Teenage girls are five-to-six times more likely to be affected by the HIV virus than boys their age.[10]

Supporting gender equality is a major goal of the UN, set forth in world summits and global conferences in the 1990s. The UN's Millennium Development Goals translate into specific reforms and programs to make a difference for women, especially those who are poor. The UN Development Fund for Women (UNIFEM) has resources to improve computerized networks for women and girls, to help organizations with gender goals, to develop databases, to fund leadership programs, and to disseminate information on women's issues.

Data on the condition of women in the developing world are continuing to improve. The data related to infant mortality, maternal mortality and life expectancy say a lot about quality of life issues. In Malawi, for example, infants and mothers die at a rate of one in ten, as opposed to one in 2,000 in the U.S. according to 2005 United Nations indicators.

Although there are small improvements in the conditions of women, life is still harsh for them in the developing world. Where there once was plenty of food, now cash crops such as tobacco and sugar are grown to support imperialist economies. Commercial forests, mines, and fisheries pushed out independent farmers, crafts and trades workers, and herders. In many places, men travel to far-off plantations, mines, and cities for work, leaving women to tend to home. Family life is fragmented. Young people, male and female, travel to cities out of economic necessity. Scarcity of food and other necessities has increased. Health services are still primitive—especially in rural areas. Women and infants suffer unusually high death rates. Coping with scarcity and with survival is now almost solely a woman's concern.

WOMEN AND GLOBALISM

Political independence and economic development are intertwined. Industrial economies, an integral component of the Western nation-states, formed the model for most of the new political entities. For the masses caught up in rising expectations, independence and nation building held great promise. A higher standard of living seemed a right that had been won through the struggle for nationhood. However, these new independent nations were vulnerable to external factors such as international economic and political ties; they were dependent on the outside world for trade, technology, economic aid, and military aid. They were weak in enforcing laws and regulating security. The governments often had little control over factors such as intimidation and corruption.

In many countries, national policies reflect a gender division of labor. Women are held to the low-paying jobs in the public economy or to the nonpaying jobs in service of the family. Poor women are forced to migrate because of economic necessity, not by personal choice. The traffic in prostitution, mail-order brides, domestic services, and slavery conditions in clothing assembly bear this out. In national, legal, and political systems, women do not have the same legal remedies available to men, and they may be forced to deal with dangerous circumstances, ending in abuse and sometimes death.

Furthermore, states have been helpless to control human immune deficiency virus (HIV) and acquired immunodeficiency syndrome (AIDS) spread through sexual activity as part of sexual tourism, especially in Africa and Asia. The United Nations reports over 38 million cases of HIV/AIDS in the world. A disproportionate number of cases are reported in women. Half of all HIV/AIDS cases affect women aged 15–49 who live in the developing world. Children make up 3 million of the population with this disease. Many contracted HIV/AIDS from their mothers before or after birth or through breast-feeding.[10] Income and human development infrastructure are related to these cases. Most of the women live in low-income countries (14 million out of 18 million) or low development situations (11.3 million of 18 million). In 2001, South Africa alone had 2.7 million cases, Nigeria had 1.7 million, India had 1.5 million, Kenya 1.4 million, Zimbabwe 1.2 million, and Ethiopia 1.1 million. Statistics for 2003 show composite percentages for the population between the ages of 15 and 49 by country. Countries with the highest percentages of HIV are Swaziland 38.8 percent, Botswana 37.3 percent, Lesotho 28.9 percent, Zimbabwe 25 percent, and South Africa 21.5 percent. In comparison, the U.S. has .6 percent HIV for ages 15–49, and more than 831,000 cases of HIV/AIDS and 501,669 deaths in 2003.

Income is related to life expectancy. In high-income countries, 89.5 percent of women live to age 65; in low-income countries they live to only 59.6. Additionally, in high-income countries, 88.3 percent of women expect to live to 65. In low-income countries, the percent falls to 41.7. In Namibia, only 30.8 percent live to 65; in Botswana, only 21.7 percent; in Swaziland, 15.2 percent; and in Zimbabwe, 8 percent. The remainder perishes before the age of 65.

Until recently, international organizations and development conferences have not concerned themselves with women's lives, but have concentrated on those of men. The Fourth World Conference on Women was held in China's capital, Beijing, in September 1995. More than 50,000 members attended and declared that women's rights are human rights. The Beijing Declaration and Platform for Action resulted. This platform encourages 100 countries and UN organizations to make commitments to improve the status of women. They look for important changes in national policies that restrict women's rights, such as changes in inheritance laws and property rights. They ask countries to improve data gathering and set targets for improving the enrollment of women in primary school and improving female literacy. They look for countries and organizations to participate in international development in a coordinated way. The conference messages underscore key concerns. The first concern is that women's rights are human rights. Second, discrimination and violence against women must end. Third, equality for women is an important goal politically, economically, and socially. Fourth, issues of population control and development that include women's voices are global concerns. The platform builds on progress made in previous UN conferences on women—in Mexico City in 1975, in Copenhagen in 1980, and in Nairobi in 1985. Each conference emphasized the role women have in development and the importance of protecting human rights.

In response to these global discussions, UN organizations, the World Bank, and the U.S. Agency for International Development have focused more attention on women as appropriate recipients of development efforts. These organizations have echoed the concerns of the Beijing conference and its call to action. A key element for many projects is increased school enrollment and literacy for girls as well as boys. Females who are educated tend to marry as adults rather than as adolescents. They have fewer children, they have access to important information on health and nutrition, and they have greater opportunities for better wages in the marketplace. Other international conferences related to poverty have also begun to give prominence to those projects that address the status of women and the feminization of poverty. The 1994 International Conference on Population and Development stressed this point in its examination of health and reproductive rights: increasing female education is necessary for population control.

It is increasingly difficult for organizations such as the UN and World Bank to ignore the plight of women. International conferences demand that women's voices be heard and that human rights abuses be addressed. In the 1990s, both the UN and World Bank chose the improvement of the lives of women as a goal. In response to pressure from women's networks, international organizations have directed themselves toward improving literacy of women and increasing female enrollments in school. They have also urged nations to dedicate themselves to the same goals. In addition, non-governmental organizations (NGOs) have begun to focus on women as being key to economic development efforts. Programs are designed to help women become knowledgeable about contraception and family planning, and to improve nutrition and prenatal care. Women's needs are considered, such as drilling new wells for drinkable water, designing improved cooking methods using little available fuel, and providing small loans to women for starting businesses that market their products and crafts. These early efforts offer much hope.[11]

Nevertheless, the data on women and development shows a crisis looming. Life expectancy and literacy are dropping in some counties, with greater drops for women. For some, economic growth is below zero, and opportunities for women are limited. A number of countries have increased child mortality, especially female children. And people still live below $1 per day; many families are headed by women.

More than 150 heads of state and world leaders at the historic Millennium Assembly of the UN in September 2000 promised to do their utmost to end poverty and to improve the lot of women. The Monterrey Consensus of March 2002 framed mutual obligations of poor countries to pursue good policies, tackle corruption, and raise domestic resources. It also calls on rich countries to support countries that demonstrate good policies. The Johannesburg Summit 2002 goals were reaffirmed as well as a summit of the industrialized countries in June 2003.

SUMMARY

The Other World is a difficult place for women. The legacy of colonialism stressed patriarchy and ignored the important economic and social roles women played in developing societies. *Nationalization* concentrated power into the hands of a few political leaders who saw women as marginal to the goals of forming a new government. Corruption also made women's lives difficult, as abuses against women often went unpunished. *Modernization* shifted populations to cities and shifted economic life from small farming plots to large agricultural businesses that pushed women into undesirable land. Sustaining human life became more difficult. *Globalization* brought international corporations into decision making on both social and economic policy. Economic opportunities have been meager. Women have been required to perform low-wage jobs. Their contributions to family economies have been underestimated. Women also have been subjected to violence, abuse, and trafficking. The high incidence of HIV/AIDS in women and children are a consequence of the spread of disease across continents and seas. International conferences, like the one in Beijing, continue to press for change in women's status and to make women's rights an important issue in the human rights struggle.

 **ISSUES FOR DISCUSSION**

1. Is development good news for women in the developing world?

Many think development will benefit all in a society. This is not always true. From the 1950s to the 1980s, women did not receive wage parity with men even in modern developing nations. Per capita income rose dramatically in many places in the Other World, but women continue to lag behind men. In some countries of Asia and Africa in particular, women have significantly less access to resources and to income opportunities. Primary school enrollment and literacy data continue to show a gender gap between women and men, even though many nations and international organization stress gender equity. In some cultures, women provide the family's basic needs. Men in the family may decide to use earned income for business or personal gain. It is women in much of sub-Saharan Africa who must provide shelter, clothes, school fees, and medical care for themselves and for their children. Men may acquire radios, bicycles, and other objects for personal consumption. Children's nutrition and health actually has worsened in some countries even when per capita income increased. This pattern exists in Guatemala, Belize, Mexico, and India.

Women's work may not always provide economic opportunity. Where jobs are created for women, wages are low and women are forced to work two jobs: one at home and one in the formal economy. Working women in developing countries often put in 12 to 18 hours a day. The World Bank, the largest international aid agency in the world, now promotes economic opportunity for women in its development efforts. The Women in Development (WID) program was created in 1977 to ensure those women were part of a project design. The program operated in a male-dominated agency with top-down directives. Later, in 1993, a Gender and Development (GAD) division replaced WID. Feminist critiques were critical of the organization. Since then the World Bank has tried to listen to women's voices in designing its programs.

2. Can women find the opportunity for increased literacy, despite their secondary status in Other World societies?

Almost every international meeting on human rights and the eradication of poverty has targeted increased literacy for women, but the reality is that in many societies, women are not valued. School fees are expensive and young girls and women are needed at home to help with chores or to work in factories and plantations so the family can afford school and job opportunities for boys. Patriarchal attitudes persist and block potential benefits for women.

The UN Population Fund continues to track the close connection between education and fertility. The more education women have, the more likely they are to have small families. In the southern Indian state of Kerala, the fertility rate is low, 2.3 children per woman. Why is it so low when others may have three or four times as many children? Most claim it is because female literacy is 66 percent—many times greater than other areas of India. In addition, women of Kerala have social and legal status. They can inherit land, and families must make a money gift to the bride's family when a marriage takes place. In other areas of the developing world, it is common for the bride's family to give money to the groom instead of receiving money. Many experts also believe that women with education appear to look for more equality in marital arrangements and for more economic opportunities for themselves and their children.

3. Can women in developing nations have a voice in government?

Today there are very few women running for political office and serving in legislatures in both the developed and developing worlds. Women's voices have been ignored, and women have been cast to the sidelines. Traditional society suggests that women restrict their efforts to the home rather than to public life. The burden of household management, childbirth, and care for children and the elderly remove women from having opportunities to learn about government offices and policy issues. Certainly low levels of literacy for females in many areas of the developing world play a big part in denying women a voice in government. International organizations have taken up the banner of equality in government and encourage women to become informed and to run for local, regional, and national offices. Feminist voices have collectively made a difference. Participating in meetings and organizations, they pressure for changes in both national and international policies that restrict women.

Economic development and literacy are prerequisites to more political opportunities. Women face a number of obstacles to gaining equity with men. In Asia and Africa, laws are often ignored. Without the ability to have voice or to protect property, women's lives continue to be determined by other persons and by other forces.

Improving the status of women is key to gender equity and to political voice. In Bangladesh, for example, the Grameen Bank gives women small loans to develop businesses. Participants become important parts of a local economy, raising domestic animals, making handicrafts, and growing important agricultural products for the market. They also have begun to pressure for a decision-making role in the life of the villages in which they live.

4. How has globalization hurt women?

Globalization has brought more job opportunities, but many of these are low-tech and low wage jobs. Manufacturing has moved from the industrialized world to the developing world because wages are low. Environmental and labor regulation often does not exist, and working conditions are unsafe and unhealthy. Because women are less valued, many women and children are hired to fill production jobs, and they are paid less than men for the same jobs. When there is a slowdown in production, women are the first to get fewer hours or to be laid off. Cuts in spending for education and health disproportionately affect women. Where cash crops are introduced into the agricultural economy, women lose their family plots and are forced to forage for food and walk great distances for essential drinking water and firewood.

5. Why is educating women so important to economic progress?

Women who are educated delay having children. They also have fewer children, and are informed about family planning. As a result, they can invest more in the few children that they have. United Nations data indicates that there are fewer infant deaths, healthier children, and higher literacy rates for the offspring of educated women. They can contribute economically to the family managing the crops and animals and developing crafts. Studies also suggest that women give more of the budget to education, health, and nutrition. School enrollment is increased for the children of educated women. These women get involved in family and community decisions to advance the well-being of others.

Review Questions

1. How has colonialism affected women in the Other World?
2. How has modernization affected women in the Other World?
3. How have nationalism and economic development affected women in the Other World?
4. What obstacles do women experience in the developing world?
5. What progress have women made in political life?

Key Terms

- **Empowerment**—Providing women with choices in their lives.
- **Globalization**—Expanding market activity across the globe.
- **Imperialism**—The extension of rule of one society over another.
- **Machismo**—Aggressive assertion of male dominance over women.
- **Mainstreaming**—Bringing women into the regular economic, political, and social life enjoyed by men.
- **Marianismo**—Assertion that women are considered morally superior to men.
- **Modernization**—Replication conditions of industrialized nations.
- **Nationalism**—Political philosophy that holds that the welfare of the nation-state is paramount.

Useful Web Sites

Feminist organization site with links: www.feminist.org
United Nations Development Programme site: www.unifem.undp.org
United Nations site: www.un.org/womenwatch
World Bank site: www.worldbank.org
World Neighbors site: http://www.worldneighbors.org

Notes

1. See the essays in Uma Narayan, *Dislocating Cultures: Identities, Traditions, and Third World Feminism* (New York: Routledge, 1997).
2. See Mary Poovay, Catherine R. Stimpson, eds., *Uneven Developments: The Ideological Work of Gender in Mid-Victorian England* (Chicago: University of Chicago Press, 1999).
3. Shiva, Vandana, *Stolen Harvest: The Hijacking of the Global Food Supply* (South End Press, 2000), pp. 48–60.
4. Ibid, pp. 316–318.
5. Ibid.
6. Winik, Lyric Wallwork, "These Women Are Changing Their Nations," *Parade*, July 3, 2005.
7. newsvote.bbc.co.uk.
8. A discussion of debt appears in the *World Development Report 2005*, pp. 268–271.

9. United Nations Development Programme, *Gender Equality: Executive Summary, November 2002*, www.undp.org.

10. *World Almanac*, pp. 88–89 and *UNDP Report, 2005*, pp. 246–249.

11. The World Bank annually provides data and analysis on both program efforts and on economic indicators, *World Development Report 2004 and 2005* (Washington, D.C.: World Bank, 2004 and 2005).

For Further Reading

Ahmed, Leila. *Women and Gender in Islam.* New Haven, Conn.: Yale University Press, 1992.

Bayes, Jane H., and Tohidi, Nayereh Esfahlani, eds. *Globalizations, Religion, and Gender: The Politics of Implementing Women's Rights in Catholic and Muslim Countries.* New York: Palgave Macmillan, 2001.

Datta, Rekha, and Kornberg, Judith, eds. *Women in Developing Countries: Assessing Strategies for Empowerment.* Boulder, CO: Lynne Rienner Publishers, 2002.

Edwards, Michael, and Gaventa, John, eds. *Global Citizen Action.* Boulder, CO: Lynne Rienner Publishers, 2001.

Jabri, Vivienne, and O'Gorman, Eleanor. *Women, Culture, and International Relations.* Boulder, CO: Lynne Rienner Publishers, 1999.

Kelley, Rita Mae, Bayes, Jane H., Hawkesworth, Mary E., and Young, Brigitte, eds. *Gender, Globalization, and Democratization.* New York: Rowman & Littlefield Publishers, 2001.

Kumar, Krishna, ed. *Women and Civil War: Impact, Organizations, and Action.* Boulder, CO: Lynne Rienner Publishers, 2001.

Narayan, Uma. *Dislocating Cultures: Identities, Traditions and Third World Feminism.* New York: Routledge, 1997.

Scott, Catherine V. *Gender and Development: Rethinking Modernization and Dependency Theory.* Boulder, CO: Lynne Rienner Publishers, 1996.

Tulchin, Joseph S. *Democratic Governance and Social Inequality.* Boulder, CO: Lynne Rienner Publishers, 2002.

Visvanathan, Nalini, Duggan, Lun, and Nisonoff, Laurie, eds. *The Women, Gender and Development Reader.* New York: St. Martin's Press, 1997.

Waylen, Georgina. *Gender in Third World Politics.* Boulder, CO: Lynne Rienner Publishers, 1996.

5

Latin America

Craig Arceneaux

[Latin] America is ungovernable, the man who serves a revolution plows the sea; this nation will fall inevitably into the hands of the unruly mob and then will pass into the hands of almost indistinguishable petty tyrants of every color and race.

ATTRIBUTED TO SIMÓN BOLÍVAR BY GABRIEL GARCÍA MÁRQUEZ IN HIS NOVEL
THE GENERAL IN HIS LABYRINTH

The capital city of La Paz, Bolivia, sits in a bowl, surrounded by spectacular mountains whose efforts to reach the heavens often leave them veiled by passing clouds. The view is awesome, and easily lulls one into a state of deep reflection. But a closer look reveals the somber reality. Reaching out from the urban center and making their way up the mountain slopes on all sides of the bowl one finds the slums and shantytowns of La Paz. Here, plumbing and electricity are scarce or nonexistent, roads sit unpaved, and the escarpments that afford such distant photogenic vistas conspire to create an ideal setting for floods and landslides. The outlying slums are the first and often last stop for the unemployed, downtrodden, and desperate who have made their way from the countryside with hopes of a better life in the city.

El Alto is the epitome of these fringe localities. Nonexistent as a city twenty years ago, today the city burgeons with some 800,000 mostly indigenous people living in squalid conditions. Some of the first settlers were the thousands of tin-miners left jobless when state-industries were privatized in the 1980s. Sharecroppers and farmhands arrived soon after, as the dictates of globalization withdrew price supports and agricultural subsidies. Seeking refuge in El Alto, their situation worsened as neoliberal reforms, arguably implemented more vigorously in Bolivia than in any other Latin American country, mandated government cutbacks on basic services.

Seven miles from the capital, El Alto is perched atop a highland plateau within eyesight of La Paz. At an elevation of 13,320 feet, it tops La Paz's already incredible elevation of 11,913 feet. But just as the clouds may gather to shield the view from the capital below, the elites of La Paz, who champion their European origins, have sought to ignore the poverty and peril of the highlands. Estranged from their fellow citizens, the elites would rather look to the newfound opportunities opened by globalization—the low inflation rate, access to capital markets, and new technologies leading to the discovery of vast oil and gas reserves—opportunities not felt by those at lower economic rungs—and higher altitudes. But El Alto is growing increasingly difficult to ignore. The city sits alongside the main road into La Paz and near the international airport. Why is this significant? Neglect allowed the population of El Alto to multiply, and it is in numbers that those in El Alto now find their power. With sheer numbers, they are able to close down the international airport, block all main roads, and crowd city streets. They can bring La Paz to a standstill. In fact, their actions have generated policy reversals, and presidential resignations in 2003 and 2005. Their support was critical to the election of the current president, Evo Morales These protests would have been unthinkable under the military governments that ruled the country from 1964 to 1982.

Such social activism is a hallmark of democracy, and opens new channels of communication where young political institutions are found wanting. But it can also overwhelm a fledgling democracy and derail vital long-term economic policies. The despondency that surrounds La Paz beckons immediate attention, but that same ambition for a swift and successful undertaking may have opened a fateful cycle of disorder as the mob moves to replace, one after another, politicians unable to ferry immediate socioeconomic gains.

The story of El Alto appears to corroborate the sentiments attributed to Simón Bolívar some two hundred years ago. And the account draws together a number of issues found throughout Latin American countries—poverty and inequality, globalization, governability, the politics of ethnicity, and social protest. These issues and others comprise the threads of similarity in Latin America. Nonetheless, these threads are woven differently from country to country, and create distinct social, economic, and political patterns. Hence, Bolivia's cycle of disorder is countered to the south by Chile, which has embraced globalization with success, and also to the north by Costa Rica, which has celebrated stable, democratic rule for almost fifty years. This chapter outlines those common threads that distinguish Latin America within the Other World as we look to the geography, demography, and the history of the region. Then, as we look to the current politics and economics of the region, variations begin to arise. These differences are illustrated most prominently in the individual case studies on Mexico, Brazil, and Cuba. Finally, in the Flashpoints section we look to international efforts to support democracy in Venezuela and the guerrilla war in Colombia.

GEOGRAPHY

Latin America comprises only 15 percent of the world's landmass, but the region stretches itself across nearly three-quarters of the globe in a north-south direction. Hence, it embraces an array of geographic contrasts that allow it both to mimic many other areas of the world, and to flaunt some environments not found anywhere else on earth. Those accustomed to the Mediterranean climate of Los Angeles, California, would feel somewhat at home in Santiago, Chile, which also sits in a mountain basin plagued by air pollution. The lush jungles of the Congo in Africa find a parallel in the Amazon region of South America. The arid heat and sterile plains of the Gobi Desert in Mongolia are matched by Chile's Atacama Desert. The highland cities of Nepal in the Himalayas have their counterparts in Bolivia. The tropical island settings of the South Pacific have their equals in the Caribbean. And, lest we forget that the southern portion of South America rests just 600 miles from Antarctica, a trip to this region will bring the visitor in contact with chilly environs populated by penguins, whales, seals, and seabirds.

But Latin America also boasts many unique natural characteristics. (See Figure 5.1.) Soaring mountains and a location near the equator have combined to give Peru most of the world's tropical glaciers. Most famously, Charles Darwin did his landmark study on evolution in the Galapagos Islands, which offers a variety of exceptional creatures and plant life. Likewise, in the coastal deserts of Chile and Peru, it is not uncommon to find a Humboldt penguin nesting near a cactus. This biodiversity is not lost on the rest of the region. Of the ten most biodiverse countries in the world recognized by the United Nations Environmental Programme, five sit in Latin America—Brazil, Colombia, Ecuador, Mexico, and Peru. And Latin America is not without its superlatives. At 22,841 feet, Mount Aconcagua in the Andes is the highest mountain in the Western Hemisphere. With its 3,212-foot descent, the Salto Angel waterfall in Venezuela cannot be bested. Meanwhile Iguaza Falls on the border of Argentina and Brazil can lay claim to being the widest in the world. The Rio de la Plata, separating Argentina from Uruguay, is the widest river in the world, at 120 miles. The entire continental United States could be placed within the Amazon River basin, which hosts the largest rain forest in the world. The length of the mighty Amazon River may be surpassed by the Nile, but the Nile would need to be combined with the Mississippi and Yangtze rivers to match the water flow of the Amazon. No one would deny that California's Death Valley is parched, with its average annual rainfall of just 1.6 inches, but this cannot compete with the 0.03 average of Arica, Chile, the driest spot on earth. Mexico's Copper Canyon is deeper and vaster than the Grand Canyon in Arizona.

Looking south from the United States, the geology of Latin America begins with the Mexican Plateau. The plateau is couched by mountains to the east and west, and comes to a rather abrupt end where it collides with a volcanic zone of mountains running east to west. Mexico City is located here, and sits below the towering volcanoes of Popocatepetl and Ixtaccihuatl. A string of volcanoes continues south, more active ones along the highlands of Central America, and less

TABLE 5.1 Characteristics of Latin American Countries

Country	Population (millions)	Population Growth Rate %	Infant Mortality Rate (per 1,000 live births)	Population Under 15 years of age (%)	Life Expectancy (in years)	Urban Population (%)	Literacy Rate (%)	Arable Land (%)	Per Capita GDP ($US)
Bahamas	0.3	0.67	25.7	29	65.54	89.5	95.6	1	16800
Cuba	11.308	0.33	6.5	20.6	77.23	75.6	97	24	2800
Dominican Republic	8.833	1.29	33.3	33.7	67.26	59.3	84.7	21	6000
Grenada	0.894	0.19	14.6	35.9	64.53	40.7	85	15	5000
Haiti	7.656	2.26	74.4	39.5	52.92	37.5	52.9	20	1600
Jamaica	2.713	0.71	12.8	29.1	76.29	67.4	87.9	14	3800
Belize	0.272	2.33	26.4	41.6	67.49	48.3	94.1	2	4900
Costa Rica	3.956	1.48	10.3	30.8	76.84	60.6	96	6	9000
El Salvador	6.587	1.75	25.9	37.4	71.22	59.6	80.2	27	4800
Guatemala	14.28	2.57	36.9	41.8	65.14	46.3	70.6	12	4100
Honduras	6.823	2.16	29.6	41.8	65.6	45.6	76.2	15	2600
Mexico	104.959	1.17	21.7	32.8	75.19	75.5	92.2	12	9000
Nicaragua	5.36	1.92	30.2	38.3	70.33	57.3	67.5	9	2200
Panama	3	1.26	21	29.6	71.94	57.1	92.6	7	6300
Argentina	39.144	0.98	15.7	26.3	75.91	90.1	97.1	9	11200

Bolivia	8.724	1.49	54.6	37.8	65.5	63.4	87.2	2	2400
Brazil	184.101	1.06	30.7	28	71.69	83.1	86.4	5	7600
Chile	1.299	0.97	25.3	24.3	76.58	38.6	86	10	5000
Colombia	42.31	1.49	21.7	31.6	71.72	76.5	92.5	4	6300
Ecuador	13.212	1.24	24.5	35.4	76.21	61.8	92.5	6	3300
Guyana	0.705	0.26	37.2	27.6	65.5	37.6	98.8	2	4000
Paraguay	6.191	2.48	26.7	38.7	74.89	57.2	94	6	4600
Peru	27.544	1.36	33	36.6	69.53	61	95.9	19	4600
Suriname	0.437	0.25	24.2	31.1	68.96	76.1	93	0	3500
Uruguay	3.999	0.47	12.3	24.4	76.13	92.6	98	7	12600
Venezuela	25.017	1.4	23	31.6	74.31	87.7	93.4	4	4800
Comparison states									
Austria	8.175	0.11	4.7	16.4	78.92	65.8	98	17	30000
Hungary	10.032	-0.26	8.7	16.4	72.4	65.1	99.4	51	13900
Ireland	3.969	1.16	5.5	21.3	77.56	59.9	100	13	29800
USA	293.017	0.92	6.6	21	77.71	80.1	97	19	37800

SOURCES: Population, Infant Mortality Rate, Population Under 15 Years of Age, Urban Population, and per Capita GDP from *The World Almanac and Book of Facts*, 2005. Population Growth Rate, Life Expectancy and Arable Land from *CIA World Factbook*, 2005.

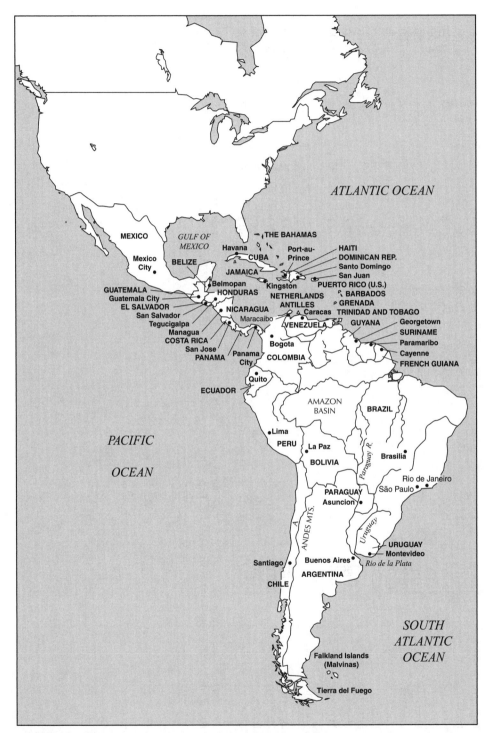

FIGURE 5.1 Political and Physical Characteristics of Latin America

active ones capping the northern cone of South America from Colombia to Venezuela. Very active volcanoes also spring up at the furthermost reaches of the Caribbean in the Lesser Antilles, and along the Andes mountain range, most prominently near Ecuador and throughout the Argentine–Chilean border.

South America is dominated by two natural features—the Andes and the Amazon River basin. The Andes form a well-defined range along the Argentine–Chilean border. But as they make their way up the backbone of the continent, through Bolivia, Peru, Ecuador, and Colombia, before they wane along the coast of central Venezuela, they break into a number of ranges, creating isolated valleys that continue to separate settlement patterns and impede trade and communications to this day. Tropical highlands are found on the eastern side of the Andes in Colombia, Peru, Bolivia, and some parts of Ecuador. The climate and remote settings of these environs are ideal for the coca cultivation and cocaine processing that has plagued these countries. The vast rain forest of the Amazon River basin cuts into the northern half of the continent from the east. To its north sits the Guiana Highlands, and to its south lay the Brazilian massif and its highlands. Ranchers covet these savannah and scrublands, and can easily expand their holdings into the rain forest through slash and burn techniques. A 2005 study by the Food and Agricultural Organization of the United Nations estimated that by 2010, expanding pasturelands would be responsible for 62 percent of the deforested area in South America.[1] Below the Brazilian highlands one finds the Paraná River system, which links the inland capital of Asuncion, Paraguay to the Atlantic through Argentina, and serves as an important source of hydroelectric power. To the west of the Paraná, the fertile, dry lowlands of the Argentine Pampas begin their march southward. Patagonia, with its barren steppes butting up against the final reaches of the Andes, comprises the southernmost area of the continent. This desolate area found its way into the lore of explorers in 1520 when Ferdinand Magellan claimed to have seen nine-foot giants he named "Patagons" (big feet). Cortés, Sir Francis Drake, and other explorers made the same claim, and labeled the land, Patagonia, or "land of the big feet."

Natural disasters have been an unfortunate byproduct of the expansive tropical areas, as well as the seismic activity in the volcanic regions. Impressive rainfalls often produce flooding in the Mexican highlands, through Central America, and in the northern cone of South America. In 1999, flooding killed 30,000 in Venezuela. Caribbean hurricanes develop regularly from July to October. Nicaragua and Honduras have yet to recover from Hurricane Mitch, whose path of destruction killed over 8,000 and left almost 3 million homeless in 1998. Over 1,000 perished in the earthquakes that rocked El Salvador in 2001, and in 1985, Mount Nevada del Ruiz erupted, killing some 21,000 in Colombia. It is important to note that much of the death and destruction in the region results from the deforestation that emerges as the impoverished masses seek resources in their surroundings, the uncontrolled land use that leads those seeking shelter to build on precarious hillsides, the lack of effective early warning systems, and an infrastructure ill-suited for rapid evacuations—all aspects of the underdevelopment found throughout the Other World. As such, one can reasonably question the term "natural" disaster, and consider if "political" disaster might be more accurate. After all, hurricanes, earthquakes, and even volcanic eruptions of similar magnitudes afflict the United States, but the numbers of those left injured or dead are miniscule in comparison.

The political geography of Latin America has been more variable than many realize.[2] Poorly documented colonial boundaries set the stage for dispute, and unstable governments both invited and ignited war. The War of the North American Invasion (1846–1848), as it is known in Mexico, deprived Mexico of half her land mass. Several of the Central American states emerged first as part of Mexico, then attempted confederacy before they went their own ways. Likewise, Colombia, Venezuela, and Ecuador united as Gran Colombia at independence, but later separated. Guatemala claims large parts of Belize, disputing the borders enforced when the country was a British colony. Venezuela lays similar claims on neighboring Guyana. The United States engineered the separation of Panama from Colombia in 1903 to facilitate control over the planned canal. Ecuador was once double in size, but Peru gobbled up her interior in the early nineteenth century. Peru would face downsizing of her own, as defeat in the War of the Pacific (1879–1884) transferred land to Chile. This same war would hand Bolivia's Pacific outlet over to Chile as well. And while Chile saw success in the north, Argentina asserted its control over the unclaimed lands of Patagonia, also coveted by Chile. Bolivia also lost land in the nineteenth century as corrupt leaders sold off large swaths to Brazil to line their own pockets, and lost yet more to Paraguay in the 1930 Chaco War. That land grab hardly substituted for Paraguay's utter defeat in the 1864–1870 War of the Triple Alliance, which pitted Argentina, Brazil, and Uruguay against tiny Paraguay. The war is still identified as a source of Paraguayan underdevelopment. The country lost about one-third of its territory to Argentina and Brazil, and saw roughly one-half of its population killed.

The emergence of U.S. hegemony in the twentieth century stifled many incipient interstate wars, but earlier territorial movements left bitter memories and stoked tensions that continue to this day. Changes in political geography are important for two reasons. First, war bred rivalry and nationalism, which aided nation building but also contributed to the rise of militaries that would later turn inward to overthrow their own governments. Second, though past unification efforts failed, they provide a traditional sense of legitimacy for new integration schemes such as the Central American Parliament, the Central American Court of Justice, the Common Market of the South (Mercosur), and the Andean Community, as well as rhetorical calls for unity like Venezuela's Hugo Chavez and his appeal for solidarity in the face of North American exploitation and aggression.

PEOPLE AND CULTURE

In dealing with an area of hemispheric proportion, we should not be amazed by the cultural and physiological variation among the indigenous present when the first Europeans arrived. Three massive civilizations dominated the region at the time of conquest. The martial Aztec Empire in the lower portion of Mexico located its capital at Tenochtitlán (modern day Mexico City) and exacted tribute from the conquered peoples of its surroundings. The Mayan civilization, acclaimed for its architectural and scientific achievements, was a looser association of chiefdoms emanating from Mexico's Yucatán peninsula, southward through Guatemala. The Incan people were an archetypal empire, with a nobility and state that controlled all natural resources. From Cuzco, Peru, their leaders oversaw city-states in the peaks and valleys of the Andes in a territory that reached from Ecuador in the north, to midway through Chile in the south.

The debate over the size of Latin America's population at the time of conquest rages on, with numbers that range from 12 million to upwards of 100 million.[3] Despite the disagreement, most studies place over 60 percent of the population within the Aztec, Mayan, or Incan Empires. The remaining were scattered chiefdoms or tribes, though other large settlements existed such as the Mapuche in northern Chile and Argentina, the Chibchas of the Colombian highlands, and the Yanomami of the Amazon. One indicator of the extent of cultural diversity is the number of languages found throughout the region. In Mexico alone there were more than 200 different linguistic groups. Another matter on which few scholars disagree is that pre-Colombian Latin America housed several very large cities. 100,000 to 200,000 lived in Cuzco, while 150,000 to 300,000 settled in Tenochtitlán. Hence, both rivaled and may have even surpassed the contemporaneous sizes of London and Paris. Tourists in Mexico City often visit the pyramids of Teotihuacán. It is fascinating to note that these pyramids were recognized as mysterious, ancient ruins even by the Aztecs (who attempted to mimic the settlement in their own capital), and represented the centerpieces of one of the largest cities in the world at its peak in 400 AD, when 200,000 lived there.

Today, the indigenous represent just 10 percent of the total population in the region, but their numbers are concentrated in Bolivia, Ecuador, Guatemala, Mexico, and Peru where they comprise between 30 and 50 percent of the population. It is estimated that the indigenous population suffered a mortality rate of 45–90 percent during the first century of contact with the Europeans, who brought with them previously unheard of diseases such as smallpox, measles, and yellow fever. The tropical highlands offered some refuge from disease and European subjugation, but the impact was especially brutal in the tropical lowlands of Mexico and Central America, as well as the Caribbean. Colonists imported African slaves, especially to the Caribbean region and Brazil, which required labor to work the newly established sugar plantations. Settlements in present-day Colombia and Venezuela served as slaving stations. The demographic legacy of the Spanish and Portuguese colonialism is clear in these countries.

Argentina sits on the other side of the demographic spectrum. Indigenous populations were historically lighter here, as was European settlement due to the lack of mineral wealth. The need for labor did not come until the turn of the nineteenth century, under a light manufacturing boom, at just the same time that many Europeans were fleeing their economically depressed continents for new opportunities in the Americas. Some ended up at Ellis Island in New York, and

Indigenous Peoples: A Mapuche woman spins wool in Santiago, Chile.
SOURCE: CRAIG ARCENEAUX

others at the port in Buenos Aires. In fact, today one in three Argentines trace their roots to Italy. Uruguay, where 90 percent of the population claims European heritage, is similar.

But today, individuals of mixed European and indigenous blood, or *mestizos*, comprise most of Latin America. The African populations have also mixed to create large mulatto groups as well. The result is a medley of peoples in the region, one that struggles to create a Latin American identity and come to terms with issues of conquest and enslavement. A plaque near the ruins of Tlatelolco in Mexico City, where the Aztecs stood their last ground, reflects this struggle. It reads: "On August 13th, 1521, Tlatelolco, heroically defended by Cuauhtemoc, fell to the power of Hernan Cortés. This was neither a triumph nor a defeat, but the painful birth of the mixed race that is Mexico today." The complicated reaction to Spanish colonialism continues to this day. In Cuernavaca, Mexico, it is not unusual to have taxi cab drivers curse the historic home of Cortés as they drive by, while in Buenos Aires, a statue of Christopher Columbus monopolizes the grounds outside the executive office. Today those of European heritage retain many elite positions, while those of native bloods continue to live in squalor. A 2005 World Bank study notes that extreme poverty in Mexico is 4.5 times higher in predominantly indigenous areas than nonindigenous areas, and sets poverty among Ecuador's indigenous at 87 percent and upwards of 96 percent in the rural highlands. It also recognizes that the trend of poverty for the indigenous continues to worsen.[4] These destitute conditions fed the Zapatista guerrilla movement in Southern Mexico, and spurred indigenous groups to play a central role in protests leading to presidential ousters in Ecuador and Bolivia.

Two in five Roman Catholics worldwide live in Latin America, so it should be no surprise that this religion predominates in the region. But because the Catholic Church so closely identified itself with the Spanish and Portuguese *conquistadores*, the colonial authorities, and later traditional and even modern elites, its link to many populations has been nonexistent, weak, or altered. At independence, to rebel against Spain also meant rebelling against the Church, and this created an uneasy relationship in many countries. As testimony, a visit to the gravesites of Chile's independence leaders requires a trip to the General Cemetery, located on the once-far outskirts of Santiago because the Catholic Church refused burial on their grounds. Likewise, though the remains of the Great Liberator, General José de San Martín, rest in the Metropolitan Cathedral of Buenos Aires, they are placed in a den, structurally separate from the hallowed interior of the church. Church affairs remained central to Latin American politics through the nineteenth century, as Conservative parties lobbied to protect religious privileges, while Liberal parties sought greater separations of church and state. Civil war often broke out between the two. More recently, the church hierarchy drew tremendous criticism as it turned its head, or even grew complicit, in the repression under the military dictatorships of the 1960s and 1970s.

But the Catholic Church has always had its progressive elements as well. Miguel Hidalgo and José Maria Morelos, heroes of Mexican independence who fought for the indigenous and social justice, were both priests. The Colombian priest, Camilo Torres, blended Christianity with Marxist thought to create Liberation Theology, and helped found the ELN guerrilla group in Colombia. Much of the progressive movement comes from the lower ranks of the Church hierarchy, whose upper level is typically quick to distance itself or historically excommunicate dissidents of traditional doctrine. Nonetheless, there are important exceptions such as El Salvador's Archbishop Oscar Romero, assassinated for his criticism of military repression in the 1980s, Guatemala's Bishop Juan José

The Metropolitan Cathedral, Mexico City: Catholicism has deep roots in Latin America, but these roots were planted on cultures that embraced their own religions. Mexico's sixteenth-century Metropolitan Cathedral was built directly on top of the Aztec's Templo Mayor, which was demolished for its construction. SOURCE: CRAIG ARCENEAUX

Gerardi, killed in 1998 after publishing a document on military abuse, and Bishop Samuel Ruiz, who defended the claims of the Zapatistas in Chiapas, Mexico.

Due to the mixed background of the Catholic Church, other faiths have moved to attract the disaffected. Many traditional African religions had an important impact on the region's religious culture. Blending African gods with Christian saints and local tradition, Latin Americans have produced such exotic rites as *Candomblé* in Brazil and *voodoo* in Haiti and Cuba. More recently, evangelical Pentecostal Protestant churches have gained a tremendous following, especially among the poorest classes in Central America and Brazil. With their focus on individual responsibility and a personal relationship with God, critics argue that they push an inherently conservative agenda that devalues questions of social justice and collective action. Though the evangelicals have not translated their growing numbers into political influence, their connection to General Ríos Montt of Guatemala (a member of the Pentecostal *El Verbo* Church) is an important exception. Christian fundamentalists from the United States sent millions of dollars to support his military government from 1982 to 1983, when he presided over a brutal counter-insurgency campaign that killed tens of thousands of indigenous persons in the name of anticommunism.

HISTORY

The Colonial Experience

The *reconquista*, the 700-year battle to expel Islamic Moors from the Iberian peninsula, set the stage for Spain's colonial exertion.[5] Eager to consolidate political control, the monarchy looked to secure overseas resources through mercantilism. Regional nobles threatened the monarchy because they had grown accustomed to local autonomy under the *reconquista*, and fighting had gained them affluence and glory. Would they now turn against royal authority? To avert such risks, the monarchy tended to send the avaricious, self-seeking, "up and coming" nobility to the New World. And so individuals such as Hernan Cortés, who conquered the Aztecs in 1521, Francisco Pizarro, who followed suite against the Incas in 1535, and other *conquistadores* were very enthusiastic about war, and set a militaristic tone as government emerged in colonial Latin America. Finally, Spain was an empire emboldened with a conquest spirit. They had militarily conquered the Moors; the Spanish Inquisition was in full swing to combat Jews, Moslems, various infidels, and later Protestants; and in the Western Hemisphere they would Christianize the Indians.

Mercantilism placed economic activity under the management of the state, and prioritized the acquisition of gold and silver. As a result, in the Americas mining was aggressively promoted, agriculture was geared toward exports (not foodstuffs for the local population, but spices and dyes), and manufacturing was actively discouraged. This economic formula would have far-reaching repercussions on development in the region.

Mexico and Peru were at the center of this mercantilist project. Their rich silver mines confirmed the Spanish hopes for wealth. But paradoxically, mercantilism would inflict its own costs on Spain. The influx of gold and silver raised inflationary pressures, which in turn undercut Spanish producers in international markets. If Spain could not compete in Europe, at least it would have its own colonies as a protected market. Over time, this raised tensions with colonists that would have rather purchased cheaper goods from the British or French. Many historians wryly note that Spain became, in essence, "the Indies of Europe." A country that, in great part due to colonialism, found itself left behind as manufacturing increased in Western Europe. Metals would come into Spain, then almost immediately leave as manufactured goods were purchased from the French, Dutch, British, and others. Spain fell into an economic situation with its European neighbors that, ironically enough, presaged that of contemporary Third World countries—it exported raw materials and imported manufactured goods.

The Spanish Empire slowly crumbled as the Netherlands broke away, and constant warfare developed between Spain and France and England (between 1650 and 1770, Spain would experience only 18 years of peace). The mercantile wall wrought round the Americas soon fell to incursions by Dutch, British, and others seeking trade with the burgeoning populations, and compelled the Spanish to expend more on defenses there. Hence, as economic malaise in Spain intensified the need for precious metals, defensive requirements abroad led more to remain in Latin America. Also, with war, shipping grew more difficult. In the mid-seventeenth century, one large fleet a year would leave Latin America for Spain. Galleons flush with bullion from Peru and Mexico would converge in Havana, Cuba, then sail together for protection to Spain. By the end of the seventeenth century, this became so dangerous that fleets would sail, or only make it, every four or five years.

Spain's gradual deterioration would have long-lasting effects on the politics of Latin America. Financial difficulties meant that Spain would have to build an empire on the cheap.[6] The sale of administrative offices in the colonies provided some revenue. To address the minimal pay, Spain conceded widespread profit-making policy authority to colonial officials. They could manipulate land-use laws, sell commercial licenses and skim port fees, and collect extra taxes on land transfers. Many also used their positions to take bribes from local merchants,

Spanish Legacies: A fort used by the Spanish Gendarme is still in use today by the police in Havana, Cuba. SOURCE: CRAIG ARCENEAUX

violating rules against intercolonial trade. The fusion between public service and private gain would breed a culture of corruption and impunity that continues to beleaguer Latin American politics today. Another enduring political impact emerged from Spanish military concerns. To advance the war effort, governmental and military roles were often united. This would ease the entry of the military into politics, a problem that would later plague Latin America.

The Wars for National Independence

Spain had a natural reaction to its imperial decline. Seeking to safeguard what it could, it allowed only the *peninsulares*, or those born in Spain but sent to America, to hold the highest colonial offices. *Criollos*, of European blood but born in the New World, were deemed less trustworthy. The move raised tensions between the two groups. And the anxiety deepened as Spain responded to continued military setbacks with calls for more military units. This meant expanding the officer corps, which traditionally had been reserved for *peninsulares*. By necessity, more and more *criollos* were allowed to enter the higher ranks. Consider what was happening. Latin Americans increasingly viewed government as something foreign, while the military began to emerge as the only truly national institution.

Still, the *criollos* were not prepared to confront the privileged status of the *peninsulares*. In the general scope of society, they too were privileged. Together with the *peninsulares*, they sat atop a social hierarchy that placed the vast majority of the population—the *mestizos*, mulattoes, and indigenous—far below. Desiring reform, but fearing revolution, the *criollos* balked and accepted the status quo. It would take a colossal blow to the Spanish Empire to shake their reticence.

That blow came in the form of the French Revolution. Napoleon's political vision rejected monarchy, and led him to invade Spain, depose King Ferdinand VII, and place his brother, Joseph Bonaparte in control in 1808. *Criollos* largely rejected the new ruler, and argued that since Spain no longer had a government, sovereignty reverted to colonies, and independence was theirs. Several local rebellions began in Buenos Aires, Caracas, and Mexico. But the end of the Napoleonic Wars reestablished the Spanish crown, and many *criollos* withdrew their support for rebellion. Spanish forces quelled the remaining rebellions, and by 1815 it seemed that all had returned to normal. But more shocks were to come from Europe.

First, Great Britain, eager to speed the fall of Spanish control in Latin America, sent troops to aid the independence movement in Caracas, and also furnished significant naval support in Peru. This gave time for the independence leaders to combine and coordinate their forces. It especially reignited the forces in the north of South America led by Simón Bolívar, who attained control of the region by 1819. Second, while Ferdinand VII did regain his position, he succumbed to reformist pressures in Spain. A liberal constitution with an anticlerical tenor appalled the conservative *peninsular* class, and led many to reinvigorate the rebellion. Their impact was felt immediately. For instance, though the Great Liberator, José de San Martín found military success across Argentina and north from Chile, *peninsulares* and *criollos* supportive of the monarchy initially forced him to stop in

Peru. But when word of the reforms arrived these same groups joined the revolt. A similar story unfolded in Mexico. Spanish General Agustín de Iturbide originally fought to put down the independence movement, but then switched sides after hearing of the reformist moves by the monarch. Mexico achieved independence in 1821, and Iturbide declared himself emperor. The Central American states, with landed elites attracted to the conservative independence movement, annexed themselves to Mexico for a time.

The independence of Brazil took a different course. On November 29, 1807, as the invading French army came in sight of Lisbon, the Portuguese court for Brazil established Rio de Janiero as the new seat of the empire. This was the only time that a king ruling from America claimed to be the head of a European state. The arrival of the Portuguese court stifled the development of local military strongmen, which had emerged everywhere else in Latin America, where the growing distance between the colonies and Spain promoted local government.

When the French were finally repulsed, the Portuguese demanded the return of their king, Dom João VI, who reluctantly departed for Lisbon, leaving his son, Pedro I, as regent in Brazil. But the independence fever persisted in Brazil. Brazilian representatives to the parliament in Lisbon were slighted by not being allowed to participate fully in debates. They remembered the recent days when they were allowed to play a more important role in the creation of policy. In the presence of this mounting resentment against the metropolis, Brazilian independence came rather quietly. Pedro I became increasingly sympathetic to the Brazilian cause and refused the summons to return to Portugal. On September 7, 1822, he heard the news that his liberalizing decrees had been invalidated and that he himself had been judged a Portuguese traitor. Pedro I stripped the Portuguese colors from his uniform and declared, "Independence or death. We are separated from Portugal."

His declaration was popularly received, and Pedro I was installed as a constitutional emperor by the council in Rio de Janeiro. The fact that Brazil had gained its independence without straining the government institutions already in place allowed it to avoid much of the internal strife that was to plague the post-independence political, social, and economic development in the rest of Latin America.

Postcolonial History and the Beginnings of U.S. Involvement

The wars for independence wrought a heavy toll. They decimated the civilian labor force, reduced livestock populations, and diverted machinery from industry to military uses. Trade virtually stood still from 1810 to 1826. Thereafter, separatist groups and lawless bands in the hinterlands hindered commerce. The public debt mushroomed under the burden of military spending. Tax collection was difficult, so governments had to pull loans, especially from Britain, that would burden them well after independence.

War also undermined traditional lines of authority as the demand for military leadership opened new opportunities for the *mestizo* class. *Peninsulares* and *criollos*, concerned first with military victory, did not mind supporting a *mestizo* if he could get the job done. But at independence, this left *mestizos* with no alternative careers in charge of large, disparate military forces. Many became *caudillos*, or military strongmen known for their avaricious ways. The *peninsulares* and *criollos* withdrew to their haciendas, where they could essentially act as self-sufficient units far off in the countryside and leave government to a *caudillo*. But *caudillo* rule typically fed the following vicious circle: a *caudillo* would assume the presidency with fanfare from his troops—they had achieved the ultimate power quest—taking the capital. But the *caudillo* would find little money in the treasury, and his troops, accustomed to war booty and expecting reward, would withdraw support. Another *caudillo* would then come forward and topple the president, and the process would begin anew. This describes the politics of much of Latin America from 1820 to 1870.

The United States had little influence during these times. On December 2, 1823, in a message to Congress, President Monroe declared what has come to be known as the Monroe Doctrine, which expressed four themes: a prohibition on the establishment of new colonies or the transfer of existing colonies in the Americas, U.S. abstention from European involvements, and the exclusion of Europe from the Western Hemisphere. In retrospect, the doctrine appears bold, and is often presented as such in U.S. school textbooks. But in reality, the Monroe Doctrine largely fell on deaf ears. The document actually grew out of a British suggestion that the United States issue a joint statement with Britain. Britain wished to restrain France from taking advantage of the Spanish retreat in the region, and desired independent states. With the world's largest navy and burgeoning commercial interests, Britain had more interest in trading than territorial conquest.

Indeed, throughout the nineteenth century, European intervention in the Americas was common. A street in Buenos Aires is named *Defensa* to acknowledge the battle against British troops, who attempted to take the city twice, in 1806–1807. French troops marched across Mexico in the 1860s in support of an Austrian duke welcomed as an emperor by Mexican conservatives. Spanish warships shelled the coasts of Chile, Peru, and Ecuador from 1865 to 1866 in a move partly spurred by postindependence animosity. British expeditionary forces landed in Nicaragua and Venezuela for long periods to enforce debt payments. U.S. intervention and influence in the nineteenth century competed with Europe, and was largely confined to Mexico and Central America. Of course, Mexico felt the full brunt of the U.S. forces, losing half its territory in the aftermath of the U.S.–Mexico War (1846–1848).

The Spanish-American War (1898) marked the true beginnings of U.S. influence throughout the region. The acquisition of Puerto Rico and Cuba symbolized a southward shift in U.S. foreign policy, as the U.S. sought to consolidate its hold on the hemisphere. The Roosevelt Corollary (1904) to the Monroe Doctrine declared that the United States would prohibit incursions by foreign creditor nations into the hemisphere by undertaking preemptive invasions and occupations of insolvent Latin American countries. Using this inflated view of its self-appointed role, the United States justified military intervention in many of the states of the

Caribbean and Central America. In response to the animosity produced by these actions, Franklin Roosevelt promulgated the "Good Neighbor Policy" to profess U.S. respect for Latin American sovereignty. But global politics soon overshad-owed the expression.

With the development of the Cold War in the late 1940s and the accompany-ing goal to contain communism, there was once again a tendency to justify inter-vention. In 1948, the U.S. declared communist groups, even if entirely home-grown, to be foreign threats. The Johnson Doctrine, pronounced in 1964, called for the destabilization and overthrow of Marxist governments even if they had been popularly elected. In the view of Latin Americans, the arrogance reached its apex in the 1960s and 1980s, when the U.S. supported brutally repressive military dic-tatorships as bulwarks in the struggle against communism—presumably in the name of freedom and democracy.

ECONOMICS

Spanish (and Portuguese) mercantilism stifled economic growth in Latin America. Then the long wars for independence and periods of *caudillo* rule interrupted economic opportunities in the nineteenth century. The region fell increasingly behind as industrialism expanded in Western Europe and the United States, but the economies of those countries would reach back and reinsert Latin America into the world economy in a subsidiary role during the late 1800s. Growing urban classes and manufacturing in the industrialized countries created demands for Latin American foodstuffs and raw materials. The demands pressured Latin American governments to cast aside *caudillo* rule so that they could stabilize and centralize. Though the new economic formula boosted national incomes, it brought with it inequality. Those with access to export markets or able to find jobs in the export sector thrived, but those without these advantages lost ground.

The newfound wealth also opened new vulnerabilities. The lack of a diverse entrepreneurial class or developed capital markets tended to push investment in a single direction, and led countries to concentrate exports within just a few, or even one, commodity. Historical data shows that by 1938 coffee comprised 92 per-cent of El Salvadoran exports, sugar amounted to 78 percent of Cuban exports, tin made for 68 percent of Bolivian exports, and coffee constituted 45 percent of Brazilian exports.[7] Other examples abound: copper from Chile, bananas from throughout Central America, oil from Venezuela, and *guano* from Peru to fertilize the agricultural fields of Europe. Later on, Uruguay would see its economy boom simply because the clothing of U.S. soldiers in the Korean War required wool from its vast sheep ranches. Such concentrated export markets placed Latin America on a roller coaster of economic swings. A 20 percent drop in the price of coffee could spark a recession in Guatemala or Colombia. An unusually poor rainy season could do the same.

Latin America would be forced to confront its export dependency when global economic demand fell during World War I. The global recession of the

1930s intensified the economic malaise, and brought with it instability that saw militaries intervene in governments throughout the region. World War II also interrupted global demands for commodities. Latin America responded with import substitution industrialization (ISI) to create more diverse economies. This economic policy called on the government to shut out imports of manufactures with tariffs so that domestic infant industries could develop behind a protective trade wall. Government also stimulated manufacturing with subsidies or public ownership of industries. And to ensure a market for their goods, governments supported wage increases and labor rights. ISI thus engendered a populist political alliance of the working class, middle class groups finding jobs in the burgeoning bureaucracy, and national industries. The primary products sector was squeezed to fund the program. Populist leaders, such as Juan Perón in Argentina or Getúlio Vargas in Brazil, presided over growing economies in the 1940s and 1950s.

But by the 1960s, the ISI model had been exhausted. The primary products sector degenerated as it was pressed to bankroll the program, and could no longer act as the cash cow it once was. The manufacturing sector did indeed develop and diversify, but protectionism allowed it to grow fat. Government found that it was subsidizing businesses that could not compete in global markets. Economic decline ensued, followed by political turmoil as business subsidies were withdrawn and wages could no longer be supported. Militaries intervened throughout the region and attempted to dismantle the ISI system from the 1960s to 1980s, but they proved incompetent—unable to devise an alternative economic formula. But the military governments did have one advantage the populist governments did not—their impeccable anticommunist credentials. Prompted by U.S. foreign policy, foreign banks saw in them trustworthy, stable allies in the effort to protect free enterprise and readily showered them with loans. But with ISI policies still anchored in place in most countries, the loans not only delayed the inevitable—they made things worse as debt accumulated. Mexico defaulted on its debt in 1982, and much of the region soon followed suit, initiating a crisis so intense that the 1980s would be tagged, "the lost decade."

If there was any silver lining to the economic devastation of the 1980s it was that it exposed the ineffectiveness of military government. The experience was so traumatic that it initiated a sea change in Latin America. Democracy not military dictatorship would guide government. The old ISI program would give way to free markets, and this push toward economic openness soon found itself backed by a sense of cooperation that began to undermine old geopolitical rivalries. The nations of the southern cone (Brazil, Argentina, Paraguay, and Uruguay) signed the Treaty of Asunción in 1991 to create MERCOSUR (The Common Market of the South). Modeled on the 1959 Treaty of Rome, which erected the framework for the European Union, MERCOSUR has reduced restrictions on trade and investment, and has served as a forum for broader integration efforts. Roads, gas pipelines, and electricity grids are being integrated, and the countries are looking to unify immigration policies and even educational systems. Bolivia and Chile are associate members of MERCOSUR. At the other end of the hemisphere, Canada, Mexico, and the United States launched the North American Free Trade

The Port at Montevideo, Uruguay: The agricultural sector dominates Uruguay's exports. Meat and wool are especially important. SOURCE: CRAIG ARCENEAUX

Agreement (NAFTA) on January 1, 1994, which focuses more narrowly on trade and investment. The countries of the isthmus created the Central American Integration System (SICA) to aid cooperation in a number of policy areas, but the new Central American Free Trade Agreement (CAFTA) with the United States may overshadow economic collaboration within SICA. Other regional groupings include the Andean Community, and the thirteen English-speaking countries that make up the Caribbean Commonwealth (CARICOM). Negotiations continue as the entire region pursues a Free Trade Area of the Americas.

The economic opening of the 1990s put Latin America on another rollercoaster, reminiscent of the commodity export economy at the preceding turn of the century. Though the extreme examples have passed, many countries remain highly dependent on a few commodities. In 2003, natural gas comprised 23 percent of Bolivia's exports, soy beans made up 41 percent of Paraguay's, and fish represented 36 percent of Panama's.[8] But investment flows are the new vulnerability of this economic opening. Countries throughout the region sold off vast government industries created under ISI, and privatized many services previously allocated by the state. Governments relaxed controls on capital markets so that foreign investors could move money across borders more easily, and with less taxation than in the past. Stock markets in Mexico, Brazil, Argentina, and Chile emerged as new sources of interest for investors throughout the world. Total private capital flows to the region increased from $13 billion in 1990, to $41 billion in 2003. As an indicator of growing confidence in governments now viewed as beholden to neoliberal economic policies, purchases of bonds increased from $101 million in 1990, to a staggering $12.8 billion.[9] The new investment flows powered economic growth in the early 1990s. But the problem was that many of those same investments could be withdrawn as easily and quickly as they came. Investors target a country when they grow confident in it. But bad news can easily erode that confidence. Moreover, a herd effect may develop as skittish investors lead others to rethink their portfolios. The withdrawal of investments dampens demand for national currencies, decreasing their value, and creating currency crises as speculators unload their currency holdings before they lose more value. This is what happened in Mexico in 1995, Brazil in 1999, and Argentina in 2001–2002. In Latin America, economic crisis seems to be an endemic feature that simply changes its stripes through time—from the commodity price fluctuations of the nineteenth century, to the debt crises of the 1980s, and the currency crises of today. The 2004 World Economic and Social Survey did predict an "incipient recovery" for the region, which was hit hard after the 2001–2002 economic downturn in the United States dampened its main export market. But while rising commodity prices buoy the region's economies, investment remains "stagnant," private consumption is "weak," and unemployment is still a "serious concern."[10]

GOVERNMENT

In the 1970s, one could count the "free" governments of Latin America on one hand: Costa Rica, Colombia, and Venezuela. The major countries of South America had military-installed bureaucratic, authoritarian regimes, while those in Central America retained a more personal and unstable rule by the armed forces. The bureaucratic-authoritarian regime was a phenomenon of the 1970s and 1980s and is distinguished from the tradition of authoritarian governments in Latin America by several characteristics. Military officers cooperated with career bureaucrats to staff government agencies. The working class was eliminated from directly influencing policy because political parties and labor organizations were curtailed or prohibited altogether. The government favored the establishment and, to some degree, the middle class because groups from these sectors were in the best position to define policy and protect their interests as the influential bureaucrats came from their ranks. This condition resulted in an acute case of bureaucratic or military myopia, which interpreted all problems as technical in nature and reducible to an administrative solution rather than negotiation. This kind of government provided the appearance of stability so satisfying to foreign investors, and often succeeded in attracting business from abroad. In time, however, it aggravated and finally alienated the members of the domestic middle class. They may have originally welcomed the military "solution" to the rising social chaos, but in time felt threatened by the growing entry of foreign investment challenging their economic status.

As the tenuous military support base of the middle sectors eroded under the strain of growing indebtedness, the ruling groups exercised several options.[11] One was to gradually transfer power to civilians through constitutional reform, as the Brazilian military did from 1964 to 1985. Another was to increase repression and attempt to install a constitutional order that incorporated military influence, as happened in Chile under General Augusto Pinochet. To his surprise, the Chilean public rejected his rule in a 1988 popular referendum, and has since modified the constitution to decrease military power. In Argentina, the military attempted to divert rising discontent and defiance through a nationalistic diversion that led to the invasion of the Falkland-Malvinas Islands. Britain defeated Argentina in this 1983 war, and the country was so humiliated that the military lost all ability and will to continue the repression.

The military regimes of the 1960s and 1980s left a traumatic legacy of human rights abuses. In some cases, the abuse was carried out within civil wars. From 1978 to 1985 the Guatemalan military implemented a "scorched-earth policy" to root out suspected insurgents from countryside villages. The campaign left some 75,000 dead, and produced more than one million refugees. Few, if any, were immune from persecution in Latin America. In 1980, the rape and murder of three U.S. Catholic nuns in El Salvador brought international attention, as did the assassination of Archbishop Oscar Romero that same year. In Argentina, labor was induced in expectant female political opponents. After delivery, the mother would be murdered and the child handed over to a military family for adoption. Sometimes fathers would be forced to witness the atrocity. In 1995 the prominent Argentine journalist Horacio Verbitsky published "El Vuelo" ("The Flight"), which documented how naval authorities would drug suspects, then take them by helicopter to be dumped over the Atlantic Ocean. In the hope they would sink quickly and never be found, the officers would slit their stomachs. A widespread tactic had officers "disappear" political opponents. In the past, detention, torture, and killing would leave a paper trail as the official records of police stations and courts documented movements. To avoid blame, military governments kidnapped individuals and disposed of their bodies in undisclosed locations. Those seeking information of their whereabouts would typically receive the same answers at police stations, or wherever they inquired: "They must have joined the subversives," or "Perhaps they left the country." The most systematic disappearances took place in Argentina. Estimates range from 10,000 to 20,000. It is important to remember that beyond those killed, many more tens of thousands survived their torture, and yet more were detained, and often deprived of their possessions or employment.

Many of the militaries received amnesties or other guarantees to coax them from government. The struggle to revoke these coerced concessions and pursue justice continues to agitate Latin American politics. That struggle has elicited ingenious legal strategies. In Chile, an amnesty prohibits prosecutions of human rights abuses committed before 1978. The courts ruled that disappearances were

The Navy Mechanics School in Buenos Aires, Argentina was a center for torture under the 1976–1983 military regime. SOURCE: CRAIG ARCENEAUX

"permanent kidnappings," and as crimes in progress they could in fact be processed. On another front, Chilean jurists have successfully argued that an amnesty cannot take effect without knowledge of the crime itself. Hence, though prosecution remains proscribed, investigation does not. Justice remains curtailed, but at least those responsible can be identified, and perhaps shamed into remorse. In Argentina, amnesty covered murder and torture, but it did not address the kidnapping of babies that took place so systematically. This allowed the courts to process generals as leaders of a criminal kidnapping network. But more dramatic changes took place in June 2005, when the Argentine Supreme Court declared the military amnesties unconstitutional.

For many, military impunity is but a symptom of more pervasive accountability issues in government. Democracy is indeed the norm in Latin America, but the lack of some basic ingredients hound democratic consolidation. Political parties remain weak and often fail to bridge societal concerns and government. Without such access to policymaking, social movements feel compelled to take more direct action through disruptive protests, labor strikes, and demonstrations. Congresses are underfunded and poorly staffed; hence, though constitutions design them to balance the presidential power, they often lack the resources to do so. This allows power to concentrate in the executive office, and provokes charges of imperial presidencies. A lack of faith in the courts has spawned a vigilante culture. A recent study found 421 reported lynchings (the actual number is certainly much higher) in Guatemala from 1996 to 2001.[12] Protestors developed the *escrache* (from *escrachar*, slang for "to uncover") in Argentina in response to the denial of justice after military rule. An *escrache* develops as the whereabouts of a perpetrator is learned. Citizens surround his house, distribute flyers and inform neighbors, write graffiti and give speeches to publicize past iniquities. Today, protestors use *escraches* in reaction to all sorts of misdeeds. In 2004, a nightclub fire killed 190 in Buenos Aires. As the public learned of code violations and blocked emergency exits, an *escrache* developed outside the owner's home, forcing the police to take him into protective custody. Could he receive a fair trial now? The *escrache*, increasingly in use throughout Latin America, emerged because of ineffective judicial systems, and there is no doubt that many deserve its wrath. But there is also no doubt that it also further undermines those same ineffective judicial systems.

🌐 CASE STUDIES

1. MEXICO

Poor Mexico, so far from God and so near the
United States.
JOSÉ DE LA CRUZ PORFIRIO DÍAZ

Under the leadership of Benito Juárez and other members of the Liberal Party in the mid-nineteenth century, Mexico experimented momentarily with republican institutions and a new constitution. The period is known as *La Reforma* (the Reform). Out of this brief republican interlude Porfirio Díaz emerged, a man cast in the mold of the traditional Latin American dictator. Under his influence (1877–1911) the country underwent its first round of economic development, as the dictator opened the country to thorough exploitation by foreigners. In four years railroad track increased fivefold as soon as Díaz granted the concession to external interests in 1880. Foreign trade increased by a factor of nine, and the United States became Mexico's chief trading partner. But the costs of progress were excruciating for the majority of the population.

Despite such progress, the Mexican middle class was excluded from decisions and became increasingly resentful of the foreigners, who flaunted a rich European lifestyle. The forces that would soon erupt into one of the few revolutions in Latin America gathered momentum with the exile of Díaz in 1911. These forces are personified by some of the famous leaders who emerged from that period: Emiliano Zapata, head of the peasant movement, who demanded land and the restoration of traditional communal holdings; Venustiano Carranza, who represented the landed oligarchy and was favored by the administration of President Woodrow Wilson; and Francisco ("Pancho") Villa, in command of countryside militias that comprised cowboys, small ranchers, and agricultural workers from the northern state of Chihuahua. Mexico remained in turmoil until the presidency of Álvaro Obregón (1920–1924), who began the tradition of peaceful transition between presidents. He also appreciated the need to reign in the turbulence unleashed by the revolution. There were hundreds of associations, armed bands, and ideological groupings that had to be organized and brought to heel if Mexico were to acquire the status of a civil society. The effort to legitimize the revolution found its expression in the formation of an official political party by President Plutarco Calles. The National Revolutionary Party would later be renamed the Institutional Revolutionary Party (PRI). This creation was initiated by the revolutionary elite and was imposed from the top down. Like many other political organizations in Latin America, it provided a structure through which the major social, political, and economic forces in the state could seek expression. It also provided a means by which they could be controlled by the establishment.

Elected in 1934, Lázaro Cárdenas is the most admired president in the hearts of the Mexican people and is seen as the embodiment of the revolution. He distributed 44 million acres of land to the dispossessed, almost twice as much as had all of his predecessors. Not all this land was turned over to individuals; much of it went into communal holdings called *ejidos* that contained hundreds of families. Today, some 3 million households live on *ejidos*, which embrace about one-half of Mexico's arable land. Neoliberal reforms enacted alongside NAFTA ended further redistribution of land and fostered privatization. The reforms caused widespread protest, and helped to feed rural rebellion, as in Chiapas in 1994. Another of Cardenas' most popular acts, and one that fueled a sense of national pride, was the nationalization of Mexico's petroleum resources. It too has been undermined by NAFTA reforms opening Mexico to greater foreign investment.

Since the 1980s, the PRI experienced increasing tension because of the growing pressures brought on by the need for development and repayment of the nation's debt. The strain tempted the party leadership to opt for a solution reminiscent of the Porfirio Díaz days—a reopening to foreign economic interests. Carlos Salinas de Gortari, elected in 1988, continued the process begun by his predecessor of moving the country's industry out of public control and into the private sector. His efforts culminated with the signing of NAFTA in 1993, which created a free-trade area with Canada and the United States. As in the days of Díaz, growth has followed, but so too has inequality. Mexico now boasts the highest per capita incomes in Latin America, but the greatest gains from NAFTA have gone to the northern and central regions of Mexico, the more educated workforce engaged in international trade, and those irrigated, more productive farms able to compete against U.S. and Canadian producers. And those unable to gain have been doubly disadvantaged, as the reduction in state subsidies and social welfare also dictated by neoliberal reform hit them hardest.[13]

But the economic reform under NAFTA would be one-half of a package that also included political reform. With democracy spreading across Latin America in the 1980s, international attention focused on Mexico. Electoral fraud and corruption by PRI to curry favor came under greater scrutiny, and grew increasingly difficult. Opposition parties, especially the right-wing PAN (National Action Party), and the left-wing PRD (Party for a Democratic Revolution) began to win more congressional seats and governorships. Events came to a head in the July 2000 presidential election, which saw the end of the PRI's 70-year lock on the presidency. PAN candidate, and former Coca-Cola executive, Vicente Fox, took the presidential sash, and committed to further economic and political reform. Nonetheless, Fox would have to deal with the new Mexican reality—democracy. Mexico was now officially a competitive multiparty state. Without a majority in congress, Fox was compelled to compromise and bargain with the PRI and PRD.

Legislative Assembly, State of Morelos, Mexico: In today's Mexico, diverse political parties, such as the PRI, PRD, and PAN, must bargain and compromise. SOURCE: CRAIG ARCENEAUX

Early on, Fox gave great priority to migration and had high hopes for some sort of amnesty program for undocumented workers, as well as a more liberal migration program. The culture of migration is something initiated and sustained by the United States, first under the *Bracero* programs beginning in the 1940s, which invited millions across three decades, and today under immigration policies that ineffectively chase migrants through deadly desert border regions, but do virtually nothing to exact punishment on U.S. businesses that hire illegals. For the reality is that the United States depends on cheap labor as much as Mexico depends on worker remittances, and though U.S. communities may be upended by the influx, U.S. businesses exert tremendous pressure to ensure political lethargy toward their cheap labor. Moreover, the U.S. fixation on terrorism after September 11, 2001, essentially wiped immigration reform from the political agenda of the Bush Administration. Though new proposals have cropped up of late, the business lobby will do its best to ensure congressional reticence, and concerns over terrorism will also dampen prospects.

The inaction on migration policy was a severe blow for the Fox administration. Fox was, in fact, the first foreign political leader invited to the United States in the first Bush administration. Many foresaw a new, harmonious relationship. A second blow came after the U.S. fell into recession in 2001–2002. Mexico's highly dependent economy followed. Impressive growth of 6.9 percent in 2000 turned to just 0.2 percent in 2001 and 0.9 percent in 2002.[14] With migration reform gone and a sluggish economy, Fox's PAN party began to lose steam. The PRI saw gains in the midterm gubernatorial elections, and congress stayed split between the PRI, PRD, and PAN parties. With inequality and economic vulnerability greater in post-NAFTA Mexico, and with a tremendous public outcry against the U.S. war in Iraq, Mexicans may be beginning to rethink their support for Fox's PAN party and its commitment to more U.S.-pressured neoliberal reform. Time will tell when Fox's six year term ends in 2006.

2. BRAZIL

God is a Brazilian.
ANONYMOUS

Brazil's transition to national independence was relatively peaceful. Brazil had no military tradition and, therefore, avoided the phenomenon of dictatorial rule until much later. The army did not become a factor until it emerged as the result of the War of the Triple Alliance against Paraguay in 1864–70. In 1889 the military declared the end of constitutional monarchy and the beginning of republican government. Since then, the military has been a dominant player in Brazilian politics.

As with the rest of Latin America, Brazil had a single commodity economy for most of its colonial history. Originally the crop was sugar, which was the force behind the establishment of slavery. Sugar plantations were concentrated in the northeast and generated as much as one-third of Brazil's foreign exchange. Later, the dominant crop became coffee, which was grown in the southern highlands. The shift in crops from sugar to coffee also represented a geographic change in the economic fortunes of the respective areas. In modern times, the northeast has become one of the most depressed regions in all of Latin America. Tremendous demographic pressure is exerted on the other areas as emigrants from the northeast populate the shantytowns overlooking large urban centers such as Rio de Janeiro. These economic refugees trek into the formerly impassable jungles of the interior, following recent inroads by teams of bulldozers. Consequently, an important ecosystem in the midst of a tropical rainforest has now been breached and laid open to wanton exploitation of resources and indigenous tribes.

Today, the government is focusing on underdeveloped regions of the fragile Amazonian ecology as a source of energy. Brazil relies on dams to provide 90 percent of its electricity. A drought in 2001 required the population to reduce its energy consumption by 20 percent. To cope with the demands of a population of 170 million whose consumption of energy has grown at a rate of 5.3 percent a year, the current government is planning the construction of the world's third-largest dam on the Xingu River. Two channels one-quarter of a mile wide and seven miles long will be carved out of the Amazon jungle to connect sections of the river to reduce the area to be flooded, which has been projected to cover 155 square miles. It is claimed that the project, to be completed by 2008, will generate 11,000 megawatts at a cost of $6.6 billion. Critics claim that in addition to the environmental damage, the dam will displace indigenous populations and settlers, and will impede navigation.

Brazil currently confronts economic and development problems similar to those facing many of the countries in the Other World. The United States and the International Monetary Fund (IMF) have continually stressed the need to privatize the economy by reducing government ownership of industries and services to encourage foreign investment and competition and diminish inflation. A country of tremendous natural resources, Brazil suffers the consequences of poor distribution. One percent of the population holds more than 50 percent of the wealth. It is a country with 12 million landless and impoverished peasants and an estimated 1.24 billion acres of arable land, two-thirds of which is owned by 5 percent of the population, which in turn farms only 15 percent of the total. Nevertheless, these powerful individuals are capable of defeating any attempt at effective land reform. Years of drought and rural hardship have driven millions to seek refuge in the urban areas, where they add to the inflationary pressure by causing the government to spend more on social services.

From 1985 to the present, Brazil has gone through five different currencies, and many years saw triple-digit inflation. Per capita gross domestic product (GDP) in 1990 was what it was in 1980, the last year of the "economic miracle." Things began to change under President Fernando Henrique Cardoso (1995–2003). He installed the *Real Plan* and inflation declined from 50 percent per month to around 3 percent. The purpose of the plan was to cut inflation by revaluing the currency (known as the *real*), tightening the supply of money and credit, and stabilizing prices by instituting wage and price freezes. But even as Brazil's economy stabilized, other problems persisted.

As President Cardoso was inaugurated in January 1995, Amnesty International reported the slaughter of thousands of "street children" at the hands of death squads. In the countryside peasant leaders and environmental organizers were murdered with impunity. Between July and October 2001, seven leaders of regional labor, religious, and environmental groups were killed. One victim was Ademir Federicci, the director of the Movement for the Development of the Trans-Amazon and Xingu. He had been warned by an illegal logger whose operations he had reported to the authorities that it was time for "Dema," as he was affectionately known, to start searching for some wood for his own coffin.

Cardoso's second term (1999–2003) was not a pleasant one. From the start, he faced a yawning fiscal deficit. The man who preceded him as president, Itamar Franco, was the governor of Minas Gerais and started the year by declaring a 90-day moratorium on the payment of his state's debt to the federal government. With the economy beginning to tilt, currency speculators bet against the Brazilian *real*. In order to defend the currency, the government raised interest rates as high as 50 percent, thereby contributing to the recession. Cardoso was on the horns of a dilemma. Should he go back on his campaign promise to control inflation, or let the *real* float and hope that the resulting devaluation would encourage exports and arrest the decline in foreign exchange?

His economic problems were compounded by the fact that he had previously secured a $41.5 billion loan from the IMF on the commitment to reduce the fiscal deficit. This was to be accomplished by raising taxes and charging taxes on pensions. If the government were to arrange more favorable interest terms for Minas Gerais, it would have to do the same for all 27 states, and that would endanger the budget deficit and create further difficulties with the IMF. President Cardoso governed with a legislative coalition that included, as one of the three most important members, Governor Franco's party, the Brazilian Democratic Movement party (PMDB). Cardoso could not afford to alienate such an ally if he hoped to institute fiscal and social reforms.

The Cardoso administration blinked. In January 1999, barely two weeks into its second term, the currency was devalued. Overnight the *real* lost 20 percent of its previous value. By the end of the month, it floated at about 1.44 to the dollar. Inflation, brought under control by Cardoso's *Real* Plan, soon revived as the price of flour for bread rose by 16 percent. The hope was that now cheapened Brazilian goods would raise exports and the increase in foreign exchange would allow a decline in interest rates to further stimulate the economy. By lowering the price of steel, however, steel manufacturers in the United States accused Brazil of "dumping" and received protection from the Bush administration. Apparently, developing nations are vulnerable in many ways.

An energy crisis resulting from a severe drought, the explosion and collapse of an off-shore drilling platform, the return of inflation, and plummeting popularity, dashed President Cardoso's hopes for social reform during his second administration. The September 11 attack on the United States and the ensuing economic recession brought more misfortune to Brazil and other economies of Latin America dependent on U.S. imports. The inability of open markets to more quickly foster economic growth prompted a growing backlash against the IMF. Brazil and others had followed the organization's dictates to impose austerity and reduce trade barriers, but instability and more poverty seemed to be the only result. Support for privatization of the economy dropped from 75 percent of those polled in 1990 to below 30 percent in 2001.

The Brazilian economy was struggling; it would grow by only 1 percent in 2001 and 2 percent in 2002. Unemployment was rising, companies were unable to borrow money, and inflation during the Cardoso administrations reached 130 percent. Midway through 2002, the International Monetary Fund agreed to loan Brazil $30 billion in an effort to stabilize its economy along the unpopular lines exacted by the IMF. As the October 2002 presidential elections approached, Luís Inácio "Lula" da Silva entered the race as he had several times before as candidate for the leftist Worker's Party (*Partido dos Trabalhadores* or PT). The one-time lathe operator, labor leader, grade-school dropout son of a family of sharecroppers, and political prisoner changed his attire and his message. Retaining his core messages—pledges to improve schools, fight corruption, create new jobs, end hunger, and restore international respect for Brazil—he pledged to honor Brazil's foreign debts and abide by the IMF agreements that Brazil's previous president, Fernando Henrique Cardoso, signed. Lula, whose lengthy alliance with trade unionists, community activists nurtured by Catholic "liberation theology," and leftist academics had earned him the distrust of business, won the presidency in a runoff election on October 27, 2002, defeating Cardoso's successor, José Serra, 61.2 to 38.7 percent of the vote.

One year into his administration he faced declining support among his devotees. Before assuming the presidency in January 2003, he promised to provide homesteads to at least 60,000 families. But the leadership of the Landless Rural Workers Movement encouraged land invasions and claimed the need for a land reform policy along the lines of the Cuban and Soviet models. To address some of the other economic problems facing his administration, he introduced a pension reform package in August 2003 similar to one that the PT strenuously opposed for nearly a decade when it was in the opposition. The proposal would affect nearly all retirees to some extent, but the country's nearly four million civil servants stand to lose the most. It would raise the minimum age for retirement of civil servants to 55 from 48 for women and to 60 from 53 for men. In addition, a ceiling of $842 a month would be placed on pensions for public workers retiring in the future. The current system pays them the same salary they were earning when they retired. Although not yet enacted, the proposed legislation generated much anger among those it would affect, causing them to denounce the president for being a traitor to those responsible for his victory.

Lula came into office with high hopes for social change, but he finds himself hamstrung by Brazil's economic commitments. Still, Lula and his Workers' Party seem to be walking a fine line with some success. The economy is growing modestly, unemployment has decreased, and Lula remains very popular. In fact, the PT's greatest problem is not economic, and largely self-created. This problem is corruption. Through 2005 allegations of widespread bribery from PT officials to pay off congressional allies for votes were confirmed. To date prosecutors have implicated some 130 politicians and more than 400 government officials, and Lula has struggled to distance himself form the scandal. The Brazilian corruption case is one example of the myriad accountability problems Latin American governments face.

3. CUBA

It is my duty . . . to prevent, through the independence of Cuba, the U.S.A. from spreading over the West Indies and falling with added weight upon other lands of Our America. All I have done up to now and shall do hereafter is to that end. . . . I know the Monster, because I have lived in its lair—and my weapon is only the slingshot of David.
JOSÉ MARTÍ

Cuba, the largest of the Caribbean Islands, was late in severing colonial ties with Spain. Although the Cubans had initiated several independence movements throughout the nineteenth century, the final attempt came on the eve of the twentieth. A mysterious explosion that sent the American battleship *Maine* to the bottom of the Havana harbor in 1898 provoked an uninvited North American intrusion into Cuba's war of independence. As a result of the North American intervention and the Spanish defeat, Cuba became a U.S. protectorate for the next 35 years.

Cuban pride was trampled when Cubans were forced to accept the provisions of the Platt Amendment in exchange for nominal independence. The amendment stipulated, among other things, that Cuba could not enter into substantial foreign agreements without approval by the United States. It ceded to the United States the right to intervene to maintain a "stable government" and the right to "acquire and hold the title to land for naval stations." Cuba was forced to incorporate the amendment into its constitution before the United States would agree to remove occupying troops. This passage provided the justification for intervention in Cuban affairs by the United States from 1906 to 1920. In 1934, the treaty was abandoned as part of President Franklin D. Roosevelt's "good neighbor policy"; however, the naval base at Guantánamo is still under U.S. control.

Until the revolution of 1959, Cuba was seen as an extension of the United States. Its economy was so integrated with that of its northern neighbor that it was treated as another of the 50 states. In 1903, Cuba and the United States worked out a reciprocal trade agreement that gave sugar a 20 percent reduction from existing U.S. tariffs in exchange for a 20 to 40 percent tariff reduction for Cuban imports from the United States. Because sugar was to become the source of 80 percent of Cuba's foreign exchange, this relationship increased dependence on the United States. The relationship also propelled U.S. investment. By 1928, Americans owned more than two-thirds of the island's sugar production,[15] a situation that contributed greatly to the growing anti-Americanism of Cuban nationalism.

U.S. meddling came again in 1933, when Washington intervened to support the rise of Sergeant Fulgencio Batista after a popular rebellion displaced the dictator Gerardo Machado. But Batista would soon evolve into a dictator of his own right, and dominate Cuban politics for the next 26 years. It was an era of rampant corruption and abuse of power that would soon give rise to protest and rebellion.

After seeing his election to a representative office nullified in the 1952 elections, Fidel Castro decided to turn to armed rebellion. He and a group of 165 youths staged a romantic and vain attack on the Moncada Barracks on July 26, 1953. The attack was a disaster. More than half of the party was killed or captured. Fidel and his brother Raul avoided harm, but were sentenced to 15 years in prison.

Good luck always followed Fidel Castro. In an attempt to appease the opposition, Batista declared an amnesty and the Castro brothers were released in 1956. They were exiled to Mexico, where the future revolutionaries were joined by others in training for the overthrow of Batista. Later that year a band of 82 revolutionaries sailed for the island. The landing was another disaster. The popular uprising that was to erupt on their arrival never materialized. After several days of mishaps, all that survived from the invasionary expedition were 12 guerrilla fighters who managed to slip into the Sierra Maestra Mountains, where they would remain pretty much unnoticed until their interview by Herbert Matthews of the *New York Times* the following year.

The interview gave "the bearded ones" the exposure they needed to mobilize the latent anti-Batista sentiment throughout the island. Every revolutionary act would elicit a repressive countermove by Batista, which in turn only stimulated further disobedience and subversion until his support dissolved and he fled from Cuba on New Year's Eve, 1959.

What accounts for Castro's subsequent rise to power? Unlike other revolutions in Mexico or China, the Cuban revolution emerged after a relatively brief period of conflict. The corrupt politics of the previous half century had thoroughly discredited the establishment. There was no one to compare in stature with the popular and charismatic revolutionary hero. The *Partido Socialista Popular* (PSP), which was the name under which the Cuban communist party operated, had been slow to back the guerrillas in the Sierra Maestra, joining in the revolutionary movement only at the last minute. The PSP was also suspect because of its long alliance with Batista and its contribution to the organization and maintenance of workers' support during his regimes. So why did Castro become a communist?

Any authentic reform of the Cuban political and economic structure would have to break the U.S. control of the sugar economy. That act would also entail a thoroughgoing agrarian reform because sugar production was the foundation of the system. The alternative would have to be a socialist or some other economic system with strong central direction from the state. Castro sought to consolidate the revolution, and to do so he availed himself of the only anticapitalist apparatus in existence at the time, the PSP. Washington's policies also contributed to Castro's communist turn. A boycott and sabotage during the Eisenhower administration were followed by the unsuccessful Bay of Pigs invasion in 1961 and assassination plots against Castro sanctioned by the Kennedy administration.

With the U.S. threat a reality, the Soviet Union stood as a ready ally. Castro drew on the communist party and Soviet advisers to replace the fleeing technicians and professionals dissatisfied with the increasing socialist direction of the revolution.

The Soviet Union supported Cuba with $5 to $6 billion in annual assistance as late as 1989. But with the fall of communism in the Soviet Union, and a move by newly independent Russia to embrace western-style market reforms, Cuba would be forced to do without Soviet aid. Ironically, despite all its efforts at agrarian re-form, Cuba found itself as dependent on sugar as before the revolution. From one of the bright spots in the Other World in terms of quality of life for the worker, Cuba has taken a plunge. The move to reinvigorate the economy with mild eco-nomic reforms and a tourist industry has brought on new social and economic di-visions. A many-layered economy has emerged with the top level reserved for those who have access to foreign currency. The consequence is that many who are employed in menial occupations, such as hotel workers and cab drivers, who fre-quently come in contact with foreigners, or those who are lucky enough to have friends and family on the outside who can send them dollars, enjoy a better eco-nomic status than others, such as doctors or teachers, who make substantial con-tributions to society through their labor but lack external contact. This latter status engenders a degree of racial tension because whites are more likely to have access to foreign remittances than the blacks. As Andrew Zimbalist comments, "Cuba has become a class society, defined by access to hard currency through work, pol-itics, or family abroad."[16] Prostitution is rampant once again as both men and women attempt to procure the hard currency from visiting tourists.

The U.S. embargo, in place but expanded since 1960, has contributed to the post–cold war economic decline. In addition, the United States has taken meas-ures in hopes that Cuban communism is nearing its end and needs only one small push. In 1992, the Cuban Democracy Act (also known as the Torricelli Bill) took effect. The statute had the effect of increasing the costs of goods transported into Cuba by prohibiting foreign-based subsidiaries of U.S. companies from trading with the island. It allows private groups to send food and medicines but forbids ships entering Cuban ports for the purposes of trade from access to U.S. port facil-ities for 180 days. This restriction annoys U.S. allies by extending the influence of the United States beyond its territory. It authorizes the president to declare any country providing assistance to Cuba ineligible for aid under the Foreign Assistance Act of 1961, ineligible for assistance or sales under the Arms Export Control Act, and ineligible under any program providing for the forgiveness or reduction of debt owed to the U.S. government. It stipulates other restrictions as well, but these were enough to cause Castro to make some economic accommoda-tions in order to attract foreign capital.

There have been some tenuous experiments with capitalism. The administra-tion allowed the use of farmer's markets where farm products could be sold di-rectly to the public. Another example would be the permission of *paladares* or small private in-house restaurants with a maximum capacity of 12 seats to be served ex-clusively by members of the household. In an effort to accumulate foreign invest-ment, Cuba has modified its economic doctrine to encourage the development of

Street performers entertain tourists on a Havana plaza in Cuba. SOURCE: CRAIG ARCENEAUX

tourism. In an attempt to accumulate foreign exchange, the government requires that investors hire Cuban labor and pay the Cuban government in foreign currency. The government then pays the Cuban worker in *pesos* at the Cuban rate. This maneuver allows the government to make a profit on the exchange rate between what the government is paid in foreign currency and what it pays its citizens.

Economic development in Cuba has been stymied further by the United States' Cuban Liberty and Democratic Solidarity (*Libertad*) Act in 1996. Also known as the Helms-Burton Bill, the statute, in part, codifies the different embargoes on trade and financial relations in effect since the Kennedy administration. It requires the president to produce a plan for providing economic assistance to a transitional or democratic government in Cuba as well as authorizing United States nationals with claims to property confiscated in Cuba (including those who were Cuban citizens at the time of the confiscation) to file suit in U.S. courts against persons who may be "trafficking" in that property (Title III). This latter provision can be suspended by the president for periods of six months at a time if he considers it necessary to the national interest of the United States and if it will expedite the transition to democracy in Cuba. The fourth title of the statute requires the denial of visas to, and exclusion from the United States of, persons who, after March 12, 1996 (when the legislation was passed), confiscate or "traffic" in confiscated property in Cuba claimed by U.S proprietors.

A move to depose Castro would not come from above. These people have too much to lose without him. Castro personifies the revolution. Those below would have an extremely difficult time trying to plot against him. Intelligence channels permeate the society in large part because of the need to maintain readiness against the omnipresent threat of an external invasion. The more the United States threatens Cuba, the easier it is for Castro to rally mass support for the defense of the revolution. The very security precautions that must be instituted against the eventuality of a U.S. invasion are the same ones that prevent the success of any domestic uprising.

Of course, Fidel Castro is not immortal. There remains the question of what will happen after the death of the 79-year-old revolutionary. It will be interesting to see how many of the social programs launched by the Cuban revolution will survive his passing. But it seems safe to predict that it is unlikely that life in Cuba will ever return to what it was before the revolution. From a U.S. policy perspective, the question is whether the normalization of relations will be conducive to a less disruptive transition. U.S. policy currently insists that Castro comply with demands that would effectively remove him from power before we relax the embargoes. That does not seem realistic. We do not have to like a government in order to deal with it. There are too many examples where we do that already, and the Cuban case by itself evidences how isolation and pressure embolden dictatorial rulers.

◆ FLASHPOINTS ◆

THE ORGANIZATION OF AMERICAN STATES (OAS) AND VENEZUELA

The Organization of American States was created in 1948 to serve as a forum for the promotion of cooperation in social, economic, and political affairs. It has always served as a medium for conflict resolution in the western hemisphere as it promoted dialogue to dissuade suspicions, as well as collaborative efforts toward a variety of common threats, from communism to environmental disasters to international terrorism. Increasingly, the OAS has directed its energy toward conflict resolution in the domestic politics of countries through the promotion and strengthening of democratic institutions. In 1991, the OAS adopted Resolution 1080, which obligated an official response in case of the "sudden or irregular interruption" of democracy in any OAS member state. The Protocol of Washington, signed the following year, strengthened that response by calling for the suspension of an implicated member state. And in 2001, the OAS passed the Inter-American Democratic Charter to spell out what constituted democratic rule, and stipulate regional responses to and penalties for *alterations*—not just *interruptions*—of democracy.

What difference have these developments made? Democratic promotion is a complex assignment, especially for an organization that has traditionally championed sovereignty—the insulation of domestic political affairs from outside influences. Indeed, sovereignty has proven a resilient force for democratic promotion. It has both blocked, and more importantly, distorted, the regional drive to maintain democracy. How? As the value of democratic promotion butts heads with the value of sovereignty, the OAS finds that it can address some democratic threats with ease, while others are deemed too sensitive—too deep within the realm of domestic politics. Hence, the OAS will show great resolve against coups. The member will be suspended and sanctions enforced. These actions helped reverse democratic threats in Guatemala (1993) and Paraguay (1996), such that today, coups seem very unlikely in the region. Another threat, that of electoral fraud, is also firmly monitored, and current elections in the region are typically free and fair. But when the more problematic concerns of democratic growth crop up—strengthening legislatures, expanding accountability, ensuring equal access to the justice—all those long-term factors so important to democratic consolidation, the OAS treads much more carefully. OAS members will condemn and/or sanction electoral mischief or coup, but mere criticisms of executive power or unresponsive judiciaries are viewed as incursions into domestic politics. That means that these problems tend to fester and grow as threats to democracy. More importantly, by only protecting democracy when risk is at its greatest, the OAS may actually shore up "low-quality" democracies, and thus undermine its own efforts. This can be seen in the case of Venezuela.

In his 1998 presidential bid, Lieutenant Colonel Hugo Chávez campaigned on a platform of wholesale political change, christening his cause the Fifth Republic Movement (MVR) to signal the opening of a new political order. True to his word, President Chávez oversaw the adoption of a new constitution, but has pushed the delicate machinery of democracy to its limits. His critics find ample fodder in the concentration of executive authority, violations of judicial autonomy, the corrosion of federal institutions, mass level groups that threaten the independence of civil society, pilfering of the state treasury for populist policies designed to curry favor, and a fiery rhetoric that all too often equates opposition with sedition.[17] But these actions do not appear on the OAS radar screen, with its concentration on coups and electoral mischief.

Chávez moved quickly to reshape Venezuelan politics. In the midst of his electoral honeymoon, he presided over a referendum to call a constitutional assembly on April 25, 1999, and, upon its success, elections for a constituent assembly on July 25. The opposition squabbled and ran far more candidates than seats, thereby splitting its vote, while government officials aided Chávez by distributing lists of favored candidates so that supporters could decipher the extended ballot. With representation from *Chavistas* at over 90 percent, the assembly took office on August 3, 1999, completed a draft by late October, scurried through debate, and presented the proposed constitution to the public on November 19. The December 15 referendum date left only 28 days for public debate on the historic change.[18]

Allegations that state funds were used to stimulate favor, and a year-end congressional investigation into fraud in the July election were quickly over-shadowed by the news of torrential flooding that would eventually kill some 30,000 people and leave hundreds of thousands homeless. The crisis became politicized as it justified greater public spending, and led to more intense re-development efforts by the armed forces.[19] With Venezuelan society still in shock and under the influence of massive public spending, Chávez went ahead with mega-elections for 6,000 public posts in the country in July 2000 (further local elections would be held in October). The elections also included the presidency, and allowed Chávez to refresh his six-year tenure when he garnered 59 percent of the vote, an outcome aided by the still-fractionalized opposition and all-time high 42 percent abstention rate.

International observers from the OAS were not absent during these developments, but they only monitored the elections, which they consistently found to be largely clean. Every assessment from the OAS endorsed the electoral outcome, and in doing so added to the legitimacy of Venezuelan democracy. If elections are the benchmark of democracy, and Venezuela consistently received a passing grade, this was a reality that certainly did not resonate with a significant sector of Venezuelan society, whose confidence in governing institutions was suffering a swift decline.

The disjuncture between Venezuelan politics and the assessments of international observers became increasingly apparent through 2001. In November, the decree of 49 "enabling laws" that significantly affected property rights with little consultation from business provided a signaling event. Middle-class groups agitated by populist policies were joined by labor unions critical of recent government interventions in their elections, and together they initiated a massive December strike that would last over a month. A February 2002 call for Chávez to resign by several high-ranking military officers spiked the opposition's mettle. But in April 2002, the Venezuelan crisis would become clear to all—those inside and outside of the country. Violent street protests led to some 20 deaths and 60 serious injuries, providing the spark for a coup led by business leader Pedro Carmona and some military units. The Bush Administration, long unabashedly critical of Chávez and supportive of the opposition, proved reluctant to condemn the action.[20] But with democratic survival clearly in the balance, other OAS members felt compelled to act. The 19-member Rio Group (a caucus within the OAS) happened to be holding its annual meeting in Costa Rica at the time, and called for a special session of the OAS General Assembly. But ultimately, the coup fell apart due to internal pressures as Carmona quickly alienated his early supporters.

Nonetheless, the antagonisms and schisms that brought about the coup remained; indeed they were deepened by the violence surrounding the three-day coup. The OAS responded with a resolution "to encourage Government of Venezuela to explore the opportunities the OAS affords for promoting the national dialogue."[21] After five months of negotiation, in October 2002, Chávez and the opposition agreed to accept a "Tripartite Working Mission" comprised of the OAS, the Carter Center, and with technical support from the UN Development Program.

Still, "dialogue" was conditioned and decided just as much, if not more, in the streets of Venezuela than in the negotiating efforts of the Tripartite Mission.[22] It was as if the opposition and government required a learning period of confrontation. That period, initiated by sporadic midyear strikes, intensified in October, when fourteen military officers marched to Plaza Altamira in Caracas to pronounce their "legitimate disobedience," and lead a protest that continued for months and swelled to the tens of thousands. Finally, a general strike beginning in December and affecting much of the oil industry, crippled the economy.

Only after these efforts failed did the opposition take the negotiations more seriously.[23] In May 2003, the government and opposition accepted a proposal to hold a referendum on the presidency. But even with the pressure to hold another vote, both sides wavered. Opposition elements in the National Assembly held up appointments to the National Electoral Council (CNE—the official electoral board), and negotiations delayed its activation until September.[24] And at that time, the body, now holding a majority of members identified with the government, refused a referendum petition from the opposition on procedural grounds. Violent protests again rocked Caracas, and more followed in February 2004, when the CNE delayed its decision on a subsequent petition with some 3.4 million signatures—almost one million above the required 2.54 million. When, in the following month, the CNE declared only 1.8 million of the signatures to be valid, the protestors found little reason to back off—despite the fact that the OAS and Carter Center officially supported the CNE decision.[25] The Tripartite Mission did play an important role as it offered to oversee a *"reparo"* (repair) period, in which signatories would verify their signatures. Though the *reparo* was marred by verified accusations of intimidation toward signatories, the process ended successfully in early June, and opened the door to an August 15 referendum.

Foreign observation of the referendum created the same trap as had previous assessments of Venezuelan elections. By focusing so squarely on the cleanliness of electoral procedures, outsiders again missed the democratic forest for the electoral trees. In the lead up to the election, the Chávez government engaged in massive spending, fueled by an opportune increase in oil prices. Other suspect strategies included naturalizing some 300,000 immigrants in the hopes of creating a new voting bloc of Chávez supporters and an attempt to stir national security concerns by coloring the arrest of alleged Colombian paramilitaries as a coup plot.[26] Meanwhile in the year leading up to the referendum, two critical reports pointed to the real problems in Venezuela: One by Human Rights Watch surveyed attacks on judicial autonomy, and another by the Inter-American Commission on Human Rights took note of "a clear weakness in the fundamental pillars of the rule of law within a democratic society," placing emphasis on the impunity with which armed civilian groups act to stifle political debate.[27] These reports exposed just some of the failures of democratic deepening in Venezuela— failures that the OAS member states paid less attention to. And in this environment, the referendum was an ill-suited mechanism for reconciliation.

The official results gave Chávez a clear victory, with 59 percent of voters rejecting his recall. Opponents were furious and questioned the outcome. The Tripartite Mission conducted an additional audit to assuage the opposition, to little avail.[28] Venezuelan politics, then, remain insecure as issues of democratic quality continue to fester. No amount of evidence could convince the opposition that Chávez won the referendum; the political atmosphere has grown too bitter. But what means nothing to the opposition could not be more important to the OAS and its members. A clear signal of "mission accomplished" has been emitted. Even the U.S. has acquiesced, portraying the vote as a chance for reconciliation. Has the OAS done a service for Venezuelan politics? Without OAS pressure, elections could have been tainted, and a successful coup would probably be much more likely. But the piecemeal approach to democratic protection also allows Chávez to use the OAS stamp of approval to further the legitimacy of the Venezuelan political system, when clearly large portions of the population feel otherwise. Is this a case in which no OAS action would be better than just some?

VIOLENCE IN COLOMBIA

The long history of violence in Colombia starts with Simón Bolívar's victory over the Spanish loyalists. Frustration with the area's incapacity to achieve civic harmony prompted the quotation attributed to the liberator with which we start the chapter. Bolívar wanted to see a strong executive elected for life. His comrade in arms, General Francisco de Paula Santander, became what is today Colombia's first president. He championed a decentralized federal system with a reduced role for the Roman Catholic Church. This became the basis for the Liberal party doctrine. Opposition to this view characterized the Conservative party and the two forces fought each other for the remainder of the nineteenth century. In the process, they made different areas of the country into their respective strongholds; the Conservatives controlling what is today Medellín and the Liberals controlling the area east and north of Bogotá.

A split within the Liberals led by Gabriel Turbay on the right and the nationalist-populist Jorge Eliecer Gaitán on the left allowed the Conservative Mariano Ospina Pérez to win with less votes than those amassed by the two Liberals in 1946. Gabriel Turbay died the following year, and Ospina Pérez began attacks against the Liberals. This started the bloody period in

Most Latin American states have had their share of violence. This outline of a human body on the Plaza of Three Cultures at Tlatelolco in Mexico is a grim reminder of the massacre that took place here when the government brutally repressed a large student protest on October 2, 1968. SOURCE: CRAIG ARCENEAUX

Colombia known as *la violencia.* In 1947 the *gaitanistas* (the followers of Gaitán) swept the congressional elections and left no doubt that Eliecer Gaitán would win the presidential election in 1948. But on April 9, 1948, Gaitán was assassinated. The assassin was mobbed, beaten to death, and his corpse was dragged to the presidential palace. Bogotá erupted into riot, burning, and looting, and the convulsion became known as *el bogotazo.*

The strife between the rival parties continued in earnest, and in a desperation move reminiscent of Hobbes' "state of nature," members from both sides asked for deliverance at the hands of the military dictator Gustavo Rojas Pinilla. He ruled from 1953 to 1957, when the Liberal Lleras Camargo met with his counterpart Laureano Gómez. Together they agreed on a constitutional reform known as the National Front, allowing the Liberals and Conservatives to alternate in office at all levels of government for the next 16 years. The elites thereby had concluded an understanding; unfortunately, even though women were given the right to vote, too many of the concerns of the majority of the population were not addressed.

The 1960s were a time of uprisings in Latin America, and the United States was anxious that other Cubas not arise; so it countered with a carrot—the Alliance for Progress—and a stick—the School for the Americas, in which the U.S. military gave instruction on countersubversion. Attempts by the Alliance to institute agrarian reform in Colombia floundered on the political maneuvering of the large landowners. Thwarted in their attempts to bring about their vision of a more equitable society and motivated by the examples of Fidel Castro and Ernesto "Che" Guevara in Cuba, young students and a sympathetic priest named Camilo Torres, took up arms. The official candidate of the National Front in the April 19, 1970 election was Misael Pastrana. The excluded groups united in the Popular National Alliance to oppose his candidacy by nominating former president Rojas Pinillas, who lost by two points. The cry of fraud rent the air, and dissatisfaction with the traditional political process engendered the organization of two rebel groups, the *Fuerzas Armadas Revolucionarias de Colombia* (FARC) and the April 19 Movement (M-19).

As a result of a subsequent peace initiative, both of these groups suspended their armed conflict with the government and sponsored legal political parties. The M-19 garnered brief success, capturing 28 percent of the vote for the special constitutional election in 1990. The Patriotic Union (UP) sponsored by the FARC in 1985 achieved limited influence by winning 14 seats in Congress in 1986. Their numbers were soon diminished by the assassination of more than 3,000 of their leaders and supporters, including two of their presidential candidates. The only UP senator winning an election was killed the day he took office, and his successor was forced into exile under threat of death. The experience discouraged further legal political participation by the reform movement.

It is easy to see why Colombia is presently considered the most violent country in the hemisphere. The guerrillas prosper because they have the support of the peasantry. Most commentators would agree that the peasants' situation has deteriorated in the last three decades. The opening up of the markets associated with the implementation of neoliberal economic policies has had a severe effect on the economics of the small landholder. The 2,299,804 small farms represent a mere 15.6 percent of the total arable land. Of these, over four-fifths are considered minifarms. The trend in Colombia is toward ever-larger farms. The world coffee price has declined, high production costs resulting from the overvaluation of the *peso*, and a parasitic infestation of the crop has made it very tempting to switch to growing coca and poppies. Official statistics indicate that the FARC operates in over half the territory. In 1985 they operated in 173 municipalities; in 1997 that number had increased to 1,071. Yet, it would be inaccurate to characterize them as narcoguerrillas, as some have tried to do. The Colombian military has used that ploy with success in extracting military assistance from the United States.

The guerrilla groups, currently comprising the FARC and *Ejército de Liberación Nacional* (ELN) or Army of National Liberation are referred to as "terrorists" for political purposes by the government of Álvaro Uribe. Combining their strategy under the umbrella of the *Coordinadora Guerrillera Nacional* (CGN), they are well armed and possess sophisticated ordinance. Initially, they supported themselves by robbery and kidnapping for ransom; now they raise revenue by taxing the narcotics operations in the areas they control. They, however, are not the narcotraffickers. The CGN merely supervises the commerce and is preferred by the *cocaleros* to the *narcotraficantes* because it maintains order and protects them from the murderous agents of the cartels.

The large landowners have always resorted to violent methods in resolving their disputes with the peasants. In control of the political apparatus, they traditionally have had access to the military and police in helping them settle disputes or, should these not be available, their own paramilitary forces or *sicarios* (assassins).

The violence is self-sustaining because, as Nazih Richani has elaborated, it has reached a "positive-sum, economy of scale."[29] A military impasse has been achieved by the belligerent factions and a "symbiotic" balance of sorts has resulted. The guerrillas provide protection for the *colonos* (small-to-middle-sized agriculturalists). The violent arena reduces the price of land, which is then purchased by the newly rich narcotraffickers looking for a means to launder their money. The military, in turn, is able to receive growing proportions of the national budget. The CGN collects a "war tax" from the corporations, landowners, and ranchers in the area. The military, in the areas in which they set up their drug extermination operations, extract a "tax" in the form of multiple bribes, which the *cocaleros* find more onerous than that paid the CGN. Narcowealth has gone into the purchase of four-to-six million *hectares* (a *hectare* is approximately 2.5 acres) used primarily for cattle grazing. The new ranchers naturally join with the established ones in opposing the agrarian reform espoused by the CGN. The military benefits by receiving salary supplements for hazardous duty in the "red zones." Retired military personnel can secure lucrative consulting fees by training paramilitary forces—often composed of former soldiers. The military and paramilitary are allies, and, hence, there is no control over the latter who have engaged in grisly massacres of suspected guerrilla sympathizers. Groups with such names as *Monchecabezas* (decapitators) have terrorized the population in an attempt to isolate the CGN from its supporters.

The violence in Colombia holds international significance. Neighboring countries, such as Panama, Venezuela, and Ecuador, feel the effects of instability as guerrillas often make their way across borders for sanctuary. The drug production fueled by the conflict spurs crime in the region through narcotrafficking and the laundering of drug profits. The United States, the world's largest market for cocaine and heroin, also feels the impact of Colombian violence. The traditional approach used by the United States to combat narcotrafficking is to address the production of drugs—their cultivation and processing. U.S. officials point to the success of the approach during the 1980s in Peru and Bolivia, where coca cultivation declined dramatically. But critics note that the supply-side focus of the United States easily falls victim to what is called "the balloon effect." Production declined in Peru and Bolivia only because it moved to Colombia. An alternative would be a stronger demand-side focus—attacking drug trafficking by concentrating on consumption in the United States. Latin Americans, noting that drug trafficking would nearly disappear without the U.S. addiction, view the focus on destroying cultivation and processing as typical U.S. arrogance because it defines drug trafficking as a problem created and sustained by Latin America.

The demand-side focus was intensified in the 2000 Andean Counterdrug Initiative, also known as *Plan Colombia* because nearly all of the funding goes to this country. The six-year program channeled some $4 billion, to combat drug production, with 80 percent of the monies devoted to military assistance. In 2005, the Bush Administration requested an extension of the program, and few doubt that the funding will continue. No politician wants to be accused of being soft on drugs. But has the program shown any success? According to the CIA's own numbers, coca cultivation in 2004 is just 7 percent below what it was in 1999. And a study by the Office of National Drug Control Policy noted that cocaine prices have not significantly changed since the implementation of *Plan Colombia*.[30] This point is important, because proponents of the supply-side focus initially argued that the focus on cultivation would decrease supply, drive up prices, and then lead to a decrease in usage. What this logic ignores is the impact of the balloon effect within Colombia (growers simply move about the country, plant smaller, less detectable plots, and/or cultivate strains of more potent coca to allow more cocaine in smaller plots). Also, should prices be affected, we should not expect addicts to react like rational consumers and decrease their use.

Review Questions

1. What are some causes of underdevelopment that are particular to Latin America?
2. How can the United States best address drug trafficking?
3. Account for the historically strong role of the military in Latin America.
4. Why are the United States and Cuba finding it so difficult to overcome their differences?
5. Employing examples from your reading, account for the endurance of violence as a way of pursuing political, social, and economic ends in Latin America.

Key Terms

◆ **Caudillo**—Literally, the "man on horseback." The history of Latin America is littered with what amounts to "war lords" who seize political power through extralegal means and govern by force of their personalities, inhibiting the institutionalization of the political process.

◆ **Criollo**—A person of Spanish descent born in the Americas and prohibited by Spanish policy from occupying the higher levels of the colonial bureaucracy. The local initiative for the independence movements came from these people who had less attachment to the metropolis.

◆ **ejido**—Communal landholdings in Mexico. A traditional source of pride for the lower classes in the peasantry, today they are viewed as an impediment to further neoliberal economic reforms.

◆ **escrache**—A form of protest meant to draw attention to individuals considered guilty of egregious crimes against society.

◆ **Fidelistas**—The followers of Fidel Castro.

◆ **Guantánamo Bay**—A United States naval installation on Cuba's southern Caribbean coast, which the U.S. obtained from Cuba as a condition for removing American troops after the Spanish-American War. This base, which is currently housing prisoners taken in the battle against the Taliban and Al-Qaeda terrorists, has been a source of irritation to Cuban nationalists. The lingering resentment associated with the memory of U.S. meddling in Cuba's war of independence provides a receptive environment for Castro's anti-*yanqui* fulminations.

◆ **Inter-American Democratic Charter**—Signed on September 11, 2001, this document commits the OAS to the protection and promotion of democracy in the Western Hemisphere.

◆ **ISI**—Import-substitution industrialization is an economic doctrine that promotes the notion of a self-sufficient national economy. The disruption of trade during two world wars and the inter-war global depression helped to establish the policy. Since then it has become apparent that the policy would have a difficult time succeeding in the face of the limited markets associated with most of the Latin American economies and the external competition from the more advanced nations. The policy has been eclipsed in recent times by the notions of "free trade," promoted by the United States and the International Monetary Fund (IMF).

◆ **NAFTA**—The North American Free Trade Agreement is a treaty initiated in 1994 establishing a free-trade area among Canada, Mexico, and the United States. It represents an attempt to promote the economic policy of free trade in contrast with the protectionism, tariffs, and quotas associated with import-substitution industrialization. Other countries of the hemisphere are experimenting with regional free-trade areas, such as that among Brazil, Uruguay, and Argentina (MERCOSUR) in the southern cone. The current talk, led by the United States, is to establish a hemisphere-wide, free-trade area known as the Free Trade Area of the Americas.

- **Organization of American States (OAS)**—The OAS emerged after World War II with the establishment of the Rio Treaty in 1947 and the 1948 Treaties of Bogotá. It took the nations of Latin America over a century after their independence to trust the United States to the point of joining it in an alliance to protect the security of the hemisphere as well as promote democratic institutions. With the waning of the cold war, the emphasis of the organization has changed from security to advancing democracy and human rights. These issues are now threatened with the problem of narcotrafficking.
- **Peninsular**—A person born in Spain who would be allowed to serve in the higher levels of colonial administration.

Useful Web Sites

The InterAmerican Development Bank: www.iadb.org
The InterAmerican Dialogue: www.iadialog.org
UTLANIC at the University of Texas: lanic.utexas.edu
The Washington Office on Latin America: wola.org/
The Political Database of the Americas: www.georgetown.edu/pdba/english.html
Organization of American States: http://www.oas.org

Notes

1. "Cattle Ranching Is Encroaching on Forests in Latin America," FAO Newsroom, June 8, 2005. www.fao.org.
2. Brian Loveman. *For La Patria: Politics and the Armed Forces in Latin America* (Wilmington, DE: Scholarly Resources, 1999), pp. 27–62.
3. David L. Clawson. *Latin America and the Caribbean: Lands and Peoples* (Boston, McGraw-Hill, 2004), pp. 141–43.
4. *Indigenous Peoples, Poverty and Human Development in Latin America: 1994–2004* (Washington, D.C.: World Bank, 2005).
5. Loveman, 1999, pp. 1–26.
6. Robert W. Patch. "Imperial Politics and Local Economy in Colonial Central America: 1670–1770," *Past and Present* (May 1994).
7. Simon Hanson, *Economic Development in Latin America* (Washington, D.C.: Inter-American Affairs Press, 1951), p. 107.
8. Economic Commission for Latin America and the Caribbean. *Statistical Yearbook for Latin America and the Carribean* (New York: ECLAC, 2004).
9. *World Development Indicators* (Washington D.C.: World Bank Group, 2005).
10. *World Economic and Social Survey 2004* (New York: Department of Economic and Social Affairs, United Nations, 2004).
11. Craig Arceneaux. *Bounded Missions: Military Rule and Democratization in the Southern Cone and Brazil* (University Park: Pennsylvania State University, 2001).
12. Angelina Snodgrass Godoy, "Lynchings and the Democratization of Terror in Postwar Guatemala: Implications for Human Rights." *Human Rights Quarterly* 24, 3 (2002): 640–661.
13. *NACLA Report on the Americas*. "Mexico's Haves and Have-Nots: NAFTA Sharpens the Divide." (January 2002) 35, 4: 32–35.

14. *World Economic and Social Survey 2004.*
15. Hugh Thomas, *Cuba: The Pursuit of Freedom* (New York: Harper & Row, 1971), p. 557.
16. Susan Kaufman Purcell and David Rothkopf, eds., *Cuba: The Contours of Change* (Boulder, Colo.: Lynne Rienner Publishers, 2000), p. 13.
17. Ronald Sylvia and Constantine Danopoulos "The Chavez Phenomenon: Political Change in Venezuela," *Third World Quarterly* 24:1 (February 2003): 63–76. Steve Ellner and Daniel Hellinger, eds. *Venezuelan Politics in the Chávez Era: Class, Polarization and Conflict.* Boulder: Lynne Rienner, 2003.
18. McCoy, Jennifer L. "Demystifying Venezuela's Hugo Chavez," *Current History*: February 2000: 66–72.
19. Ibid., 69–70.
20. "Chávez Ouster Draws U.S. Backing, Then Opposition," *Associated Press Worldstream*, April 17, 2002, Lexis-Nexis Online.
21. "Declaration on Democracy in Venezuela," AG/DEC. 28 (XXXII-O/02), 2002.
22. López Maya, Margarita (2003): "Las insurrecciones de la oposición en el 2002 en Venezuela: causas e implicaciones", XXIV Congress of the Latin American Studies Association, March 27–29, 2003, Dallas, Texas.
23. Ibid., xxx.
24. "Opposition Squabbles, Deadline Passes," *Latin American Weekly Report*, May 20, 2003; "Deal May Break 'Fifth Man' Impasse," *Latin American Weekly Report*, July 8, 2003.
25. "Venezuela: Opposition Shuns CNE and Takes to the Streets," *Latin American Weekly Report*, March 2, 2004, Lexis-Nexis Online; "Venezuela: Opposition May Scuttle the Referendum," *Latin American Weekly Report*, April 20, 2004, Lexis-Nexis Online.
26. Regime Change or Bust: Venezuela," *The Economist*, March 13, 2004. Lexis-Nexis Online; Venezuela: Opposition denounces 'fraud by naturalisation'," *Latin American Weekly Report*, July 13, 2004, Lexis-Nexis Online.
27. "Rigging the Rule of Law: Judicial Independence Under Siege in Venezuela," Human Rights Watch, June 2004 (New York: Human Rights Watch); "Report in the Situation of Human Rights in Venezuela," Inter-American Commission on Human Rights, December 2003. Available online at www.oas.org.
28. These assessments can be found in: "Auditoria de los resultados del procesos del referéndum revocatorio presidencial Venezuela," OAS and Carter Center, August 26, 2004. Available online at www.oas.org; "Last Phase of the Venezuelan Recall Referendum: Carter Center Report," Carter Center, August 21, 2004, available online at www.cartercenter.org; also see "U.S. Firm Defends Exit Poll," *Associated Press Online*, August 20, 2004, Lexis-Nexis Online.
29. Nazih Richani. "The Political Economy of Violence: The War-System in Colombia," *Journal of Inter-American Studies and World Affairs* 39, no. 2 (1997): 37–81.
30. "Memorandum: Rethinking Plan Colombia," Washington Office on Latin America, Washington, D.C. Available at www.wola.org.

For Further Reading

Arceneaux, Craig. *Bounded Missions: Military Regimes and Democratization in the Southern Cone and Brazil.* University Park, PA: Penn State University Press, 2001.

Arceneaux, Craig, and David Pion-Berlin. *Transforming Latin America: The International and Domestic Origins of Change.* Pittsburgh: University of Pittsburgh Press, 2005.

Atkins, G. Pope. *Latin America in the International Political System.* 3rd ed. rev. Boulder, CO.: Westview Press, 1995.

Blouet, Brian W., and Olwyn M. Blouet. *Latin America and the Caribbean: A Systematic and Regional Survey.* Hoboken, NJ: John Wiley, 2005.

Camp, Roderic Ai. *Politics in Mexico: The Democratic Transformation.* New York: Oxford University Press, 2003.

Crandall, Russell, Guadalupe Paz, and Riordan Roett. The Andes in Focus: Security, Democracy, and Economic Reform. Boulder, CO: Lynne Reinner, 2005.

Franko, Patrice. *The Puzzle of Latin American Economic Development.* Lanham, MD: Rowman and Littlefield, 2003.

MacDonald, Gordon J., Daniel L. Nielson, and Marc A. Stern. *Latin American Environmental Policy in International Perspective.* Boulder, CO: Westview Press, 1997.

Mainwaring, Scott, and Arturo Valenzuela, eds. *Politics, Society, and Democracy: Latin America.* Boulder, Colo.: Westview Press, 1998.

Molineu, Harold. *U.S. Policy toward Latin America: From Regionalism to Globalism.* 2nd ed. Boulder, Colo.: Westview Press, 1990.

O'Donnell, Guillermo. *Modernization and Bureaucratic-Authoritarianism: Studies in South American Politics.* Berkeley: Institute of International Studies, University of California, 1973.

Purcell, Susan Kaufman, and David Rothkopf. *Cuba: The Contours of Change.* Boulder, Colo.: Lynne Rienner Publishers, 2000.

Roniger, Luis, and Mario Sznajder. *The Legacy of Human Rights Violations in the Southern Cone: Argentina, Chile, and Uruguay.* New York: Oxford University Press, 1999.

Rouquié, Alain. Translated by Paul E. Sigmund. *The Military and the State in Latin America.* Berkeley: University of California Press, 1987.

Skidmore, Thomas E., and Peter H. Smith. *Modern Latin America.* 6th ed. New York: Oxford University Press, 2005.

Smith, William C., and Roberto Patricio Korzeniewicz, eds. *Politics, Social Change, and Economic Restructuring in Latin America.* Boulder, Colo.: Published by the North-South Center Press at the University of Miami and distributed by Lynne Rienner Publishers, Inc., 1997.

Stein, Stanley, and Barbara Stein. *The Colonial Heritage of Latin America.* New York: Oxford University Press, 1970.

Sub-Saharan Africa

Ira Reed

Seek ye first the political kingdom and all other things will be added unto you.

KWAME NKRUMAH

Viewed in the new millennium, these words from one of Africa's liberation leaders in the post–World War II generation seem quaint or naive. Independence from colonial rule did not bring "all other things." As emphasized in this chapter, Africa's problems have multiplied in the past few decades. In addition, foreign interests have often focused elsewhere in the world. The political instability, economic decline, social unrest, and environmental degradation that became commonplace in most of the states of the region will not quickly improve, despite some hopeful developments.

From 1957 to 1993, more than three dozen African colonies achieved independence, some peacefully and others violently. Despite the different roads taken, a common theme ran through these new states in their early years: hope, excitement, deliverance.

This early enthusiasm struck a responsive chord in the West. Some leaders were genuinely supportive of the new order. British Prime Minister Harold Macmillan declared that "the winds of change" were blowing through Africa and would have to be accommodated. Youthful President John F. Kennedy embraced the notion of a Peace Corps, with Africa a major recipient of hundreds and then thousands of practical idealists. Furthermore, it was believed that the East-West conflict would be fought in the Other World, and the battle for the hearts and minds of the people of Africa was seen as an important objective.

If this earlier period was one of optimism and gains in Africa, then the 1980s was a period of pessimism and losses. In fact, the period has been described as "the lost decade." Although there are success stories and some recent encouraging signs, the overall situation is disheartening. While it is true that the 1990s witnessed a modest increase in participatory political systems, these changes have yielded mixed results at best. As will be seen in the Case Studies and Flashpoint sections of this chapter, several of the wars in Africa have abated or ended, but other violent conflicts continue to fester, and many African nations remain unstable. In a number of African countries, either military rule or strict civilian governments persist, in which democracy, at least as we understand it in the West (e.g., freedom of speech and press, fair and competitive elections, and an independent judiciary), is significantly restricted or nonexistent. In a few states or areas within states, warlords or rebels have taken over and real governments of any sort have ceased to exist.

By virtually any index, the economic situation has worsened. Per capita income, already the lowest in the Other World, actually declined during the 1980s to gain little in the 1990s. (For recent figures, see Table 6.1.) The international monetary debt of most African states soared through those decades. Unemployment or underemployment continued its upward climb. Most agricultural products and minerals are fetching lower world prices than 20 years ago, causing even those states rich in resources to face periods of declining prices. Millions simply do not get enough to eat.

The picture is not any brighter in other areas. The population explosion continues with a few significant exceptions, and is again far higher than in the rest of the Other World. Food production has not kept pace with population growth, and despite rising food imports, the average African has less to eat now than in 1980. Environmental degradation increases yearly, and the underlying support systems sag under the onslaught. More and more species are endangered as impoverished humans encroach on their habitat, sometimes killing the animals for profit. Similarly, the quality of education is in serious straits, and newer health problems such as acquired immunodeficiency syndrome (AIDS) dwarf older ones, some of which have been curbed or eliminated, while others, such as malaria, polio, and tuberculosis have resurfaced.

History and geography provide some clues to the plight of Africa. A discussion of the political, social, and economic realities within and beyond Africa today provides additional explanations. The Case Studies illustrate the dilemmas the peoples of Africa are facing. The chapter concludes with Flashpoints on current trouble spots and issues. (Discussion of the five North African states bordering the Mediterranean is included in Chapter 8.)

GEOGRAPHY

Africa, second in size only to Asia, has some of the world's mightiest rivers and abundant mineral resources. Nevertheless, the region has more than its share of natural impediments to development, including its relative isolation from other areas of the world. The Atlantic Ocean is located to the west of the continent and

TABLE 6.1 Characteristic of African Countries

Country	Population (millions)	Population Growth Rate %	Infant Mortality Rate (per 1,000 live births)	Population Under 15 years of age (%)	Life Expectancy (in years)	Urban Population (%)	Literacy Rate (%)	Arable Land (%)	Per Capita GDP ($US)
Algeria	32.129	1.22	32.2	33.5	73	58.8	70	3	5900
Egypt	76.117	1.78	33.9	33.96	71	42.1	57.7	2	3900
Libya	5.631	2.33	25.7	35	76.5	86.3	82.6	1	6400
Morocco	32.209	1.57	43.3	33.8	70.66	57.5	51.7	21	4000
Tunisia	9.974	0.99	25.8	27.8	74.89	63.7	74.2	19	6900
Benin	7.25	2.82	85.9	47.2	50.51	44.6	37	13	1100
Burkina Faso	13.575	2.53	98.7	47.3	43.92	17.8	26.6	13	1100
Cape Verde	0.415	2.53	49.1	41.40	70.45	55.9	76.6	11	1400
Cote d'Ivoire	17.327	2.06	97.3	46	48.62	44.9	50.9	6	1400
Gambia	1.547	2.93	73.5	45.1	55.2	26.1	40.1	18	1700
Ghana	20.757	1.25	52.2	40.4	56	45.4	74.8	12	2200
Guinea	9.246	2.37	91.8	42.8	49.86	34.9	36	2	2100
Guinea-Bissau	1.388	1.96	108.7	41.9	46.97	34	55	11	900
Liberia	3.39	2.64	130.5	43.3	47.69	46.7	57.5	1	1000
Mali	11.956	2.74	118	47.2	45.09	32.3	46.4	2	900
Mauritania	2.998	2.9	72.4	46.1	52.73	61.8	41.7	0	1800
Niger	11.36	2.63	122.7	47.9	42.13	22.2	17.6	3	800
Nigeria	137.25	2.37	70.5	43.6	46.74	46.7	68	33	800
Senegal	10.852	2.48	56.5	43.5	56.75	49.6	40.2	12	1600
Sierra Leone	5.883	2.22	145.2	44.7	42.52	38.8	31	7	500
Togo	5.556	2.17	67.7	45.1	52.64	35.1	60.9	38	1500
Burundi	6.231	2.22	70.4	46.5	43.5	9.9	51.6	44	600
Djibouti	0.466	2.06	105.5	42.8	43.1	83.7	67.9	0	1300
Ethiopia	67.851	2.36	102.1	47.2	48.83	15.6	42.7	12	700

Country	Population	Population Growth	Infant Mortality Rate	Population Under 15 Years of Age	Life Expectancy	Urban Population	Literacy Rate	Arable Land	Per Capita GDP
Kenya	32.021	2.56	62.2	41.1	47.99	39.4	85.1	7	1000
Madagascar	17.501	3.03	78.5	45	56.95	26.5	68.9	4	800
Malawi	11.906	2.06	104.2	44	36.97	16.3	62.7	18	600
Mauritius	1.22	0.84	15.6	25.4	72.38	43.3	85.6	49	11400
Mozambique	18.811	1.48	137.1	42.5	40.32	35.6	47.8	4	1200
Rwanda	7.954	2.43	101.7	41.7	46.96	18.3	70.4	35	1300
Seychelles	0.08	0.43	16	27.8	71.82	49.9	84	2	7800
Somalia	8.304	3.38	118.5	44.7	48.09	34.8	37.8	2	500
Sudan	39.148	2.6	64.1	44.2	58.54	38.9	61.1	5	1900
Tanzania	36.588	1.83	102.1	44.6	45.24	35.4	78.2	3	600
Uganda	26.404	3.31	86.2	50.9	51.59	12.2	69.9	25	1400
Zambia	10.462	2.12	98.4	47.1	39.7	35.7	80.6	7	800
Zimbabwe	12.671	0.51	67.1	37.9	36.67	34.9	90.7	7	1900
Angola	10.978	1.9	192.5	43.3	36.61	35.7	42	2	1900
Cameroon	16.063	1.93	69.2	42.1	47.84	51.4	79	13	1800
Central African Republic	3.742	1.49	92.2	43	41.01	42.7	51	3	1200
Chad	9.538	2.95	94.8	47.8	47.94	24.9	47.5	3	1200
Congo	2.998	1.31	93.9	42.4	48.97	31.6	65.5	0	700
Democratic Republic of Congo	58.317	2.98	94.7	48.2	49.35	53.5	83.8	3	600
Republic of Equatorial Guinea	0.523	2.42	87.1	42.4	55.56	48.1	85.7	5	2700
Gabon	1.355	2.45	54.3	33.3	55.75	83.3	63	1	5500
Sao Tome and Principe	0.181	3.16	44.6	47.7	66.99	37.8	79.3	2	1200
Botswana	1.561	0	70	40	33.87	51.6	79.8	1	8800
Lesotho	1.865	0.08	85.2	39	36.68	17.9	84.8	11	3000
Namibia	1.954	0.73	69.6	42.6	43.93	32.4	84	1	7100
South Africa	42.718	−0.31	62.2	31.6	43.27	56.9	86.4	10	10700
Swaziland	1.169	0.25	68.4	45.5	35.65	23.5	81.6	11	4900

SOURCE: Population, Infant Mortality Rate, Population Under 15 Years of Age, Urban Population, Literacy Rate, Arable Land, and per Capita GDP from *The World Almanac and Book of Facts, 2005*; Population Growth and Life Expectancy from *CIA World Factbook, 2005*.

the Indian Ocean to the east. Prevailing wind patterns on the west coast minimized maritime contacts between Africans and Europeans until the fifteenth or sixteenth century. With the Sahara (the Arabic word for desert) in the north, it is easy to understand why overland transportation from Europe and North Africa was and is spotty. The Kalahari Desert in the southern part of the continent is an additional obstacle.

Africa's great rivers—Nile, Zaire (Congo), Niger, Zambezi, and Orange—all have cataracts, sand bars, or other obstructions, which also undermine rather than enhance communications. The continent's smooth coastline, and thus its lack of natural harbors, has been another problem, although today coastal cities such as Dakar, Lagos, Luanda, and Dar es Salaam are highly important.

Most of the region's interior is flat or gently undulating. The major exception is the Great Rift Valley system in eastern Africa, which runs north to south for hundreds of miles and features deep trenches, 20 to 50 miles wide, carved into the Earth. Inactive volcanoes, frequent Earth tremors, and occasional earthquakes occur in the area. Lake Victoria is the largest lake in Africa, and Mount Kilimanjaro is the continent's highest mountain, 19,340 feet above sea level.

Whatever the focus, African geography runs the gamut from scarcity to abundance. Although temperatures are generally high, rainfall, when abundant, gives rise to lush vegetation; more often, the absence of rainfall contributes to a parched landscape. Varying soil quality also helps produce rainforests, savannas, or deserts. Mineral resources follow the same oscillating pattern. Some areas in central and southern Africa are uniquely blessed, whereas other locales are virtually void of substances valued in the modern world (see Figure 6.1).

The complex interaction of temperature, rainfall, population growth and distribution, and soils is of crucial significance in Africa today. The human habitat was once more hospitable. Thirty-five hundred years ago, what is now the Sahara was green. Just 40 years ago the Sahel, which includes the area lying just south of the Sahara, was able to sustain a population of perhaps 20 million. Today, famine is an ever-present danger. Millions of nomadic herders, traders, and small farmers have been turned into refugees trying to eke out a living in an increasingly unforgiving environment.

As a result, both the farmer, whose land becomes more difficult to till, and the herders are forced to move to overcrowded cities. Nouakchott, for instance, the capital of Mauritania and on the edge of the Sahel, has grown from 20,000 people in 1960 to more than 735,000 today. Many of its people barely survive; some starve. The same might be said of Khartoum, the capital of Sudan, some 3,000 miles away. In the last few years, eastern and southern Africa has been affected in a similar way. In fact, the encroaching desert, aided by drought, has affected some two dozen African states. In 1998, the flooding Nile meant that hundreds of thousands of people near Khartoum were victimized by both an absence of rain and a deluge of water. In 2004, the problems of the northern desert areas were compounded by hordes of devastating locusts, leading to a severe famine and humanitarian crisis in Niger the following year. A severe 2005 draught brought famine to Malawi, a nation also mired in partisan political turmoil.

FIGURE 6.1 The Physical Geography of Africa

In the past, Africa's strategic importance rested on its mineral wealth in the central and southern parts of the continent and its geographic "chokepoints" on the perimeter of the region. High-tech industries of the West relied on platinum, chrome, and vanadium, which are found almost exclusively in Africa. Gibraltar, the Suez Canal, Bab el Mandeb, and the Cape of Good Hope at the southern tip of the continent were strategic areas of interest to both East and West. With the end of the cold war, both the economic and geopolitical standing of the region declined.

PEOPLE

Africa's people have been divided by many factors, including race, ethnicity, religion, country, and class. The importance of race was established as early as the fifteenth century. Later, it was tied to class when positions in society became dominated by Europeans. Because of the colonial legacy, the belief that one race is superior or inferior to another still has considerable significance in Africa. The emphasis on race was clearest in South Africa, where apartheid, a form of separate development based on race, was officially proclaimed by whites in 1948 and rescinded only in 1990.

Race remains important in many other African countries. In several former French colonies, there are almost as many Europeans now as there were at independence more than three decades ago. There, as elsewhere, Europeans have many of the most prestigious and best-paying jobs. Often, being white gets one a better seat in a van or truck or allows one to be waved through a checkpoint while others with a darker skin must wait. For the present then, Europeans, a name often given to all whites, still enjoy a high social status and lifestyle far above that of most of the indigenous population.

Between the Europeans and the Africans on the ladder of success are the Indians of East and South Africa and the Lebanese of West Africa. Both groups are major forces in retail and wholesale merchandising and in the economy generally. Because of their positions, both are also targets of protest from those below them on the ladder.

When discussing language, ethnic groups, cultures (and subcultures), and religions, the key concepts are diversity and complexity. There are, conservatively, many hundreds of different ethnic groups. (Because of the negative connotations of the words *tribe* and *tribalism*, the terms *ethnic group* and *ethnicity* have replaced them.) Thus, there are many hundreds of distinct languages and cultures. Although some groups number in the millions of members, others have only hundreds. The sheer number of such groups throughout Africa makes this dimension unique to the continent. Ethnic divisions are a powerful force today. Struggles in such diverse states as Angola, Burundi, Congo, Ethiopia, Kenya, Liberia, Mauritania, Nigeria, Rwanda, Sierra Leone and Sudan may be explained, in part, by deep-seated ethnic divisions.

African religions, again diverse and complex, have generally accommodated external religions, accepting some aspects and modifying others. Christian missionaries, who preceded colonial officials, remained after their government's departure. Although numbers are hard to confirm, there is a consensus that the number of people embracing either the monotheism of Christianity or Islam in some form is growing rapidly. The Roman Catholic population, for instance, has grown considerably in the last decade to more than 120 million, and the late Pope John Paul II visited the continent no fewer than 12 times. Some Church experts thought that an African Pope, specifically a respected Nigerian Cardinal, might be elected this time, but the College of Cardinals elected a German instead. Local customs and beliefs have challenged Rome's pronouncements; indigenous churches therefore abound. Islam has been an important political factor in many countries in the Sahel, the Horn of Africa, spreading deeper into Central and West Africa also, and militant fundamentalist movements have made inroads.

Most people in the West give their primary support to the nation-state, but such a commitment is rare in Africa. Race, ethnicity, and religion have historical and deep-seated appeals that compete with the nation-state. With a large majority of Africans still continuing to live in the rural areas, developing support for the nation-state is a challenge. Only rarely do state and ethnic boundaries coincide. Nationalism is further hampered by the small size and population of many of the countries, as well as their lack of resources.

A belief in a shared past or shared future, in myths or traditions, in joint economic or social institutions, or in a common culture is in short supply on the national level. Rarely is there a common indigenous language. In fact, in most African states, the official language is a European tongue. In conflicts between personal, family, village, or ethnic ties on the one hand, and a national perspective on the other, the larger focus usually loses. National leaders and others in the intelligentsia have the media at their disposal in their call for increased support for the state, and expanding education for children and adults helps. Nevertheless, developing a broadly based nationalism is proceeding slowly.

As in the former Soviet Union (including the Other World nations treated in Chapter 9), and Eastern Europe, class formation is expanding and perhaps sharpening. With few exceptions, the emergence of a small elite class, often tied to one ethnic group, has become the norm. For the time being, a comfortable lifestyle is beyond even the aspirations of the great majority. With the move to privatization described in the section on economics, some will improve their lot dramatically, but many others will become more embittered as the good life passes them by.

At the beginning of the twentieth century, the continent of Africa had fewer than 100 million people. Its population now is more than 873 million (over 710 million of whom live in the Sub-Saharan region). During the 1970s and 1980s, the population growth rate increased to more than 3 percent a year. Different sources say that the region's annual population increase has moderated to around 2.5 percent. That means over a billion people on the continent by 2025, but some factors, including population control policies and the ravages of AIDS in southern Africa, might curb this rate in certain areas. Despite the regional differences, Sub-Saharan Africa maintains the dubious distinction of the highest population growth rate in the world.

The birthrate in sub-Saharan Africa declined slightly in the last generation, but the death rate had declined more. By 1995, the gap had become immense, with an annual birthrate per thousand of 43.1 and a death rate of 14, but by 2005, these figures had changed to 40 and 16, respectively. Since the infant mortality rate has declined dramatically there is one less reason for parents to want more children, lessening the traditional preference for large families. Botswana, Kenya, Côte d'Ivoire, Tanzania, Djibouti, Guinea, and Zimbabwe have achieved varying degrees of success at population control. Kenya, which a decade ago was averaging close to 4 percent growth per year, then the world's highest, is now just above 1 percent, and average family size there declined from eight in the 1970s to 5.4 in 1998. Only a small percentage of married African women used modern contraceptive methods, even in the midst of the AIDS crisis. In most countries, the status of women is low and their sex education lags behind that of men. The religious admonition calling for large families is another factor driving population growth and hindering condom use. It is feared that the continent's life-support systems will be overwhelmed and the mortality rate will increase. Over the last 30 years, economic growth has barely kept pace with population growth. Life expectancy at birth in sub-Saharan Africa in 2003 stood at only 46.1 years, by far the lowest in the Other World. Of the 31 nations categorized as having "low human development" in the 2005 United Nations (UN) Human Development Index, a widely recognized measure of the quality of life that combines life expectancy and educational statistics, all but two (Haiti and Yemen) are sub-Saharan African, including the lowest-ranked 24 nations. (Liberia and Somalia are not ranked.) Of the sub-Saharan nations on the African continent, South Africa holds the highest ranking on this index at 120. The UN has established the Millennium Development Goals, eight ambitious targets for positive human change by 2015; sub-Saharan Africa will certainly face the greatest hurdles of all the Other World regions to reach them.[1]

HISTORY

Africa's history before the arrival of the Europeans was rich, varied, and complex. It involved many types of political systems, social structures, and economic patterns. It also involved considerable interaction with the peoples of North Africa, the Arabian Peninsula, and even China. Africa has been called "the cradle of human history," "the cradle of mankind," and "the first habitat of man." These phrases apply, because the oldest human remains, dating back at least 3 million years, were found in eastern Africa. Nevertheless, many people did not think Africa had a history because, to them, history was based on written language. This bias has now been corrected. In certain areas south of the Sahara, written Arabic was in use 1,000 years ago. More important, we now realize that oral traditions, archaeological exploration, comparative linguistics, art styles, ethnography, radio carbon dating, and a host of other tools can provide a rich history, predating the written word.

The domestication of cattle is 6,000 to 7,000 years old in Africa. Working with metal and iron, planting crops, and engaging in long-distance trade are occupations that go back millennia as well. In fact, there is a lot of discussion today about how much Egypt, often referred to as the cradle of civilization, was influenced by areas further south. The KhoiKhoi (Hottentots), San (Bushmen), and Twa (Pygmies) had long inhabited much of central and southern Africa until incursions from West Africa around the eleventh century began to reduce their spheres.

African kingdoms of great size and wealth predate the European colonial presence by many hundreds of years. Some of the best-known empires—Ghana, Mali, and Songhai—which together lasted over 1,000 years, were in the western Sudan, south of the Sahara. Here, Islam made its presence felt, especially among the rulers of Mali and Songhai. Great Zimbabwe in southern Africa, with its imposing stone structures, reached its apex in the fifteenth century. New archeological research is uncovering more evidence of other sophisticated, well-organized sub-Saharan African civilizations.

By the eighth century, Arab traders had brought Islam to the Horn of Africa, from which it gradually spread south and west. The Arab presence, however, went back much further, especially along the east coast. In succeeding centuries, traders pushed into the interior, although African culture remained dominant throughout. The Arab influence was great, however, from the formation of towns along the Indian Ocean to the rise of Swahili as the most important language in the region. The arrival of the Portuguese, with their superior military power, at the end of the fifteenth century signaled the rapid decline of Arab culture in the area.

Until the latter half of the nineteenth century, there were few Europeans in sub-Saharan Africa, especially in the vast interior. Despite their small numbers, they had a profound and lasting impact on African life. The institution of Western-style slavery cost the continent anywhere from 12 to 50 million men, women, and children. (See the Flashpoints section.) In the seventeenth and eighteenth centuries, slaves were the major export from the west coast of Africa.

By 1850, the European presence in Africa had existed along narrow coastal strips for over 350 years. The Portuguese in the fifteenth and sixteenth centuries, the Dutch in the seventeenth century, and the British in the eighteenth and first part of the nineteenth centuries had been dominant because of sea power. By about 1850, newfound European attention to the "Dark Continent" coincided with turbulence in several parts of Africa and resulted in greater penetration of the interior than ever before. The European objectives in Africa included raw materials to feed the Industrial Revolution, new markets, promising investments, naval bases, the renewed drive to "save souls," and a multifaceted quest for new knowledge.

THE COLONIAL EXPERIENCE

Despite the increasing presence of the Europeans, 90 percent of the continent was ruled by Africans until the last two decades of the nineteenth century. The European powers had not thought the benefits of occupation were worth the costs. As the foreigners jockeyed for power and prestige on the continent and around the globe, the situation quickly changed. The European states moved to establish a series of colonies in the region, and the possibility that the new competition would result in war was seen as a real danger. From October 1884 to February 1885, a conference to discuss the future boundaries of Africa was held in Berlin, at which almost all of the important European powers (but, tellingly, no Africans) were represented. The decisions reached there—and elsewhere in Europe in the remaining 15 years of the nineteenth century—established the basic political map of the continent to this day.

Africa was artificially divided to suit the objectives of the colonial governments. Preexisting ethnic, linguistic, and cultural units were ignored. The maps in Figures 6.2 and 6.3 are only 11 years apart, but the contrast is striking. Throughout Africa, closely knit people speaking the same language were suddenly separated. It was from these diversions that future generations' secessionist movements and border claims, known as *irredentism*, would spring.

The heyday of European colonial rule in Africa lasted for only 50 or 60 years; however, those few decades changed the face of the continent forever.[2] The impact of colonialism depended on the type of rule instituted, the presence or absence of white settlers, and the particulars of the African elite. Most importantly, each African ethnic group had its own political and social system. Each responded to colonial rule in a different way, ranging from willing acceptance to bloody resistance of the outside powers. The Baganda people of East Africa welcomed the European presence. In contrast, the Ndebele-Shona Rebellion (1896–1897) against English-speaking settlers in what is now Zimbabwe, the Ashanti and Fulani resistance against the British in West Africa (1900–1901), and the Maji Maji rebellion contesting harsh German rule in East Africa (1905–1907) all resulted in a strong European show of force followed by occupation.

The British generally practiced indirect rule, a system in which they were removed from day-to-day activities; instead they used the traditional authorities, who were now responsible to them. The other colonial systems employed direct rule, in which the European administrators played a much more extensive role in everyday African life. The British, concerned about costs, emphasized the economic dimension and were more aloof; the French, the leading practitioners of direct rule, were more intimately involved, held out the slight possibility that their subjects might become French citizens, and had a more lasting effect on their colonies.

Whatever the differences, the similarities were more important. The colonial powers' dominance occurred everywhere. Different peoples were divided or united by fiat, and long-time trading patterns were subject to fundamental change as the societies themselves were transformed in a hundred different ways. The indigenous populations suffered altered political arrangements, alien tax structures, forced labor, and directed changes in individual wants and societal norms. By shifting the roles and selection processes for traditional political leaders, the colonial authorities unintentionally sowed the seeds for far greater political changes in years to come. Much of the economy fell under the influence, if not control, of the

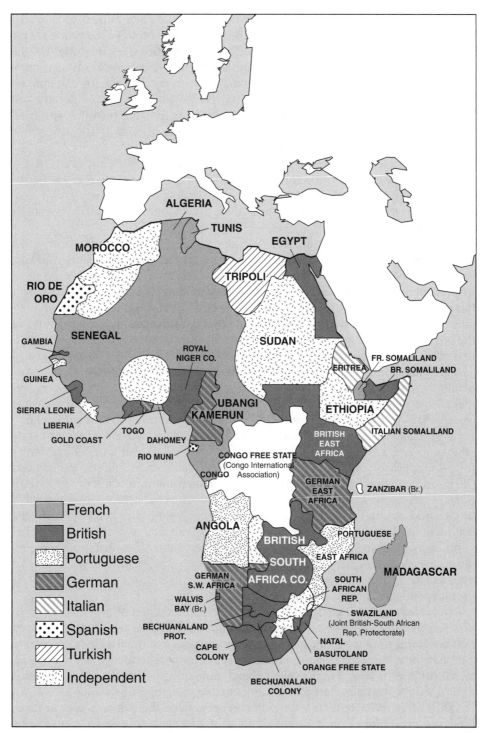

FIGURE 6.2 European Colonization in Africa, 1895

Europeans, who wished to substitute one or two cash crops or minerals for subsistence farming. Foreign goods and the widespread use of colonial currencies were also introduced. Cities, roads, and railroads were constructed for the benefit of the colonial rulers' administrative and economic interests. This colonial infrastructure tended to divide Africa rather than link it together; even today, the African map reflects the extractive goals of the imperial powers. In addition, the missionary and soldier added their particular persuasions to that of the administrator and merchant. By 1920, only Ethiopia, Liberia, and the Union of South Africa were free from formal European control, and the last was run by a white minority.

The new order scarcely touched the lives of the masses in many of the colonies. The people had little contact with Europeans, except when it was necessary to pay some new tax, live under some new law, or adopt a new plan for local land use. For the majority living in the rural areas, change or adaptation was to be a very gradual thing.

In the Portuguese, German, and Belgian colonies, the rule was far more harsh and the impact was often far more devastating. Villagers were routinely taken, with or without their leaders' approval, to work on roads or other projects. Impressment, however, was the least of it. The Congo Free State, for instance, was the private preserve of the Belgian king, whose control was so inhumane that after about 20 years he was forced to cede his 900,000-square-mile playground to the government of Belgium, which then established an only slightly more benevolent rule over this mammoth colony in the middle of Africa.

The movement to independence can be described in one of two ways: structurally or chronologically. Among the most important structures in the movement, especially to the generation coming of age at the turn of the century was the church. This institution was part of the white establishment, with its distinction between superior and inferior values, but it was also a source for Western-style education and a breeding ground for future nationalists. Although Christianity first undermined local cultures and traditions, later, independent, indigenous Christian churches came to question colonial government policies. Other institutions of change were located in the fast-growing cities. These included the tribal unions and associations; trade unions or workers' solidarity organizations; the rudimentary mass media; the soldiers and ex-servicemen, who had traveled beyond the colony; and finally, overt political movements. All contributed to the requests for greater responsibility by the local, African elite; to calls for autonomy or power sharing by the growing nationalist movement; and ultimately, to demands for independence, now backed by the masses.

In both World Wars, African troops participated on behalf of their European masters, gaining valuable training and combat experience. They also observed that the Europeans were not invincible. Chronologically, the trickle of restrained nationalism before 1885 became a torrent of calls for independence in the years after World War II. West Africa moved ahead more quickly than East Africa, which in turn led the southern part of the continent. Overall, the British colonies were in advance of the French, who led the Portuguese. Even the British were cautious, however, expecting at most a slow devolution of power. The British anticipated that black parliamentary governments would be established by local leaders, who would be "properly" educated and trained. For the French, those few Africans who gained political power would do so not in African political structures, but as overseas representatives in the French National Assembly in Paris. The other European powers believed that any growth of political consciousness would change the status quo and thus was unthinkable.

When World War II began in 1939, no one would have guessed that independence for most of the African colonies was only a generation away. Despite the depression of the 1930s, colonial rule appeared immutable. Certainly, there were the firebrands who agitated for greater rights for Africans, but they were few in number and cautious in method, despite an occasional protest or even riot at a particular location.

The war, however, had a tremendous effect on all parties. Tens of thousands of soldiers saw action beyond the continent. They returned home with newly honed skills and ideas and settled in the cities rather than returning to their homes in the rural areas. They became a part of the mass independence movements that were destined to sweep the continent. The new militancy was fueled by large numbers of students returning to Africa from overseas, the demands of an increasingly urbanized population, and a new generation of political leaders. The battered European powers, meanwhile, were simply hoping to hang on at home and had little interest and few resources for the colonies, thousands of miles away.

Africans under French rule were ready for a new day. Early in the war, General Charles de Gaulle had promised greater local autonomy (but not self-government) and increased rights for the peoples of French West Africa (FWA) and French Equatorial Africa (FEA) if they supported him in his battle against Vichy France and Nazi Germany. Similarly, in 1941, U.S. President Franklin Roosevelt and British Prime Minister Winston Churchill promised in the Atlantic Charter "to respect the right of all peoples to choose the form of government under which they will live." At the end of the war, the newly founded UN called for self-determination, and the two emerging superpowers—the United States and the Soviet Union—both supported changes in the existing colonial order.

The beginning of the end for colonial rule came with a railway workers' strike in FWA in 1946, followed by disturbances over economic issues in the Gold Coast, a presumed model British colony in West Africa, in early 1948. This latter protest, in which ex-servicemen played a major role, spread to the other British colonies in the area. In those postwar years, a new law and a new constitution in Paris also accelerated change throughout FWA and FEA. In the years that followed, Africans that lived thousands of miles apart, spoke hundreds of different languages, and were subjects of several colonial powers took up the unifying cry of self-government.

Independence came first to the Gold Coast (renamed Ghana) in 1957. The next year, President de Gaulle angrily accepted Guinea's vote to follow suit.[3] At the same time, the other colonies that had been carved out of FWA and FEA chose federation with France, allowing Paris continuing control of foreign affairs, internal security, and defense. In 1960, the logjam broke as the remaining 11 French-speaking colonies became independent. The same year, Nigeria ended its colonial

FIGURE 6.3 Political Map of Africa, 2006

relationship with Britain to become a regional magnet. For the next 20 years, the march to independence continued, and by the end of 1980, only Namibia, on the southwest coast of Africa, remained in a dependent status (see Figure 6.3); South Africa, despite UN resolutions, refused to give up its controlling interest over the former German colony it had inherited as a mandate after World War I. Finally, in 1990, even this dependency ended, as a general agreement on regional relations in southern Africa was reached.

Independence throughout the region had been achieved. But if this was a time for celebration, it was also a time of great concern because there was never a consensus on future directions within each state, let alone within regions or the continent as a whole. Older animosities that sometimes had been kept under wraps by the colonial power burst forth. Opposing local, national, and supranational forces threatened the stability of the fragile new states. Furthermore, the economic dimension was no more secure than the political, as local economies remained vulnerable to both domestic and international interests. The former colonial states were independent, but their governments lacked the sustained support of the people or, in some cases, the international community. Without such support, unity and economic well-being were unlikely.

GOVERNMENT

To understand African government in the early 2000s, one must realize that there has been an incredible compression of major political events. The older Africans of today grew up in the heyday of colonial rule, lived through World War II and the nationalist rush to independence, and finally, have experienced the instabilities of the postindependence years. The scholar Ali Mazrui quoted former Tanzanian President Julius Nyerere as saying that while some countries are trying to reach the moon and beyond, many Africans are still trying to get to town.[4] Such traditional institutions and values as the extended family and communal ownership of property are under attack while a new set of institutions and beliefs is not yet in place.

Instead of rule by the people, African independence has usually resulted in the continued rule of the few, though the new elites are indigenous, not foreign. The urban community, not the majority in the countryside, gets the bulk of state-run programs. In the cities, it is the small middle and upper classes that benefit from government. Despite a long history of group participation in decision making in many societies, pronouncements in the decades after independence were usually made by and for the few. The result was too often an elite driven by self-interest and even greed, while the many were disregarded. A view of politics as a means of extraction and personal enrichment, fostered under the experience of colonial rule, continued into independence, often with devastating results, as corruption among elected and appointed officials became commonplace.

Political solutions tried elsewhere in the Other World have faced opposition and indifference from societies in Africa. A major problem for the social elites is that the people have little faith in them. Although a few traditional authorities such as Chief Gatsha Buthelezi of the Zulu people in South Africa exercise considerable political influence, such examples are rare. Almost all African states comprise many ethnic groups, and traditional authorities may be unsuccessful in reaching out to those who owe them no special allegiance. Moreover, few of these authorities have real political power. They may also carry the baggage of colonial days, when their functions were usually altered by their European overlords, thus leading to the loss of respect from their subjects.

By the early 1980s, competitive political party systems in Africa were a rarity. This fact would have surprised earlier generations because, in many cases, the political party was in the forefront of the march to independence, and in doing so, gained mass support. Some parties managed to gain the grudging blessing of the colonial rulers, who looked fondly to their own political parties as models.

As the twentieth century ended, there were two schools of thought regarding African political systems. One was stated by Susan Rice, Assistant Secretary of State for African Affairs, in an address to the African Affairs Association in late 1997:

> Africa stands at a crossroads. . . . There is now more reason for optimism about Africa's future than at any time since the wave of independence over 30 years ago. . . . Democracy is ascendant. . . . Economic growth is also increasing. . . . Regions of stability are . . . emerging throughout the continent . . . [I]n many countries . . . reconciliation is supplanting confrontations as the means of bridging differences rooted in the past.[5]

The other was summarized by Judith Matloff, reporter for the *Christian Science Monitor,* as she wrapped up almost six years in the region in early 1998:

> I'd like to leave Africa saying that it had turned a corner into peace and prosperity and that most of the countries were on the right track. But that would be myopic and downright dishonest. The poverty and lack of education are so endemic, the access to arms so easy, and the democratic institutions so fragile that it's unlikely that the world's poorest continent will change overnight.[6]

Phrases such as *African Renaissance* and *Africa's second independence* are bandied about, but others see scarce improvement. Analysts come up with very different assessments of perceived democratic trends in the region. And Westerners often see Africa as cut from one piece of cloth, not as distinct states. Through the media, it is usually the wars, the poverty, the human rights abuses, and thus, the resignation that stand out. As far-removed states back off, the international lending institutions and nongovernmental aid agencies have become more prominent. Such institutions and agencies, however, have a long way to go. United Nations Secretary General Kofi Annan, from Ghana, elected to a second term and also awarded the Nobel Peace Prize in 2001 for the UN's peacekeeping efforts, bemoaned both divisive and draining colonial systems and more recent African leaders who had too often resorted to "heavy centralization of political and economic power and the suppression of political pluralism."[7] Centralized and personalized forms of government, patterns of corruption, ethnically based decisions, and human rights abuses, asserted Annan, were all too common. Even in the emerging African democracies, elections are often viewed as tainted and the winners as lacking legitimacy. Recent elections in Ethiopia, Madagascar, Nigeria, Togo, Uganda and Zimbabwe have been disputed or come under suspicion. (The 2005 Liberian presidential election might be seen as an exception to this pattern.) Rarely has a recent African election gone unchallenged, often through violent protests, and many elections fall far short of generally accepted norms of free, fair, and competitive.

BOX 6.1 ◆ WANGARI MAATHAI

Originally trained as a biologist, Kenyan Wangari Maathai became active in women's rights and founded the innovative environmental organization, the Greenbelt Movement (GBM), in 1977. Through GBM, women plant trees to restore damaged ecosystems, empowering the women and giving them purpose and self-esteem in the process. Despite strong opposition from the Kenyan government under Daniel Arap Moi, Maathai's GBM grew in popularity and stature. With a change in administrations in the 2002 elections, Maathai was elected to parliament and later appointed Assistant Minister of the Environment, Natural Resources and Wildlife, a post she currently holds. Her work with GBM emphasized the connections between human rights, environmentalism, democratization, and peace, leading to the award of the prestigious Nobel Peace Prize in 2004. In citing her for the award, the Nobel committee wrote:

> She has taken a holistic approach to sustainable development that embraces democracy, human rights and women's rights in particular. Her efforts have been adopted by other countries as well. We believe that Maatahi is a strong voice speaking for the best forces in Africa to promote peace and good living conditions on that continent.[8]

As an African woman holding a high position in government, Maathai is a rarity.

Most commentators agree that any long-term strategy for the future of Africa that does not consider women prominently is doomed to fail. Women figure strongly as victims in nearly all of Africa's most serious dilemmas; they must now be brought to the forefront in the decision-making processes that will lead to solutions. As Chipo Lungu, executive director of the Zambia National Women's Lobby Group put it, "The men haven't done a good job of running our countries, so maybe now we are looking for a Big Woman, not a Big Man, to do the job. The list of corrupt, incompetent and just foolish male leaders is a long one."[9]

Despite the fact that GBM has planted 30 million trees in Kenya alone and accomplished much good, environmentalists in sub-Saharan Africa face enormous challenges. Civil wars and careless profiteers exact terrible tolls on the environment, threatening, for example, the famed mountain gorilla population in Congo and invaluable rain forests in much of Central and West Africa. Life-support systems throughout the continent are at risk. Still, as some African writers have noted, all environmental problems do not rest with the Other World, and Africa faces human issues that cannot yield to simple admonitions from the developed nations to protect nature and end pollution. Africa's capabilities to protect its own environment, given the pressures of conflicts, health issues, and the debt crisis, among other factors, are limited without understanding and substantive assistance from those in the developed world with the means and technology to make a difference. To learn more about Wangari Maathai's work, visit her Web site at www.wangarimaathai.or.ke

Wangari Maathai
SOURCE: AFP GETTY IMAGES

Pan-Africanism and Regional Cooperation

In July 2003, the recently formed African Union held its second annual summit meeting in Maputo, Mozambique. African heads of states and other political representatives came together to continue to chart a new path for African integration roughly along the lines of the European Union. Few ordinary Africans seemed to be paying close attention, however, to these potentially momentous deliberations. Tens of millions of Africans were simply too busy trying to make their daily way, or worse, survive the threats of famine, disease, or civil war. (Even President Bush, visiting the continent during these sessions, did not bother to attend.) An estimated thirty million Africans, on the other hand, were preoccupied that summer with a new reality TV show, "Big Brother Africa," which brought together twelve young adult Africans, each from a different country, for several months, living under the constant glare of cameras in a TV format popularized in the U.S. and Western Europe.[10] To many African fans, the show represented hope for the future, breaking down national stereotypes and pointing to the possibility of positive cooperation across borders. To its critics, though, the program negatively reflected on African values with its casual relationships in the midst of the AIDS pandemic, its voyeurism, and its depiction of an upscale, urban lifestyle out of reach for most Africans. Which, (if either) of these events better represents the future and promise of pan-Africanism, the solemn gathering of men in suits issuing declarations and decisions on new integrative directions for Africa, or the Western-style reality TV show with a distinctively African twist?

This chapter highlights some, but by no means all of the many conflicts in sub-Saharan Africa in the early 2000s. Guinea-Bissau, Chad, Congo (Brazzaville), Namibia, Lesotho, Zambia, Burundi, Kenya, and Uganda are among the states not prominently mentioned in these pages that have been beset by instability and violence. In several cases where opposing forces initially have been unwilling to seek solutions except through violence, there have been attempts by outside individuals, countries, or organizations to stop the fighting. The notion of a common heritage, common values, and a common future kindles interest among those grown weary from the upheavals. After all, pan-African congresses had been held during the early decades of the last century.

Back in the 1960s, there was a struggle between more militant governments who wanted to work for continental fusion and Mother Africa, and those who, having just gained independence, did not wish to be swallowed up by some larger entity. Antagonistic blocs of countries formed. Trying to stem the hostilities, 30 African states met in the Ethiopian capital of Addis Ababa in May 1963. The result was the creation of the Organization of African Unity (OAU), the principles of which included

United Nations Tragedy: The wreckage of a UN plane shot down while on a peacekeeping mission in the Congo. SOURCE: EMMIT B. EVANS, JR.

1. National independence over continental unity,
2. Nonintervention in the affairs of another state,
3. The sanctity of national boundaries,
4. The responsibility of Africans for peacefully solving their own problems,
5. The adoption of a nonaligned or neutralist stance, and
6. Equality of all sovereign states.

Support for liberation movements was agreed to in a resolution, but it was not a principle on which the organization was founded.

In the ensuing years, OAU membership swelled as more colonies became independent. Annual meetings of heads of state and foreign ministers were held, often amid great pomp and ceremony, to promote political, economic, and cultural cooperation. But, as in the UN, hard decisions involving action were in short supply.

In the last decade, financial problems and coming to grips with the traditional unwillingness to intervene "in the affairs of another state" were stumbling blocks. In any case, as we know from the Balkan region in East Europe, regional intervention is difficult and perilous. The OAU was all but invisible in the civil wars in Somalia and Rwanda in the first half of the 1990s and has played a peripheral role in other trouble spots since then, preferring rather to cede responsibility to smaller entities. Equivocation on the "noninterference issue" remained, despite support for collective action by national leaders at a 1993 OAU conference.[11]

Given its mixed and often disappointing record, the OAU undertook in 1999 an ambitious and far-reaching program of reform. Beginning in 2002, the body changed its name to the African Union and initiated steps over a number of years that, if successful, will lead to much closer cooperation and eventual integration among the member states.[12] One factor inhibiting progress in the old OAU was the requirement that all major decisions be unanimous; reaching agreement on matters of substance among dozens of disparate states is notoriously difficult. The reforms are to introduce some majority voting, a permanent legislative body, and, eventually, a common currency similar to the European Union's euro. Most of the planned institutions and programs have yet to be implemented, although there has been progress. It remains to be seen if the new reforms can stay on track and make a real difference in the continent's ongoing political and economic problems. Critics contend that early results have not been encouraging given the limited role the AU has played in its formative years in resolving the crises Africa has faced, but its ongoing peacekeeping efforts in Darfur (see the Flashpoints section) have been more substantive.

Smaller geographical organizations have been somewhat more active, albeit not always successful, in political-military matters. The Economic Community of West African States (ECOWAS) played an important role in the long-festering conflict in Liberia in the early 1990s, in Sierra Leone later, and more recently in Liberia again. In most of these cases, Nigerian soldiers were instrumental in curbing the fighting. Similarly, the Southern African Development Community (SADC), under its Chair, South African President Nelson Mandela, tried to broker a cease fire in the 1998 Congo war (see Central Africa and the Great Lakes Region in the Flashpoints section), but achieved minimal results.

Especially in economic matters, SADC has been the most important and successful of the regional entities, with numerous linkages established. South Africa and its former President Mandela, however, by their very prominence, have produced a wariness or even hostility from some of the other members. The economic clout of South Africa is both a hope and a concern for other member states. Leaders such as Zimbabwe President Robert Mugabe appear to resent being upstaged by the charismatic Mandela. There is still much the SADC can do to help the region's southern tier of countries, but national sensitivities and personalities loom large. Otherwise, the more than 200 additional organizations for regional cooperation have simply not been very effective.

African Relations with Outside Powers

Over the last century, Africa's relations with outside powers have gone through several stages and may now be entering a new stage. As the earlier discussion in this chapter suggested, the colonial powers consolidated their control over most of the continent in the 1890s. At least through World War II, the United States, the Soviet Union, and China did not challenge the domination of the existing order. Even the advent and pursuit of the cold war did not at first change this order. The Other World, and especially Africa, was not seen as a major theater of competition. Conflicts might flare around the perimeter of the Soviet Union and even to a limited degree in Latin America, but Africa was a backwater.

As African states began to achieve independence in the late 1950s, however, this situation began to change. The U.S.-Soviet rivalry became global, and soon the Chinese entered the maneuvering. In addition, the French continued their strong economic and military presence in the region. For 20 years the jousting continued unabated.

By the 1980s, this foreign competition began to ebb. The superpowers and China became more selective in their involvements. The ideological orientation of any one state was not viewed as very important. The Soviet Union was the largest supplier of military aid to the region, but then, under Mikhail Gorbachev, it reduced military material bound for Mozambique, helped broker the Cuban pullout from Angola, played a supportive role in achieving Namibia's independence, and withdrew its commitment to what had been its closest ally in the region, Ethiopia.

The Western influence had been much in evidence economically. France was the country that had long had close relations with its former colonies. By the mid-1990s, this had changed. Almost all of the first generation of African postindependence leaders who embraced France passed from the scene. More important, in late 1993, France greatly reduced its support for the common currency used in almost all of French-speaking Africa. These former colonies thus became more vulnerable to the shifts in world markets. Furthermore, France later decided to withdraw its garrisons from the continent, but in 2003, it sent thousands of troops in a perilous and controversial mission to end a civil war in the Cote d'Ivoire and led a special UN mission to curb ethnic violence in the Democratic Republic of Congo.

Sub-Saharan Africa and the United States

The United States enjoys enduring, deep, and rich connections of culture and heritage with sub-Saharan Africa. Most Africans would probably agree that maintaining close and friendly ties with the United States is crucial to a positive future for Africa. However, most Americans are not well-informed about African affairs, and the American media rarely covers Africa except in times of political or economic crisis or natural disaster. Normally, it is difficult to find hopeful or positive images of Africa in our mainstream media outlets. This contributes to a sense that Africa is a lost cause teeming with corrupt, greedy politicians, endless civil wars, and horrible epidemics and famines, deserving perhaps of humanitarian attention, but a futile case for more foreign aid or direct intervention.

After the cold war, the United States abandoned anticommunism as the linchpin of its African policies and with it went its support for corrupt leaders. Longtime ally Sese Seko Mobutu, president of Zaire (now the Democratic Republic of the Congo), was rebuked for activities that made him one of the richest men on the continent, if not the world, while silencing any potential opposition. There is an African proverb which says that "when the elephants fight, it is the grass that gets trampled." This proverb was often applied to the cold war, with the two superpowers in the role of elephants and Africa the grass. As some African commentators pointed out, things do not improve for the grass when elephants "make love" instead of fight; things have improved little if any for Africa since the end of the cold war. On a more positive note, Washington played key diplomatic roles in long-festering civil wars in Angola, Ethiopia, Liberia, and now, perhaps, in the Darfur region of Sudan.

While the Clinton administration paid considerable attention to Africa, arguably with mixed results, many African advocates feared that a Bush administration would neglect the continent. The former Texas governor's remarks during the 2000 presidential campaign were not encouraging; he seemed much more interested in relations with Mexico and the rest of Latin America than with Africa, and argued against U.S. intervention and involvement in Africa. However, the Bush administration, with the leadership of secretaries of state Colin Powell and Condoleeza Rice, perhaps the two most influential African-Americans in any U.S. administration, has not ignored Africa. Emphasis has been placed on coping with the AIDS crisis, the threats of international terrorism, development of free markets, and democratization. President Bush had appointed respected former Senator John Danforth to be his Special Envoy to address the issues of the Sudanese civil war before the events of September 11, 2001, and rejuvenated this mission before his 2003 Africa trip. In February 2006, President Bush urged renewed efforts to curb the continuing violence in the Darfur region of Sudan and called for an increase NATO role, but he stopped short of commiting U.S. troops to the mission. Secretary Powell visited Africa in the spring of 2001, and later that year made these remarks at the annual dinner of Africare, a prominent U.S. non-governmental organization (NGO) that raises funds and promotes humanitarian causes in Africa: "AIDS could kill a continent. It is a catastrophe. It is a disaster. It is a pandemic of the worst kind."[13] (The Bush Administration $15 billion package to combat AIDS is discussed in the Flashpoints section.) Powell also gave assurance that U.S. focus on international terrorism, the subject of another Flashpoint, would not distract it from paying attention to Africa's other problems.

During his July 2003 whirlwind trip to Africa, when he visited five nations in as many days, President Bush repeatedly emphasized that Africans "are not alone" in facing their problems. Despite the words, Africa still ranks low in America's priorities, with U.S. exports to and imports from the region constituting 1 percent of total U.S. foreign commerce. With the global economic downturn, U.S. trade with Africa declined 15 percent from 2001–2002; further, 90 percent of that trade rested with only four nations, mineral-rich and industrial South Africa and oil-producing Nigeria, Angola, and Gabon. New initiatives are being shaped, however, including the New Partnership for Africa's Development (NEPAD), which involves a commitment from AU nations' leaders to promote good governance, peace, and economic reform with assistance from G-8 nations. These conditions are similar to those contained in President Bush's Millennium Challenge Account, which would provide additional development aid only to those needy other world nations that practice good governance and embrace free enterprise. Perhaps nothing dominated President Clinton's Africa policy as much as working "to accelerate Africa's full integration into the global economy;"[14] the Bush Administration has announced similar goals. For countries embracing Washington's prescription for development, special trade preferences in modest amounts of public funds have been available through the much-vaunted African Growth and Opportunity Act, passed in 2000 (its provisions and developments can be monitored at www.AGOA.gov). Funds to strengthen democratic institutions also are being made available. Since 1996, the United States also has sponsored the Africa Crisis Response Initiative, which trains and advises indigenous troops in peacekeeping activities.[15] In a related program, Operation Focus Relief provides training and equipment for Nigerian and other forces assigned to peacekeeping duties in Sierra Leone. (See also the Flashpoint on international terrorism.) Former U.S. Secretary of the Treasury Paul O'Neill and activist–rock star Bono went on a highly publicized tour of Africa in May 2002 to assess the extent of the continent's poverty and survey its development needs. Washington also focuses on the African dimension of such global issues as weapons proliferation, drugs, infectious diseases, terrorism, air navigation, education, and the environment.

The United States, after encountering serious problems while intervening in Somalia in 1993, curbed its interest in Africa. Getting bogged down in quagmires that involve revamping police and security forces, reestablishing basic services, rebuilding infrastructure, and creating jobs did not have support in Washington. The Republican Congress was intent on slashing foreign aid, especially to most African states, where no vital American interests were seen to be at stake. Only four sub-Saharan African nations, Eritrea, Ethiopia, Rwanda, and Uganda, belatedly joined the "Coalition of the Willing," those nations that morally or materially supported the U.S.-British led 2003 Iraq War that ousted dictator Saddam Hussein. Originally, all African nations favored instead the position championed by French President Jacques Chirac that UN weapons inspectors in Iraq should be given more time to search for weapons of mass destruction.

In early 1998, President Clinton set off on a six-country, 12-day tour of sub-Saharan Africa, the longest period of time that a serving U.S. president had ever spent in Africa. The president spoke of what he saw as a "new African Renaissance" in which democracy and economic reform would flourish. His tone was optimistic, like that of President Bush later, although no major new aid pronouncements were made during the trip. (U.S. annual aid for the entire region is much less than the amount contributed to Israel or Egypt alone and constitutes a far lower percentage of the gross national product than that of most advanced nations, such as France or Japan).

President Clinton's trip and President Bush's briefer sojourn five years later were intended to show that the years in which Africa was merely a cold war sideshow were history. President Bush visited four of the six nations also on his predecessor's itinerary—Uganda, South Africa, Botswana, and Senegal—and ended in oil-rich Nigeria, included reportedly to show support for democratization and peacekeeping efforts there. His trip, delayed because of the Iraq War, came with the backdrop of possible U.S. intervention in the Liberian civil war. Both U.S. presidents, speaking after visits to Goree Island, the infamous slave-trade transit depot in Senegal, stopped just short of a formal apology for slavery in the United States. Botswana was chosen by both presidents because of its political stability and remarkable economic growth despite the ravages of AIDS. In Rwanda, Clinton said the United States and the world were to blame for doing nothing during the 1994 genocide that took up to 1 million lives. In South Africa, Clinton acknowledged that Washington had been very late in actively working to end apartheid (though he also said that, although belated, the country finally took a leadership role to end white rule). The presidential trips to Africa carry major symbolic importance, a statement that Africa matters to the United States today and would matter more tomorrow, but Africans look to concrete results beyond the rhetorical goodwill.

ECONOMICS AND NATURAL RESOURCES

It has already been suggested that African physical geography, including temperature, rainfall, coastlines, rivers, soils, and the like, created difficult conditions for its peoples. Moreover, foreigners exploited the natural habitat in many parts of the region. For instance, the colonial powers instituted cash crops and the export of livestock, which in turn meant widespread clearing of the land and sometimes depletion of the soil. Similarly, Europeans carving up the continent created or heightened local rivalries, which resulted in conflicts that also affected

*Divided Highway Ends: The main road between Malindi
and Lamu, Kenya.* SOURCE: EMMIT B. EVANS, JR.

the landscape. The decline of large areas of present-day Africa has been caused more by human than natural factors. Exploding populations, the movement from countrysides to cities, the devastating civil wars, and the shift from a nomadic to a sedentary way of life have major ramifications.

Economic patterns established in Africa a century ago continue to have great relevance today. The search for legitimate trade in the decades after the abolition of slavery resulted in the introduction of such cash crops as cocoa, coffee, tea, cotton, ground nuts, and palm oil, as well as renewed exploration for minerals. Gradually, a shift from subsistence farming to exports took place. In almost all cases, the colonies depended on no more than three crops or minerals for almost all of their earnings. Thus was Africa gradually drawn into the global capitalist system, albeit as a minor player. This pattern remains true today.

After independence, the future at first looked promising. Some countries followed the Western model of letting free enterprise dominate the economy; others chose to have the state play the major role. In either case, the 1960s and early 1970s was a period of growth throughout the continent. Unlike Asia, most of the countries were feeding themselves; unlike Latin America, most of the land was either communally owned or run by small farmers. Foreign investment was forthcoming and commodity prices were high.[16]

With the first oil price shock in 1973, this rosy picture began to change. Only a few African states had appreciable amounts of oil; others were forced to spend more of their precious capital and then to borrow money at high rates of interest to secure oil for industry. By the late 1970s, prices had peaked and were beginning to fall for both agricultural products and minerals. Deindustrialization resulted from declining domestic demand brought on by reduced income and shortages of foreign exchange. Poor maintenance and lack of spare parts, the protection of inefficient basic industries, and political considerations accelerated the economic decline. Drought became more pronounced in the Sahel region south of the Sahara. Sub-Saharan Africa's total debt, which had been $6 billion in 1970, rose to $125 billion by 1987.

By the early or mid-1980s, stagnation had been replaced by economic decline. Governments were living way beyond their means. African per capita income began to decline. Millions who had only barely been eking out a living now fell deeply into poverty and, in some cases, faced starvation.

These problems give a sense of the enormity of the economic disaster Africa is weathering. By 1990, 325 million people, or 62 percent of the region's population at the time, minus South Africa, were living in absolute poverty.[17] Per capita income hovered in the $300-a-year range (U.S. dollars). Fifteen years later, only the population figure had substantially changed.

How can this situation be altered? For more than a decade, the answer most often given by foreign governments and international lending agencies is privatization. That is, outside help, including additional loans and the restructuring or even writing off of outstanding loans, will only be made available to African countries if they agree to major policy reforms that substitute market forces for state-directed economies.

Reforms focusing on currency devaluations, reductions in government expenditures, and limits in domestic credit were begun by the International Monetary Fund (IMF) in the early 1980s. The World Bank, noting that little had been accomplished, added other "structural adjustments." It sought to increase producer prices, reduce or eliminate subsidies and trade restrictions, improve education and health systems, pay far more attention to the environment, encourage foreign investment, and champion small producers. A domestic bicycle industry or low-cost local roads for non-motorized vehicles were looked on favorably. Above all, it emphasized private enterprise.

By the mid-1990s, more than two dozen countries in Africa adopted major economic policy reforms. These states embraced the reforms or capitulated to Western prescriptions. Outside criticisms of these programs included the reduction in the quality and quantity of government services; the introduction of user fees, which disproportionately hurt the poor; and the increased cost of basic foodstuffs and transportation.

Structural adjustment at the national level may be inadequate unless the Western countries open their markets, pay decent prices for African goods, and curtail or suspend debt repayments. Any benefits for African states are likely to take years, if not decades, whereas adverse effects of reform are instantaneous. If discontent rises, government instability and repression will be the likely results. The IMF and World Bank argue that states taking the plunge have done better than those that have not. That is small consolation to millions of individuals who have experienced worsened conditions.

On balance, sub-Saharan African economies early in the new century are a bit improved over the beginning of the 1990s, if not over 10 or 20 years earlier than that. "Better fiscal policies, greater trade liberalization, and more-realistic foreign exchange rates in sub-Saharan Africa have helped lead to the rising per capita income—an average of 1 to 1.5 percent a year the past two years,"[18] though economic growth was not as strong in the early 2000's with the general world economic downturn. The World Bank estimates that a 6 percent economic growth rate is necessary for real improvement; Botswana is the only African nation in recent years to attain that figure.[19]

There are major problems, specific and general, and the economic turnaround is sputtering. Government debt is simply crushing many states in the region. The following statistic provides just one example: Africa spends four times as much servicing debt as it does on health and education. The region also pays out more in interest on the debt than it receives in trade and other flows. There is a concerted movement, particularly on the part of the creditor G-8 nations, to provide debt relief to the Heavily Indebted Poor Countries (HIPC) without stringent conditions, such as the preparation of detailed Poverty Reduction Strategy Papers, and thus better tend to their social needs. Critics contend that debt relief and aid alone are not panaceas for the economic ills of those countries because they do not alleviate the plight of all the poor, and must be accompanied by sound, sustainable development programs. There is good news: Although public monies are declining, they are more than offset by private funds. There is also bad news: The flows only go to a few countries, including South Africa. Furthermore, global economic instabilities, insufficient market shares by small countries to attract major investors, skill deficiencies, inadequate infrastructure, downbeat coverage of Africa by the media, and chance events such as the bombing of two American embassies in East Africa in 1998 are detrimental. Arms purchases, often with kickbacks, "crony companies" that lack competence, payments to security forces or the military, "white elephant" projects, and ruling elites engaging in capital flight exacerbate the financial drain.

Much of the modern global economy is driven by high technology, but Africa is the least-wired continent with the fewest Internet subscribers. In the UN Human Development Report of 2001, which focused on high technology and telecommunications, Africa ranked last on virtually every indicator of all the regions of the Other World. Africa's Internet users are made up of the region's elite and foreigners. Africa has by far the lowest number of phone lines per capita in the world, computer usage is minimal, and online users, a majority of whom live in South Africa, number in the low millions.

Internet access, however, is growing, cell phones, now estimated to be used by one in 35 Africans, are commonplace in capital cities. Numerous Western government agencies, foundations, universities, and corporations are supplying financial material, and training aid to speed Africa's entry into the high technology information age. There is growing optimism that "Africa in cyberspace" will dramatically increase in the early years of the twenty-first century as technology costs become cheaper and more congruent with the continent's needs, making the region far more competitive in the tough global market and facilitating exciting new connections within and outside of Africa. Mike Jensen, a South African widely acknowledged as a leading authority on Africa's entry into the "wired" world, noted in 2000,

> The development of the Internet is at a critical point in Africa. Web-based services could help accelerate the continent's economic growth and poverty alleviation, but these tools place large demands on an underlying infrastructure that is currently incapable of servicing them. . . . It will require greater commitment by African leadership to open up the telecommunication sector to ensure that the potential of the Internet is fully exploited.[20]

Progress in Africa's online activities is evident, but with only 12 personal computers per thousand people (2003), much work remains to be done in closing the "digital divide."

Sub-Saharan Africa has great natural resources, much of them untapped. The United States gets almost as much of its foreign oil from the region as it does from the Middle East. In addition to the major petroleum sources along the coast of West Africa, there are also promising prospects in Chad and Sudan. Similarly, natural gas in commercial amounts appears to exist in Angola, Congo, Equatorial Guinea, Gabon, Ghana, and Cameroon. New resources used in the Western high-technology industry are being exploited in Africa, but not always for the benefit of the people as a whole. The risks of investing in natural resource extraction are great, but so are the potential profits. Corruption, weak environmental protection (which permits groundwater contamination and unknowing populations coming into contact with uranium waste), and lax miner safety are some of the hazards to be overcome. Overfishing by European fleets is another reality. Although foreign access fishing agreements bring in hundreds of millions of dollars, which help service the debt, the payments come at the price of depriving millions of local inhabitants of a vital food source. On balance, it is fair to say that globalization, with the accompanying influence of multinational corporations based far from the continent, has not been kind to sub-Saharan African resources and economies

CASE STUDIES

1. SOUTH AFRICA

The key point about South Africa is that although blacks outnumbered whites by five to one, political power remained with the minority until 1994. Over the generations, white domination wore many faces. At the turn of the twentieth century, the British defeated the Afrikaners in a bloody civil war. The Afrikaners were a people whose ancestors came mainly from the Netherlands beginning in the seventeenth century. For the next few years there were four separate states, with Great Britain in charge of them all; then in 1910, the four fused into one Union of South Africa, and London became all but invisible. Fearing for the future of blacks in the country, a forerunner to the African National Congress (ANC) arose two years later. However, it could do nothing to prevent the Land Act of 1913, which prohibited blacks from owning land in most areas and from owning quality land in all parts of the country. Another important date is 1948, the year that the Afrikaner-backed National party won the whites-only national elections. The newly elected party formally instituted a policy of apartheid, or separate racial development. From then on, blacks (and to a lesser extent, Indians) and those of mixed race, called coloreds, were treated as inferior beings. Brute force, including the arrest of the leaders, legislation, and custom enshrined the new order. For the next 36 years, despite nonviolent protests and occasional acts of sabotage, the status quo of white domination and black subordination prevailed.

Significant resistance to apartheid increased through the 1960s and 1970s. Beginning in late 1984, disturbances became more widespread, and violence by both the state and opponents of apartheid intensified. Arrests numbered in the thousands. A year later, the government declared a state of emergency in much of the country. Authorities tried to keep order by imposing controls on dissidents, including the media. The economy began a downward spiral, helped along by damaging strikes. Limited sanctions imposed by several governments, including the United States, and the loss of many foreign companies were also detrimental. Nevertheless, the white ruling class held firm.

In the late 1980s, the South African government tried both the carrot and the stick to impose its will. The authorities offered minor reforms, and relations improved with some surrounding black-run states; however, several thousand people died because of political unrest, and a second emergency decree resulted in tens of thousands of additional arrests. A change of direction seemed impossible.

Change did come, however, and it came rapidly. There are several explanations for the shift. First, Frederik W. de Klerk, succeeding P. W. Botha as president and head of the National party in 1989, gradually moved his forces in a different direction, including calls to prepare a new constitution and share power.

At the same time, the situation fundamentally improved in neighboring Namibia and Angola. South African leaders perceived that the abating U.S.-Soviet confrontation would lessen the threat of communism within their own borders. Many in the country also noticed democratization in other parts of the world. Both the South African government and the ANC, the pan-African Congress, saw a military solution to the internal unrest as unlikely. In addition, the economy continued to sag, and Western powers warned that tougher sanctions were a possibility. Demands for change came from all directions.

The winds struck with gale force. Nelson Mandela, jailed in the early 1960s for promoting the violent overthrow of the government, was dramatically released by Prime Minister de Klerk in 1990, along with other dissidents. The government also lifted the 30-year ban against the ANC, the South African Communist party, and many other organizations. Over the next few months, the government rescinded the state of emergency throughout the country, curbed the secretive state security system, reduced the military budget, and ended political censorship. It also repealed the Separate Amenities Act, thus opening public hospitals, restaurants, libraries, buses, and parks to all.

The first half of 1991 shook apartheid to its roots. Its pillars—the Lands Acts, Group Areas Act, and Population Registration Act—were repealed, and the Internal Security Act was severely amended. It took three more years of maneuvering, however, before the ultimate goal of one person, one vote was achieved. The ANC and the rival Zulu-based Inkatha movement, led by Chief Gatsha Buthelezi, clashed, resulting in thousands of deaths. There were divisions among the whites as well, with a small minority refusing to consider any changes. But in late April 1994, the people of South Africa, including millions of black citizens, went to the polls for the first time in the country's history. As expected, the ANC was the big winner, receiving 63 percent of the vote as Nelson Mandela became president. Because they did not receive two-thirds of the vote, the victorious party had to work with non-ANC members in Parliament in the writing of a new constitution. The National party finished second and became the official opposition. In addition, de Klerk became one of two vice presidents. The Inkatha Freedom party finished third. In a bid to form a government of unity and reconciliation, Mandela offered a number of cabinet positions to members of the other two parties. Buthelezi became the Home Affairs minister.

Many people predicted that given the struggle that preceded the election, the following months would be ones of upheaval. It did not work out that way. There were growing pains, yes, but both in political circles and throughout the country there was relative tranquility based on a foundation of gradual change. The move from international outcast to liberal democracy in one year was phenomenal. Although some complained that Mandela was moving too slowly to institute reforms, most were supportive of the pace and direction of change. Racial strife gradually eased. Economic growth caught up with population growth for the first time in a decade. Of course, South Africa still faces very serious problems. Gaining political power is a lot different from gaining economic power. Major economic disparities along racial lines continue as poverty cuts deeply across the black majority while a majority of the wealth remains in white hands.

> For many the situation has not yet changed much—the landless; the homeless; the black African majority, more than 40 percent of whom live in absolute poverty; women and children, who are the majority of those living in deprivation, especially in rural areas; and the growing numbers of those who are unemployed, underemployed or living on less than $1 a day.[21]

Land reform or redistribution is a deeply felt issue by many landless farmers. The government promulgated its land restitution program in 1995, but was hesitant to promote widespread change for fears of alienating white farmers and undermining the agricultural sector. The one million homes that the government, with private-sector backing, committed itself to building by 1999 were not completed. There are also disagreements with traditional authorities over what to do with tribal lands.

Economic growth is not keeping pace with population growth and formal unemployment is running at more than 30 percent. The national currency has been in rapid decline, while foreign investments have only been a fraction of the amounts expected. University tuition has climbed, and many who looked to the new government to set things right have been acutely disappointed. Credit, especially for the poor, has been hard to come by and global competition for foreign assistance is intense.

Another major problem is dealing with South Africa's past. The Truth and Reconciliation Commission, headed by Archbishop Desmond Tutu, was created by a parliamentary act in 1995. It delved into the dark corners of the apartheid years. The commission's goal was to bring the past to closure by inviting those who had transgressed to testify in public. Toward that end, the commission had the power to grant amnesty to those who gave an account of their crimes and who could show that the struggle over apartheid was behind their acts. It was not necessary for the perpetrator to show remorse. There were confessions of terrible acts on both sides. Although some refused to testify and many South Africans were not reconciled, it was a remarkable attempt to put the past in the past.

Since the end of apartheid, political violence has abated, but criminal violence has increased. The crime wave transcends race, ethnicity, and class. The murder rate is several times that of the United States, and rape has been an especially severe problem. Lawlessness, though, is nothing new in South Africa. How can the country "restore an ethic of lawfulness" after the ANC encouraged people to long defy the white authorities? (There are also disgruntled white farmers and white police officers, disaffected ANC members, and long-standing ethnic conflicts.) Police corruption and low rates of arrest and conviction have caused many to lose faith in the criminal justice system. A statistic indicates that "two-thirds of Johannesburg's citizens and half of Cape Town's were victims of crime between 1993 and 1997 alone."[22]

After six years of work, a new constitution was inaugurated in 1997. A balance was struck between a strong central government and devolving considerable powers to the states. There are strong statements protecting individual rights. Private property rights are balanced by the need to redress past discrimination. The 1999 election results showed that the ANC had lost none of its popularity, receiving over 66 percent of the vote, just a sliver away from the two-thirds mark that would have allowed it to make certain changes in the constitution if it so wished. Thabo Mbeki succeeded Mandela as president. President Mbeki was widely regarded as a very able, experienced administrator, even though he obviously lacked Mandela's international stature and charisma. Mbeki has been unable, however, to control South Africa's mounting economic, social, and health problems, and many are disturbed with his idiosyncratic views on human immunodeficiency syndrome (HIV) and AIDS, which have hit his nation especially hard. (See Africa and AIDS in the Flashpoint section.) Concerns have also been raised over Mbeki's adherence to external and historical reasons to explain his administration's lack of economic progress for his nation. The corruption that has long plagued the politics of much of the continent has now also reached

South Africa, where a top parliamentary leader of the ANC was charged with fraud, corruption, and committing perjury in 2001. Still, the ANC won an overwhelming majority of 70 percent of the votes in the nation's 2004 parliamentary elections, returning Mbeki for his second five-year presidential term. Deputy President Jacob Zuma, seen by many as Mbeki's most likely successor in 2009, was fired in June of 2004 under suspicion of corruption and accepting bribes, a scandal that has rocked the ANC political establishment at the very top. Rape charges have also been brought against Zuma, and his trial which began in early 2006 threatens to divide the ANC and possibly disrupt political stability as his many supporters believe all the charges are false and politically motivated.

What of South Africa's image beyond its borders? Mandela himself remains much revered, though he had clashed with the United States over his kind words for Cuba, Iran, Libya, and Syria—countries that gave support to the antiapartheid struggle at a time when the cold war made the United States timid. Mbeki is a more controversial figure. In southern Africa, there is disquiet over one country so obviously more powerful than the others. The South African military's intervention in neighboring Lesotho in 1998 to deal with unrest there underscored this concern. Although South Africa has been a champion of a regional common market, some of the other countries are concerned about being in that country's orbit.

2. NIGERIA

Next to South Africa, Nigeria is viewed as the country in sub-Saharan Africa with the greatest potential. Recurring political instability, corruption, ethnic strife, and economic mismanagement for the past 45 years, however, have taken their toll.

Nigeria's population of 130 million people is the largest on the African continent. Twenty-five years ago, the country was an economic powerhouse. In 1977, per capita gross domestic product (GDP) was $1,000. Ten years later, the figure had dropped to $370; in 1992 it was $320. For the period 1980 to 1992, Nigeria's economic growth rate was negative 20.4 percent. In that period, the country slipped from the Other World's middle-income to low-income group. By 2004, per capita GDP had climbed to $800, still below the figures of a quarter century before.

A major factor in the decline was the precipitous drop in oil prices. The government and many upwardly mobile people lived way beyond their means during the oil boom. Yet the masses saw little of the new wealth; current high oil prices are not expected to improve the situation. As the last decade drew to a close, the international debt soared to $35 billion, and the government agreed to begin a very stiff structural adjustment program (see Economics and National Resources section). In this environment, social unrest further undermined foreign investment.

The military government that came to power in a 1985 coup (there have been seven coups since independence in 1960, and many more attempted coups) promised elections and the return to civil rule at the beginning of 1993. Indeed, elections were held, but when the military rulers, who had run the country for all but 12 years since independence, did not like the results, they simply annulled them. After that, strikes, riots, additional instability in the military, rule by decree, summary executions of the regime's opponents, and a seemingly never-ending economic downdraft occurred. The election victor, billionaire Mashood Abiola, went to jail, was placed in solitary confinement, sentenced to death, and finally had that sentence commuted. The military, then under the control of General Sani Abacha, ushered in five years of brutal rule while defying global condemnations. General Abacha, who rapidly became a billionaire, also attempted to head off further criticism by belatedly promising a return to civilian rule by late 1998.

Before 1995 ended, nine dissidents, including Ken Saro-Wiwa, a prominent author and playwright, were executed. The government charged that they had fomented strife that led to the murder of several rivals in a major oil-producing area. Saro-Wiwa had protested that the production had resulted in serious pollution in the area. He also railed against the refusal of the corrupt government to give even a fraction of the riches to his poor Ogoni people living in the oil-rich coastal sector. Worldwide condemnation followed the hangings, with none other than South African President Nelson Mandela calling for an embargo on Nigerian oil. Under the best circumstances, however, it is difficult to get approval for such a global action and even more difficult to enforce it. Nigeria, for instance, is the fifth-largest foreign supplier of oil to the United States and owed over $30 billion to Europe and Japan.

In June 1998, Abacha died of a heart attack. A month later, Abiola, still in prison, also died. With the despised head-of-state and his main nemesis gone, the question simply was "What now for Nigeria?" Abacha's replacement, General Abdusalami Abubakar, gradually moved in a new direction. Many political prisoners were released from jail and the officers' sentences were commuted. A start was made to face up to the omnipresent corruption, with several leading figures including Abacha's security advisor arrested. Most important, national assembly and then presidential elections were held in February 1999. Olusegun Obasanjo was chosen to lead the new civilian government that formally took power three months later. Obasanjo had headed a military regime in the late 1970s before voluntarily yielding power to an elected civilian government. More recently, he had been jailed from 1995 to 1998 on a dubious claim that he was plotting to overthrow Abacha. Although some felt that the newly elected Obasanjo was too close to the military leaders he was replacing, others thought he was the right man for the troubled times in the troubled country.

Sweeping poverty as well as ethnic and regional tensions is deeply rooted. British colonial rulers favored Moslem northerners because they were seen as more obedient and conservative than southerners were. After independence, northerners continued to rule at the national level, whether the country was under civilian or military rule. Yet the oil and the major financial, commercial, and industrial centers are in the south. The hope was that President Obasanjo would be able to quell the country's long-time divisions. Despite good intentions and promising pronouncements, this goal has proved elusive. Deadly ethnic clashes continued, some involving government troops and most pitting northern Moslems against southern Christians. For example, more than 200 died in rioting resulting from a controversy over the staging of the Miss World pageant in Lagos in November 2002 when a newspaper reporter suggested that Mohammed himself would have wanted to marry a contestant. Frightened pageant officials hurriedly moved the contest to London. Sparked in part because of the adoption of Islamic Sharia law in many of Nigeria's northern states, more than 10,000 people have died in ethnic/religious violence since the return of democracy in 1999.

Nigeria has vast oil reserves; it is the world's sixth largest producer of oil, with revenues running $30 billion a year. The country also has many minerals, fertile land, and more than 30 universities. Nigeria, however, also has a run-down infrastructure (the nickname for the National Electric Power Authority, or NEPA, is Never Expect Power Again). Chronic unemployment plagues the nation's young people. The nation has not come to terms with the abuses committed by some members of the military during its troubled past. In December 2001, Nigeria's Minister of Justice was assassinated by gunmen invading his home, another indication of Nigeria's ongoing instability.[23] International observers cited widespread irregularities in the nation's April 2003 state, national assembly, and presidential elections, but these questionable electoral practices might not have changed the ultimate outcome of the vote that returned Obasanjo and his ruling People's Democratic Party to power. Ethnic violence persisted into the mid-2000s, and in January of 2002, suspicious explosions rocked an army munitions depot in Lagos, causing over 1,000 civilian deaths in the ensuing panic. Early 2006 brought more serious challenges, including rebellions and hostage-taking over regional control of oil resources and sectarian violence between Moslems and Christians sparked by the volatile Danish Mohammed cartoon incident. Nigeria, which survived the deadly Biafra secession war in the late 1960s and has seen a succession of corrupt military and civilian governments, is trying to get back on track. It will not be an easy task.

3. ZIMBABWE

Zimbabwe became independent in 1980 after a lengthy struggle to end white-minority rule. In the 1997 edition of *The Other World*, the country was considered a relative success story because economic growth had more than kept pace with population growth, family planning programs had made great strides, and ethnic disputes between the majority Shona and minority Ndebele had faded. Literacy rates were among the highest on the continent, racism had been contained, there was a good healthcare system, a thriving tourism industry, a police force that no longer generated fear, a functioning infrastructure, and environmental issues were being successfully met. Finally, there was a reasonable level of political stability.

The downside, always present, has worsened in the last nine years. The economy has continued to slump, with inflation and interest rates rising. Many foreign investors are leaving because of what they believe are ruinous government policies; unstable or even collapsed banks; a declining stock market; falling prices for such domestic commodities as gold, other minerals, and tobacco; a high debt load; and tax increases that many claim line the pockets of President Robert Mugabe's supporters or favorites. Unions have risen up in opposition, as have students who claim government corruption. The press, one of the few institutions willing to speak out against the ruling elite, has suffered threats, arrests and torture, and the president threatened journalists who criticized the violent, lawless actions of his supporters. Minorities, especially gays, are chastised by the president himself. In 2005, the International Monetary Fund threatened to suspend Zimbabwe's membership because of its irresponsible economic and fiscal policies, a move unprecedented since communist Czechoslovakia suffered that fate in 1954, but the IMF gave the Mugabe government a six-month reprieve to initiate reforms. The country's membership in the British Commonwealth of Nations was suspended indefinitely in 2003.

Charges of favoritism, luxurious living for the few, and crony capitalism are widespread. *The London Times* reported that "after a relatively slow start from independence in 1980, the Nigerian model has been adopted with alacrity; senior politicians take control of state contracts and licensing, violate all procedures, and pass on the right to politically well-connected businessmen."[24] There are bitter feuds between Mugabe's dominant Zimbabwe African National Union and the opposition party, the Movement for Democratic Change. Public and international support has plummeted. The country continues to have one of the highest HIV-positive rates in Africa.

As in South Africa, probably the most volatile issue in Zimbabwe is land ownership. Until recently, 4,500 white farmers owned more than 70 percent of the country's most fertile land, leaving the 7 million black farmers to engage in mainly subsistence farming. In the midst of rising discontent, President Mugabe announced that he intended to seize millions of acres of white-owned land and undertake a radical land reform program; he further stated the government would not compensate those who stood to lose their property and livelihood. The land-grab, begun in 1997, ended in 2002 with more than 35 million acres of white-owned farms seized. Damage to the economy from this policy has been catastrophic; the main beneficiaries are Mugabe supporters. In 2005, the Mugabe government undertook a disastrous policy of "urban renewal," termed "Operation Drive Out the Rubbish," which bulldozed poor neighborhoods of mostly anti-Mugabe residents and resulted in hundreds of thousands of displaced, jobless, and homeless city-dwellers.

Zimbabwe's involvement in the Congo war of 1998 was another unanticipated financial cost. The expanded war also brought the cool relationship between Mugabe and South African President Nelson Mandela into the open. The latter urged a cease-fire, but this was dismissed by the Zimbabwe president.

By mid-2005, the earlier promise of a stable, tolerant democratic regime in Zimbabwe seemed thwarted; instead, political repression, famine, disease, and chaos held sway. Mugabe's supporters continued intimidation and attacks against his political opponents, white settlers, and blacks who worked on their farms. New measures designed to suppress opposition groups and the press were introduced before the 2002 presidential election. In March 2002, President Mugabe won reelection in a vote widely denounced by outside observers as unfair; he promptly had his major opponent arrested on charges of treason. Such tactics, along with other human rights violations, continued unabated through the following years. Many analysts now agree that the aging Mugabe, eager to cling to power, has become one of the despotic "Big Men" who littered the history of Africa's postindependence leadership.

FLASHPOINTS

AFRICA AND AIDS

Recent estimates indicate that approximately 60 percent of the world's total HIV/AIDS cases afflict sub-Saharan Africans who comprise only 10 percent of the world's population, according to 2004 UNAIDS data.[25] In other words, approximately 25 million of the people suffering from AIDS are African, with several million new cases reported in the region each year and an estimated 2.3 million deaths in 2004 alone. Because 9 of the 10 countries with the highest infection rates are in Africa, these grim statistics will not improve on a regional basis any time soon.[26] Besides the terrible toll in human life, the epidemic will inevitably have a drastic effect on economic productivity in heavily affected areas for many years to come.

Unlike other parts of the world, over 50 percent of HIV-positive adults in sub-Saharan Africa are women, and the infection rates are especially high for women in the critical childbearing years. UNAIDS officials thus reluctantly decided that women infected with HIV should consider feeding formula instead of breast milk to their babies. Throughout the region, more than 12 million children are orphans because of AIDS, a figure projected to reach 20 million by 2010.

Although statistics from different sources are not always congruent, the numbers are overwhelming. Dealing effectively with the epidemic is also overwhelming. There is too little money for tests, drugs, or directed support networks. Even in South Africa, health services are totally inadequate to provide treatment for AIDS. The costly combinations of drugs that help keep the virus in check among infected people in the north have been largely out of reach in the south, where other problems press the population every day. President Mbeki of South Africa, where one in four women in their twenties is infected with HIV, caused much controversy with his challenges of accepted scientific studies on the relationship of HIV and AIDS, claiming instead that poverty and imperialism were the causes of the disease. His administration's policies hindered modern treatment of AIDS in his country.

Can anything be done to combat the disease? Many major international organizations, such as the UN and World Bank, have rallied to address just this issue through special programs, conferences and the Global AIDS Fund. Despite a lack of financial resources, the African Union has been active on this front, as have many private-sector and nongovernmental organizations. On the positive side, access to the expensive drug treatments is improving, and a Fall 2001 ruling from the World Trade Organization (WTO) relieved desperate nations of patent infringements in making or acquiring generic substitute drugs. UNAIDS has emphasized two recent programs: "The Three Ones," intended to coordinate and integrate national efforts on anti-AIDS:

1. Actions and policies
2. Authority and responsibility
3. Monitoring and evaluation to avoid wasteful overlap and fragmentation

and "3 by 5," a concerted effort to extend antiretroviral treatment to 3 million worldwide by the end of 2005. Unfortunately, an interim UNAIDS report in June 2005 concluded that the ambitious 3 by 5 goal would fall far short of expectations despite accelerated treatment programs in the first six months of that year that doubled (to 500,000) the number of sub-Saharan African AIDS victims with access to the drugs.

Education is the one word most often offered in proposed strategies, and in Uganda the education is broad and multisectoral. The nation has been widely acclaimed for the success of its ABC policy—emphasizing abstinence, being faithful to one's partner, and condom use whenever appropriate. Even with its success in curbing the spread of the virus, however, Uganda has insufficient funds to treat those already afflicted. President Bush lauded Uganda's strong public programs in his 2003 trip to Africa, where he also promoted his five-year, $15 billion assistance program to combat the disease, to be directed primarily at afflicted African nations. There is no magic bullet, but a multifaceted approach can produce encouraging results. Finally, the global community has mobilized resources to cope with this urgent epidemic, but the many generous international commitments of support and money must be realized. Care must be taken also, not to lose momentum in combating Africa's other major health scourges, such as malaria, tuberculosis, and polio ($2.3 billion of the five-year, $15 billion package will in fact target such diseases), in confronting the enormity of the AIDS crisis. Fears have also been raised that Africa might be particularly vulnerable to the deadly form of Avian flu virus, since human cases of the disease began surfacing in Nigeria, Niger, and elsewhere in the region in early 2006.

SLAVERY AND HUMAN TRAFFICKING

Slavery, both historical and modern, remains one of the most controversial, sensitive, and compelling subjects in sub-Saharan Africa. Questions about the impact of the historical slave trade on present-day Africa continue under hot debate. Was the European and American slave trade, which robbed West and Central Africa of millions of its young, able inhabitants over the course of several centuries, so devastating economically and psychologically that it has contributed materially to Africa's current state of underdevelopment? Should those areas in Europe and the Americas that benefited from slave labor hundreds of years ago, now all relatively rich, pay reparations to the victimized nations today? Many argue that the former slave-holding nations should not only apologize for these abominations against humanity, but also pay substantial sums to try to set things right. Others contend that the historical slave trade was a regrettable but distant chapter of the past, perpetrated by ancestors long since gone, which has little relevance to the pressing issues of a new millennium. Questions also arise around the Arab-based slave trade in East Africa.

These issues arose in proposals and debates at the UN conference on racism and xenophobia held at Durban, South Africa, in 2001. The United States boycotted the conference, in part because of the controversial slavery reparations proposal, but also because of a proposal from the Arab delegation equating Zionism, the movement for the state of Israel as a Jewish homeland, with racism. Ultimately, the conference proceeded with much acrimony and little resolution of the slavery issue. Condemnations of slavery were adopted that fell far short of a call for direct reparations; a redistributive cause whose time is not likely to come.

Aside from the debate over historical slavery, a few regions of Africa suffer from various forms of modern slavery and human trafficking. In Sudan and Mauritania, the two nations most often cited, traditional forms of chattel, or ownership, slavery persist into the twenty-first century. Usually, this slavery takes the form of wealthier Arab owners holding poorer black Africans in bondage, sometimes through generations and sometimes as a result of capture in war. Both governments deny the existence of such slavery and deem it formally illegal, but human rights activists insist that tens of thousands of slaves are held in the two nations. Furthermore, testimonials of escaped and liberated slaves confirm the practice. International awareness and outrage against the practice, perhaps less brutal than historical slavery but nonetheless invidious, is on the rise. Organizations such as the American Anti-Slavery Group in Boston are agitating and taking action against modern African slavery; other groups and concerned individuals, using a controversial approach, are raising funds to buy slaves' freedom directly from their masters.

Another form of modern African slavery exists in West Africa, in which youths, usually boys from the more deprived nations such as Benin or Togo, sign fraudulent work contracts and become indentured or bonded laborers, usually with no pay, in large agricultural enterprises in the better-off West African nations such as Ghana. The good news about modern slavery in Africa is the heightened publicity, exemplified in the extensive coverage of the decrepit slave ship turned away from several West African ports in the summer of 2001, and the resultant calls for action from many quarters across the globe to abolish these anachronistic, inhumane practices once and for all.

CIVIL WARS AND COMMUNAL VIOLENCE

This Flashpoint surveys the causes and circumstances of significant cases of war and violence in various African regions. These conflicts include some apparently settled conflicts but also others, notably the wars in Sudan, Uganda, Burundi, Cote d'Ivoire, and the Democratic Republic of Congo that were ongoing into mid-2005, despite international efforts at pacification. Arguably, persistent violence has been one of the greatest man-made obstacles to Africa's growth and progress.

Pessimistic observers of Africa's conflicts might simply designate the whole region as a flashpoint candidate. For example, the cover of a May 2000 issue of the influential weekly newsmagazine *The Economist* portrayed a photo, filling an outline African Map, of a man with a rocket launcher on his shoulder. The issue is entitled "The Hopeless Continent." This represents a gross exaggeration of the real situation. Several African countries, such as Mauritius, have suffered relatively little if any recent violent conflict; others have seen long- or short-term violent conflicts resolved without new outbreaks, as in Mozambique, and, more recently, Angola, Liberia, and Sierra Leone. Still, few sub-Saharan African nations have avoided some form of civil, ethnic, or religious violence, coups, riots, or wars at some point in their postcolonial histories.

It is notoriously difficult to generalize about the root causes of violent conflict in sub-Saharan Africa. In earlier days, cold war rivalries played a prominent role, and the apartheid regime in South Africa destabilized much of the region beyond its borders. Some analysts point to the colonial heritage of violent conquest and coercive power. Greed and personal ambition have often been evident. Many of the more recent civil wars seem to arise from disputes over a volatile mixture of control and exploitation of valuable resources combined with ethnic animosities rather than differing political ideologies or approaches to national development.

Child Soldiers

A disturbing development in African civil wars over the last several years has been the increasing use of very young combatants, usually boys (but sometimes girls as well) in their early teens or even younger, fighting for rebel forces and, in some nations, government militias. For example, recent civil wars in Liberia, Sierra Leone, the Democratic Republic of Congo, Burundi, and Sudan have seen widespread use of child soldiers. This is a departure from the practices of earlier African civil wars, where professional soldiers, adult insurgents and guerrillas, and hired mercenaries were the usual participants. Many African nations, including Liberia and Sudan, have yet to sign or ratify the international protocol on children in armed conflicts, which, among other provisions, forbids the military conscription of children under the age of 18.

While some of these underage, naive troops appear to join the fights willingly for reasons of self, family, or village protection; ethnic or religious motivations; financial gain; or perhaps adventure, many more are coerced into enlisting through threats against themselves or family members if they do not cooperate. Child soldiers are also recruited as orphans after their parents have been slaughtered. Drugs and alcohol are widely employed as further means of control and as incentives to fight viciously without regard to their personal safety. Under fear for their own lives and the lives of their families, child soldiers have been forced to participate in horrible atrocities against civilian victims. Field commanders frequently prefer child soldiers in Africa's civil wars because they are easier to manipulate and discipline, cost little to maintain, and are often fearless in battle, lacking a mature understanding of the value of life.

Children who have been swept up as participants in Africa's civil wars have, if they survived, lost their childhood and the opportunity for an education and a productive life. Instead, they have learned how to kill wantonly and brutally. In nations with settled conflicts, such as Sierra Leone, efforts are underway to rescue the former child combatants and teach them to rejoin a peaceful society. The successful methods used for this slow process are similar to those in psychological deprogramming of individuals who have fallen under the sway of cults; they require patience, resources, and skill. Fortunately, the UN and many NGO human rights groups are attuned to the issues of child soldiers and are taking aggressive steps to educate the public and bring an end to this objectionable practice.

Weapons in Africa's Wars

One factor that has facilitated the use of child soldiers, discussed above, is the ready availability of inexpensive, simple, lightweight firearms, such as the AK-47, that can be carried by a child as young as 8. The cold war is over, ending U.S.-Soviet competition in Africa. Americans are no longer backing one side in Somalia while the Soviets back neighboring Ethiopia. The United States no longer supports one side in the Angolan civil war while the Soviet Union embraces a competing group. Has there been an end to the bloodletting in Africa with the end of the U.S.-Soviet conflict? The answer is a stark no, as peace has failed to follow the demise of the superpower rivalry. Many of the weapons introduced into the continent during the cold war era remain, only to menace new generations of Africans. Additionally, many industrialized nations, including the U.S., Russia, and others, continue to produce and sell weapons to Africa for profit. Today, civil wars in some African nations are waged more for control of valuable resources, such as diamonds in Sierra Leone or col-tan, a mineral found only in the Congo used in computer-chip production, than for the political or ideological reasons of the past. Control of the resources provides power and funding for continuing armed struggles.

There is money to be made in African conflicts. Countries as diverse as France, Romania, Egypt, Russia, and South Africa supplied arms to the warring parties in Rwanda during the post–cold war 1990s. In Angola, a cease-fire led to a partial demobilization of soldiers, causing small arms to fall into the hands of civilians. In southern Africa generally, "there is no doubt that the region is flooded with weapons [as] decades of warfare and violent political struggle have given rise to a pervasive gun culture."[27] South Africa, without a civil war, has the highest rate of civilian deaths from firearms in the world.

In Sierra Leone and Liberia, local warlords have traded diamonds, timber, iron ore, and agricultural products for small arms. In Rwanda, it was tea for weapons. In Zimbabwe, the commodities were ivory and rhino horns whereas the commodity of choice in Angola was diamonds.[28] As the Somali government disintegrated in the early 1990s, some half-million weapons were spirited to competing factions. Landmines, a focus of much international concern, are present in abundance in Africa, particularly in war-torn nations such as Somalia and Angola. Cheap small arms have also upset traditional balances between ethnic groups on more local levels, as in western Kenya, where raids between the Pokot and Marakwet peoples have become much bloodier with the infusion of AK-47s.

Weapons sometimes jump from one country to another. Foreign mercenaries brought their own arms to Sierra Leone, Angola, and Zaire (now Congo) and attempts have been made to disarm combatants with gun-buyback programs. Cross-border police cooperation between the South African and Mozambican police has had some effect. In 2001, delegates from nearly 180 nations worldwide began negotiating the first international treaty aimed at curbing the illicit trade in small arms, but this process will take time to bear fruit. In the meantime, the bottom line is that light weapons are easily available in great abundance, and innocent civilians are the main casualties in the continuing carnage. This Flashpoint now turns to examples of several settled (at least for the present) and active national and regional African conflicts, beginning with Angola.

Angola

Angola's history has been highlighted by first, a very harsh colonial government, then a bitter struggle for independence, which was attained in 1975, and then an almost constant civil war that finally came to an official end in April 2002. Abundant resources include diamonds, oil, rich soil, and fish off the coast. The resources, however, especially the diamonds and oil, only exacerbated the tensions and the stakes in the protracted battle for control of the government and of the country's riches.

The brief statement regarding Portuguese rule is that, in the late sixteenth century, they were the first European power to come to sub-Saharan Africa and the last to leave, and then only when opposition became too strong, both on the battlefield and back in Lisbon. The ensuing battles from 1975 to 1991 between the Popular Movement for the Liberation of Angola (MPLA) and the National Union for the Total Independence of Angola (UNITA) took some 300,000 lives. In addition, starvation afflicted more than a half million people; one-half of the country's export earnings went for the war; the economy, even with oil revenue and considerable outside assistance, remained in tatters; and refugees numbered in the hundreds of thousands. With the cold war still going strong, 50,000 Cuban fighters entered on the MPLA side and a lesser number of South Africans supported UNITA. The Soviet Union and the United States lent their support in important but less overt roles as they supplied intelligence and weapons to the warring parties.

In 1991, a peace treaty was signed in Angola, officially ending the 16-year-old civil war. The agreement called for the former enemies to build a unified armed force, promote a multiparty political system and market economy, and plan for elections monitored by a UN observer force. When the votes were counted a year later and the MPLA claimed victory, UNITA refused to recognize the results, claiming it had lost because of fraud and ballot stuffing.

In the succeeding two years, thousands more were killed in renewed fighting. Another treaty was signed in November 1994. This time 7,000 UN peacekeepers monitored the cease-fire, and the opposition force was to have a share of the power. Again, there were hopes that the contestants would be able to come together in a grand coalition, but again it was not to be.

The on-again, off-again war continued to wreak havoc on the country, drain the economy, and cause tens of thousands of people to flee to refugee camps in neighboring Congo and Zambia. Although the MPLA was not blameless, it was UNITA that had been hit by international sanctions for routinely violating the 1994 agreement, including not fully carrying out the demobilization of its forces. The number and intensity of the clashes increased and intensified during 1998–2001 as the Angolan government of national conciliation collapsed. Generally, the MPLA forces through this period were able to gain the upper hand over UNITA, but the civil war looked to be far from resolution. The UN finally pulled its peacekeeping mission, acknowledging there was no more peace to keep. Even in the Congo war (see Central Africa subsection), MPLA and UNITA backed different sides. With the death of long-time UNITA leader Jonas Savimbi in a government ambush in

February 2002, negotiations led to the end of this decades-old civil war less than two months later. The people's hopes turned to rebuilding this ravaged nation, where, besides the awful loss and displacement of lives, the great mineral wealth had been squandered for over twenty-five years.

Wars in the Horn of Africa: Sudan and Darfur

Ethiopia, Eritrea, Djibouti, Somalia, and Sudan—five different countries, all poor, with five different histories that affect one another—comprise the Horn of Africa. All have known war recently, and in one, the fighting continues. Drought, soaring populations, and depleted natural resources are endemic to the Horn of Africa. Ethiopia is one of the oldest countries in the world and Eritrea is among the newest; both are carving out new directions. After decades of unrest Djibouti appears relatively stable in the early 2000s, while Somalia struggles to rebuild a fractured, decimated state, and Sudan having resolved one of Africa's longest and ugliest civil wars, faces new challenges.

From the 1890s until independence in 1956, Sudan was formally under joint Anglo-French control. In 1958, a coup brought a change of regime and ushered in an era of unrest and military uprisings, the most recent of which occurred in 1989. The sporadic civil war raged for over 35 years. The opposing forces comprised 30 million people in the mainly Moslem north and 8 million in the non-Moslem south. The northern-based government, dominated by Islamic fundamentalists, imposed itself on an evermore hostile south. Both sides used food as a weapon. To make things more complicated and more terrible, those opposing the government split into two groups and spent as much time fighting each other as the common enemy; there were divisions in the north also. In 1993, the United States added Sudan to its list of countries that aided terrorism, claiming that the government helped individuals and groups bent on destabilizing other states in Africa and beyond, but the regime, once the home of Osama bin Laden, has provided some intelligence to the United States in the war on terrorism. The tragedy in Sudan rivaled that in Central Africa, but, until recently, received even less attention by the media or the nation-states of the world.

In 2002, the government and the two contending rebel groups signed a protocol calling for a six-year interim period followed by an internationally supervised referendum on self-determination for the south, but hostilities continued nonetheless. Hopes for a brighter tomorrow, fueled by dramatic accords signed by government and southern rebel negotiators in January 2005, were tempered first by brutal attacks from government militias on the inhabitants of the remote Darfur region of western Sudan, the site of another insurgency, and then by the tragic death in July 2005 of the former rebel leader John Garang, recently installed as vice-president under the terms of the peace agreement. The Darfur attacks, formally labeled as genocide by the U.S. government, resulted in thousands of deaths, tens of thousands of rapes, and hundreds of thousands displaced in spartan refugee camps, creating a humanitarian crisis. The African Union, the UN, and the international community generally focused much attention on the disaster, but not before a terrible human toll was extracted with further deterioration possible. One U.S. official admitted that attacks on villages finally abated largely because "there were no villages left to attack." By mid-2005, several thousand AU peacekeepers, supported with financial and logistical aid from the West, were in place, but much of the damage had been done. To make matters worse, the national elation over the end of the long civil war came to a bitter end with the mysterious crash of John Garang's helicopter near his home in southern Sudan. The long-term rebel leader was instrumental in brokering the peace accords and was seen as a key figure in attempts to resolve the separate conflict in Darfur. Riots sparked by suspicions over the circumstances of his death killed 140 in the capital of Khartoum. Garang was soon succeeded as vice president by his rebel comrade and some-time rival Salva Kiir Mayardit, but many doubt whether he has the political experience and stature to carry on Garang's delicate work of rebuilding the shattered nation. Finally, there is the politics of oil. More than 3.5 billion barrels of high-quality crude have been discovered in the southern part of the country, and a $1.2 billion pipeline has been built over nearly 1,000 miles of extremely harsh terrain to get the product moving toward global markets. The oil is in production, but there remains concern over whether its proceeds will be used to improve the lives of all Sudanese citizens as agreed.

Because of inhospitable terrain and no obvious exportable economic resources, Ethiopia was able to keep its independence and its monarchy until conquered by Italy in 1935. Six years later, the British drove the Italians out and restored Emperor Haile Selassie to power. In seeking to enlarge his diverse state and alter the country's landlocked status, the emperor, with British approval, in 1952 claimed the former Italian colony of Eritrea without asking the Eritreans. A military coup in 1974 swept away the old Ethiopian order. Ethiopia then endured a brutal period of Marxist rule under President Mengistu Haile Mariam before his regime collapsed under pressures from nationalist guerrilla fighting units and the end of Soviet sponsorship.

By the time Mengistu fled in the spring of 1991, 2 million people had died under his 17-year reign. In the following months, representatives of 27 ethnic and political groups, including the Ethiopian People's Revolutionary Democratic Front (EPDRF) and the Eritrean People's Liberation Front (EPLF), met to work out the future of the country. Meles Zenawi of the EPDRF headed a transition government. Despite new programs, food shortages and severe rural poverty continued as population growth outstripped grain production by ever-widening amounts. The promised democracy under a 1994 constitution has made limited progress, and in a pattern repeated in many African elections, the fairness of the 2005 Ethiopian national elections has been hotly disputed. Still, most observers agree that internal political conditions are much improved over the pre-1991 era.

The region of the Horn has suffered from droughts and famines exacerbated by civil violence. Ethiopia experienced a severe episode in 1984–1985 that cost an estimated one million lives as starving villagers futilely migrated to poorly supplied feeding stations. Massive international aide eventually arrived, but too late for many victims. Threats of a similar tragedy loomed in the summer of 2003 but this time hopefully tempered with lessons learned from past bitter experience.

With Ethiopia's consent, Eritrea invoked its right to self-determination in 1993. Following almost 30 years of war in which 250,000 people were killed, it became the first territory in Africa to secede successfully from another African country. In a referendum, 99.8 percent of the voters opted for independence, and the new nation embarked on a democratic transition, earning high marks for its political sensitivity and self-reliant economic programs.

In mid-1998, again in early 1999, and in May 2000, the two states waged a border war, complete with planes, tanks, and considerable casualties, belying the stated friendship between the two countries' leaders, Meles Zenawi and Issaias Aferweki. Rebellions by Eritrea had gone on since the early 1960s, when the actual annexation by Ethiopia had taken place. For the next 30 years, there was minimal cooperation between the national government and its embittered province. Nevertheless, the leadership of both entities worked together to overthrow the hated Mengistu government. But the fraternal relations could not survive the peace. On one level, this conflict was simply a disagreement over who owned a border area that had been drawn by Italy in 1885, but there were serious economic disputes as well. After the renewed fighting in May of 2000, the two nations agreed to a cease-fire including UN peacekeepers in a buffer zone. The UN mediated a final demarcation of the disputed border in 2002, but, by early 2006 renewed tensions threatened the fragile peace, a test for the African Union's goal of peacefully resolving conflicts between its member states.

Southern Italian Somaliland and northern British Somaliland were fused at independence in 1960. Nine years later, Mohammed Siad Barre seized power and became a ruthless president for the next 22 years. Even though the overwhelming majority of the people are from the same ethnic group, competing clans and subclans formed the basis for challenges to Barre and each other.

During the time of U.S.-Soviet rivalry, the United States first backed Ethiopia, while the U.S.S.R. supported Barre's version of socialism. When Marxist Mengistu took power in Ethiopia, the two superpowers switched sides, both supplying their new beneficiaries with more weapons. Despite Barre's deplorable human rights record, the United States continued to funnel military and economic aid to Somalia until the late 1980s.

In 1991, Barre was finally ousted and a struggle for power between sub-clans began, bringing with it hardship and famine. As pictures of starving children filled television screens followed initial UN hesitation, the world body began to supply food to hundreds of thousands of people. With provisions being hijacked or blocked at the capital of Mogadishu, UN observers, and then U.S. troops, arrived to assist. Gradually, the mission's objective changed (so-called "mission creep") from ending starvation to establishing a measure of peace and security to the country by ending the struggle for power. Later it was hoped that the UN could rebuild the infrastructure, the economy, and finally the government itself. This change in objective involved the UN as a participant in the conflict.

By 1993, there were 25,000 American military personnel, thousands of other UN peacemakers, and countless private parties, all attempting to provide assistance. In October of that year, 18 U.S. Army Rangers lost their lives in a futile attempt to capture a Somali leader who was accused of fomenting strife. This incident has become fixed in popular memory through graphic video and in global popular culture through the 2001 movie, "Black Hawk Down." The international community beat a measured retreat and within two years all military personnel were gone, though a few relief agencies braved the dangers and stayed. Some saw the operation as saving great numbers of lives and offering hope during a time of misery; others believed that UN members came too late and became too enmeshed in local politics and in "nation building."

Since then, there was no operating government in Somalia until fall 2000, when negotiations led to the beginnings of a return to law and order. Success is far from assured, however, as rival warlords and break-away groups maintain their armed militias outside government control which seems to center in the capital of Mogadishu, where danger and instability forced the prime minister and his cabinet to spend seven months in virtual exile in Kenya from late 2004 to mid-2005. Both floods and drought have taken their toll as the world became donor-fatigued and turned its attention elsewhere, but concerns over international terrorism might refocus attention on struggling Somalia.

Central Africa and the Great Lakes Region

Without a doubt, events in Central Africa at the new century's onset were the most tumultuous, the most complicated, and the most dangerous in all of sub-Saharan Africa. Personal rivalries, ethnic antagonisms, cross-border conflicts, and precolonial and colonial currents mix in unpredictable ways. In the Democratic Republic of the Congo (formerly Zaire), the third largest country on the continent, the last several years have witnessed the overthrow of a president who had ignominiously ruled since the 1960s, a successor who barely clung to power amidst charges of incompetence, an assassination leading to a young, untried president, and a war in which troops from several surrounding countries joined local forces. One humanitarian nongovernmental organization (NGO), the International Rescue Committee, estimated that 3.3 million people have died as a result of the civil war in rebel-held Eastern Congo through 2002.[29] Some sources add estimates of hundreds of thousands of more victims to that staggering figure in the following years. In Rwanda, a terrible 1994 civil war that took hundreds of thousands of lives has been followed by continuing bitter ethnic hostilities across borders, with no final end to the killings. The mass killings in tiny Rwanda, stemming in part from long-standing ethnic rivalry between the dominant Tutsis and the majority, lower-status Hutus, led to refugee disasters, reprisals and second-guessing of UN and Western power inaction. Prosecutions of alleged war criminals from this horror continue to this day, and the world witnessed moving 10-year memorials of the massacre in 2004. Many neighboring countries, especially Angola, Burundi, Uganda, and Zimbabwe, already struggling with major political and economic problems, were pushed to the limit by convulsions emanating from Congo (then Zaire) and Rwanda. Burundi, which has been plagued by ongoing ethnic clashes similar in some respects to those of Rwanda, has experienced outbreaks of civil war in 2003. The international community is rushing to avoid the mistakes that led to the awful massacres in its northern neighbor nearly a decade ago. Amidst all the swirls, there was the fear that the turbulence of this region could lead to boundary changes on a scale not seen for more than a hundred years.

In the mid- and late nineties, events in Rwanda became ever more closely entwined with those of neighboring Congo (both were under Belgian colonial rule). The huge state in the middle of the continent was a prize, with its lush forests, fertile croplands, and prodigious mineral deposits; however, its painful colonial experience as the Belgian Congo made it totally unprepared for independence in 1960. Not surprisingly, chaos resulted, in which racial, ethnic, and ideological conflicts brought the country close to disintegration. Outside states threatened to intervene, but a UN peacekeeping operation, despite many problems, provided the glue that kept the country together. After the UN departure in 1964, however, instability grew again. A year later, General Joseph Mobutu staged a coup and began to put his mark on the country, a mark that has become all-pervasive.

Thirty years later, Congo was going back in time. It was a country where political and economic conditions had gotten about as bad as they could get. In a change he dubbed African "authentication," the nation had been renamed Zaire and the general had become President Sese Seko Mobutu, but he ran a "kleptocracy," government by theft. Although Mobutu was a billionaire who maintained several residences in Europe, the World Bank declared Congo bankrupt in 1994. Massive corruption including diamond smuggling, hyperinflation, and hunger were among the symptoms of his sick regime. Mobutu's promoting tensions and divisions among the country's 250 ethnic groups to ensure his own longevity in office was another. Because of the disintegration of the government infrastructure, civil servants and soldiers were not paid and staged mutinies.

Because of the cold war, Congo for many years was the largest recipient of U.S. aid in sub-Saharan Africa. Indeed, Mobutu came to power with the help of the Central Intelligence Agency (CIA), which used the country as a staging area for activities throughout the continent while turning a blind eye to the endemic decay and corruption. Several attempts at democratic reform during the 1990s came to naught, and in the end the malaise was so advanced that a Tutsi-supported revolt, which started along the border with Rwanda in October 1996, swept the country in just seven months. The OAU principle of nonintervention in the affairs of another state had been ignored during the overthrow of Mobutu in which several neighboring nations collaborated.

The president, already terminally ill with prostate cancer, fled the country in May 1997 and died in exile four months later. Laurent Kabila, who was from southern Congo and had been a longtime opponent of the regime, was anointed to lead the rebellion and become the new president. Expectations ran high for a better tomorrow, but it was not to be, as his corrupt, chaotic and war-torn term ended abruptly with his assassination by a disloyal bodyguard in January 2001.

His son Joseph Kabila, a 31-year-old army officer with little political or administrative experience, assumed the presidency. Many observers feared that the awful situation would deteriorate even further. On the contrary, the young and untried president showed stability and competence, and he spoke of building a peaceful, democratic future for his country. A failed 1999 cease-fire accord regained momentum. In the wake of several negotiated cease-fires, peace initiatives, and conferences, sometimes boycotted by one or more of the key parties, the efforts of international mediators such as Nelson Mandela, and the presence of UN peacekeeping forces, the civil war moved to an interim, transitional settlement in the summer of 2003. While Joseph Kabila retained the presidency, he accepted four vice presidents from the contending factions, and the long-suffering nation was poised to move toward reconciliatory measures. A new constitution was ratified in 2005, with elections to be held no later than June of the next year.

Even with these hopeful developments and the presence of the largest UN peacekeeping force in the world, ethnic strife, rebel guerilla and militia attacks, and cross-border incursions continued. Often these actions targeted civilians for ruthless slaughter; child combatants were prevalent. Women were raped both by insurgents and by some of the peacekeepers. In a move that, if successful, could lead to a major reduction in the violence, President Kabila vowed to push all foreign militias, (including the dreaded Interahamwe, the Hutu extremists responsible for much of the killing in the 1994 Rwandan massacre) out of the country by the end of September 2005. Is this regions' troubled past destined to follow it into the near future, or has it truly turned a new page? Time will tell, but the violence continues despite the formal end of the civil war.

West Africa

Long one of the most politically unstable regions of Africa, littered with civil wars and coups, conditions in West Africa at the turn of the last century were relatively calm. For example, Nigeria, Senegal, and Ghana were showing signs of participatory democracy, while civil wars and coups in Cote d'Ivoire, Liberia, and Sierra Leone were in various stages of abatement. Much of this superficial calm, however, preceded more gathering storms. Deteriorating ethnic relations in Nigeria are noted in the case study, and the rebel insurgencies in Cote d'Ivoire and Liberia reignited. Free elections in Senegal and Ghana, on the other hand, resulted in peaceful changes of power, and a long, brutal civil war in Sierra Leone was settled with ECOWAS and UN peacekeeper intervention so that reconstruction could begin.

During Francophile President Felix Houphouet-Boigny's twenty-three-year term, Cote d'Ivoire, with a large French presence, enjoyed considerable stability and prosperity, if limited freedom and democracy. With his death in 1993, things began to unravel, and in September 2002, the nation experienced a renewed military rebellion that divided it along religious and sectarian lines, particularly the more Moslem north and Christian south. French military intervention and a brokered truce in Paris in the spring of 2003 failed to resolve the conflict. Despite other peace-making attempts, new violence ensued. In April 2005, the civil war was officially settled through a power-sharing and disarmament agreement, but slow implementation forced cancellation of the planned October elections. The AU promised to convene a summit over the issue, and it remains to be seen when Cote d'Ivoire will return to the political stability and economic success enjoyed in earlier years.

Sierra Leone suffered a particularly vicious decade-long civil war that centered in part over control of the nation's lucrative diamond trade and was fomented by Liberian rebel intervention. The main Sierra Leonean rebel force, the Revolutionary United Front (RUF) under its leader Foday Sankoh, appeared to have little political plan for the nation beyond exploiting resources; brutally intimidating and recruiting civilians, often children, as combatants; and seizing power. Attempts by neighbors through ECOWAS and various international actors, including the U.S., to broker cease fires and arrange a power-sharing settlement in the late 1990s fell through, but renewed efforts by the UN, British and ECOWAS forces (termed ECOMOG and consisting mostly of Nigerian troops) bore fruit in later years with the capture of Sankoh and the surrender and disarmament of most of the rebel fighters. Sierra Leone established a Truth and Reconciliation Commission based partially on the South African model to deal with the horrors of its past and try to rebuild for the future; trials of alleged war criminals began in 2004; Sankoh himself died of natural causes while in prison awaiting trial. With the war-ravaged nation ranking next to last in the world on the latest UN Human Development index, much work remains to be done.

While the capital of Sierra Leone, Freetown, was established in 1787 by freed African slaves from Britain and its colonies, neighboring Liberia was founded early in the nineteenth century as a home for freed slaves repatriated from the United States. This group of "Americo-Liberians" comprised no more than 5 percent of the total population, nonetheless controlled Liberian politics and wealth through their True Whig Party and related Masonic Temple. The behavior and conduct of the True Whigs mirrored in many ways the society of the plantation masters they had left. Their aloof, arrogant rule came to a decisive and bloody end in 1980 in the form of a coup led by Sergeant Samuel Doe. Sadly, this regime change heralded the beginning of more problems for Liberia as the next two decades would be marked by civil wars that killed hundreds of thousands, left many refugees and internally displaced persons, and ruined the faltering economy.

A ruthless rebel force led by Charles Taylor, now under indictment for war crimes in connection with illicit diamond trading in Sierra Leone's civil war, emerged in the late 1990s. His regime was soon challenged by other rebels, such as the Liberians United for Reconciliation and Democracy (LURD), whose brutal battlefield tactics against civilians belied their high-sounding name. By mid-summer of 2003, with a beleaguered Taylor holding only the capital city of Monrovia, desperate Liberians cried out for international peacemaking assistance, especially from the United States, whose forces had just toppled a dictatorial regime in Iraq. Liberians, with so many ties of heritage and economy to the U.S., felt this special relationship should prompt U.S. forces to the rescue. Angry Liberians displayed the bodies of their slain relatives in front of the U.S. embassy after the Americans hesitated to respond and the killing escalated. Taylor finally left the country for reluctant exile in Nigeria, as the U.S. and others had demanded, but evidence mounted that he still tried to run Liberia, including its army and business interests, from abroad. Meanwhile, some 3,000 multinational ECOWAS troops, especially Nigerians based in Sierra Leone, intervened to stop the fighting in the capital. The U.S. administration promised assistance to help end the slaughter by sending more than 2,000 Marines to the Liberian coast to support the coming ECOWAS and UN peacekeepers, but only a couple hundred actually landed. The U.S. called for a large UN force to relieve the ECOWAS troops. As the death toll mounted, the patience of Liberian citizens across the nation was wearing thin. Calm finally prevailed under the ECOWAS troops, and the beleaguered nation held presidential elections in October 2005 that resulted in a runoff between George Weah, a renowned former soccer star, and Ellen Johnson-Sirleaf, a former World Bank official.

(Interestingly, some of the campaigning among the 22 candidates took place in the U.S. Liberian community; although these citizens would not be allowed to cast absentee ballots, they had ample and needed funds for campaign contributions.[30]) Johnson-Sirleaf won convincingly in the run-off, an election judged as fair and free, to become Africa's first female president. Her initial policy moves in early 2006 aimed at rooting out corruption and reconciling rival factions; it will be interesting to see whether she succeeds where so many male leaders have failed.

More than 40 years after independence, many nations of Africa continue to experience ethnic and religious violence and civil wars and insurgencies. All the news is not grim. On the contrary, many clashes of the past have been settled, and reconstructive efforts are ongoing in numerous nations, such as Angola, Liberia, Mozambique, Uganda, Rwanda, Sierra Leone, and soon, perhaps, Burundi and the Democratic Republic of the Congo, all previously afflicted by awful violence and unspeakable atrocities. As the examples in this Flashpoint prove, though, it is risky to declare these African conflicts resolved for good, and all African and international actors need to learn hard lessons from the mistakes of the past.

SUB-SAHARAN AFRICA AND INTERNATIONAL TERRORISM

After the striking events of September 11, 2001, the attention of the United States and much of the rest of the world was riveted by the vexing phenomenon of international terrorism, but Africa had already seen its awful impact in two related attacks. In early August 1998, powerful bombs exploded adjacent to U.S. embassies in Kenya and Tanzania, and resulted in the deaths of more than 260 people, including 12 American citizens. More than 5,000 were injured.

In this case, it appeared that the terrorist acts had their origin in the Middle East or Afghanistan. The perpetrators were taking vengeance against the United States for its pro-Israel policies and its support for what were seen as despotic governments in the Arab world. More generally, there was a backlash against the intrusion of American and Western culture and values into Islamic countries.

For Kenyans and Tanzanians the price was high. First were the many killed or injured and the ripple effect on their families. Many of the deceased or those seriously hurt were breadwinners. Thousands, therefore, had their lives uprooted. There were the economic impacts such as tourists staying away in droves and many shops and buildings destroyed, which could only be slowly reconstructed, if at all. To add to the bitterness, there was criticism that U.S. servicemen who were deployed in the hours and days after the bombings were indifferent to the plight of the Africans who were injured, focusing only on American casualties.

Two weeks later the United States struck back, launching surprise missile strikes on terrorist bases in Afghanistan and a factory in Sudan, which allegedly produced chemical weapons, although that evidence remains in question. In the meantime, Kenyans and Tanzanians tried to get on with their lives while Africans in other countries wondered if they would be next. An attempt by Kenyan citizens to sue in U.S. courts for compensation for damages from the embassy attack did not succeed. In November 2002, Kenya suffered a related terrorist attack, on a resort hotel in Mombassa frequented by Israeli tourists. This suicide car bomb attack, linked to Al Qaeda, claimed the lives of ten Kenyan and three Israeli victims. On the same day, two "stinger" type missiles narrowly missed an Israeli airliner bound for home with 271 aboard.

Sub-Saharan Africa's ties to the crisis of international terrorism are many and appear to be growing. Virtually every African government expressed sympathy and offers of aid to the United States following the September 11 attacks, and several African nations, such as Sudan, once a headquarters for Al-Qaeda operations, were able to provide important intelligence assistance. Some critics fear, though, that closer ties with authoritarian regimes for help in the war on terrorism could have negative consequences later, as they did with anticommunism in the cold war.

Because Africa has many nations with large Islamic populations, it should not be surprising that there are also substantial followings for militant, fundamentalist Islamist groups among the discontented and disaffected, especially youth. Susan E. Rice, Assistant Secretary for African Affairs in the second Clinton administration, wrote in the *Washington Post*:

> What has Africa got to do with Osama bin Laden or terrorist finance networks? This: Africa is the world's soft underbelly for global terrorism. If we intend to win—and not just fight—the war on terror, we cannot view Africa as separate from our comprehensive, global war. . . . Al Qaeda and other terrorist cells are active throughout East, southern and West Africa, as well as North Africa. These organizations plan, finance, train and execute terrorist operations in many parts of Africa, not just Sudan and Somalia.[31]

Al-Qaeda presence in Sudan and Somalia is widely acknowledged in intelligence circles. The Khartoum government, which has had difficult relations with Washington over the last decade because of alleged sponsorship of terrorism, previously hosting Osama bin Laden, its long civil war with the black, partially Christian south, the more recent violence in Darfur, and allegations of modern human slavery, chose to avoid confrontation with the United States in the war on terror and instead became a source of intelligence. Somalia, still highly unstable with little central governmental authority, is reputedly a safe haven for Al-Qaeda operations and might even provide some sanctuary for terrorist fighters escaping from the United States in Afghanistan. With help from Ethiopian authorities on the border, U.S. officials conducted scouting missions in Somalia late in 2001 for possible later actions against terrorist activities there. The U.S. maintains a contingent of Special Forces in Djibouti to deal with terrorist activity in the region. A new Trans-Sahara Counter Terrorism Initiative, begun in 2005 with very limited funding but to be funded at $100 million annually, starting in 2007, provides U.S. Special Forces trainers on counter-terrorist tactics for troops from Chad, Mali, Mauritania, Niger, Nigeria, Senegal and three North African states.[32]

In an article entitled "Blood on the Diamonds," *Washington Post* reporter Holly Burkhalter examined the illicit trade links of Al-Qaeda terrorists, some of whom are linked to the 1998 embassy bombings, in securing diamonds at wholesale prices from Sierra Leonean rebels by way of contacts in neighboring Liberia, and then trafficking the diamonds at windfall profits to the world markets in Belgium. Legislative and other efforts to intercept and close down such lucrative terrorist financial dealings are underway.[33] Nigeria experienced deadly riots by extremist Moslems against Christians in northern cities such as Kano following the U.S. bombing of Taliban and Al-Qaeda positions in Afghanistan. Clearly, official positions in African countries are supportive of U.S. efforts to combat international terrorism, but opinions of the people "on the street" in African Islamic nations may not be so favorable to U.S. positions. Whether the attention on Africa resulting from concerns over international terrorism will be good for African interests in the long term remains to be seen, but short-term disruptions are likely.

SUMMARY

Don't Worry. It's Africa. Nobody cares about Africa.
FROM THE MOVIE "SAHARA" PARAMOUNT PICTURES, 2005

The line above was spoken by a villainous warlord in an action-adventure, Indiana Jones-like film set in the deserts of Mali and in Lagos, Nigeria. Like most Hollywood movies, "Sahara" was intended to entertain rather than to inform, but it is replete with stereotypes, including the ruthless, greedy warlord intent on victimizing innocent indigenous peoples who oppose him (in this case with the slight variation that the warlord is black and the victims are Islamic "Tuareg" tribesmen). The warlord believed he could get away with his schemes because no one in the "outside world" would pay any attention. The truth, as it is hoped this chapter has shown, is that many in the U.S. and the world at large do care a great deal about Africa, but it is too easy to remain uninformed, under-informed, or misinformed about the realities of sub-Saharan Africa. The entire issue of the September 2005 *National Geographic* magazine is devoted to Africa, with thoughtful articles that concentrate on resources, the environment, and changing patterns of human life. Instead of the characteristic photograph, the front cover simply states, in large letters, "Africa," and beneath, "Whatever you thought, think again." This is sound advice both for the student new to the study of Africa and for those who consider themselves to be "old hands," because the region is in flux, and the outcomes should matter to all of us.

Natural geography and history impede positive change in Africa. Population, health, education, food, energy, and environmental concerns are troubling problems. Politically, the continuing quest for legitimacy, the social diversity and conflict, embedded corruption, the uncertain effectiveness of regional and pan-African cooperation, and varying international interest in Africa do not bode well for the years ahead. Finally, by many indicators, economic well-being is very tenuous for most Africans, while dependency on external agencies that prescribe privatization has increased.

As Africa moves into the twenty-first century, there has been no dramatic turnaround for the region; however, politically and economically there are glimmers of hope. Throughout the 1990s into the early 2000s, particularly gruesome civil wars, marred by many atrocities against civilians, raged in Congo, Liberia, Rwanda, Sierra Leone, Angola, and Sudan. Côte d'Ivoire, long one of the most stable governments in former French West Africa, suffered a violent military coup, and corrupt dictatorships held sway in several other West African nations. In addition to the shift to civilian rule in the important nation of Nigeria described in the Case Studies previously discussed, the civil wars have abated in Angola, Liberia, Sierra Leone, Rwanda, part of Sudan, and hopefully Burundi, where elections were held in 2005. Some disarmament and rebuilding has begun. Both Congo and Côte d'Ivoire have begun implementation of agreements for power sharing, and Ghana, Senegal, and Kenya experienced relatively peaceful and significant transfers of power to opposition leaders through free and fair elections. Kenya's electoral success, where "big man" Daniel Arap Moi held authoritarian sway for nearly 25 years, is especially significant because of its size and potential, but citizens complain that governmental corruption continues despite highly touted reform efforts, and, as a result, well-intentioned international aid still fails to reach its intended audience. Despite ongoing problems, developments in South Africa are still exciting.

The AIDS crisis continues to rage and take an awful toll, but more international donor attention is on the way, and some national programs, notably those of Botswana and Uganda, have shown success. Fears that the Bush administration would put Africa on the backburner have proven unfounded, but Africa awaits concrete results from promised new programs and financial help competing with other U.S. priorities, such as the Iraq War and rebuilding after the Katrina hurricane disaster.

Among African leaders and scholars, there is a major debate about whether the causes, and thus the implied cures of Africa's current ills are largely external (such as slavery, colonialism, imperialism, and globalization) or internal (such as poor leadership, corruption, and ethnic conflict). President Mbeki of South Africa is considered a strong proponent of the externalist position, while President Obasanjo of Nigeria has made statements along the internalist lines. Although these are useful distinctions for analysis, many would agree that action for Africa is needed on all fronts, both outside and inside the continent. All must work together to cure Africa's ills.

People in many cases still fear their own governments, but they are no longer suffering in silence. Literacy is rising; technology is making inroads in the most distant villages, and, from Senegal to Nigeria to Kenya to Zimbabwe, the people, including women, "will be heard." More people are standing up to mismanagement and corruption. Some see promise in the development of the African Union. Western powers, including the United States, seem to be paying increased attention to the region. Africa has great potential, but there is much to do and there may be little time left to do it.

Review Questions

1. What are the effects of the European Colonial Period, including the earlier slave trade on the current political and economic situation in sub-Saharan Africa?
2. Why do many Africans believe that their own governments and leaders have not served them well? Are there exceptions to this pattern?
3. Why has regional cooperation in Africa proved so elusive, and what are the goals and prospects of the new African Union?
4. What parts of Africa continue to suffer episodes of civil war and ethnic violence? Why? What previous civil wars have been resolved in recent years?
5. Why is there a special relationship between the United States and Africa? Why do some Africans fear that their interests have at times been marginalized in U.S. foreign policy?
6. What contributions has Wangari Maathai made to African development? Do you believe that she is a good role model for other Africans? Why is the political and economic participation of women vital for Africa's future success?

Key Terms

- **The African Union (AU)**—Founded in 2002, the association of all independent African nations that succeeded the Organization of African Unity (1963) to build new institutions and agreements leading to African integration and solutions to Africa's problems.
- **Apartheid**—The policy of racial discrimination and separation practiced by the white Afrikaner regime in South Africa until the coming of majority rule in the 1990s.
- **The Berlin Conference**—The notorious meeting of European imperial powers to divide Africa for colonial exploitation without the participation of Africans. This division is still reflected in today's political map of Africa; see Figures 6.2, and 6.3.
- **"The Elephants and the Grass"**—From a Swahili proverb that claims that grass is trampled when elephants fight, with Africa cast in the role of the grass and

the Western powers (formerly, also the Soviet Union) and financial institutions in the role of elephants.

• **Externalists and internalists**—Those who explain Africa's problems and possible solutions on the basis of factors outside Africa (external), such as historical slavery, colonialism, the cold war and globalization, as opposed to factors within Africa (internal) such as corrupt leadership, ethnic conflict, and civil war.

• **The Great Lakes Region**—The area that includes much of Central Africa comprising the northeastern part of the Democratic Republic of the Congo, western Kenya, northern Tanzania, southern Uganda, and all of Rwanda and Burundi that has witnessed much ethnic violence, civil war, and refugee problems.

• **The Horn of Africa**—The region of Northwest Africa consisting of Djibouti, Ethiopia, Eritrea, Somalia, and Sudan that has seen much instability, war, and disaster, both natural and man-made.

• **Modern slavery**—The practices of indentured servitude of youths and of chattel (ownership) slavery of black Africans in Sudan and Mauritania.

• **Pan-Africanism**—The idea, often associated with Kwame Nkrumah, the charismatic first president of Ghana, that African nations and peoples need to unite for their common good and survival; an ideal not yet realized in practice.

• **The politics of extraction**—A concept closely associated with corruption that holds that political power is intended for acquiring material well-being rather than serving the people, as practiced by the colonial powers and allegedly learned by some of Africa's own leaders, such as Mobutu of Zaire, after independence.

Useful Web Sites

Africare (U.S.-based charitable organization promoting aid to Africa): www.africare.org
Africa Action (U.S.-based advocacy organization for Africa): www.africaaction.org
All Africa Global Media (consortium for African news media): allafrica.com
The African Union: www.africa-union.org
The University of Pennsylvania's African Studies Program:
www.sas.upenn.edu/African_Studies/AS.html

Notes

1. For details of UN Millennium Development Goals, see www.un.org/millenniumgoals/; for the recent UN Human Development Reports, visit hdr.undp.org/reports/.
2. For example, A. N. Wilson writes of the British in the 19th Century colonial era in *The Victorians* (New York, NY: W. W. Norton), 2003: "Theirs was the period of the most radical transformation ever seen by the world. . . . Large tracts of the world, especially in Africa, were unmapped. After them, the 'Dark Continent' had been penetrated by European powers; the destiny of Africa had changed . . ."; p. 1.
3. "Angrily" is an understatement. With independence, France cut all ties with Guinea and withdrew, taking with them everything from government vehicles to telephones.
4. Mazrui related the anecdote in the 1986 television series, *The Africans*.

5. Susan Rice, "A New Partnership for the 21st Century," address to the African Studies Association, November 14, 1997.

6. Judith Matloff, "African Anthem: Where Life Goes on, No Matter What," *Christian Science Monitor,* 6 January 1998, p. 9.

7. Robert Reid, "Annan: Africans Must Share Blame," *Associated Press,* 16 April 1998.

8. Quoted from the Nobel Peace Prize Award Citation, Norwegian Nobel Committee, November 27, 2004.

9. Quoted in Emily Wax, "Africa's Women Beginning to See Progress in Politics," *The Washington Post,* June 6, 2003, A6.

10. Emily Wax, "An African 'Big Brother' Unites and Delights," *The Washington Post,* 14 July 2003, A1.

11. For a fuller discussion on this subject, see Herman J. Cohen, "Conflict Management in Africa," *CSIS Africa Notes,* February 1998, pp. 1–7.

12. The official progress of the AU, including joint actions, programs established and annual summit meetings, can be followed through its Web site, www.Africa-Union.org.

13. Peter Carlson, "Powell, on Another Front," *The Washington Post,* 7 November 2001, p. C1.

14. Susan Rice, Assistant Secretary of State for African Affairs, "U.S.-Africa Policy," address to the National Association for the Advancement of Colored People, 14 July 1998.

15. In 1998, U.S. soldiers joined their Kenyan, Tanzanian, and Ugandan counterparts in Kenya to show that their hypothetical country of Sumang could be returned to calm after upheaval. Small-scale training and exercises involving U.S. troops and African peacekeeping forces continue into the early 2000s.

16. Jennifer Seymour Whitaker, *How Can Africa Survive?* (New York: Council on Foreign Relations, 1988), pp. 30–31.

17. Alan B. Durning, "Ending Poverty," in Lester R. Brown et al., *State of the World, 1990* (New York: Norton, 1990), p. 139.

18. David Francis, "World Reaps Benefits of Economic Reform," *Christian Science Monitor,* 10 February 1998.

19. John Koppisch, "Lessons from The Fastest Growing Nation: Botswana?" *Business Week,* 26 August 2002, pp. 116, 118.

20. Mike Jensen, "Making the Connection: Africa and the Internet," *Current History;* reprinted in ed. E. Jeffress Ramsey, *Global Studies: Africa* (Guilford, Conn.: Dushkin, 2001), p. 196.

21. Human Development Report 1997, p. 103.

22. R. W. Johnson, "A Brutal Brush with Gun Law in South Africa," *The Sunday Times* (London), 6 September 1998.

23. "Nigerian Justice Minister Shot Dead at Home," *The Washington Post,* 25 December 2001.

24. Jan Raath, "Mugabe's Grace and Favours," The Times (London), 18 July 1998.

25. These grim statistics and many others on the ravages of the epidemic and the effort to combat it in Africa can be found at UNAID's Web site, www.unaids.org. UNAIDS is a joint United Nations program created to fight the global epidemic.

26. In Zimbabwe, for example, where as much as 25 percent of all adults may be infected with HIV, average life expectancy, which was 62 in 1993, plummeted to less than 34 years by 2002. Of course, other factors besides AIDS, such as famine, contributed to this disturbing decline.

27. Michael Renner, "An Epidemic of Guns," *Worldwatch Magazine,* July/August 1998, p. 25. Most of the specifics in this Flashpoint come from the same article.

28. Michael Renner, "Small Arms, Big Impact: The Next Challenge of Disarmament," *Worldwatch Paper 137,* October 1997, p. 34.
29. This staggering figure cannot be verified, since access to the remote areas of the conflict by outside observers has been impossible, and many of the deaths have resulted from disease and famine related to the conflict, rather than from actual combat. Regardless of the exact figure, few Americans are aware of the enormity of this tragedy, a situation that Ted Koppel's ABC *Nightline* program had hoped to correct in September 2001 through a five-part series entitled "Still in the Heart of Darkness." Unfortunately, the last four parts of the broadcast were preempted by the September 11 terrorist attacks, but the series finally aired in late January 2002.
30. Sudarsan Raghavan, "After Shattering Civil War, Liberians See Hope at Polls," *The Washington Post,* 9 September 2005, B-1, 8.
31. Susan E. Rice, "The Africa Battle," *The Washington Post,* 11 December 2001.
32. Ann Scott Tyson, "U.S. Pushes Anti-Terrorism in Africa," *The Washington Post,* 26 July 2005, pp. A1 and A14. The color photograph accompanying this front-page feature story shows U.S. Special Forces trainers using GI-Joe action figures to demonstrate tactics to Chadian troops.
33. Holly Burkhalter, "Blood on the Diamonds," *The Washington Post,* 6 November 2001, p. A23.

For Further Reading

Ali, Taisier, and Matthews, Robert. *Civil Wars in Africa.* Toronto: McGill-Queen's University Press, 1999.

Ayittey, George B.N. *Africa Betrayed.* New York: St. Martin's Press, 1992.

———. *Africa in Chaos.* New York: St. Martin's Press, 1999.

———. *Africa Unchained.* New York: Palgrave Macmillan, 2005.

Bayart, Jean-Francois. *The State in Africa: The Politics of the Belly.* London and New York: Longman, 1993.

Bratton, Michael. *Democratic Experiments in Africa: Regime Transitions in Comparative Perspective.* Cambridge and New York: Cambridge University Press, 1997.

Davidson, Basil. *The Black Man's Burden: Africa and the Curse of the Nation State.* New York: Times Books, 1992.

Decalo, Samuel. *The Stable Minority: Civilian Rule in Africa.* Gainesville, Fla.: Florida Academic Press, 1998.

Gourevitch, Philip. *We Wish to Inform You that Tomorrow We Will Be Killed with Our Families: Stories from Rwanda.* New York: Farrar, Straus and Giroux, 1998.

Hochschild, Adam. *King Leopold's Ghost.* New York: Houghton Mifflin, 1998.

Kapuscinski, Ryzard. *The Shadow of the Sun.* Translated by Klara Glowczweka. New York: Alfred A. Knopf, 2001.

Leach, Melissa, and Mearns, Robin, eds. *The Lie of the Land: Challenging Received Wisdom on the African Environment.* Westport, Conn.: Heinemann, 1996.

Mazrui, Ali. *The African Condition.* New York: Cambridge University Press, 1980.

———. *Cultural Forces in World Politics.* Westport, Conn.: Heinemann, 1990.

Meredith, Martin. *The Fate of Africa: From the Hopes of Freedom to the Heart of Despair; A History of Fifty Years of Independence.* New York: Public Affairs, 2005.

The National Geographic Society. *National Geographic.* "Africa" Special Issue, September 2005.

Roe, Emery, *Except Africa: Remaking Development, Remaking Power.* Somerset, N.J.: Transaction, 1998.

Soyinka, Wole. *The Open Sore of a Continent.* Oxford and New York: Oxford University Press, 1996.

————. *The Burden of Memory, The Muse of Forgiveness.* Oxford and New York: Oxford University Press, 1999.

Young, Crawford. *The African Colonial State in Comparative Perspective.* New Haven and London: Yale University Press, 1994.

7

Asia

Joseph N. Weatherby

And at the end of the fight is a tombstone white with
the name of the late deceased, and the epitaph drear:
"A fool lies here who tried to hustle the East."

RUDYARD KIPLING, 1892

INTRODUCTION TO ASIA

For almost 2,000 years, Westerners have looked to Asia. Here the West has sought a source for luxury goods including spices, porcelain, tea, and silk. Since early times hardy adventurers like Marco Polo and Vasco da Gama have risked hardships and death to gain access to the wealth of Asia. During the last four centuries, profit has been the primary motivation for the rise of Western imperialism in Asia. As early as 1687 this aim was clearly expressed in directions sent to the East India Company's British agent in India. The company is quoted as ordering him to "establish such a polity of civil and military power and create and secure such a large revenue . . . as may be the foundation of a large, well-grounded sure English dominion in India for all time to come."[1]

Throughout most of this period, the West has also had good reason to fear the military power of Asia. On many occasions fierce warriors have ridden out of Asia to crush kingdoms, sack cities, and take slaves. Names like Attila the Hun, Genghis Khan, and Tamerlane still strike fear in the hearts of Europeans hundreds of years after their invasions took place. When the adventurer Marco Polo met Kublai Khan in 1275, the Khan's empire stretched from Korea to Hungary.

It was not until the Europeans developed efficient ships and effective guns that the military dominance of Asia was broken. Technology allowed Western imperialists to dominate large parts of Asia for almost 500 years. Hilaire Belloc's nineteenth-century comment about Africa could also be applied to Western imperialism then taking place in Asia. He is quoted as saying, "Whatever happens, we have got the Maxim Gun and they have not."[2]

Much of the story of modern Asia has been one of the Western search for wealth followed by imperialism that was made possible because of superior military technology. Now that technology is being challenged by the emerging powers of Asia.

It is not an understatement to assert that if the nineteenth century belonged to Britain and the twentieth century was American, the twenty-first century is likely to be Asian. Western policymakers are already recognizing this fact. In referring to the growing importance of China, former United States Deputy Defense Secretary Paul Wolfowitz has put it this way, "I think the right way to think about China is that it's a country that is almost certain to become a superpower in the next half-century, and maybe in the next quarter-century, and that's pretty fast by historical standards."[3]

A brief review of the information contained in Table 7.1 does much to illustrate the great variety of conditions in Other World Asia. Such diversity makes it impossible to analyze the region state by state. This chapter will briefly discuss geography, then focus on the major states of the area.

GEOGRAPHY

Where Is Asia?

Viewed from space, there is no Asia! Asia is simply a subdivision of a single Afro-Eurasian "island" that stretches from the Cape of Good Hope all the way to Cape Dezhnev (North Cape) in Russia. Within this great landmass Asia forms the largest part (see Figure 7.1).

The separation of the continent of Asia from that of Africa and Europe is more cultural and historic than geographic. To identify Asia, most geographers arbitrarily draw a line along the Ural Mountains of Russia down through the Caspian Sea. The line then takes in Turkish Anatolia and the eastern shores of the Mediterranean and Red seas to include the Arabian Peninsula. This marks the western boundaries of Asia. All the lands east of that line into parts of the Pacific are considered to be Asian.

The Asian Continent is subdivided into five regions: Southwest Asia or Asia Minor, South Asia, Southeast Asia, East Asia, and Russian Asia or Siberia. Here the authors have included Southwest Asia in the chapter on the Middle East and North Africa. Because, as it is defined in Chapter 1, Russia is not part of the Other World. Russian Asia is not discussed here. Admittedly, this definition of Asia is subjective. Places like the former Soviet Republics of Central Asia along with Afghanistan, and Pakistan could have been put in several places. Here the former Soviet Asian Republics and Afghanistan are discussed in Chapter 9. Because of Japan's unique history of development, it is not considered an Other World state. For our purposes, Other World Asia includes Pakistan as part of South Asia. Southeast Asia and East Asia make up the remaining portions of this chapter.

TABLE 7.1 Characteristics of Asian Countries

Country	Population (millions)	Population Growth Rate %	Infant Mortality Rate (per 1,000 live births)	Population Under 15 Years of Age (%)	Life Expectancy (in years)	Urban Population (%)	Literacy Rate (%)	Arable Land (%)	Per Capita GDP ($US)
Middle South									
Bangladesh	141.34	2.092	64.3	33.8	62.08	24.2	43.1	73	1900
Bhutan	2.185	2.11	102.6	39.8	54.39	8.5	42.2	2	1300
India	1065.07	1.4	57.9	32.7	64.35	28.3	59.5	56	2900
Maldives	0.339	2.82	58.3	45.3	64.06	28.8	97.2	10	3900
Nepal	27.07	2.2	68.8	40	59.8	15	45.2	17	1400
Pakistan	159.196	2.03	74.4	39.9	63	31.4	45.7	27	2100
Sri Lanka	19.905	0.79	14.8	25.6	73.17	21	92.3	14	3700
South East									
Brunei	0.365	1.9	13.1	30.2	74.8	76.2	91.8	1	18600
Myanmar	42.72	0.42	68.8	28.6	56.22	29.4	83.1	15	1900
Cambodia	13.363	1.81	73.7	40.7	58.87	18.6	69.9	13	1700
Indonesia	238.452	1.45	36.8	n/a	69.57	45.6	88.5	10	3200
Laos	6.068	2.42	87.1	42.5	55.08	20.7	52.8	3	1700
Malaysia	23.522	1.8	18.4	34.1	72.24	63.9	88.9	3	9000
Phillippines	86.241	1.84	24.2	36.6	69.91	61	95.9	19	4600
Singapore	4.353	1.56	2.3	17.6	81.62	100	92.5	2	23700
Thailand	64.865	0.87	21.1	23.3	71.57	31.9	96	34	7400
Vietnam	82.689	1.04	29.9	31.6	70.61	25.7	94	17	2500
East Asia									
China	1298.847	0.58	25.3	24.3	72.27	38.6	86	10	5000
Korea, N	22.697	0.9	7.2	21.4	71.37	80.3	98	19	1000
Korea, S	48.598	0.38	24.8	25.4	75.82	61.1	99	14	17700
Comparison States									
Japan	127.333	0.05	3.3	14.5	81.15	51.2	100	11	28000
Belgium	10.348	0.15	4.8	17.3	78.62	97.2	98	24	29000
Italy	58.057	0.07	6.1	14.1	79.68	91.6	98.6	31	26800

SOURCE: Population, Infant Mortality Rate, Population Under 15 Years of Age, Urban Population, Literacy Rate, Arable Land, and Per Capita GDP from *The World Almanac and Book of Facts, 2005.* Population Growth Rate and Life Expectancy from *CIA World Factbook, 2005.*

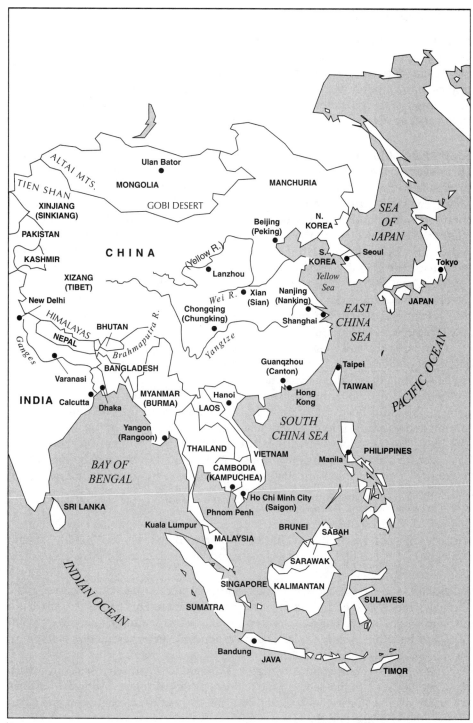

FIGURE 7.1 Political and Physical Characteristics of Other World Asia

What Is Other World Asia?

Even limited to South, Southeast, and East Asia, the continent is the world's largest. As might be expected, the land is both physically and climatically complex. Here there are high mountain ranges, important passageways, vast deserts, tropics, and important rivers. In terms of human geography, for thousands of years important civilizations have thrived in both China and India. Until about 500 years ago, China was arguably the most advanced civilization in the world.

South Asia   Most of South Asia is part of a peninsula that stretches from the Himalayas to the southern borders of India. Only Sri Lanka is outside of this peninsula. In the north are found the world's highest mountains, with the famous Mount Everest soaring to a height of 29,028 feet. These mountains are part of a continuous highland region stretching west to Switzerland. Here the range includes the Hindu Kush and the Karakorum separating Pakistan, Afghanistan, and India before becoming the Himalayas of Nepal and Butan. The mountain ranges have made travel in this region difficult.

The Great Deccan Plateau of India lies south of these mountains. This large tableland makes up most of the peninsula. The central parts of the plateau have arid conditions. Below the mountains of the eastern and western Ghats lies a coastal area with tropical forests.

Both India and Pakistan have great river systems that support some major areas of population. The Ganges is considered to be a sacred river by Hindu Indians. Rising in the Himalayas, the river flows past the great cities of Allahabad and Varanasi for 1,560 miles before joining the Brahmaputra to reach the Bay of Bengal. The Indus headwaters are in Tibet. The river flows for 1,800 miles through Jammu and Kashmir into Pakistan, where it eventually reaches the Arabian Sea. The Indus has a number of hydroelectric and irrigation systems that are a source of power for Pakistan. The control of some of these systems has been a source of conflict between India and Pakistan since they were granted independence in 1947.

The major cities of South Asia are Karachi, Pakistan (10,032,000), and Islamabad, Pakistan (698,000). India, the second most populous state in the world, has a number of great cities including Mumbai (Bombay) (16,088,000), Kolkata (Calcutta) (13,058,000), Delhi (12,441,000), and Hyderabad (5,445,000).

Southeast Asia: Southeast Asia is the land that lies to the east of India and to the south of China. Most of the climate is tropical monsoon. This means that there is a wet and a dry season. The trees are typical of a warm, humid climate, with palm trees and bamboo common. Rice is grown almost everywhere and is a staple in most of Southeast Asian diets.

The terrain of the region is complex. Mountains separate river valleys, with most people living in the deltas of the region's principal rivers. Southeast Asia has six major river systems: the Brahmaputra, the Irrawaddy, the Salween, the Chao Phraya, the Mekong, and the Hong (Red).

Southeast Asia is a region with large cities. Major Southeast Asian cities include Dhaka with a population of 11,560,000 and Chittagong (3,271,000) in Bangladesh, Rangoon 3,874,000) in Myanmar, Bangkok (6,486,000) in Thailand, and Ho Chi Minh City (4,619,000) and Hanoi (3,977,000) in Vietnam. Finally, Singapore is a city with a population of 4,253,000.

East Asia   Other World East Asia is made up of China and Korea. Of these, China is by far the most important. China is the world's most populous and third-largest state in area. One out of every five people on the planet is Chinese. China may be divided into six parts: China, the lands to the east and south of the Great Wall; Manchuria; Inner Mongolia; Sinkiang; Tibet; and Taiwan. Today Taiwan is held by the Nationalist Chinese who were driven from the Mainland in 1949. However, most Chinese in both Taiwan and on the Mainland consider Taiwan to be part of "greater" China.

As might be expected, China has a complex geography. High mountains, deserts, and endless forests surround China, except along the 4,000-mile east coast. All of this has contributed to China's historic isolation from the states to the north and west.

In the west the Tibetan Plateau reaches heights of 12,000 feet. The part called Sinkiang (Xinjiang) is an isolated flat land surrounded by mountains. It is dry land inhabited by Turkic-speaking peoples. Here are located some of the world's highest mountains. Much of this region is underpopulated because it is too cold, too dry, too high, and too remote.

The northeast includes Inner Mongolia and Manchuria. This area has cold, long winters. Manchuria was the site of the puppet-state called Manchukuo. Established by the Japanese in 1932, Manchukuo served as a cover for the Japanese occupation of Manchuria and the later invasion of the Chinese heartland. While it existed, the last surviving member of the Manchu Dynasty, Henry Pu Yi, ruled Manchukuo. With the defeat of Japan in World War II, Manchukuo was abolished and China reestablished control. Today Manchuria is known for agriculture, mining, and manufacturing.

Most people live in the Chinese heartland. Although there are many cities here, most people live in the valleys of China's great rivers, the Huang Ho (Yellow), the Yangtze, and the Xi. Two of these rivers, the Huang Ho and the Yangtze, rise in the same area as the Mekong and Brahmaputra. Finally, the Xi is not important because of its length, which is only about 300 miles, rather it is an important source of river commerce between the great city of Guangzhou and the Macao-Hong Kong areas. Once known as the Pearl, this river was one of the entry points for European imperialists during the nineteenth century.

About 32 percent of China's 1.2 billion people live in urban areas. It should not be surprising to learn that China has more megacities than any other Other World Asian state. The largest and most important cities are in order of size: Shanghai (12,887,000), Beijing (10,848,000), Tianjin (9,156,000), Hong Kong (6,855,125), Chongqing (4,900,000), Shenyang (4,828,000), and Guangzhou (3,893,000). The former Portuguese colonial city, Macao, has a population of only 461,833.

Other Asian Names   In Asia there are different names that have been used to describe regions or the continent as a whole during different historic periods. Two examples are the Orient and the Far East.

The Orient: In ancient times, the Latin root word Orient referred to the rising of the sun. Gradually the word came to mean eastern lands. At times it could mean anything to the east of Venice. During the eighteenth and nineteenth centuries, Europeans thought that anything along the eastern coast of the Mediterranean to the Pacific to be the Orient. So in old Constantinople (Istanbul), one could cross from "the West to the Orient" while remaining in the city, by crossing the Bosporus Strait. Today, the term *Orient* is usually used to refer to East Asia.

Far East: The Far East is simply a designation given to the general area of East Asia by Western imperialists. Like the terms "Near East" and "Middle East," the Far East designates the distance from the colonial capitals in Europe. Today this term is considered to be offensive to some nationalists.

RELIGION IN ASIA

As might be expected in a region so large, Asia has a complex religious heritage. There are at least five major religions or philosophies that have mass appeal. The major sects of Asia are Buddhism, Confucianism, Daoism (Taoism), Hinduism, and Islam. In addition to these major faiths, there are a number of others that are of local importance.

Buddhism

Both a religion and a philosophy, Buddhism was founded by an Indian prince, Gautama, around 550 B.C. Today there are more than 372 million Buddhists worldwide.[4] Buddhism is an acquired rather than a revealed religion like Christianity and Islam. Buddhists view life as a cycle of tribulation. The aim of the believer is to overcome life's suffering through following a series of steps or paths to reach nirvana. To the Buddhist, nirvana is a state of liberation from earthly desires. Buddhists also believe in reincarnation based on one's previous behavior. Although Buddhism began in India, the modern religion has the largest numbers of believers elsewhere. Centers of Buddhist worship are located in Sri Lanka, Tibet, China, and Southeast Asia.

Confucianism

Confucius was born around the same time as Buddha: 551 B.C. He was concerned with how society should be arranged. His ideas of social order have played an important part in the administration of Chinese society for over 2,000 years. Although Confucianism was originally a philosophy, temples and a ritual had developed by the first century A.D. Many emperors even proclaimed Confucianism as a state religion. Confucianism declined because of its association with the old imperial regime. Under Mao, Confucian temples were destroyed and believers severely persecuted. However, in recent years the government of the People's Republic has been more tolerant of this traditional Chinese system of belief. At the present time there are 6.4 million Confucians.

Daoism (Taoism)

Founded by Latose in the sixth century B.C., like Confucianism, Daoism was not supposed to be a religion but a way of finding peace in solitude. Later writers developed an elaborate ritual and built temples around what became the Daoist religion. Over time Daoism involved alchemy, magic, ghosts, saints, and gods. One major aim was to find the secret of immortality. Daoism has absorbed practices from both Buddhism and Confucianism. As a native Chinese religion, Daoism has had a great influence on art and literature. Daoists have survived revolution, communism, and the modern world to maintain a small foothold in modern China.

Hinduism

Originally a religion of India, Hinduism today has an estimated 837,262,000 believers worldwide, making it larger than either Buddhism or Confucianism.

The Ganges: The river is of great religious significance. Here at Varanasi, Hindus bathe in its sacred waters. SOURCE: EARL HUFF

Hinduism is one of the world's oldest religions, reaching back 4,000 years. It has no founder, and recognizes numerous traditions and gods, making Hinduism a religion of great diversity. Most Hindus would emphasize that while using different paths, they strive to attain liberation for the soul from a series of lifetimes. The ultimate goal of this cycle reincarnation is to achieve a purity and union with God. One of the features of Hinduism has been the emergence of a caste system that includes four classes: priests, rulers, peasants, and artisans. Sometimes called a fifth class, the untouchables have been discriminated against since early times. Author Stanley Wolpert has described the emergence of the untouchables class in India in the following way, "In all probability the subclass of untouchables emerged in the late Aryan age, recruited first perhaps from those . . . who performed tasks that were considered "unclean" such as the work of tanners, associated with animal carcasses, and that of sweepers, especially among the ashes of cremation grounds."[5] Although officially outlawed in employment in modern India, the caste system still remains a social feature of Hindu life.

Islam

The basic ideas of Islam are discussed in some detail in Chapter 8. Islam became an important force in South Asia through invasion in the sixteenth century. Traders along "the Silk Road" spread the religion into China. Today there are 869 million Moslems living in Asia. The most important Moslem majority states are Afghanistan, Bangladesh, Indonesia, and Pakistan. However, there are large Moslem minorities in India, China, and the Philippines.

 CASE STUDIES

1. THE PEOPLE'S REPUBLIC OF CHINA: THE DRAGON

The History of Old China

Many in China place an emphasis on fate. People living in China during the last 175 years would be quick to point out that fate has not been kind to them during this period.

In its preface, a Chinese publication states their frustration in the following way:

> The year 1840, the gate of feudal China was opened by the rumble of gunfire in the Sino-British Opium War, turning the country into a semi colonial and semi feudal society that lasted for more than a century.

Writing about the same subject, the author states further:

> Heavy is the heart whenever looking back to this period of history: The corrupted rulers, the endless wars, the slowly developed economy, the people in deep distress, and the foreign policies humiliating the country and forfeiting its sovereignty.[6]

During the nineteenth century, China fought and lost the so-called "Opium Wars." In these conflicts, Chinese authorities attempted to stop the importation of opium, which was being used by British businessmen to pay for their purchases of tea and other luxury goods. In 1860, during one of these conflicts, the British burned the Emperor's Beijing summer palace in retaliation for the Chinese execution of Western hostages.[7] In 1900, a nationalist called the Society of Righteous and Harmonious Fists, or Boxers, moved against foreign missionaries, businessmen, and diplomats in China. The Chinese leadership attempted to take advantage of the Boxer uprising to oust foreign interests from China. The humiliating defeat of the Boxers resulted in a fatal weakening of the imperial government, leading to its complete collapse in 1911.

After the empire, China degenerated into a land of warlords and conflict, culminating in the famous civil war between the communists and the nationalists. That war began in 1927 and did not end until the final defeat of the nationalist forces in 1949.

To make matters worse, the Japanese forces took advantage of Chinese disunity to occupy Manchuria in 1931. It was there that they established the satellite state, Manchukuo.

In 1937, the Japanese invaded China proper. They did not leave China until the Japanese surrender in 1945.

The civil war between the Chinese communists and nationalists continued until the communists' victory in 1949. The leader Chiang Kai-shek took the surviving nationalists to the island of Formosa, setting up a dispute over the island's sovereignty that continues to the present day. The civil war and World War II cost untold millions of Chinese lives. These conflicts also set back Chinese economic development for a generation or more.

New China Under Mao

We communists never conceal our political views. Definitely and beyond all doubt, our future or maximum program is to carry China forward to socialism and communism.[8]
MAO ZEDONG

In 1949, the Chinese Communists under the leadership of Mao Zedong (Mao Tse-Tung) were able to unify the mainland under one rule for the first time in half a century. Early on, Mao had recognized that the Chinese experience was different from that of Russia. The strength of the party was in the peasants of the countryside, not the urban proletariat! Mao argued that in "semi-colonial and semi-feudal" China, "the broad peasant masses" had simply "risen to fulfill their historic mission to overthrow the rural feudal power." He further stated that, "Every revolutionary comrade should know that the national revolution requires a profound change in the countryside."[9]

With the arrival of Chinese communist rule on October 1, 1949, struggle and pain for the average person in China did not end. During the rule of Mao, at least three traumatic events overshadowed any accomplishments of the regime. These horrible trials for the Chinese people were the Korean War, the Great Leap Forward, and the Cultural Revolution.

China entered the Korean War against the United States when 2.3 million "volunteers" crossed into Korea on October 25, 1950. Using the slogan "Resist America, Aid Korea," the Chinese fought the United Nations (UN) forces to a stalemate along the 38th parallel until a truce was signed in July of 1953.[10]

The human cost of this conflict was terrible for both the Chinese and the Koreans. Geoffrey Stern has put the losses this way:

> In a war of firepower against manpower, the U.S. put Chinese and North Korean deaths at 1.5 million. If this seems incredible, there are Chinese sources which put it even higher.[11]

The Great Leap Forward (1958–1960) was a disaster for the Chinese economy. Mao and the party leadership attempted to bypass the traditional steps of the development process to create a modern industrial and agricultural state overnight. Planners in the cities ordered Chinese farmers to ignore traditional agricultural methods to create communes. Workers in the cities were told to industrialize in ways that were sometimes called "backyard steel mills" by detractors in the West. The result of this misadventure was famine in the countryside and economic disaster in the cities. Mao quietly abandoned this experiment in 1960.

What the Great Leap Forward did to the economy, the Cultural Revolution (1966–1976) did to Chinese civilization. This campaign began as an attempt by Mao to purge China of any opposition. It quickly spread to an attack on intellectuals, teachers, artists, professionals, and progressives not adhering to Mao's authority in the party. Before it ended with Mao's death, the Cultural Revolution had resulted in the imprisonment of thousands and the destruction of China's art and architecture.

China After Mao: The "Ka-Ching" Dynasty

To get rich is glorious.
DENG XIAOPING[12]

Deng Xiaoping was fond of the story of the black cat and the white cat to illustrate his change in the economic course of China. He would point out that the color of the cat did not matter so long as it caught the mouse. China was opened to the West for development when Deng began what became known as the second revolution in 1978. In 1979, he led a delegation to the United States with the purpose of increasing trade. In an ever-increasing process, Western business interests embraced the opportunity to do business with China.

To be sure, there have been setbacks in this development. The most serious event was the 1989 suppression of the pro-democracy movement in Tiananmen Square. However, China's admission to the World Trade Organization (WTO) and the selection of China to host the Olympic Games both signal that China will be a major economic player during the first half of the twenty-first century.

Deng's rule can be characterized as one that moved the economy away from the old communist dogma and central planning toward a more modern free-market mechanism. However, as the Tiananmen Square tragedy demonstrated, he would not tolerate any political reforms that would set in motion a challenge to the rule of the Communist Party.

China today is a paradox. It is still a state controlled by the Communist Party. At the same time China has an economy that is rapidly becoming one of the most "free-wheeling, rough and tumble" capitalist systems in the world! How can these two seemingly contradictory positions be reconciled? The position taken here is that the People's Republic is in the transitional stage of moving from a totalitarian to a one-party authoritarian state. In this case, twenty-first century China is following a course already largely completed on Taiwan. The outcome of this process may be something like fascist Spain during the final years of General Franciso Franco's rule. In this case the party will continue to hold on to power by opposing any organization or group that could evolve into a force that might challenge the party organization's grip on power. At the same time the economy will be left largely free to continue to grow at one of the world's fastest rates. Unlike other states in Asia, China is also insulated from world economic downturns because of a huge domestic market with unmet needs.

China's Future: Snow is a fifth-grade student who lives 100 miles south of Beijing in Shandong Province. SOURCE: FORREST

Pepsi Street: Shanghai's famous shopping street, the Nanjing Road, is called Pepsi Street by the locals because of the large Pepsi Cola signs that are placed on every lamppost.
SOURCE: JOE WEATHERBY

American companies have been quick to recognize the potential of the Chinese marketplace. In a statement made in 2005, Myron Brilliant, vice president for East Asia, U.S. Chamber of Commerce said, "The United States ranked second among China's global trading partners in 2004 and China was again the third largest trading partner for the United States." He went on to point out that, "U.S. exports to China have grown by 114 percent since 2000, five times faster than to any other country."[13]

To be sure there are potential sources of unrest. Perhaps the greatest threat to stability is the disparity of income between rural and urban China. However, the euphoria generated by China's admission to the WTO and being selected to host the Olympic Games should buy the authorities time to stabilize the situation before serious problems can develop.

Addressing the problem of inequality, Joseph Caron, Canadian Ambassador to China said, "There are ongoing debates on change and stability in China." He then stated that,

> Stability is linked to representative institutions and accountability, rule of law and good governance. On the ground, at the level of individuals, this means rights and individual freedoms, equity, justice and probity, the free flow of information and the end of endemic corruption. It also means freedom from undue influence by those in power.[14]

Anyone who has not been to China within the last 10 years cannot imagine the kind of growth that has occurred in places such as Hong Kong, Shanghai, and

Beijing. Even provincial towns such as Suzhou and Taian have modern high-rise buildings.

In China, the Communist Party is attempting to expand economically while keeping a tight grip on all forms of political expression. The question remains, can a modern economy develop while ignoring political expression?

Ambassador Caron also pointed out that, "Among the top twenty developed countries in the world, no country has achieved and sustained its standards of living without respect for individual rights, rule of law, and representative institutions." [15]

What the Chinese citizens want is stability. Will they be content if the Party remains so long as it provides the kind of environment that will allow them to enjoy the material benefits of the modern world? What they fear is the kind of uncertainty and chaos that occurred with the collapse of communism in Russia. No one can predict if this model of political control and economic openness will succeed.

In addition to its domestic problems, China also has two difficult security problems that must eventually be dealt with. First and foremost is the problem of a prosperous, democratic Taiwan that might make moves toward formal independence. Here the mainland party leadership must respond to the concerns of mainland nationalists who oppose any talk of separation while avoiding provoking the United States into resuming a formal military backing of Taiwan.

A nuclear North Korea is another thorny foreign policy issue for China. Here a desperate "saber-rattling" Korean leadership could force the introduction of nuclear arms into Japan and South Korea. The specter of a forward-deployed American nuclear force projecting a viable presence off the Chinese coast as the result of Korea's behavior provides additional headaches for Chinese planners. Either of these two issues could resume China's isolation and cause a strengthening to all the economic gains recently made. This could cause social unrest and result in the downfall of the current regime.

2. INDIA: THE ELEPHANT

Although Vasco da Gama opened the European route to India, it was the English who were to exercise primary rule over the subcontinent. At first, European penetration of this part of the world was hindered by the previously mentioned Treaty of Tordesillas, which had divided the colonial world between Portugal and Spain. However, after the Protestant Reformation, Holland and England were no longer restrained from challenging the Portuguese and the Spanish monopoly of Asian trade.

Few could have imagined that when Captain William Hawkins sailed his flagship, *Hector*, to India, on the East India Company's first visit, that the English would grow in power until they ruled all of southern Asia! The English presence in the region lasted from the *Hector*'s arrival in 1608 until India and Pakistan gained full independence in 1947.[16]

The English arrived in India only a year after the founding of Jamestown in 1607. However, they stayed in India more than 350 years. The British impact on

Indian culture is profound. Today India is the world's largest English-speaking nation. Although there are many Indian dialects, English is still the only universally understood language. The schools, universities, hospitals, courts, and even government have an English base.

The British East India Company came to India solely for trade when it established its first factory at Surat in 1612. The first century of British trade in India was accompanied by struggles with both Indian and European leaders. To British thinking, this situation required a military response. This period resulted in the conversion of the East India Company from a mere trading company into the de facto rulers of India. This situation of private company colonial rule was to last until Queen Victoria appointed the first Viceroy of India in 1858.

Under British colonial rule, nineteenth-century India achieved a measure of economic development. In the cities, the emergence of an Indian industrial class was well underway. The British also brought new lands under irrigation, thereby increasing agriculture.

A side effect of this activity was the emergence of a Western-educated Indian middle class. These "new Indians" demanded a greater role in political affairs. In 1885, the self-appointed Indian Congress movement first met to discuss social and political issues. In a manner not unlike the earlier American Continental Congress, these educated Hindu Indians demanded reforms from Britain, not revolution. However, by 1906, a more radicalized national congress was demanding nothing less than self-rule for India. By 1920, even relatively pro-British Indians such as Mohandas Gandhi were openly and actively opposing continued British rule. Gandhi's nonviolent resistance movement provided a base for mass support that complemented the political efforts of the Indian National Congress.

In the same year that the Indian National Congress first demanded self-rule, another organization of nearly equal significance was formed. The Moslem League demanded that the British create a separate Moslem state in Pakistan.

During World War II India supported the British by sending large numbers of troops to fight for the Empire. At the same time, the Germans and the Japanese tried to foment rebellions in India by attempting to recruit Indian prisoners of war into nationalist armies of liberation. The Japanese movement was called the Indian National Army and was led by Subhas Chandra Bose. The Germans sponsored a movement called the Free Indian Legion. Although these movements may have had as many as 40,000 volunteers, it is believed that no more than 7,000 ever were committed to combat. These nationalist movements were discredited by the defeat of fascism and became only a footnote to the history of World War II.[17]

As World War II ended, Britain reluctantly recognized its inability to continue governing South Asia. It announced that it was going to shortly withdraw from the region. In February 1947, amid growing Hindu–Moslem violence, the British Labor government announced a withdrawal date. The Hindus under Mohandas Gandhi and Moslems led by Mohammed Ali Jinnah tried but failed to reach agreement on the establishment of a single Indian state. In August 1947, British India was divided into a Moslem Pakistan and a majority Hindu India. Because large minorities of Hindus and Moslems were caught on the wrong side of the new borders, a population exchange became necessary. During this process, 16 million people were forced to move, while another 500,000 people died in the religious violence that followed independence. This period provokes anger in both India and Pakistan more than 50 years after partition.

The creation of two states did not end communal strife. Just as conflicts between Moslems and Hindus were instrumental in the division of British India into two states, later tensions between the Punjabi of West Pakistan and the Bengalis of East Pakistan resulted in the 1971 creation of a separate state in the east called Bangladesh. Pakistan remains as a Moslem state in the West.

India became free of British rule in 1947. The Chinese mark their independence from colonialism with the establishment of the People's Republic in 1949. At that time most observers would have considered India to be ahead of China. Since that time China has endured major wounds that have resulted in the deaths of millions. Despite these setbacks, why is China economically ahead of "democratic" India today? Several answers should be apparent to the reader. First, China abandoned its state planning in favor of moving toward an open free-market system starting in 1979. India has only begun to reform its creaking, inefficient socialist system.

In spite of all, India has begun to see some improvement. In recent years, Indian reforms have been recognized by the outside world for increased growth and stabilizing prices. The electronics business is now world class.

India still has a long way to go before challenging China. The per-capita income of India is only one third that of China. India is still ranked by the World Bank as 90th out of 146 countries on the corruption index.[18] It will be almost impossible to make lasting improvements in India before these problems are addressed.

Despite talk of economic reform, the climate for business investment is far better in China than in India. Unlike China, India has failed to get control of the growth of its population. India's population is increasing at the astounding rate of 50,000 people a day. No developing country will be able to secure economic prosperity for its people without controlling birth rate. China has often been criticized for its almost draconian birth control methods. Nevertheless, the government has reduced the Chinese population growth to around 1 percent. At the present time, more than 250 million people in population-growing India still live below the government's official poverty line.[19]

The other great internal problem in India is, like it was in 1947, sectarianism. In recent years, a Hindu movement called the "Saffron Tide," the Hindu color, has come to prominence. The Hindu nationalist Bharatiya Janata Party became a rival to the old Congress Party as the ruler of India. Like European nationalists of the 1930s, the BJP focused on "scapegoats" to gain most Hindu support. The more than 100 million Indian Moslems were particularly targeted, but the movement also singled out Christians and Jews.

After several years of BJP rule, a new coalition called the U.P.A. (United Progressive Alliance), dominated by the old Congress Party, has been elected and taken power. The coalition promises to repair India's secular fabric and restore India's prestige abroad. Internationally, Prime Minister Manmohan Sing has taken steps to "cool down" the continuing dispute with Pakistan over Kashmir.

On the domestic front, Congress Party Chairman Sonia Gandi recently said, "We are out to repair India's secular fabric." She then added, "We are proud that we are once more a society that celebrates its diversity, led by a government that stands by its commitment to defeating prejudice and discrimination."[20] In a country with dozens of religions and a long history of sectarian conflict, the threat of parties like the BJP returning to power is always present.

Finally, the Indian political system is democratic in name only. Political offices are regularly bought and sold. The courts operate with a system of "rule by law" not "rule of law" making judges and high officials above the law. There is widespread police corruption rendering many personal freedoms, including the "freedom from fear," meaningless. Until the "world's largest democracy" is ready to address these issues in a straightforward manner, there will be little chance for India to become a major player in world affairs.

3. THE FOUR ASIAN TIGERS: TAIWAN, HONG KONG, SINGAPORE, AND SOUTH KOREA

Introduction

With one exception—Thailand—the nations of Southeast and East Asia share a common past: colonization by outside powers. Burma, Malaysia, Singapore, Brunei, and Hong Kong were ruled by the British; Indonesia was Dutch; Indochina (Vietnam, Cambodia, and Laos) was French; the Philippines were first under Spanish rule then under the Americans. In both the nineteenth and twentieth centuries parts of China were controlled by foreign powers including Britain, Russia, Germany, Japan, Portugal, and the United States. In the twentieth century both Korea and Taiwan were occupied by Japan. Typically, boundaries drawn by the colonial powers paid little attention to the ethnic makeup of the lands they administered, so people with well-established cultural identities were often divided. Just as often, diverse ethnic groups were combined into larger political units. This ethnic mix was often complicated by the addition of large Chinese and Indian minorities who were either transported or encouraged to settle there by the colonial powers. Consequently, when the regions were granted independence, the newly formed states often lacked the sense of nationhood in terms of a nation-state. Cohesion, when it existed, was often nothing more than the common impulse to rid the region of the taint of colonial rule. In the process of forming modern entities, these new Asian nations have strongly opposed any outside pressures as interventions into their rights as sovereign states. The memory of the humiliation of colonial rule dies hard. As author Aeba Takanori has put it,

> The negative perception of foreign control remains as if explosive magma flows within the hearts of the people in these regions.[21]

Thus far, four states have been able to channel a new self-confidence in their ability to compete with the best that the developed world now has to offer. Called the Asian Tigers, these states can serve as models for their neighbors still wallowing in anger and self-pity.

Taiwan

On the mainland, Taiwan is called Chinese Taipei. The confusion over the island's name recalls one of the world's longest-lasting disputes: over which China rules China? Both the People's Republic of China (communist) and Taiwan (nationalist) officially endorse the concept that Taiwan is part of China. After more than 50 years, they still disagree over who is the legitimate ruler of China.

When 2 million members of the defeated nationalist (Kuomintang) fled from the mainland to China's smallest province, Formosa (Taiwan) in 1949, few observers gave them a chance for long-term survival. The United States, their principal supporter, was braced to abandon the nationalists to their fate. However, when North Korea attacked South Korea in June 1950, the Nationalists received a "new lease on life." The Truman administration recognized that an active nationalist movement could serve as a sufficient threat to the mainland to check Chinese intentions in Korea. The United States placed elements of the Pacific Fleet between the mainland and the nationalists, thus preventing an almost certain communist occupation of the island.

Since the Korean War, Taiwan has not only survived but also prospered. Economically, the Republic of China's development has been remarkable. Taiwan's economy is made up of textiles, clothing, electronics, processed foods, and chemicals, along with agricultural products and fishing. This means that the average citizen of Taiwan earns as much or more than his counterpart in South Africa, Greece, Portugal, or the Czech Republic. *The Economist of London* Economic Freedom Index ranks Taiwan ahead of rival Japan.[22]

Politically, the Republic of China has evolved from an authoritarian state under martial law headed by the Nationalist Party, to a fairly open democracy where, for the first time, an opposition candidate was elected president in 2000. The president, Chen Shui-bian, is a fervent nationalist who in the past has opposed unification with the mainland. Traditional politicians like their mainland counterparts advocated a one-China policy. They simply disagreed over who should run the "one China." The communist government has consistently offered to consider a one China, two systems formula similar to the one applied to Hong Kong.

Like their counterparts on the mainland, the leaders of Taiwan face a dilemma both politically and economically. Almost half of the Taiwanese people seem to favor more political contact with the People's Republic. At the same time, they continue to elect supporters of the presidents who are for independence.

Economically, contact with the mainland is exploding. Since 2002 China has passed the United States as Taiwan's largest trading partner. In 2004, China accounted for 18 percent of Taiwan's foreign trade.[23] According to He Sizhong, director of the economic bureau of the Taiwan Bureau of Affairs of the State Council (PRC), Taiwan-funded businesses in China exceed 65,000. Contracted Taiwan investment in China is more than 82 billion U.S. dollars.[24]

Many members of the defeated Nationalist Party have grown to accept eventual reunification with the mainland. President Chen has advocated a "no haste, be patient" policy in furthering ties with the mainland. In this potentially explosive situation, the United States has attempted to play an important role in resolving this conflict. In 1949, the Nationalists talked of retaking the mainland. Now they talk of defensive engagement with the mainland. The American role is to reassure the Taiwanese that they will remain militarily strong enough to deter an attack, but not so strong as to encourage more talk of independence. The main American hope is that economic integration will, over time, heal the bad feelings and suspicions on both sides, leading to a peaceful settlement.

It is clear that Taiwan has actually if not legally recognized independence. Taiwan maintains political separation while increasing economic integration with the mainland. It is in everyone's interest to continue to maintain the status quo with the "ideal of one China two systems." The alternative to a peaceful evolution is almost too serious to contemplate. The leaders of the United States, the People's Republic, and the Republic of China have each made the danger of the situation abundantly clear.

President George W. Bush stated on a Cable News Network (CNN) broadcast that while he supported a one China policy uniting China and Taiwan, the United States would do whatever it took to defend Taiwan from attack. In the same interview, he was quoted as saying, "We need a peaceful resolution. . . . Our nation will help Taiwan defend herself. . . ."[25] The American ability to balance the twenty-first century interests of the People's Republic of China and the Republic of China promises to be very interesting indeed.

Hong Kong

The story of Hong Kong is one of the most interesting in Asia. When it was ceded to Great Britain by the Treaty of Nanjing in 1842, Hong Kong was a barren island. Prior to the British arrival, fishermen and pirates had mainly used the harbor. When it became British, Hong Kong's future was assured. Author Trea Wiltshire has described the British arrival in the following way,

> When Hong Kong became one of the spoils of the Opium War, merchant princes such as William Jardine and John Dent were quick to relocate.

Later the author states,

> The secure base enabled the merchants to form banks that would service these rapid developments of the colonial island and its Treaty Port Sisters. It also provided a convenient headquarters for the fledgling consular services that took root in each of the coastal outposts and for the British Army and Navy.[26]

The growth of Hong Kong as a British colony was accelerated by two events. In 1860, Kowloon and Stone Cutters Island were ceded to the colony by China's signing the Beijing Convention. In 1898, the New Territories, a large area adjacent to Kowloon, was leased to the colony for 99 years. The additions of land allowed the inhabitants to expand past the limits of Hong Kong Island.

During the twentieth century the colony prospered as a door to China until the Japanese occupation during World War II. The British reoccupied the colony in 1945.

It has been said that the greatest postwar event contributing to the growth of capitalist Hong Kong was the communist victory over the mainland in 1949. Why can this be viewed as a positive event in Hong Kong? Simply stated, the communist victory ended the dominance of Shanghai as China's window to the outside world.

After 1949, China's isolation allowed Hong Kong to become the "transshipment point" for most goods and services passing to and from China. Hong Kong became one of the world's leaders in container shipping, and the manufacture of clothing, toys, calculators, radios, travel goods, handbags, and artificial flowers.

In the 1980s it became clear to the British that the lease on the new territories would not be renewed when it ended in 1997. After months of negotiation, the Chinese and the British agreed to Hong Kong's return to Chinese sovereignty under the "one China two systems" arrangement. Under this arrangement, sovereignty would be transferred from Britain to China, but a great deal of autonomy would remain in the hands of the Hong Kong people for 50 years.

Thus far one China two systems has worked, but with mixed results. Economically the two systems have been able to thrive side by side. Politically, Hong Kong has had an often bumpy relationship with China. Politically, it is still possible for the U.S. Department of State to report,

> Hong Kong with a population of nearly 7 million remains an international city and one of the world's most open and free economics. Hong Kong residents enjoy a strong respect for the rule of law and civil liberties.[27]

However, the authorities in China have recently questioned some of the "free wheeling" political protests that occur in the former British colony. Recently China's President Hi Jintao compared Hong Kong to the more politically subdued Macau, saying that the people of Hong Kong "should summarize your experience, look for your shortcomings, and constantly raise your governance ability." This mild criticism masked the threat of a more heavy-handed Chinese involvement, should Hong Kong politics ever get out of hand.[28]

When the 1997 British handover took place, many businessmen assumed that Hong Kong would slip into economic decline. Even stalwarts like Jordine and Matheson moved its corporate headquarters to Bermuda after a 170-year stay in the colony. The most optimistic observers believed that Hong Kong would be eclipsed by a resurgent Shanghai; they were all to be proved wrong!

In 2005 Hong Kong was listed first in the world on the index of economic freedom.[29] Other reports list Hong Kong as the world's eleventh largest trading entity. The average income of residents of Hong Kong in 2005 is more than $25,000.[30]

Thousands of Hong Kong businessmen expanded into Chinese manufacturing located in centers near Hong Kong. Michael de Goiyer of Hong Kong Baptist University estimated that as many as 250,000 workers cross the border between China and Hong Kong every day.[31]

Hong Kong has been able to reinvent itself as one of Asia's most important centers for service. Today Hong Kong focuses on shipping, banking, and finance.

The city is noted for rule of law, efficient service, and freedom from corruption. With exploding economic growth in China, Hong Kong could rival New York and London as financial centers within the coming years. Hong Kong also remains particularly advantaged to capitalize on the resources of China. It will continue to remain a major Asian tiger in the twenty-first century.

Singapore

According to Dorothy Perkins, the name *Singapore* literally means "the lion city" when translated into Indian Sanskrit.[32] Modern Singapore is one of the Asian tigers. Situated at the end of the peninsula of Malaysia, this city-state of 4 million people is one of the world's most important trading centers. Because of its location at the mouth of the Strait of Malacca, which leads from the Indian Ocean, Singapore is called the Gateway to the Pacific.

Although the area now called Singapore had been a trading town in early times, it was only a loosely populated island when the Malacca Sultanate ceded it to the British East India Company in 1819. It was then that the company representative, Sir T. Stamford Raffles, founded the city of Singapore. In 1824, the trading post came under the control of the British government. It was to remain a British colony until 1942 when the Japanese captured it. The British reoccupied the island with the defeat of Japan in 1945. Singapore gained full independence from Britain in June 1959.

When the British first established it as a trading post, few could have guessed that a century and a half later Singapore would be one of the world's most important commercial centers. Today, this multicultural city-state has a per capita income of $23,700 U.S. This makes the 4 million residents the third most prosperous people in Asia after Japan and Hong Kong.

The key to Singapore's success is more than just strategic geography. The political system is noted as paternalistic. Although a republic with free elections, the government keeps a tight hold on public order. The civil rights group, Reporters without Borders, ranks Singapore in the bottom fourth of countries on press freedom. Considering the diversity of Singapore's society both ethnically and religiously, this kind of control is understandable.

Singapore occupies a land area of only 255 square miles. Still, according to the *Economist*, Singapore ranks as the world's second highest on the Economic Freedom Index.[33] Observers have asked how a city-state with so few resources could become one of the world's centers for business. Kevin O'Conner, market analyst at CLSA Asia-Pacific Markets in Hong Kong replies, "They have to shape up to compete in the environment or die."[34]

Singapore has overcome its environment to create an investment-friendly atmosphere, making it a leader in corporate location, banking, technical manufacturing, and shipping. In 2004 the economy grew at an astounding 8.4 percent. Because the economy is only expected to grow by 3 to 5 percent in 2005 even the prime minister has called for even more business competitiveness. Prime Minister Lee Hsien said recently, "Our economy is at a turning point . . . restructuring has to continue." He then pointed out that because of the rise of China and India, Singapore had to become more lean and efficient.[35]

Singapore—not the United States or Japan—is the model for development currently being followed by the People's Republic of China. The Chinese hope to avoid the chaos of post-Communist Russia by keeping a tight hold on politics while letting a free-market economic system develop.

South Korea

Like the other tigers, Korea experienced both European and Asian colonial rule during the nineteenth and twentieth centuries. In 1900, Tsar Nicholas II ordered his troops into Northern China and Korea.[36] The Russian hold on these territories was strengthened by their participation in putting down the Boxer Rebellion in China. However, Russia lost everything when they were defeated in the Russo-Japanese War of 1904.

Japanese colonial rule was consolidated by 1910 when they annexed Korea. Korea was not to see the end of Japanese rule until their final defeat in World War II. At the Yalta Conference held in February 1945, the Allied Powers agreed to a number of secret provisions regarding Asia that were not made public until 1947. Among the Asian agreements was Russia's commitment to declare war on Japan within three months of the defeat of Japan. In return, Russia would get footholds in Manchuria and Korea to the 38th parallel. Hans Morgenthau graphically pointed out the continuing role that Korea has played in the great power struggle for Asia.

> The rivalry between Japan and Russia for control of Korea ended with the defeat of Russia in the Russo-Japanese War of 1904–1905. Japanese control of Korea, thus firmly established, was terminated with the defeat of Japan in World War II. From then on, the United States replaced Japan as a check upon Russian ambitions in Korea. China, by intervening in the Korean War, resumed its traditional interest in the control of Korea.[37]

The Korean War lasted from 1950 to 1953. Although the first great military conflict of the cold war, it ended in a stalemate with the opposing parties stretched along the 38th parallel in essentially the same place that they were before the war began. The war firmly divided North and South Korea into the separate states that exist today.

1953 saw South Korea completely devastated both socially and economically. The struggle on both fronts to become an important player in East Asia has been difficult for the South. With the exception of its military power, the communist North is almost a complete failure.

Today South Korea ranks fourth among the Asian tigers. However, considering the recent past, fourth is an impressive accomplishment. With an average income of $17,200 US, Koreans can boast that their individual earnings exceed those of both China and India in Asia, Argentina and Brazil in the Americas, and Poland and Latvia in Europe. Korea is third of the Asian states exporting products to the United States. Despite the global economic slowdown that occurred after the

September 11 attacks in New York and Washington, South Korea expects to continue to have both growing shipbuilding and automobile industries.

As South Korea enters the twenty-first century, two potential problems loom on the horizon. First, there is the economic threat coming from China in the market for low-cost goods. To compete, Korea must follow the examples of Japan, Taiwan, and Singapore by moving into the fields of high technology where their higher labor costs can be utilized effectively.

The second problem is in the often-hostile relations that the South has with North Korea. This conflict is one of the world's most dangerous flashpoints. However, there have been some halting moves on both sides aimed at improving relations. Nevertheless, the 38th parallel remains one of the most militarized borders existing today. It is clearly in the interest of both parties to move toward a normalization of relations, possibly leading to eventual reunification.

Everyone is familiar with the difficulties that have come with German reunification. The differences between North and South in Korea are far greater than those that existed between East and West Germany. Whether this conflict can be resolved in the foreseeable future is impossible to predict.

◆ FLASHPOINTS ◆

KASHMIR (JAMMU AND KASHMIR)

Kashmir has been called the "Switzerland of Asia." This area is probably the most beautiful spot in Asia. Here, there are lush valleys and shimmering lakes surrounded by the rugged mountains of the Karakorums and the Himalayas. It was to this region that the British colonials sent their families during the fever-ridden hot months in India. Like middle-class Americans who relocated to the mountains during the polio epidemics, the English believed that Europeans were safer from the tropical diseases common during the hot seasons if they were in the cool climate of Kashmir. Srinagar became the de facto British capital of India during the summer months.

Kashmir had been a Moslem state since the Mogul empire overran it in 1586. When the British occupied the area in 1846, they recognized Kashmir as a semi-independent state but placed a Hindu prince in charge. Hindus continued to rule locally under British tutelage until British withdrawal from South Asia in 1947.

When India and Pakistan were created out of old British India, most semi-independent states had to choose between joining India or Pakistan. At first the *maharaja* of Kashmir attempted to keep his state neutral, but large portions of the Moslem population revolted, forcing him to flee to India. Once in India, the Hindu *maharaja* declared Kashmir to be Indian against the will of the majority Moslem population. Indian troops were rushed to Kashmir to secure India's claim.

The result was the start of a conflict that continues to the present time. After three wars, Pakistan occupies about one-third and India two-thirds of Kashmir. In the 1980s, Moslem separatists renewed their fight for linking Kashmir with Pakistan. The result has been the continuation of a low-intensity war between the Moslem population, supported by Pakistan, and India. The conflict has ended the tourist trade and devastated the region. Now that both India and Pakistan have nuclear weapons, the small area of Kashmir constantly threatens to ignite a major conflict in South Asia.

In the spring of 2002, the conflict again reached a crisis level as both India and Pakistan alerted their nuclear forces and sent armies to the border. War was averted, but just barely. Everyone knows that a nuclear war in the Indian subcontinent would kill millions and possibly plunge the entire world into an economic depression.

In many ways, the dispute over Jammu and Kashmir is not unlike the one between Israel and the Palestinians. In both cases the parties to the dispute can cite "chapter and verse" to justify their particular points of view. Until recently both India and Pakistan used the inhabitants of the disputed territory as the foot soldiers for their larger conflict.

A 2004 return of a coalition with the Congress Party leading was elected to power in India. Pakistan returned to favor as a supporter of America in the war on terror. The United States and the allies occupied Afghanistan. These three events put a new emphasis on solving the Kashmir dispute. To avoid the spread of conflict from Afghanistan, the United States made it clear that India and Pakistan should move ahead on breaking the logjam over Kashmir.

Kashmir Peace Plan

Following a series of meetings between Indians, Pakistanis, and the Kashmiris, several peace plans had emerged. One of the most promising makes the following assumptions and proposals.

1. A totally independent Kashmir is not possible.
2. No party will agree to making the current boundary permanent.
3. The areas administered by India, Kashmir, Jammu, and Ladakh will become self-governing entities.
4. A loose federation of Kashmir, including both sides, will be created.
5. An all-Kashmir body representing both sides would handle regional issues such as tourism, water, environment, and transportation.
6. This federation would be completely demilitarized with each entity having only local police.
7. India and Pakistan would handle a joint foreign policy.
8. There would be open borders between India and Pakistan through Kashmir.
9. All parties to the conflict would agree that no plan could be implemented without the approval of the residents of the disputed territories.

Plans are easy to propose. This dispute is one of the longest running in the world. It will not end before all sides recognize that there must be a settlement before there can be a lasting peace.

CHINA'S BORDERS

It should not be surprising that with a state as old as China, the borders have changed many times. During times of power the Chinese borders have expanded and during periods of weakness the reverse has occurred. Three examples of Chinese border problems are offered here.

China and India: In the high mountainous border between India and China a dispute has existed since a savage territorial war broke out between the parties in 1962. At that time Chinese forces soundly defeated the Indian army. The Chinese forces were poised to advance into the Indian heartland when they suddenly halted. Forty years later it is believed that the Chinese intention may not have been territorial but political. The Chinese used this border dispute to assert political dominance over Asia while clearly relegating India to a distant second place. This action solidified the Chinese hold on Tibet and sent a warning to the Indians to tread carefully in their dealing with the mini states located on their northeastern border.

Today the strategic and economic relations between India and China are cooperative. In this new improved atmosphere, both parties signed a series of groundbreaking agreements in April 2005. One of these agreements was aimed at resolving the boundary dispute between the parties. In the agreement both sides agreed to resolve this dispute through peaceful means. They also agreed to make "meaningful and mutually acceptable adjustments to Boundary question, so as to arrive at a package settlement to the boundary question . . .".[38] There is hope that in this new atmosphere the old border issue can finally be settled.

China and Russia: In the nineteenth century Russia acquired more contiguous territory than any other state except the United States. Much of this new land was seized at the expense of a weakened China. Part of the border in Asia was finally fixed along the Amur River. As in other parts of the world, rivers change course and this causes conflict. Although the Russian presence has been guaranteed by treaties going back to the mid-nineteenth century, there is a great fear that a weakened Russia will eventually be forced out of Soviet Asia.

The sluggish, winding Amur opposite the city of Khabarovsk is the current source of tension. Here two strategic islands, Bolshoi Ussuri and Tarabarov, have been formed by the joining of the Amur and Ussuri Rivers. Although geographically part of China, they have been controlled by Russia since the 1930s. The running conflict over control of these two small islands almost led to an all out war in 1969.

For the Chinese who were in political ascendancy, control of the islands represented the rewriting of a historical injustice. For the Russians, who had only 6 million people in Asia, there was a fear that the loss of the islands was the first step that would lead to the eventual Chinese claim to all of Russian Asia.

An agreement on the border was signed in Beijing on October 4, 2004. This agreement was later ratified in both China and Russia. Under this agreement the border is the middle of the rivers and also a line crossing the middle of the islands. The actual demarcation of the 375-square kilometers was expected to be completed shortly. This agreement marked the first time in 300 years that the Chinese Russian border was entirely established.

Russian Foreign Minister Sergei Lavrov said, "The geopolitical significance of the document is that it closes the last border issues with China that have been open since the times of the Soviet Union."[39]

The South China Sea: China has laid claim to more than 80 percent of the South China Sea. Chinese military forces seized control of the Paracel Islands at the end of the Vietnam War. They expanded their influence by driving off Vietnamese naval forces and occupying the Spratly Islands in 1988. Chinese claims in the region conflict with those of Taiwan, the Philippines, Malaysia, and Vietnam.

This dispute is a classic one about previously unimportant rocks and other spots on the ocean that suddenly became important because of the potential for oil recovery. In this case, China is the big power. This has prompted unlikely smaller players like the Philippines and Vietnam to unite to challenge unilateral Chinese moves in the South China Sea. If oil is discovered in large quantities this could become one of the Other World's new areas of conflict.

KOREA: NORTH AND SOUTH

North Korea

Although North and South Korea share a common language, history, and culture, they remain bitterly divided politically. While the South Koreans have developed into a major Asian powerhouse, the North Koreans have declined into an economic "basket case." North Korea's foreign trade could be as low as 1 percent of South Korea's. It is known that North Korea must import almost half of its food from China. Even so, the people of the North are in an almost constant threat of starvation. Fifty years after the end of the Korean War, most observers would consider North Korea either a failing or a failed state.

North Korea's leadership presides over a state that caused international concern when its intention to develop nuclear weapons became known. North Korea agreed to halt the development of a nuclear program in 1994, but denounced that agreement when subjected to charges of cheating in October 2002. North Korea resumed its nuclear program in 2003. In response, the West ended foreign aid and technical help on safe nuclear power.

A nuclear North Korea is a direct threat to South Korea and Japan. Any conflict would most certainly draw the United States into it. Although most believe that the South, backed by the United States, would prevail, millions would be killed. There is hope that this crisis may yet see a peaceful resolution. Six-sided talks between North Korea, South Korea, China, Japan, Russia, and the United States resulted in a statement that foreign aid would be linked to a verifiable agreement given by the North that it had ended its nuclear weapons program.

An interesting development occurred in 2005. Earlier, the six power talks with North Korea had ended with a Korean walkout. As they resumed, the European Community was improving its offer of aid and technology transfers to Iran if they abandoned parts of their nuclear program. Some observers speculated that the European offer made to Iran might be a model that could be used in negotiations with North Korea.

The fear of a desperate, nuclear-armed North was twofold. First, a nuclear armed North would force both Japan and South Korea to either develop or allow the storage of similar weapons on their soil. Second, a cash-short North Korea might be tempted to sell nuclear weapons or technology to other states, leading to the proliferation of these weapons of mass destruction throughout the Other World.

The one bright light on the political horizon is the idea that the cultural contacts between the North and South will have a life of their own. The road to reconciliation may be long and halting, but if successful, one of the world's most dangerous flashpoints will become history.

SUMMARY

Asia is the world's largest and most diverse continent. The lands of Asia include the world's highest mountain ranges, great river systems, foreboding deserts, rich agricultural regions and steaming jungles. China and India are the world's two most populous countries.

China and India are also the two major political powers on the continent. The four smaller political and economic "powerhouses" are Taiwan, Hong Kong, Singapore, and South Korea.

Politically, the Peoples Republic of China is emerging from the political and economic sterility of a communist command economy into one of the most dynamic states in Asia. With other smaller states matching China's growth, the twenty-first century is likely to be an Asian one.

Review Questions

1. Briefly outline the tension between India and Pakistan.
2. What is the policy of "one China two systems"?
3. What is the dispute over Taiwan about?
4. What is the Paracel Islands dispute?
5. Who are the Asian tigers?

Key Terms

* **1949**—Date that Chinese communists drove the Nationalists off of the Mainland to Taiwan. This date is called "Liberation Day" on the Chinese Mainland.
* **Boxer Rebellion**—A rebellion at the end of the nineteenth and beginning of the twentieth centuries against foreign influence provoking military intervention by eight nations.
* **Buddhism**—The only major religion of China that was imported from the outside.
* **Cultural Revolution**—A period under Mao when the party used mob rule to eliminate opposition, and in so doing, destroyed much of the cultural heritage of China.
* **Daoism**—One of the three main religions of China. Along with Confucianism, Daoism is native to China
* **Great Leap Forward**—A period in the 1950s when the Chinese under Mao attempted to industrialize overnight.
* **Kashmir Dispute**—A conflict between India and Pakistan over the largely Moslem region of Indian Kashmir.
* **Marco Polo**—An early European visitor to China who wrote down his adventures and opened up knowledge of China to Western readers.
* **Opium Wars**—A series of nineteenth-century conflicts fought primarily between China and Britain to force China to trade goods in exchange for Western supplies of opium shipped from India.
* **The Silk Road**—Several land trade routes that were used to carry goods between China, India, and the West.

Useful Web Sites

China: www.china-embassy.org/eng
Taiwan: www.roc-taiwan.org
Pakistan: www.embassyofpakistan.org
India: www.indianembassy.org
Singapore: www.gov.sg

Notes

1. *Who Said What When: A Chronological Dictionary of Quotations* (London: Bloomsbury Publishing, 1988), p. 95
2. Ibid, p. 200. Also note that the Maxim machine gun was the first truly automatic gun. Adopted in 1884, it was the standard British infantry support weapon until after World

War I. It, and other guns like it, ended the horse cavalry as a serious instrument of war. See Eric Morris, Christopher Chant, Curt Johnson, H.P. Willmott, *Weapons and Warfare of the 20th Century* (Secaucus, NJ: 1976), p. 13.

3. Bill Gertz, "China Future Superpower," *Washington Times,* 29 August 2001. Accessed from Lexis-Nexis Academic database.
4. Sources for all figures on religion adherents taken from: *The World Almanac and Book of Facts 2005,* World Almanac Education Group, Inc., New York: 2005, p. 734.
5. Stanley Wolpert, *A New History of India,* 5th ed. (New York: Oxford University Press, 1997), p. 32.
6. *A Glimpse of Old China* (Beijing, China: China Pictorial Publishing House, 1995), p. 1.
7. Trea Wiltshore, *Encounters with China: Merchants, Missionaries, and Mandarins* (Hong Kong: Form Asia Books Ltd., 1995), p. 42.
8. Chairman Mao Tse-Tung, *Quotations from Chairman Mao Tse-Tung* (Peking: Foreign Language Press, 1966), p. 24.
9. Chairman Mao Tse-Tung, "Report of an Investigation into the Peasant Movement in Hunan," *Selected Works of Mao Tse-Tung, Vol. I* (Peking: Foreign Language Press, 1954), pp. 23–59.
10. Dorothy Perkins, *Encyclopedia of China: The Essential Reference in China: Its History and Culture* (New York: Checkmark Books, 2000), p. 259.
11. For more information on Chinese losses in Korea see Geoffrey Stern, *Atlas of Communism* (New York: Macmillan Publishing Company, 1991).
12. Quote attributed to Chairman Deng Xiaoping. J. D. Brown, *China: The 50 Most Memorable Trips* (New York: Macmillan Publishing Company, 1998), p. 532.
13. "U. S. China Economic Relationship," Testimony by Myron Brillant, Vice President U. S. Chamber of Commerce, House Committee on Ways and Means, *Congressional Quarterly,* Washington D.C., April 14, 2005.
14. Joseph Caron, "The Business of Doing Business with China: An Ambassador Reflects," *Ivey Business Journal Online,* May 2005, University of Western Ontario, Canada, p. 1.
15. *Idem.*
16. For an interesting account of the Portuguese, Dutch, and English struggle to control trade with India, see Wolpert, op. cit., pp. 135–148.
17. Don McCombs, Fred L. Worth, *World War II: 4,139 Strange and Fascinating Facts* (New York: Wings Books, 1938), pp. 278–279.
18. "Two Sides of India's Economic Miracle," India Express Online, Media Ltd., *Financial Express,* taken from Lexis-Nexis, the Academic Universe, April 20, 2005.
19. "Sino-Indian Economic Ties," *The Hindu* (India), 25 October 2000. Accessed from Lexis-Nexis Academic Universe.
20. "Indian Ruling Party Says Coalition Government A 'Historic Endeavor'," *Indian News Agency PTI.* Accessed from Lexis-Nexis, the Academic Universe, May 22, 2005.
21. Aeba Takanori, *Asian Magma and Japan-U.S. Relations: Journal of Japanese Trade and Industry,* 1 May 2001. Accessed from Lexis-Nexis Academic database.
22. *Pocket World in Figures 2005 Edition, The Economist* in association with Profile Books, London UK, 2005, p. 30.
23. "Taiwan-China Trade Up 33.1 Percent in 2004," *Agence France Press News,* Paris, taken from Lexis-Nexis, the Academic Universe, March 2, 2005.
24. "Mainland Approves Over 65,568 Taiwan-Funded Businesses," Xinhua News Agency, PRC, taken from Lexis-Nexis, the Academic Universe, June 29, 2005.
25. "Bush Says U.S. Will Defend Taiwan," *United Press International Dispatch,* 25 April 2001. Accessed from Lexis-Nexis, the Academic Universe.

26. Trea Wiltshire, *Encounters with China: Merchants, Missionaries, and Mandarins* (Hong Kong: Form Asia Books Ltd., 1995), pp. 170–171.

27. "U.S.-Hong Kong Policy Act Report," United States Department of State, U.S. News Service. Taken from Lexis-Nexis, the Academic Universe, April 1, 2005.

28. *Tiger on the Doorstep: Management Today*, Haymarket Publishing Services, Ltd., London, February 7, 2005.

29. Economic Freedom Index, *Pocket World in Figures, 2005 Edition*, *The Economist* in association with Profile Books, Ltd., London, 2005, p. 1.

30. *The World Almanac and Book of Facts 2005*, World Almanac Books, New York, 2005, p. 764.

31. Peter Godspeed, "Hong Kong Reborn: With a Form of Democracy and a Burgeoning Economy, What's Not to Like About the Hand Over?" *National Post*, Canada, March 12, 2005, p. A13.

32. Perkins, op. cit., p. 466.

33. Economic Freedom Index, *Pocket World in Figures, 2005, The Economist* in association with Profile Books, Ltd., London, 2005, p. 31.

34. "How Success Turns Local Heroes Into World Heroes: Companies in Energy and Service Sectors Draw Investors," *International Herald Tribune*, Paris, France, April 9, 2005, p. 16.

35. "Continued Economic Restructuring: A Key to Singapore's Future," P.M. Lee, Agence France Press, Paris, taken from Lexis-Nexis the Academic Universe, May 3, 2005.

36. Elizabeth Heresch, *The Empire of the Tsars: The Splendor and the Fall, Pictures and Documents 1896 to 1920* (Vienna: Stroitel Pub., 1991), p. 54.

37. Hans J. Morgenthau, *Politics Among Nations: The Struggle for Power and Peace*, 5th ed., Revised (New York: Alfred A. Knopf, Inc), pp. 183–184.

38. "China and India Sign Accord Aimed at Resolving Border Dispute," Agence France Press, taken from Lexis-Nexis the Academic Universe, April 11, 2005.

39. "Duma to Consider Ratification of Border Agreement with China," ITAR-TASS News Agency, Russia, taken from Lexis-Nexis the Academic Universe, May 19, 2005.

For Further Reading

Connor, Mary, *The Koreans: A Global Studies Handbook,* ABC-CLIO, Santa Barbara, CA, 2002.

Feigon, Lee. *Mao: A Reinterpretation,* Ivan Dee Publishing, Chicago, 2002.

Lijun, Seng. *China and Taiwan: Cross-Strait Relations Under Chen Shui-Bian,* Macmillan, New York, 2003.

Murthy, Ranjani. *Gender, Poverty, and Human Rights in Asia,* Macmillan, New York, 2003.

Saieh, Tony. *Governance and Politics of China,* Macmillan, New York, 2001.

The Middle East and North Africa

Joseph N. Weatherby

My own ambition is that the Arabs should be our first brown dominion, and not our last brown colony.

LAWRENCE OF ARABIA, 1919

Both the East and the West want to corrupt us from within, obliterate every distinguishing mark of our personality and snuff out the light which guides us.

MUAMMAR AL-QADDAFI

*E*verything in the Middle East changed on September 11, 2001. But the more that things in the Middle East change, the more they stay the same.

There is a saying in the West that the Middle East is a region too important to the outside world to allow it to be governed by Middle Easterners. The Middle East has played a pivotal role in world affairs since ancient times. Forming the land bridge between Asia, Africa, and Europe, the Middle East has the strategic attention of both the East and the West (see Figure 8.1).

The Middle East is also the birthplace of the world's three great monotheistic religions: Judaism, Christianity, and Islam. For more than 1,000 years, Islam has been the religion of 90 percent of the region's inhabitants. The effect of religion on politics is more pronounced in the Middle East than probably in any other region in the world.

The twentieth century witnessed one of the greatest transfers of wealth in history, as vast supplies of oil have been discovered in both the Arabian Peninsula and North Africa. This development prompted the bitter Western comment that

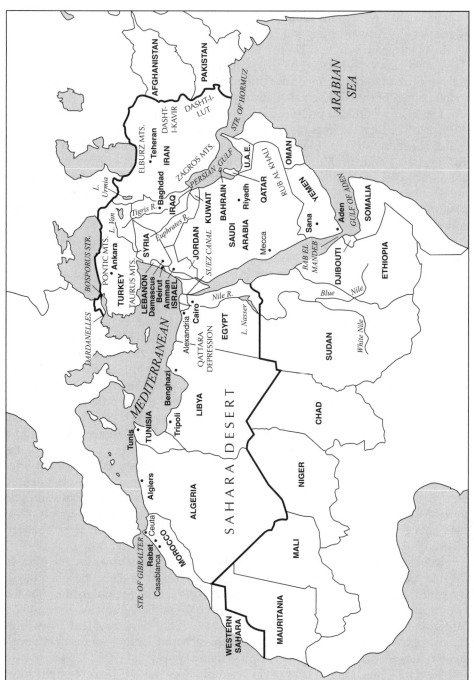

FIGURE 8.1 Political and Physical Characteristics of the Middle East and North Africa

"where there are Middle Easterners, there is oil." In the twenty-first century, Saudi Arabia, Kuwait, Iran, and Iraq accounted for more than 53 percent of the world's petroleum reserves. This oil is a primary fuel for the industries of Europe, the United States, and Japan. As newspaper headlines indicate, more issues critically important to the future of the United States and the Western world converge in the politics of the Middle East than anywhere else in the Other World.

This chapter offers a brief introduction to the Middle East and North Africa. After a discussion of geography and economics, we trace the history of the Middle East; the story of Islam; and the subsequent rise of nationalism in Egypt, Turkey, Iran, Saudi Arabia, and Israel. The essential aspects of Arab nationalism are also discussed. Finally, the central points of the Arab-Israeli dispute are outlined in the Flashpoints. The data in Table 8.1 illustrate the vast differences in population, wealth, and conditions of life in the North African and Middle Eastern countries.

Although most Americans can point to a map and identify some countries located in the Middle East, few have any idea what nations are actually included in the region. Even scholars fail to agree on the subject. The U.S. Department of Defense states categorically that there is no precise, generally accepted definition of the region variously called the Near East or Middle East.

Because, at times, all the area from the Atlantic coast of Morocco to Afghanistan has been included in this region, no one term seems to describe adequately the whole. The terms *Middle East* and *Near East* are inadequate, misleading, and culturally biased. They are misleading because they have been used to describe different places at different times in history. Originally, the Near East referred to the lands of the eastern Mediterranean, and the Middle East described the Indian empire controlled by Britain. The terms converged geographically only during World War II, when the British based their Near Eastern and Middle Eastern operations in Cairo. Because the active involvement of the United States in the region began during this period, Americans have tended to use the term *Middle East,* whereas Europeans continue to use the more traditional designation, *Near East,* to describe the same area. Even in the absence of this confusion, the terms *Middle East* and *Near East* are culturally biased from the standpoint of inhabitants of the region. Both terms describe the Other World in ways that are meaningful only in reference to the former colonial powers in Europe.

In an effort to avoid these pejorative labels, writers sometimes use the phrases *the Arab world* and *the Islamic world* as substitutes. Unfortunately, these words often confuse as much as they inform. *The Arab world* cannot accurately describe the region as a whole because the phrase ignores 67 million Iranians, 68.8 million Turks, and 5 million Jews living in Israel. Much of the same problem arises with the use of *the Islamic world.* Although Moslems account for most of the area's population, large Christian and Jewish minorities play pivotal roles. This term also implies a religious unity in Islam, which simply does not exist except on the most superficial level.

Despite these concerns, the terms *Middle East* and *North Africa* will be used in this chapter because of their common usage in the United States. The Middle

TABLE 8.1　Characteristics of Middle Eastern and North African Countries

Country	Population (millions)	Population Growth Rate %	Infant Mortality Rate (per 1,000 live births)	Population Under 15 Years of Age (%)	Life Expectancy (in years)	Urban Population (%)	Literacy Rate (%)	Arable Land (%)	Per Capita GDP ($US)
Middle East									
Bahrain	0.677	1.15	17.9	29.2	74.23	90	89.1	1	17100
Iran	67.503	0.86	42.9	31.6	69.96	66.7	79.4	10	7000
Iraq	25.374	2.7	52.7	41.1	68.7	67.2	40.4	12	1600
Israel	6.199	1.2	7.2	27.1	79.32	51.8	95.4	17	19700
Jordan	5.611	2.56	18.1	36.6	78.24	79	91.3	4	4300
Kuwait	2.257	3.44	10.3	28.3	77.03	96.3	83.5	0	18100
Lebanon	3.777	1.26	25.5	27.3	72.63	87.5	87.4	21	4800
Saudi Arabia	25.795	2.31	13.7	42.4	75.46	87.7	78.8	2	11800
Syria	18.016	2.34	30.6	39.3	70.03	50.1	76.9	28	3300
Turkey	68.893	1.09	42.6	27.8	72.36	66.3	86.5	32	6700
United Arab Emirates	2.524	1.54	15.1	27.7	75.24	85.1	77.9	0	23200
Yemen	20.024	3.45	63.3	47	61.75	25.6	50.2	3	800
Algeria	32.129	1.22	32.2	33.5	73	58.8	70	3	5900
Egypt	76.117	1.78	33.9	33.96	71	42.1	57.7	2	3900
Libya	5.631	2.33	25.7	35	76.5	86.3	82.6	1	6400
Morocco	32.209	1.57	43.3	33.8	70.66	57.5	51.7	21	4000
Tunisia	9.974	0.99	25.8	27.8	73	63.7	74.2	19	6900
Comparison States									
Canada	32.507	0.9	4.8	18.7	80.1	80.4	97	5	29700
Poland	38.626	0.03	8.7	17.9	74.41	61.9	99.8	47	11000
Italy	58.057	0.07	6.1	14.1	79.68	91.6	98.6	31	26800

SOURCE: Population, Infant Mortality Rate, Population Under 15 Years of Age, Urban Population, Literacy Rate, Arable Land, and Per Capita GDP from *The World Almanac and Book of Facts*, 2005. Population Growth Rate and Life Expectancy from *CIA World Factbook*, 2005.

East will be understood to include the Arab states of Arabia and the eastern Mediterranean, Turkey, Israel, and Iran. It will also contain the North African states of Egypt, Libya, Tunisia, Algeria, and Morocco. This selection may seem arbitrary because it omits Afghanistan, Somalia, the Sudan, and Mauritania, which form transition areas between the Middle East, North Africa, and other adjacent regions.

In the Middle East, one encounters strange-sounding names with a regional significance. The Holy Land, Maghreb, Levant, Judea, Samaria, and the Fertile Crescent are all examples of special places that require more explanation. The *Holy Land* was traditionally associated with pilgrimages and crusades to the sites venerated by Christians because of their association with the life of Jesus. Today, the term also includes sites sacred to Jews and Moslems, most of which are in or near the city of Jerusalem.

The Maghreb is a phrase literally meaning, and implied by tradition, "the setting sun in the west." This term is used to describe the North African countries of Morocco, Algeria, and Tunisia, and some writers also include Libya and Mauritania. Like the Maghreb, *the Levant* signifies a direction, the eastern point of the compass. The Levant is generally understood to include the present states of Lebanon and Israel.

Judea and *Samaria* are ancient Hebrew names currently applied by the government of Israel to the former Jordanian-held territories on the West Bank of the Jordan River. The old biblical names are used to remind the world that Israel claims a historic right to bring Jewish settlers into these Arab-populated territories. These terms are used by those Israelis who support the expansion of the borders of Israel to include all of the territories that biblical tradition teaches were promised by God to the ancient children of Israel.

The term *Fertile Crescent* is familiar to many in the West because it is the traditional site of the birthplace of Western civilization. It includes the present countries of Israel and Lebanon as well as Syria and Iraq. Some writers say that the Fertile Crescent arches like a bow from the eastern Nile delta to the mouth of the Shatt-al-Arab River in Iraq. Other authorities hold that the western terminus of the bow is Palestine, not the Nile delta. What is important to remember is that this is an area of relatively good agriculture, low population, and a reasonable climate. As in ancient times, this area offers the best hope for the development of a non-petroleum-based economy.

GEOGRAPHY

Western perceptions of the Middle East are simultaneously accurate and misleading. The greatest expanse of desert in the world exists here, but although there are still camel-mounted Bedouins in parts of the Middle East, most people now live in villages, towns, and cities. Even those Bedouins who have not settled into permanent residences are now likely to be exchanging their "ships of the desert," camels, for Toyota trucks. Like many parts of the Other World, the Middle East is an area of both variety and dynamic change.

In its simplest form, the Middle East can be divided into three distinct geographic regions: the plains of North Africa and Arabia, the Fertile Crescent, and the northern tier. These areas are surrounded by five seas and five straits and are bisected by two of the world's great river systems.

The Plains of North Africa and Arabia

The vast deserts of the Sahara and the Rub al Khali cover more than 95 percent of this region. Because of their immense size, it should not be surprising to learn that the surfaces of these two deserts vary from gravel to rock to sand.

The Qattara Depression, larger than 4,000 square miles, is located near the Mediterranean in Egypt's portion of the eastern Sahara. From time to time, proposals have been made to divert the waters of the Mediterranean over the precipice to the Qattara floor, which is 400 feet below sea level. Engineers estimate that enough falling water could be diverted through generators to create an electric power complex that would rival the Nile's Aswan High Dam. A combination of environmental concerns and a shortage of capital in Egypt have postponed serious consideration of this project for the foreseeable future. There has been another, perhaps more feasible, Qattara proposal to tap an abundant ancient water supply, believed to exist beneath the depression floor, to create a new Nile delta in the desert. Whether the Egyptian government will find the development funds that would be required to attempt either of these ambitious schemes is doubtful at present.

The Rub al Khali of Saudi Arabia is famous for sand mountains that are hundreds of feet high. This desert contains the largest area of sand on earth. The Rub al Khali is about the size of Texas, extending from Yemen in the east to the United Arab Emirates in the west. For the first time since the ancient caravan routes flourished, Westerners are again penetrating the unknowns of the Rub al Khali, but this time in modern vehicles and engaged in the search for oil.

The Sahara: Camels gathered around one of the government-prepared watering holes in the Sahara Desert. SOURCE: JOE WEATHERBY

The Souk: Located next to the coral-colored walls of the old kasba, the market, or souk, *is the focal point of life in this Moroccan town.* SOURCE: JOE WEATHERBY

The remaining 5 percent of the plains of North Africa and Arabia is a transitional territory that includes two distinct areas: desert scrub country and a rich Mediterranean coastal zone. This zone stretches from the Nile delta westward for most of the length of North Africa and to the Atlantic coast of Morocco as far south as Casablanca. The desert scrub country contains some soil, moisture, and vegetation, and much of it resembles the high plains of the western United States. The conditions that produce desert scrub occur elsewhere in the Middle East, including southern Turkey, western Iraq, western Iran, and parts of Jordan and Syria. The nomads live in the desert scrub with their ever-migrating herds of sheep and goats.

Most of the residents of the plains live in the narrow coastal zone of the Mediterranean rather than in the deserts. The North African coast of the Atlantic and the Mediterranean generally conforms to what is known as the Mediterranean climate. This climate features hot, dry summers, with brown or dormant vegetation, and cool, wet winters, when the plant life has its growth period. In North Africa, this coastal zone ranges from only a few miles in width in parts of Egypt and Libya to as much as 50 miles in Algeria. In Egypt, the coastal zone and Nile valley and delta combined average 2,700 people per square mile, representing one of the world's densest populations. Remarkably, unlike other high-density areas, such as the Netherlands, the people of Egypt are still largely engaged in traditional Other World occupations, including subsistence agriculture (see Box 8.1).

BOX 8.1 ◆ WATER

The greatest shortage in the Middle East is water. Since ancient times, Mediterranean people have used ingenious methods to carry water to the fields. Following are several traditional irrigation methods still used in the region.

> The *qanat* is a tunnel sometimes over 10 miles long that taps the groundwater in the foothills and transports it to the fields in the valleys. This system is used in Iran and other mountainous countries in the northern tier.
> The *shadoof* is an ancient system using a goat-skin bag attached to a pole that is pivoted from the river to the field. This water system is used extensively along the banks of the Nile River in Egypt. The water wheel is a device used to lift and transport water. This system is usually animal-powered.
> The *Archimedes* screw is a portable gear used to raise water from a river or pond to the fields.

Some of the great cities of Africa and the Middle East are located in or near the Mediterranean coastal zone. Cairo, with a population of over 10.8 million people, is the largest and most important city on the African continent. Other important North African cities are Alexandria, Egypt (3.5 million); Tripoli, Libya (2 million); Benghazi, Libya (912,000); Tunis, Tunisia (1,927,000); and Algiers, Algeria (3 million). Both Rabat (1.7 million) and Casablanca (3,357,000) are located in the coastal zones of Morocco. Saudi Arabia in the Arabian Peninsula contains the historic cities of Mecca (1,335,000) and Medina (500,000). The commercial centers of Jedda (3,192,000) and Riyadh (5,126,000) are also located in Saudi Arabia.

These statistics may have more meaning if we compare the size of North African and Arabian cities with those found in the United States. Cairo has about the same population as New York City; Alexandria and Casablanca are larger than Houston; Tunis and Mecca are the same size as San Antonio; Jedda, Rabat, and Riyadh are all larger than San Francisco.

The North African and Arabian plains contain a number of mountains, including the Atlas and Rif of Morocco and the Tell Atlas of Algeria and Tunisia. The highest point in Egypt is the 8,600-foot Jabal Musa (Mount Sinai), located in the southern Sinai. Tradition holds that God gave the Ten Commandments to Moses on Mount Sinai. The Arabian Peninsula is mountainous in Yemen and Oman. In both places, peaks reach heights of 12,000 feet.[1]

The Fertile Crescent

Perhaps nowhere in the world has so much human history been tied to one single geographic area as in the Fertile Crescent. Everywhere the visitor looks, on the hills or in the valleys, important events in the history of humankind have occurred.

Here are the ruins of ancient civilizations, the land of prophets, and the birthplace of Judaism and Christianity. Geographically, the Fertile Crescent includes a narrow coastal zone flanked by the sea on one side and a rather low coastal range of mountains, running north to south, on the other. Along the southern border of Turkey, the Fertile Crescent arches eastward through a gap in the mountains to include the desert scrublands of Syria and Iraq before joining the rich river basins of the Tigris and Euphrates rivers. The region terminates at the northern end of the Persian Gulf.

The coastal zone of the Fertile Crescent is similar in many respects to the coast of California. Although this analogy has limitations apparent to any geographer, it may be useful to consider the following comparisons. If we were to travel the coastal route south from San Francisco to Los Angeles, we would pass through countryside that is similar in many respects to the coastal zone of the eastern Mediterranean, with Beirut being comparable to the Bay Area, Haifa to Monterey and Carmel, the Lebanon Mountains to the California coastal range, the Bekaa Valley in Lebanon to the Salinas Valley, and Tel Aviv to the area between Santa Barbara and Los Angeles.

The cities of the eastern Mediterranean do not rival either those of North Africa or the interior of the Fertile Crescent. Tel Aviv has a population of 2,752,000 and Jerusalem 686,000. Tripoli, the second-largest city in Lebanon, has a population of 245,000 people. The population of Beirut, Lebanon's capital, is 2,115,000.

The two major cities of the Fertile Crescent are Baghdad, Iraq, and Damascus, Syria. Baghdad, with a climate similar to the southwestern United States, has a population of 5,620,000. The population of Damascus is over 2,228,000. Syria and Iraq are the most important states of the Fertile Crescent. Both are considered to have a good chance to develop well-rounded economies, maintain low population densities, and establish reasonable standards of living. Presently, their problems are mainly political, not geographic or economic.

The Northern Tier

The northern tier is an area of mountains and plateaus linked to a mountain system that stretches from the Alps in the west to the Himalayas in the east. Although Afghanistan and Pakistan are often included in this region, this discussion of the northern tier is limited to Turkey and Iran.

Both countries are located on high plateaus surrounded by mountains. Turkey is situated on a peninsula jutting out into the Mediterranean. Turkey is about the size of Texas and Arkansas combined. The Anatolian Plateau, a high, dry region about 3,000 feet above sea level, is located in the center of Turkey. Here, the Turks produce most of their wheat and cereals. Two mountain ranges run east to west along the edges of the plateau. The Pontic Mountains are located on the north and the Taurus Mountains on the south of the peninsula. Eastern Turkey is extremely mountainous along the Iranian border. Mount Ararat, the traditional site of the landing of Noah's ark, is near this border. It is worth noting that Turkey has a long, varied coastal region that includes both a Mediterranean climate along the south and west and a wet area near the Black Sea city of Rise. This city receives as much as 100 inches of rain a year. With such climatic variety in the coastal zone, Turkey raises a number of crops including tea, tobacco, and cotton. Although most people live in villages, Turkey has several large cities. Istanbul, with a population of 8.9 million, is the largest. Ankara, the capital, has a population of 3.4 million, and Izmir has 2.2 million people.

Nature has played a cruel trick on Iran. Larger than Alaska, Iran consists of a high desert surrounded on all sides by rugged mountains that prevent moisture from penetrating into the interior. The Zagros Mountains run along the length of the eastern shore of the Persian Gulf, and the Elburz Mountains are located along a line parallel to the southern coast of the Caspian Sea. The jewel of the Elburz is a partially snowcapped volcano 18,376 feet high. This volcano, Mount Damavand, is clearly visible from Tehran. Tehran is built in the foothills of the Elburz and has a setting and climate closely resembling Salt Lake City, Utah.

Most of the interior of Iran consists of two terrible deserts, where some of the world's highest temperatures have been recorded. The Dasht-i-Kavir, or "Salt Desert," and the Dasht-i-Lut, or "Sand Desert," popularly called the "Desert of Death," are largely untraveled even today. The hostile environment in Iran's interior has caused over 70 percent of the country to remain uninhabited. The people of Iran live either along the narrow coastal plain of the Caspian Sea or in scattered urban centers in the north and west. Tehran, the capital, totally dominates these urban centers with a population of over 7.2 million people. The nation's second-largest city, Meshed, has a population of less than 2 million.[2]

Strategic Geography

The Middle East contains two of the world's great river systems: the Nile and the Tigris and Euphrates. The area also has two lesser waterways that are important in the politics of the region: the Suez Canal and the Jordan River.

Flowing 4,037 miles, the Nile is the world's longest river. Rising in Ethiopia and Uganda, it crosses the Sudan, enters Egypt at Lake Nasser, passes through the dam at Aswan, and flows past Cairo to the delta and the Mediterranean. If there is a central feature to Egypt, it is most certainly the Nile, which has been the life-support system for this nation's residents for more than 5,000 years. The need to secure the Nile in upper and lower Egypt is as important today as it was when the pharaohs ruled the nation in ancient times. As in the past, today's Egyptian leaders pay particular attention to politics in the Sudan. To the Egyptian, the fate of the Sudan still affects the security of the Nile.

Both the Tigris and the Euphrates begin their journey to the sea in central Turkey. The Euphrates passes through Turkey, Syria, and Iraq, and the Tigris through Turkey and Iraq. The Karun flows from Iran to join with the Tigris and the Euphrates, forming a new river called the Shatt-al-Arab just before reaching the northern shore of the Persian Gulf. It is in this meandering delta of the Shatt-al-Arab near Basra where much of the war between Iraq and Iran was fought during the 1980s.

The Suez Canal has been strategically important since its opening in 1869. One hundred and one miles long, the canal joins the Red Sea with the Mediterranean, saving ships the costly and time-consuming trip around the tip of southern Africa when traveling from the Persian Gulf and points further east to and from Europe. For further information on strategic waterways, see the Flashpoints section at the end of this chapter.

The Jordan River and its system of lakes and seas are historically significant as the site of many events sacred to Christians and Jews. The Jordan is also politically important because it is the disputed border between Jordan and Israel. The river flows through a valley for about 80 miles between the Sea of Galilee (Lake Tiberias) and the Dead Sea. The Jordan's economic significance is limited. Ranging from 50 to a few hundred feet in width, its potential for irrigation cannot possibly meet the exaggerated hopes for agricultural development of either the Arabs or the Israelis.[3]

No area of the globe is as strategically located as the Middle East. For centuries, it has been the invasion route of Egyptians, Persians, Romans, Christians, and Moslems. Today, its important location as a passageway between Africa, Europe, and Asia is without challenge. Five easily traversed seas surround the Middle East: Arabian, Red, Mediterranean, Black, and Caspian. There are three gulfs of importance: the Gulf of Aden, located at the tip of the Arabian Peninsula; the Gulf of Oman, situated between Oman and Iran; and the famous Persian Gulf. Entry and egress to all but two of these bodies of water are controlled by narrow straits: the Straits of Gibraltar, controlling the western Mediterranean; the Dardanelles and the Bosporus, dominating entry to the Black Sea; the Bab el Mandeb, controlling the southern end of the Red Sea and the Suez Canal; and the Straits of Hormuz, which must be passed to enter the Persian Gulf. Strategic straits do not dominate the Arabian Sea, which is part of the Indian Ocean, and the Caspian Sea, which has no outlet.[4]

PEOPLE

A popular misconception is that there is a homogeneous race of people in the Middle East. This notion is fostered by some of the region's religious institutions, whose traditions allude to Arab, Jewish, or even Aryan races. These terms, however, have little meaning in the Middle East today, unless they are limited to linguistic or cultural associations.

Although there are no recognizable groupings about which everyone would agree, authorities acknowledge that the region contains Semitic, Turkish, and Persian-speaking people. Of the Semitic-speaking population, the Arabs are the most numerous. Although there are many dialects, written modern standard Arabic is understood by educated Arabs everywhere. Arabic is spoken from the Atlantic coast of Morocco to the shores of the Persian Gulf. By this definition, approximately 200 million Arabs live in the region. Although there is a single Arab nation in theory only, the common bond of language has meant that unification is an aspiration of many of the region's inhabitants.

The other large Semitic group lives in Israel. Reviving a formerly ritualistic language as a symbol of their nationalism, the more than 5 million Jews living in Israel have again made Hebrew a living language.

The ancestors of the 60 million Turkish-speaking people in modern Turkey came to the Anatolian Peninsula in the eleventh and twelfth centuries from central Asia. They have lived in a single identifiable state since the Turkish Republic was created from the breakup of the Ottoman Empire following World War I.[5]

Persian is an Indo-European language written with a modified Arabic alphabet. There are about 36 million Persian-speaking Iranians in Iran. Finally, it should be pointed out that the region also contains people who speak different languages, including the Kurds, Armenians, and Greeks.

RELIGION

Two great forces are shaping the character of the modern Middle East. One is the Islamic religion and the other is nationalism.

Islam is the youngest of the three great monotheistic religions that arose in this region; the other two are Christianity and Judaism. Islam has been the dominant religion in the Middle East for more than 1,000 years. Today less than 10 percent of the population is non-Moslem. Thus, to understand the Middle East, it will be necessary to have some knowledge of Islam.

First, however, a distinction should be made between what is often referred to as the popular or folk religion and the formal religion of mosque and church. It is next to impossible to generalize about Middle Eastern folk religions except to point out that the popular practices of Christians, Jews, and Moslems are similar. All have their local saints, sacred places, and symbols. Many of these traditions spill over from one religion to another. For example, people of all religions in the Mediterranean traditionally paint the doors and shutters of their homes blue to ward off the evil eye. The distance between this popular practice and the formal religion of the scholars is often as great as that of the Pentecostal snake handler in the Appalachian Mountains and the pope in Rome. This inquiry will be limited to the formal religious practices of the majority religion, Islam.[6]

Much of the universal appeal of Islam is found in its straightforward simplicity. Unlike Christianity, there are no priests dispensing sacraments, no catechism, and no complicated theology. Islam demands a belief in only one God, called *Allah* in Arabic. Moslems believe that Mohammed is the prophet of God. The word *Islam* means "submission"; thus, a Moslem is a believer who has submitted to the will of God. This simple theology may be summarized as belief in the oneness of God, the prophecy of Mohammed, judgment day, and life after death.

Islam is more than a religion, as that term is generally understood in the West. It is a way of life, 24 hours a day, 7 days a week, 365 days a year. Moslems do not concern themselves with what is the truth because truth is contained in the profession of faith and the word of God as revealed through Mohammed in the Koran. The great questions of Islam are centered on how a good Moslem should

The Growth of Islam: With more than 1,207,148,000 adherents, Islam is one of the fastest growing religions. Located on the docks in Doha, Qatar, this portable mosque serves the needs of local dockworkers and fishermen.
SOURCE: JOE WEATHERBY

live and relate to others, not what a Moslem should believe in order to enter paradise. Although it is easy to make a profession of faith in Islam, it is difficult to live the life of a good Moslem. As a guide for living, Moslems observe five religious obligations, called the Five Pillars of Islam: professing faith, observing ritual prayer, giving alms, fasting during the month of Ramadan, and making a pilgrimage to Mecca.

The Profession of Faith (*Shahadah*)

Moslems believe that there is no god but God and that Mohammed is his prophet. The implications of this profession are threefold. First, in contrast to most Christians, who believe that there is one God, expressed as Father, Son, and Holy Spirit, Moslems hold to an uncompromising monotheism: "There is no god but God." Second, Moslems believe that although other prophets, including Jesus, have received revelations, Allah's words as revealed through Mohammed are the final, complete message from God to humankind. Third, Moslems believe that this message is contained, in full, in a book called the Koran.

Prayer (*Salat*)

Traditionally, Moslems pray at five prescribed periods a day: in the morning before sunrise, noontime, afternoon, sunset, and late evening. The prayer is ritualistic and keeps the believers in constant contact with God. Islam differs from those forms of Christianity in which believers pray through mediators inasmuch as Moslems believe that they have direct access to God.

Alms Giving (*Zakat*)

Moslems believe that they are obliged to pay a percentage of their income to the poor and needy. They do not believe that poverty is a crime. For Moslems, there is little or no stigma attached to this system of voluntary religious welfare. Many Moslems give to Islamic charities that then provide help for people who are in need. In recent years, the West has accused some Islamic charities of providing cover for the funding of international terrorism.[7]

Fasting (*Sawm*)

During Ramadan, the ninth month of the Islamic calendar, all Moslems are called on to observe the fast by abstaining from all food, drink, and other earthly pleasures during daylight hours. This month-long fast, longer than anything practiced in either Christianity or Judaism, teaches Moslems self-denial and moderation.

Pilgrimage to Mecca (*Hajj*)

If possible, all Moslems are enjoined to visit the Great Mosque in Mecca at least once. Here, facing the Ka'bah and wearing the same ritual white, Moslems from every station in life, from every country in the world, both male and female, pray as equals before God.[8]

Holy Struggle (*Jihad*)

Many consider the *jihad*, or holy struggle, to be almost a "sixth pillar of Islam." This duty, often misunderstood in the West, has two meanings: one inner and one external. The inner meaning calls on Moslems to fight constantly against their own evil inclinations. The external command offers salvation to those Moslems who fight to promote a universal Islamic doctrine. The confusion concerning *jihad* arises because the term has been used in a political manner by some Islamic leaders to further their own purposes.

The Moslem community is governed by a hierarchy of principles expected to guide the faithful in all matters of life. These principles, or authorities, are collectively called the *Shari'ah*, or "the path to be followed." This path includes, in descending order of importance, the Koran, the tradition (*Hadith*) of how Mohammed lived, consensus (*Ijma*) of the religious scholars on issues, and deduction (*Qiyas*) where there is no precedent. Not all Moslem communities accept this hierarchy in its entirety.

The great split in Islam began because of a dispute over how the successor (caliph) to Mohammed should be selected. The Shiia branch of Islam is centered in Iran. Shiites believe that the first caliph should have been Ali, the son-in-law of

Mohammed, and that successive caliphs should have come exclusively from the descendants of Ali. Sunnis, who make up approximately 80 percent of the world's Moslem population, believe that the caliphs should have been chosen by election of the faithful from members of Mohammed's tribe. Over the centuries, many other differences have developed between these two branches, and their disputes still color Middle Eastern politics hundreds of years after the original split occurred.

HISTORY

Since the seventh century, the history of the Middle East has been inexorably bound to the history of Islam, which includes at least five distinct Suni periods: the life of Mohammed, the rightly guided caliphs, the Umayyads, the Abbasids, and the Ottomans.

The Life of Mohammed (A.D. 571–632)

Mohammed was born in A.D. 571 in the city of Mecca. Orphaned as a child, he was reared by a grandfather who was a leader of the Meccan Quraysh tribe. Mohammed is traditionally believed to have traveled with caravans to other parts of the Middle East as a young man. His visits may have exposed him to other religions. When he was 40 years old, he started receiving revelations commanding him to tell the world that there was one God, that Mohammed was his prophet, and that there would be a judgment day. These revelations were revolutionary ideas that threatened existing society in Mecca. In the summer of 622, opposition from the Meccans forced Mohammed to flee from Mecca 200 miles north to the city of Medina. The date of Mohammed's flight, called the *Hijra*, marks the beginning of the Islamic calendar. After converting Medina to Islam, Mohammed lived to see not only Mecca but also the entire Arabian Peninsula become Moslem before his death in A.D. 632. It should be remembered that Moslems do not ascribe divine qualities to Mohammed. He is considered to have been a human being who, while living a perfect life, served as a messenger from God.

The Rightly Guided Caliphs (A.D. 632–661)

Mohammed's death left the movement without a clearly designated successor. This vacuum initiated a struggle for power that ultimately led to the Sunni-Shiia split. Although some of the faithful believed that Ali had been designated by Mohammed as his successor, Abu Bakr (the prophet's father-in-law) was chosen to be the caliph. After only two years, Abu Bakr chose Umar to be the caliph, and under Umar's leadership, Islamic armies conquered the Fertile Crescent, Persia, and Egypt. Much of what is familiar to Westerners about Islam, including the veiling of women and the ban on alcohol, was institutionalized during Umar's tenure. Uthman succeeded Umar, who was assassinated in 644, but he too was assassinated 12 years later. Ali was finally selected as the fourth caliph, only to be

Mosque of Mohammed Ali: Located on the Citadel towering above Cairo, this mosque was begun in 1824. Today, it remains the most imposing landmark in the city.
SOURCE: JOE WEATHERBY

challenged by the powerful Umayyad family from Mecca. The Umayyads backed another leader named Mu'awiyah. There was a civil war between the Umayyads, who had the support of Moslems in Syria, and the Moslems who supported Ali. Eventually, Ali was assassinated in 661. Shiites still maintain that Ali was the only legitimate successor to Mohammed.

Moslems look with fondness at the period of the first four caliphs as a time when the religion had a purity of purpose that ultimately was lost. Modern Moslems tend to stress the exertions of the period, the justice, and the humanity, and ignore the disturbing reality that three of the four "rightly guided caliphs" were assassinated. Nevertheless, if there ever was a time that Moslems long to return to, it is this one.

The Umayyad Dynasty (A.D. 661–750)

Under the first Umayyad caliph, Mu'awiyah, the election of leaders was ended in favor of a dynastic approach, and the political capital of Islam became Damascus. During the almost 100 years that the Umayyads ruled, the Islamic faith spread to three continents. However, it was only a question of time until the non-Arab elements of the empire began to believe that they were being treated as second-class members of the Damascus state. In 750, the non-Arab dissidents of the empire arose and ended the Arab domination by destroying the Umayyads. In place of the Umayyads, a new multicultural system was established, called the Abbasid dynasty.

The Abbasid Dynasty (A.D. 750–1258)

With the rise of the Abbasids, the so-called Golden Age of Islam began. The empire's new capital in Baghdad saw Moslems lead the world in philosophy, literature, mathematics, and medicine. Many developments that were to bear fruit in the explosion of the arts and sciences during the Renaissance in Europe originated in the streets of Abbasid Baghdad. The rule of the Abbasids came to an end in the year 1258, when Mongol armies from central Asia conquered Baghdad. After the fall of the Abbasids, no single power was able to dominate the Middle East until the Ottoman period.

The Ottoman Empire. (A.D. 1453–1918)

Tradition holds that the Ottomans came to Anatolia from central Asia in the early Middle Ages. By the mid-1300s, they were in the process of establishing an empire that would again extend Moslem control to parts of Europe, Africa, and the Middle East. Although it is difficult to generalize about an empire that lasted for over 600 years, it is safe to state that many of the conditions found in the modern Middle East began in the practices of the Ottomans. For example, the Ottomans were able to rule a diverse multicultural empire stretching over much of the Mediterranean world because they established a system of religious and cultural autonomy called the Millet. Sectarian separation was institutionalized and even encouraged by the Ottomans as long as loyalty and taxes were paid to the caliph. This system of religious toleration resulted in the survival of small Christian and Jewish groups, which otherwise would have disappeared. Middle East groups still divide along sectarian lines after the fashion of the Millet.

During the eighteenth and nineteenth centuries, Ottomans were in retreat in the face of increasing Western power. Many of the negative stereotypes that westerners have about the Middle East come from this period of Ottoman weakness. The Ottomans survived the nineteenth century but collapsed with the defeat of the Central Powers in World War I. The subsequent partition of the non-Turkish elements from the empire resulted in the creation of the modern Turkish Republic.

Shi'ite Islam

Most people in the West see Islam as monolithic. In reality, Islam is no more monolithic than Christianity. Like most Christians, there is agreement on a few fundamental beliefs, but after that there is diversity.

The Shi'ia are the largest minority in Islam. They have a different history and traditions. First the Shi'ites argue that upon the death of Mohammad, Ali should have been selected Caliph. Second, Shi'ites believe that the Shiia Imam (caliph) must be a direct descendant of the Prophet Mohammad and Ali, the first Imam. Most believers recognize twelve Imams in history. The twelfth Imam called, "the Lord of the Age," has been "hidden" but will eventually return at the end of the world to establish a perfect and just society.

Until the twelfth Imam returns, his successor, called a *Muijtahid* or *Ayatollah*, has the right to interpret religion for the Shi'ite community. It is believed that as successors of the twelfth Imam, the decisions of the Ayatollahs have special force over the community of believers.

Unlike Sunai Islamic leaders, Ayatollahs continually make religious and political pronouncements. This explains how the religious leadership in places like Shi'ite Iran can "veto" the actions of elected secular leaders. This tradition gives extraordinary power to the senior religious leadership in Shi'ite Islam.

Islam Today

Much has been written in recent years concerning the resurgence of Islam as a unifying force in the Middle East. Although it can be said that Islam is not a form of nationalism, it is clear that Islamic attitudes and symbols are used and manipulated by nationalists in the Middle East to legitimize their respective political objectives.

It is possible to identify certain important attitudes that Moslems have concerning non-Moslems. Islam victoriously entered the world scene over 1,400 years ago and remained so for almost 1,000 years. This long period of dominance has led to a collective mindset that is reflected in the commonly used Moslem expression "Islam dominates and may not be dominated." Thus, for Moslems, some religions may be tolerated, but none will be allowed parity, much less dominance, if there is power to prevent it.

Although some Moslems view the defeats of the recent past with the rationalization that "Islam gains strength with every testing," there is no denying that it is particularly galling to have unbelievers dominating believers after all these centuries. This attitude is reflected in the responses of many people from the Middle East when they come in contact with the outside world. In the nineteenth century, the early military defeats administered by the West were rationalized on the grounds of Middle Eastern technological inferiority. Attitudes eventually evolved into a conspiratorial view of history in which the West was blamed for every problem in the region.

In the 20th century, continuing defeats, both external and internal, have led to a further sense of helplessness that is reflected in an almost irrational rage against anything Western or modern because it is believed to represent colonialism in a new form. This attitude can be seen in a number of ways, including the actions of students studying in the West, Islamic resurgence movements in the region, and the return to conservative Islamic dress by many university-educated women. Although it is difficult to forecast the direction these frustrations will take, it is safe to say that they have a real basis in fact and can only become a major unsettling element in Middle Eastern politics.

It is popular to focus on "Islamic fundamentalism" when referring to the resurgence of Islam in the Middle East. What is often ignored is that fundamentalist movements exist in all major religions. Like their counterparts in Christianity and Judaism, the fundamentalist movements in Islam represent only a fraction of the total number of believers.

What cannot be ignored since the September 11 attacks is the reality that while there is not a monolithic fundamentalist movement using world terrorism as a strategy, there are many well-financed and organized fundamentalist groups that do. Furthermore, many Moslems who would not engage in terrorism do provide a fertile field of support for those fundamentalists advocating violence as a solution to Other World problems.

Islamist political movements have received positive receptions in many parts of the Middle East where the inhabitants have suffered the experiences of colonialism and neocolonialism, social injustice, poverty, and governmental ineffectiveness. These Moslems resent the harsh life, lack of jobs, and the culture of corruption that has created a wide gap between the rich and the poor. The fundamentalist movements offer hope for change and a new sense of worth to an often-bankrupt society tired of experimenting with imported solutions to problems. Fundamentalists have won many friends by taking leading roles in assisting the sick, the widowed, the poor, and the unemployed. They have been active in reforming the schools and universities. They have even been involved in such diverse activities as blood drives and providing financial aid for funerals. All of these fundamentalist movements call for a moral sense of purpose that offers alternative solutions to the ones advocated by the secular nationalists and the traditional Moslem leaders who currently make up the Middle Eastern establishment.

The lesson of the Iranian revolution should now be clear to everyone. The Islamic reformers captured that revolution from secular nationalists because they offered the masses a chance to put an end to the evils of the past. The Iranian revolution should serve as a warning to the establishment in every state of the Middle East. If the injustices of the past are not addressed, there will be a rise in militant Islamic fundamentalist movements throughout the region.

In part, the Islamic resurgence has occurred because Islam avoided the stigma of failure that accompanied the secular philosophies. In the twentieth century, capitalism, socialism, Marxism, and secular nationalisms have all been tried, and each has ended in failure. Only Islam offers hope for a renewal of Middle Eastern society without the taint of defeat, corruption, or association with colonialism. In whatever form it takes, Islam is today, as it has always been, the central factor in the lives of millions of people.

THE COLONIAL EXPERIENCE

For the better part of 1,300 years, Christians from Europe have fought Moslems from the East. During the last 200 years, this traditional conflict has been worsened by the impact of Western colonialism. It began with the French invasion of Egypt in

1798. Although this occupation was cut short by the British victory over the French fleet at the battle of Aboukir Bay,[9] it signaled a growing European interest in the area. Soon Britain, France, Italy, and Spain pursued their imperial objectives. Germany and Russia were absent only because their ambitions were frustrated by the British and the French. The British began their imperial adventure on the periphery of the Middle East by developing a series of strategic colonies on the shores of the Persian Gulf. By the opening of the Suez Canal in 1869, Britain controlled colonies stretching from Aden, at the mouth of the Red Sea, across southern Arabia all the way to India. Later the British leased the Ottoman island of Cyprus and used it as a naval base to check the Russian attempts to enter the Mediterranean.

The British military occupied Egypt in 1882 because of a fear that the Egyptian government would not pay debts owed to foreign investors. This occupation was considered to be temporary, but the British did not leave Egypt until 1956. They were also interested in expanding their influence along the Red Sea. After much fighting, the Anglo-Egyptian forces occupied the Sudan in the last decade of the nineteenth century. By this time, Britain was the European country with the most extensive presence in the Middle East. When the Ottoman Empire was disbanded at the end of World War I, the British gained custody of Iraq, Palestine, and Transjordan. Semi-independent, these territories were administered by the British as mandates until the end of World War II. For the most part, British colonies in the Middle East were established as strategic colonies either to protect the lifeline to India or to create a stable environment for business investment.

After earlier French occupation of Egypt, French imperial activity was limited to the establishment of a colony in Algeria in 1830. Throughout the nineteenth century, French settlers expanded this colonial bridgehead until it included a large portion of North Africa. In the twentieth century, these holdings grew to include the southern portion of Morocco. France gained control of Syria and Lebanon as part of the partition of the Ottoman Empire. Regardless of their official status, the French administered these territories as colonies.

Spain and Italy developed imperial ambitions in North Africa during the early part of the twentieth century. Italy began a military occupation of Libya in 1911, when the territory was taken from the Ottomans. Building on several ancient enclaves, the Spanish joined the French in the partition of Morocco by occupying the northern portion in 1912. Although established largely for prestige purposes, these colonies proved difficult to completely pacify and expensive to maintain. It is doubtful whether these colonies ever justified the blood and treasure required to hold them.

Although Germany never actually controlled any territory in the Middle East, it did play an active political role as a participant in the great power struggles of the nineteenth and twentieth centuries. Before World War I, it sent military advisors and agents to both the Ottoman Empire and to Persia. It also participated in the planning and partial construction of the Berlin-Baghdad railway. Because the Germans were only in the Middle East in a financial or advisory capacity, and because they were opposed to the British and French, they were the most admired Europeans active in the region.

With the exception of the navy in the war against the Barbary pirates, the United States avoided involvement in the Middle East until the end of World War II. Before President Truman played a leading role in the establishment of the state of Israel, the United States escaped the colonial stigma applied to most other developed countries. Since that time, the United States has been blamed for almost every ill that plagues the region.

During the last 200 years, almost every area in the Middle East has suffered under colonial occupation. Many of these areas fell under European control after World War I. As a result of this experience, the worst forms of imperialism are well remembered. At times, the Western powers have denied that they were officially in the Middle East in an imperial capacity. Nowhere in the Other World was Western imperialism implemented in a more hypocritical or cynical fashion.

There is no question that American intervention against Iraq in the two wars have heightened regional suspicions about the intentions of the United States. To many in the Middle East, American actions look very much like the past colonial activities of Britain and France.

GOVERNMENT

By the last quarter of the twentieth century, the countries of the Middle East had received formal independence. The end of colonialism resulted in the creation of one of the most politically complex regions in the Other World, containing democracies, authoritarian civilian states, military-dominated regimes, and monarchies. Morocco, Saudi Arabia, Jordan, and the Arab states of the Persian Gulf are authoritarian monarchies. Libya and Syria are regimes in which the military plays an important role. Egypt, Tunisia, and Turkey are civilian authoritarian states. Iraq, at this writing, is under an American military occupation arguably not unlike periods of British colonial rule during the twentieth century. Iran is an Islamic republic. In the past, both Israel and Lebanon have been considered Western-style democracies, but a civil war, Palestinian intrigues, Syrian military intervention, and the 1982 Israeli invasion combined to kill any short-term hope for an independent democracy.

By 2005, both Israel and Syria had officially withdrawn from Lebanon. The Lebanese held what was termed by many as the first free elections in many years. There is still much foreign intrigue being played out in Lebanon. Only time will tell if the Lebanese can truly return to the active democracy that once existed.

It is important to remember that since independence, few Middle Eastern regimes have demonstrated a sustained commitment to constitutional government. During periods of crisis, decision-making has often reverted to informal systems that exist outside the formal mechanisms of government. Thus personalities and politics rather than law dominate the Middle East, as it is understood in the West, where following procedure is more important than winning. Middle Eastern government institutions must be considered as only a part of a greater cultural whole that is involved in political decision-making. Traditional social, cultural, and religious institutions still play a disproportionate role in the politics of the region.

ECONOMICS AND NATURAL RESOURCES

It is popular to state that with the exception of petroleum there are no significant mineral deposits in the Middle East. Although it is true that the resources of the region are limited, it is also true that much of the Middle East has not been thoroughly surveyed. Nevertheless, important mineral resources have been found in limited areas. Phosphate deposits are mined in Morocco, the former Spanish Sahara, Tunisia, Jordan, and Egypt. Iron ore is found in both North Africa and Turkey. Some gold has been discovered in Egypt and Saudi Arabia.

Clearly, oil is the great natural resource of the region. The Persian Gulf states provide significant amounts of the oil needed by Europe, Japan, and the United States.[10] What is perhaps more important is the realization that the oil states of the Middle East and North Africa control more than 60 percent of the world's proved reserves of oil and 25 percent of the reserves of natural gas. Because of these resources, this region will play an important economic role in world affairs for a very long time.

There is a vast contrast between oil-rich states with low populations and non-oil-producing states with high populations. For example, the United Arab Emirates per capita gross national product (GNP) is about $23,200 (U.S. dollars); that of the most populated Arab country, Egypt, is only $3,900. This discrepancy is a destabilizing element for the entire region. Former Iraqi President Saddam Hussein cited economic inequity as a justification for his 1990 invasion of Kuwait:

> The malicious Westerners intentionally multiplied the number of countries with the result that the Arab nation could not achieve the integration needed to realize its full capability. When fragmenting the Arab homeland, they intentionally distanced the majority of the population and areas of cultural depth from riches and their sources.[11]

In an effort to redress some of this economic inequity, Saudi Arabia has donated more than 120 billion dollars in aid to the Other World during the last half of the twentieth century. This aid went to a total of 70 states including 38 in Africa and 25 in Asia. The principal dollar recipients were friendly, poor Arab states.[12] Saudi Foreign Minister Mosaad Bin Mohammad Al-Aiban recently reported that since 1973, $83.7 billion was assistance for developing countries. He said, "This represents more than four percent of the average Saudi GDP during those years and equals six folds of the target required by the United Nations of the GDP of the donor countries."[13]

The scarcity of water is the most serious impediment to improving agricultural production in the region. In an experiment, the Gulf States and Saudi Arabia have made great strides, at high cost, to start an agricultural industry. There have been calls from some of the poor states to use Arab oil money to make the non-oil-producing states breadbaskets for the region. This pan-Arab agricultural vision for the present is still a dream.

Turkey, with a better supply of water than the Arab states, has a well-developed agricultural system. The Turks rank among the top 20 nations in the world in the production of wheat, potatoes, barley, olives, tomatoes, sunflower seeds, cotton, tea, and wool. Iran produces wheat and grapes, and Egypt is famous for its high-quality cotton and oranges. Grain products and oranges are also produced in the Levant.

 CASE STUDIES

ON MIDDLE EASTERN NATIONALISM

Despite their diversity, the countries of the Middle East underwent similar experiences that shaped their attitudes toward the outside world. All of them felt the humiliation of Western colonialism in one form or another. As was the case elsewhere in the Other World, reaction to the colonial experience served as a spark that ignited the fires of nationalism. Much of the force of Middle Eastern nationalism has centered on a resistance to Western colonialism.

Over the years, the competing nationalism of the Turks, Iranians, Egyptians, and Israelis has resulted in irredentist claims against one another. When one looks at the territorial aspirations of Turks, Kurds, Iranians, Iraqis, Israelis, Palestinians, Jordanians, Egyptians, and Libyans, it becomes obvious that if all of their hopes are to be realized, the people of the Middle East will have to stack countries on top of one another. Reaching a satisfactory solution for these competing nationalistic objectives is one of the great political problems of the twenty-first century.

The traditional goal of Middle Eastern nationalism has been to achieve independence. Certainly, here, as elsewhere in the Other World, there is no agreement about what independence means or how it can be realized. The case studies in this chapter demonstrate that Middle Eastern nationalists have used a variety of approaches to achieve their objectives. Some have totally rejected the political and religious institutions of the past, as in Turkey, whereas others have sought independence by returning to what they believe to be the traditions of early Islam, as in Saudi Arabia and Iran. Finally, some nationalists have sought to chart a middle course similar to that of Egypt.

Although included in this discussion, the experience of Israel cannot readily be identified with other nationalism in the region. Israel is a settler state based on Western traditions. The Israeli experiment, however, is interesting because the Zionist form of nationalism is becoming more sectarian and Middle Eastern in its point of view.

In Chapter 2, nationalism was described as it has developed in the West. Among the features discussed were exclusivity and suspicion of others. Nationalism also supported the establishment and maintenance of the modern nation-state. We will see from the case studies in this chapter that this process also occurred in the Middle East. Some Middle Eastern nationalism, however, is moving in new directions, making it difficult to categorize in traditional terms. Some nationalistic movements no longer identify with the state boundaries that currently exist. They favor a new unification through supranational units such as the Levant or the Maghreb.

Many of the new nationalists view their own governments as illegitimate, and they almost repudiate those goals of their fathers 40 or 50 years ago. At that time, nationalistic efforts were directed at the overthrow of the colonial rule of Britain and France. Some Islamists express their opposition to Israel, the United States, and the Arab establishment, have articulated this changed attitude. They are voicing opposition to Arab governments of the left and right, and they are hoping to use the Islamist revolution as a catalyst to spread change to all of the states of the Middle East. Recently, this point was forcefully made by the popular dissident Saudi cleric Sheik Hamoud al-Shuaibi. When asked about Arab governments that cooperate with the United States, he replied, "I don't specify any person or group of persons. But everyone who supports America against Islam is an infidel, someone who has strayed from the path of Islam."[14]

Middle Eastern nationalistic sentiments are primarily products of the urban centers. In much of the countryside, people still have loyalties similar to those found in prenationalistic Europe. To these people the first contact with the authority of the state is often a point of contention and not an expression of loyalty. The villagers' contact with the government is limited to paying taxes and watching the state take their village sons away to the army. In many of the rural areas, the values of the central government have little or no legitimacy.

Traditional nationalism has failed to fulfill regional aspirations, so it is being either modified or discarded. In the past, nationalistic goals included political unity and freedom from both colonial and neocolonial domination. Arab nationalism also hoped to establish a classless society, a democratic political system, and an effective challenge to Israel. After years of formal independence, these stated goals remain unfulfilled dreams.

1. TURKEY

 Emerging from the Ottoman defeat of World War I, Turkish nationalism drew on the struggles and writings of the previous 50 years to create a movement based on the unifying aspects of the Turkish language and Turkish identification. This idea succeeded in ways in which the similar Young Turk movement had failed. In the nineteenth century, the Young Turks failed because the multinational character of the old Ottoman Empire rendered the appeal of being Turkish ineffective. Modern Turkish nationalists succeeded because the geographic limits of the new Turkish republic coincided with areas where people identified with being Turkish instead of Ottoman.

The new movement was led by a military hero named Ataturk (Mustafa Kemal). He was determined to break Turkey out of the backwardness of the Ottomans by creating a modern, secular Eastern European republic that could compete on equal terms with any country in the West. At the time, Ataturk's revolution was expected to be as significant as those of his contemporaries: Hitler, Mussolini, and Lenin. Seventy years after the founding of modern Turkey, Ataturk's reforms are not considered as revolutionary as they once were. Since the 1950s, Turkish nationalism has abandoned some of its more controversial themes. For example, Islam is a resurgent force in what was once considered to be a secular state. Nevertheless, as they have done for a half-century, Turkish nationalists still turn away from the Middle East and look toward Europe for their future. We should remember that the central feature of Turkish nationalism has been the rejection of the failed institutions and solutions of the past to create an entirely new system.

Throughout the second half of the twentieth century, Turkish politics continually revolved around heated disputes between competing civilian forces, often interrupted by military takeovers. After the passions of the moment cooled, the military would return to the barracks until the next time. During this period the military even removed Suleyman Demirel, the seven-time prime minister, from office on two occasions.

In domestic affairs, Turkey is a state with a population that is 99 percent Moslem. Most Turks still support the move to Westernize the country and join the European community. They fear fundamentalist movements like those that developed in Iran and Afghanistan. They do not want to see a civil war like the one taking place in Algeria. This paradox between Islam and westernization forces the government to walk a fine line.

The fears of the secularists came true in the spring of 2000 when the "near Islamist" Justice and Development party came to power. In spite of a dispute with the United States over using Turkish bases for the invasion of Iraq in 2003, this party is more popular than ever. This triumph of the conservative Moslems over the traditional secular leaders represents a real shift in Turkish politics.

The JDP remains in power in 2006. During the party's tenure, several policies have continued to complicate Turkish relations with the West in general and the United States in particular. Turkey has established closer relations with both Syria and Iran. There is also a deep frustration in Turkey with the failure of the United States to control Kurdish cross-border activities in the northeastern part of the country.

Turkish foreign policy focuses on three issues. First, the Turks hope to see more positive moves by the European Union toward setting a specific time for their admission to the Union. Second, the government believes that the positive votes on the 2004 UN reunification plan of Turks on Cyprus followed by the negative vote by the Greeks should merit a relaxation of trade restrictions on the Turkish Republic of North Cyprus. Third the Turkish authorities want the United States to move to restrict the activities of Kurdish terrorists over raiding in Turkey from safe havens in Iraq.

Although Turkish importance to the West may not be what it was during the cold war, it is still important for several reasons. Although it is sometimes a "rocky one," Turkey is still democratic and secular. In March 2005, Foreign Minister Abdullah Gul signaled that there would be little change in Turkish policy when he said, "We do not plan to have an agenda that includes Islamic policies and laws."[15]

Cyprus

In 1974, an Athens-supported *coup d'etat* overthrew the multicultural government of Cyprus in an attempt to link the island to Greece. This action provoked a Turkish military intervention. The Turkish victory divided the island between Greek and Turkish *Cypriots.*

The Turks justify their action by pointing out that the London treaties of 1959 and 1960 allowed Turkish action. The treaties also prohibited Cyprus from joining any other state or group of states without the consent of all the interested parties, including Turkey.[16]

Starting in 2001, more contact between Greeks and Turks on the island occurred. The Turks opened their border with Greek Cyprus in 2003. In 2004, the majority of Turkish Cypriots accepted the UN-sponsored reunification plan. Although the Greek population rejected the proposal, there still remained hope that some form of agreement might eventually take place. In the meantime, a divided Greek Cyprus became a member of the European Union in 2004.

Kurdistan

Kurdish aspirations for independence pose threats to several states, including Turkey, Iran, Iraq, and Syria. In the case of Turkey, there have been low-intensity conflicts with the Kurds taking place for years. Many Turks are fearful that the American defeat of the government of Iraq could lead to the establishment of a Kurdish state in northern Iraq. If that event were to occur, that conflict would almost certainly spread to eastern Turkey.

The Turkish parliament has recently passed a number of measures designed to support the effort to join the European Union. These constitutional reforms include limiting the death penalty and relaxing prohibitions on Kurdish language broadcasts. These reforms are among the requirements that the European Union (EU) has obliged Turkey to meet.[17]

Turkish Political Realities

As the twenty-first century begins, two opposing nationalists' visions of the future are contending for power in Turkey. Governmental establishment represents one. The residents of the cities and the university-educated elites who support the secular nationalist principles of the republic that Ataturk founded defend Westernization, want Turkey to remain a member of North American Treaty Organization (NATO), and work for Turkish admission to the European

Community. Others, including Islamic traditionalists and rural conservatives, believe that the country has deserted a rich Middle Eastern heritage. These conservatives support efforts to control the excesses of modern Turkish society. Today Turks are deeply divided over the direction that nationalism should take. Should Turkey continue to push for a place in Europe or should Turks return to their traditional place of leadership in the Middle East and Central Asia?

2. IRAN

Like the Ottomans, the Persian Empire (Iran) was an Islamic monarchy, except that Shiite Islam was the state religion. Iranian nationalism developed during Anglo-Russian interventions in Persia in the early days of the twentieth century. The history of nationalism in Iran can be divided into three periods: the reign of the Pahlavis, the Mossadeq crisis, and the Islamic Republic.

The first Pahlavi, Reza Shah, was an army officer who seized power in 1921 and had himself crowned king (Shah) in 1925. His rule lasted from 1925 to 1941. Reza Shah believed that a modern state, like Turkey, could be created in Iran. Although many proposed changes emulated those of Ataturk in Turkey, Iran was far less Westernized and change came slowly. Unlike Ataturk and Lenin, who destroyed the old to create a new system, Reza Shah wrapped himself in the traditions of the old Persian monarchy to establish his legitimacy. In the late 1930s, he indicated a sympathy for Adolph Hitler that provoked a Russian-British-American intervention in Iran once World War II began. Reza Shah was deposed, and with the approval of the Western powers, his young son, Mohammed Reza, was placed in power.

Mohammed Reza's reign was uneventful until the Iranian oil crisis of 1951. At that time, a popular nationalist leader, Mohammed Mossadeq, formed a political organization known as the National Front. He gained control of the government and then nationalized the British-owned Anglo-Iranian Oil Company. The Western oil powers responded by boycotting Iranian oil. Deprived of oil revenue, by 1953 the Iranian economy was in such bad shape that the Shah used this crisis to attempt to have Mossadeq removed. The Shah's action failed and he was forced into exile in Switzerland. In one of the most interesting periods in modern history, supporters of the Shah were persuaded—it is now believed, with CIA help—to stage a counterrevolt.[18] Mossadeq's allies failed to respond effectively, and the Shah was returned to power within days. The downfall of Mossadeq ended the rule of one of the only truly popular, secular nationalist leaders in modern Iranian history. Returned to power, the Shah ruled in an increasingly arbitrary manner until he was forced into exile in 1979.

When the Ayatollah Khomeini assumed power in Iran, he enjoyed the support of both the secular nationalists abroad and the religious nationalists at home. The Western-educated elites, who accompanied him on his return flight from exile in France, carried foreign passports. Khomeini's first cabinet was made up of these secular nationalists. Many of these officials expected to bring liberal democratic rule to Iran. Within three years, all of these officials had disappeared from the political scene. Ayatollah Khomeini built his political base among the poor and the dispossessed who also happened to be the religious conservatives. In this way, he was able to shape the Iranian revolution into a struggle that was both religious and class oriented.

Totally reversing two millennia of Iranian monarchy, the Islamic Republic of Iran has represented a temporary victory for the religious nationalists over the secular nationalists of the 1950s. The leaders make effective use of the symbols of Shiite Islam to maintain authority over the Iranian people. According to the rhetoric of the regime, this movement represents an attempt by Shiism to gain the leadership of the Islamic world. The progress of the Islamic revolutionary model developed by Iran is being watched with interest by many states of the Other World.

In 1997 a moderate Shiite cleric was elected president of the republic gaining almost 70 percent of the vote. Although this victory was confirmed in Mohammad Khalami's reelection four years later, the struggle between reformers and traditionalists continues. In a blow to the reformers, Iran elected a hard-line president, Mohmoud Ahmadinejad, in 2005. Preceding the election, the opposition had largely been marginalized by the conservative religious leadership called, "the guardians." Dozens of opposition politicians were disqualified and their newspapers were closed before the election took place. *New York Times* columnist, David Sanger, stated that, "the Bush administration declared the process rigged."[19]

The results of the 2005 election suggest that Iran will move away from the moderate policies that the previous reformist president proclaimed. As an example of the hard-line change, new President Ahmadinejad, quickly announced that Iran would resume the development of its nuclear programs that had been previously halted while talks with the West took place.

The real power in Iran is not held by the government or its officials; it is welded by the conservative clerics or guardians under the leadership of the Supreme Leader of the Islamic Revolution, who is elected for life, Ayatollah Sayyed Ali Khamenei. He controls the political apparatus of the country and, in practice, overrules the president and the assembly. The presence of an American army on the borders cannot help but remind the clerics of the repeated Western interventions into their country during the last century. They are playing a very dangerous game as the leaders of Iraq found out.

The real test for the long-term success of the Iranian revolution depends on the ability of the state to make measurable improvements in the lives of most Iranians while, at the same time, avoiding a conflict with the United States. This revolutionary balancing act "will not be an easy one to accomplish."

3. EGYPT

Egyptian nationalism emerged as a reaction to Napoleon's invasion in 1798. The national movement is almost as old as the French Revolution. Experiencing both peaks and valleys during the nineteenth century, nationalists later championed the call to end the British occupation of Egypt that had begun in 1882. In the 1920s, a middle-class anti-British political movement called the Wafd emerged to dominate Egyptian politics until the rise of Nasser in 1952.[20]

Probably no man in the history of the modern Middle East has successfully captured the hearts and minds of Other World peoples of all social classes and political philosophies as did Gamal Abdel Nasser. Espousing a militant nationalism of Arab socialism and social reform at home, Nasser also called for independence from foreign domination, opposition to Israel, and Arab unity abroad. He is best remembered by Middle Easterners for his successful challenges to the policies of the United States and the former colonial powers of Western Europe. It is important to note that Nasser's continuing contribution to Egyptian nationalism is symbolic and transcends specific successes or failures of his policies while he was the country's leader. Following Nasser's death in 1970, Anwar el-Sadat assumed control.

Anwar el-Sadat's 11-year rule over Egypt is extolled in the West as an example of what an enlightened Other World nationalist can accomplish. Sadat expelled the Russians in 1972, fought Israel to a standoff in 1973, and then went to Jerusalem to begin a process that resulted in the 1979 peace agreement with Israel. Sadat's assassination in 1981 is still viewed in the West as a great setback to peace efforts in the region. Surprisingly, Egyptians rarely discuss the tenure of Sadat. In Egypt, he is considered to have frustrated the cause of Arab unity by stressing the separateness of Egypt and peace with Israel over the greater good of the Arab people. Sadat's virtual surrender of the Egyptian economy to Western investment raised new fears of a return to neocolonial status. The danger of an erosion of independence, whether direct or indirect, has become central to the thinking of many Egyptian nationalists who were opposed to Sadat.

President Hosni Mubarak sought to develop a nationalism that steered a middle course between the economic excesses of Sadat and the political adventurism of Nasser. He worked hard to end Egypt's isolation in the Arab world. Expelled after the Camp David agreement, Egypt was restored as a member of the Arab League and the league's headquarters was returned to Cairo. The Egyptians continued to honor the peace agreement with Israel. They reestablished diplomatic relations with Russia and remained a close Arab ally of the United States. The thrust of all of these diplomatic efforts was aimed at establishing Egypt as a bridge between competing states in the region.

In domestic policies, Mubarak remains firmly entrenched in power. When he first assumed the role of president after Sadat, Mubarak asserted that he would remain in office until the end of his term. In 2005, he announced that he planned to, again, stand for election. There were rumors that he planned to eventually pass the office to his son, banker Gamal Mubarak.

Other observers speculated that in allowing opposition candidates to stand for president for the first time in 7,000 years, Mubarak was beginning the slow transition away from the present authoritarian state that had operated under emergency laws since 1981.

There is no question that elections in Iraq, Lebanon, and Palestinian territories has put pressure on the Egyptian authorities to make changes. In allowing limited opposition to Mubarak, they faced enormous difficulties, not the least being more than 24 years of political stagnation. The problems of Egypt were accelerated by a series of terrorist attacks on the infrastructure of the tourist industry. One of the most serious of these attacks occurred at Sharm el Sheik where more than 80 people were killed in July 2005. These terrorist operations represent a major threat to the continued domestic stability of the regime.

In 2003, Egyptian foreign policy was directed at convincing Israel that no normalization of life would be possible until both the Palestinian situation and the status of Jerusalem were resolved satisfactorily. At the same time, Mubarak tried to convince the Americans that no peace in the Middle East would occur without forceful leadership from the United States. To successfully pursue these often-contradictory policies, Mubarak had to avoid offending the United States while recognizing that the majority of people in Egypt were anti-Israel.

In a sense, Egyptian policy toward the United States is schizophrenic. On the one hand the media mouths a political rhetoric that is anti-American. At every opportunity the United States is portrayed as the protector of Israel. Furthermore, American interest in the Arab world is limited to easy access to low-cost oil. On the other hand, Egyptian economic interests are closely tied to maintaining good external relations with the United States. Egypt cannot afford to ignore the major aid package dispersed every year by the Americans. Egyptians learned in 2003 when they backed the European Union's position against the importation of American beef into Europe that the United States can "bite back." The United States abruptly suspended talks on a U.S.-Egypt free trade agreement. The message was clear. The neocolonial phrase "one should not bite the hand that feeds you," still applies.

In the Arab world, Egypt still tries to maintain a leadership role as Arab spokesman. Again, however, the American invasion of Iraq clearly demonstrated the limits of Egyptian persuasion when a major power decides that its national interests are threatened.

Of all the states of the Middle East, Egypt is the one that authorities speak of in the most pessimistic terms. Beset by a population explosion that is uncontrollable without using unacceptably draconian measures, no Egyptian government can hope to make significant improvements in the lives of the people in the foreseeable future. The question being asked by all who look at Egypt's problems is: How long will the Egyptian masses wait before turning to more radical solutions to their problems? Because Egypt is the most populous Arab state, the direction that it takes will determine the future of much of the Middle East. Is time for Egypt growing short? Egypt's leaders have many problems and few solutions. The miracle is that Egypt continues to limp on, surviving each gloomy forecast.

4. SAUDI ARABIAN "BEDO-NATIONALISM"

It is popular to speak of the British royal family as "the family business." Perhaps no better example of a family business exists than that of the House of Saud. Since the alliance between a clan chief, Muhammad ibn Saud, and the religious leader, Muhammad ibn Wahhab, in 1744, the House of Saud has played the defining role in Arabian politics. Whether in or out of power, Sauds have always been a force to be reckoned with.

The modern story of Saudi Arabia began in 1901, when the famous leader, Abdul-Aziz Ibn Abdul Rahman Al-Saud (Ibn Saud), rode out of desert exile in Kuwait to capture the fortress of Riyadh. From that base he gradually increased his hold on the Arabian Peninsula until he was able to unite all the major tribes and their territories to create the present state of Saudi Arabia (called the Kingdom) in 1932.

In 1933, Ibn Saud rejected British advice and granted a 60-year petroleum concession to Standard Oil of California. When a great pool of oil was discovered, this arrangement became one of the most profitable business deals in history. The oil company first evolved into the Arabian American Oil Company (Aramco) and later, under Saudization, into Saudi Aramco.

Ibn Saud's greatness was in his ability to first win military victories, and then consolidate power by linking his family through marriage and alliances to the other major families in the region. This tribal linkage has remained intact to the present day. Furthermore, he was able, in his international politics, to skillfully balance his role as an Arab leader with that of a world leader.

Using the Kingdom's vast oil wealth, he and his sons were able to wrench the Arabian people out of the Bedouin system into the modern world. All of this was

Incense: A Resident of Jedda, Saudi Arabia, demonstrates the proper use of an incense burner. Sandalwood is used as fuel for the burner. SOURCE: JOE WEATHERBY

accomplished without sacrificing the region's traditional values. Saudi Arabia became the world's best example of the premise that a state did not have to be Western to be modern. Because of the leadership from the House of Saud, residents of the Kingdom were able to enjoy the benefits of the modern world while remaining true to the religious and cultural traditions of their Bedouin roots.

At first glance the Saudi government is authoritarian. However, this is dismissing the complexity of Arabian politics by substituting Western models of government. Politics in Arabia are true to the traditions of that region. The West separates religion from government and focuses on problem-solving strategies. The Kingdom combines religion and government by placing all issues within an Islamic context. These issues are dealt with on the basis of personal relationships backed by family honor.

Although updated many times in this century, The Kingdom is organized around the complex interaction of powerful tribes and families, often having blood ties to the House of Saud. At each level from district to province, there is room for input offered to local leaders through an unstructured meeting called the *majlis*. In the "bedo-democracy" of a *majlis*, the leader is the first among equals. Appointed governors called *amirs* repeat this process at provincial levels. The national Majlis al-Sura is composed of 90 members who advise the king. The king rules; he does not reign as in the English monarchy.

Because of the linkage of the state with Islam, the Kingdom does not have a constitution in the Western sense. The Koran is the constitution of Saudi Arabia. The state does have a basic law that covers many items found in Western constitutions. These provisions include general rules for the organization of the financial system, the eligibility for succession to king, and the organization of the judiciary. The basic law also provides for a citizen's bill of rights, the protection of private property, and the protection from arbitrary punishment.

The Future for Bedo Nationalism

In 2005, Abdullah bin Abdulaziz became king of Saudi Arabia. The question being asked is: How long can this system of tribal leadership last? Demographics indicate that the future for the system is not promising. Like the king, who was born in 1924, most of the Saudi leadership comes from the 2.4 percent of the population that is over 65 in age. At the same time almost 40 percent of the population is under 14! To many observers, there is a clear disconnect between the old and one of the fastest growing youth populations in the world. This disconnect is complicated by a decline in economic opportunity within the kingdom. It is only a matter of time before the Saudi young, both male and female, demand a greater voice in Saudi affairs. Will the current system be able to reinvent itself to meet these new demands or will another system emerge to guide Saudi Arabia through the first half of the 21st century?

September 11 exposed a dark side of the Saudi story. A significant number of the terrorists who bombed the World Trade Center that day were Saudis. When the United States traced the plot back to Saudi Osama bin Laden's organization in

Afghanistan, it was found there was more Saudi involvement. The question of why Saudis and others from the wealthy Gulf states would actively participate in terrorism needs an answer.

The Arabian Peninsula has been very religious since the time of Mohammed. In the eighteenth century, the Sauds adapted Wahhabism. The Wahhabi interpretation of Islam is probably the most conservative in the Moslem world. For most of this time, Arabia remained isolated and poor. In this environment it was easy for a ruler to impose a conservative system.

The problem started to occur with the discovery of oil in Arabia. This influx of wealth also brought foreigners and other ideas along with technical expertise. Saudis welcomed the wealth but not the Western ideas on cultural and political issues. Rationalizing the contradiction between Wahhabi religious zealotry and opposition to materialism, while at the same time acquiring great wealth was a problem. The House of Saud maintained its power by saying one thing abroad while saying something different and catering to religious conservatives at home. Domestically, the government tolerated no formal political or religious dissent. They established state-supported mosques everywhere. The clerics were required to remain supportive of government policy. Through this strategy the House of Saud was able to walk a fine line between being supportive of the West abroad while maintaining a certain tolerance for the radical elements of Saudi society at home.

Two events have brought this policy into question. First, the Russian war in Afghanistan mobilized large numbers of Saudis to go and fight there. However, when the veterans returned to their homes, many were committed to adopting a military solution to solve their social problems.

The second problem occurred as a by-product of the Western intervention in the effort to expel Iraq from Kuwait. When the war was over, the Americans did not go home. The fact that America, Israel's greatest supporter, continued to base large numbers of troops in the region is a source of great resentment to many Saudis.

Working through religious clerics who remain largely outside the state religious establishment, an underground of radicals emerged. These militants often were wealthy and many were Afghan war veterans. All saw that the oil business had corrupted the purity of Islam. Saudi and Gulf leaders were compromising their principles to deal with the West. Typical of the radical clerics who have inflamed these militants is Sheik Hamoud al-Shuaibi. He directs his criticism against America, Israel, and anyone who supports them. The sheik has been quoted as saying, "It is the duty of every Moslem to stand up with the Afghan people and fight against America."[21]

Because the normal political and media outlets are closed to them, the religious militants have coalesced around "house mosques." Clerics like Sheik al-Shuaibi who remain outside the official religious establishment.

Although not yet powerful enough in Saudi Arabia to threaten the survival of the government, these militants can cause social unrest if the government attempts to implement the serious crackdown that America would like to see. Saudi Arabia today has a young, potentially volatile population. Whether the

Saudi version of Bedo Nationalism can survive the rise of these Moslem militants remains to be seen.

In the aftermath of the events of September 11, the war in Afghanistan and the invasion of Iraq, American support of the ruling regime has been severely shaken. American troops have largely been redeployed outside the Kingdom. American press accounts of some Saudi involvement in terrorist acts against the United States have shaken the "special relationship" between America and the Kingdom.

As Saudi Arabia enters the twenty-first century, the Kingdom faces many other challenges. The birthrate is one of the highest in the Middle East. There are far too many guest workers taking jobs that Saudis should be prepared to occupy. The parallel society established for women in the workforce is both costly and inefficient. The Kingdom must broaden the economic base before the oil revenue declines. Finally, Saudi Arabia's geographical location dictates that the Kingdom must be prepared to play a major role in the Gulf long after the Americans have sailed over the horizon.

5. THE ARABS

The political scientist Karl Deutsch once said, "A nation is a group of people united by a common dislike of their neighbors and a common misconception about their ethnic origins."[22] If one looks at the spirit of the nation from the perspective of the Arabs, it is clear that Deutsch's observation applies to the Middle East.

Arab nationalism is often characterized as xenophobic, negative in international outlook, and dependent on a historical past that is often more myth than fact. Arabs are suspicious of others because of what they perceive to be more than 200 years of lies and deceit by the colonial powers. Throughout the nineteenth century and well into the twentieth, this pattern repeated itself with cynical regularity. For example, the British promised the Arabs independence during World

Business: A young bicyclist carries a load of chairs to be sold in the Cairo market.
SOURCE: JOE WEATHERBY

War I, only to carve up the region into colonial mandates when the war was over. Arab nationalists from Gamal Nasser to Osama bin Laden have seen this event as a treacherous act, ensuring that the Arabs would remain a divided people who could be controlled by outsiders. Many Arab nationalists see both American support for the state of Israel and the occupation of Iraq as fresh attempts to divide and dominate the Arab people.

The history that forms the basis of Arab nationalism is characterized by the gap between aspiration and reality. The aspiration is the reestablishment of a single, united Arab nation similar to the nation that existed during the early days of Mohammed. The reality is that this kind of unity never existed. Even during its early days, the Islamic state was characterized by civil wars and assassinations. In modern times, the aspiration has been to free the Arab people from foreign domination. The reality has been a reliance on foreign influence, aid, and military support to accomplish Arab political goals. For example, Arab opposition to Israel caused nationalists to embrace almost any outside power that was perceived as being willing to aid in this effort. The reality of this approach has been to mortgage Arab sovereignty to external obligations. Finally, the aspiration that oil can be used to achieve Arab economic independence has clashed with the reality that Arab oil must be sold abroad for hard currency. Instead of unifying the Arabs, wealth generated by oil has divided rich and poor Arabs across the region. Although Arab nationalism is a potent force, it has failed to meet the aspirations of those who seek the rebirth of a great, unified Arab nation.

6. ISRAEL

Israel may be described as a settler state with a European ideology transplanted into the Middle East. This impression may be less true today than it was in the past. Modern Israel is more conservative, militaristic, sectarian, and Middle Eastern than it once was. With U.S. financial aid more important than ever before, Israel reflects many of the same neocolonial fears and suspicions that are found in other Middle Eastern states.

Founded in Basel, Switzerland, in 1897, modern political Zionism is a form of nationalism that calls for the establishment and maintenance of a Jewish state in Palestine. The return to Palestine is based on Jewish traditions that go back 2,000 years. The specifics of this call have been modified to fit the changing needs of the movement. Today, Zionism generally means that the survival of the State of Israel must be guaranteed as a symbol of refuge for Jews everywhere, whether they choose to immigrate or not.

Over the years, two factions of nationalists emerged to contend for power. The Israeli Labor Alignment represented secular nationalists who were interested in the establishment of a modern state with viable borders. These nationalists included some of the great names of Israeli history, such as David Ben Gurion, Golda Meir, and Abba Eban. They represented the ideas of the European founders of Israel, and their party alignments dominated the policies of Israel from the nation's founding until 1977.

In 1977, the demographic changes in the Israeli population tilted politics in favor of non-European Jews. Continuing Palestinian hostilities and new demographics created conditions that brought a conservative coalition, called the Likud, to power. The Likud represented the second direction taken by the Zionists. Their view argued for the creation of a "Greater Israel" or a "Promised Land" that would include those portions of the Middle East that tradition held were promised by God to the ancient Hebrews. In recent years, non-European Jews who had experienced Arab domination also tended to support Likud's hardline policies toward the Arabs.

At the beginning of a new century, Israeli nationalism is in a state of transition. No one can predict with certainty the final direction that the movement will take. On the one hand, Israel can pursue the maximalist goal of recovering and then holding all of "the land of Israel." To the outsider this course seems to be not only impractical but also sure to doom the state to entering into an endless cycle of debilitating wars with the Arabs, followed by costly occupations. To many, this is a process in which Israel cannot hope to prevail.

The other nationalist approach is accommodation with Israel's neighbors. This choice is also dangerous and difficult. It involves making painful concessions on issues that are of primary concern to most Israelis. This course is made all the more difficult because it means that Israel will have to give up the most when exchanging "land for peace." It is analogous to sacrificing several chess pawns in order to win the game. Here, winning for Israel is survival as a Jewish state with secure borders and peaceful neighbors.

The Palestinians and Israelis came tantalizingly close to a negotiated settlement in the summer of 1999 only to have the Palestinian leader Yassar Arafat reject the peace plan at the last minute. To outsiders this plan had possibilities because it offered Palestinian statehood, a return of most of the West Bank and Gaza, plus a foothold of some kind in Jerusalem. In return, the Palestinians would have had to give up all disputed claims in Israel and agree to a permanent peace. In short, the Palestinians would have largely gained politically what they had lost on the battlefield.

Following this disappointment, a hard-line Likud, under the leadership of Ariel Sharon took power in Israel. Many observers stated ruefully that "the Palestinians had never missed an opportunity to miss an opportunity." Certainly the deal offered by the Israelis in 1999 would not likely be repeated. This deadlock ushered in the beginning of more than four years of low-intensity conflict that embittered parties on both sides.

Following the death of Yassar Arafat in 2004, Ariel Sharon announced to the world that Israel would impose a "temporary" solution by extending an already begun wall of separation in the West Bank and by a total withdrawal from Gaza. The withdrawal from Gaza was complete in the summer of 2005.

Israel has bought some time by withdrawing from Gaza. Still, the major problems separating Palestinians and Israelis remain: the future of the West Bank and Arab Jerusalem. These issues are so great that any major moves by the Israelis to meet Arab demands could result in domestic unrest in Israel itself.

Politically, the Labor Party had been largely marginalized since the failure of the 1999 peace talks. However, Likud threatened to split over what had to be done to achieve peace with the Palestinians in Gaza. On November 21, 2005, Ariel Sharon, the former war hawk, turned Israeli politics upside down, when he announced that he was resigning from Likud and forming a new center political party dedicated to a peaceful settlement of the conflict. Shortly after the founding of his centrists party, Kadima, Prime Minister Sharon suffered a massive stroke! He was replaced by Ehud Olmert, as acting Prime Minister and the Kadima head. Kadima won the election held in March 2006. The party can be expected to follow the path laid out by Sharon. In the absence of the settlement with the Palestinians, Israel will unilaterally establish a border between the two parties. They will extend the security wall that they are building to enclose all the West Bank of the Jordan that they intend to hold. All Israeli civilians will be relocated to permanent settlements within the wall. The Israeli army will continue to remain active in those areas evacuated. Kadima leaders call this a civilian disengagement with a military buffer remaining in the abandoned areas.

In 2006, there are the secular Israelis who want a return to normalcy. The sectarian nationalists in the Likud settlement movement want no further concessions made to the Palestinians. Some even threaten violence against their own government if more concessions are made.

Will the rise of the Kadima center party bridge the gap between the Israeli right and the left? Regardless of the outcome of this political conflict, the Israelis can be expected to strike a tough bargain. At the present time, most observers say that while Israel may have proposed a return of 90 percent of the lost West Bank in 1999, Palestinians can expect less than 60 percent today.

►LOOKING AHEAD

Trust everybody, but cut the cards.
FINLEY PETER DUNNE

As will be seen in the Flashpoints at the end of this chapter, many of the region's conflicts are indigenous and based on long-standing cultural and geographic factors. On the surface, each of these issues should stand alone. In the Middle East, however, the Arab-Israeli conflict and the Western occupation of Iraq dominate the politics of the region.

What are the prospects for peace? Two scenarios illustrate the difficulty in attempting to forecast the future for any political issue in the Middle East.

THE PESSIMISTIC SCENARIO

It is not the big armies that win battles; it is the good ones.
MAURICE DE SAXE, MARSHAL-GENERAL OF FRANCE

Without a settlement to the Arab-Israeli dispute, those parties on both sides who prefer the status quo to peace can be expected to continue their present policies.

The status quo benefits those Israeli factions that believe that any settlement will force Israel to make concessions in territory. Palestinians are fearful that the Arab states might be willing to sacrifice the Palestinian nation to regain territory previously lost to Israel. Many Arab leaders continue to use their dispute with Israel as an excuse to prepare for war abroad and to avoid reform at home.

If the deadlock continues, acts of terrorism will increase. The Arabs will accelerate the arms race to achieve qualitative military parity with the Israelis. This military development will be achieved at the expense of funds that could be made available for social development. The likely result of this scenario will be the continuation of Arab regimes that are volatile and unstable.

If the Israeli leadership continues to encourage more Jewish settlement in the West Bank, the Arabs will resist it with any means available. The continuation of the status quo means that bloodshed will continue on both sides. Because of the destructive capability of modern weaponry, there is always a chance that one of these sharp conflicts will escalate into a major war.

If the American and allied efforts fail in Iraq, the outcome is almost too grim to contemplate. There could be a collapse of central authority followed by a civil war. The more numerous Shiia will likely separate and move in the direction of the Iranian model. Those Sunnis who survive such a conflict will link with Syria. An "independent" Kurdish region will almost certainly provoke a Turkish invasion followed by an occupation. Iraq will cease to exist, and the balance of power in the Middle East will be fundamentally changed.

THE OPTIMISTIC SCENARIO

God willing, there will be peace.
A PALESTINIAN EXPRESSION

The 2003 Iraq War involved hundreds of thousands of American soldiers. In this conflict, the Arab-Israeli dispute was a secondary but important aspect. If it was not understood before, it became obvious that the issues in the Middle East were interrelated. This event shattered the complacency of those in the Bush administration who had wished to avoid direct involvement in the affairs of the Middle East. Badly frightened at the prospect of a permanent Vietnam, many Americans became active in attempts to eliminate the conditions that could lead to a new American military involvement in the region. The result was that the United States applied pressure on all of the parties involved to force them to negotiate.

The end of the cold war also freed the hands of those leaders in the West who had used the policy of containing communism as a test for dealing with the governments in the Middle East. For the first time, there was agreement that it was in the interest of Russia, the United States, and the other Western powers to encourage a settlement between Arabs and Israelis. The major powers combined with a majority of other states in the world to encourage the parties of the region to talk seriously about peace. Although Palestinians and Israelis continued to play the game of attack and reprisal in the Second Intifada, there might still be some hope. Both the Israelis and Palestinians have nowhere to go. The Second Intifada had no plan B. Eventually the issues dividing the parties would have to be resolved if either party is to survive in peace.

In Iraq, a successful democratic state in the heart of the Arab world will energize democratic movements everywhere. An oil-rich, stable, and peaceful Iraq will exert great positive influence on the entire region. The result will make the blood and treasure expended by the West worth the price.

◆ FLASHPOINTS ◆

PALESTINE

At the beginning of the twenty-first century, a twentieth-century problem is still the central feature of Middle Eastern politics. This dispute is between Jews and Arabs over the control of Palestine. Since 1948, the Palestinian focus has been on opposition to the State of Israel. At the same time, Israeli Jews have consistently opposed the creation of a Palestinian state. The result has been a series of Arab-Israeli wars fought in 1948, 1956, 1967, 1973, and 1982. In addition, there have been a number of continuing low-intensity conflicts that are characterized by the cycle of attack and retaliation. Israelis call Palestinian bombers and hijackers "terrorists;" Palestinians call the attacks by the Israeli military and settler shootings and bombings acts of "state terrorism."

Before discussing the specifics of the dispute, several assumptions need to be made. First, the leaders on both sides have raised their demands to the heights of irreducible principles. This has had the effect of painting both parties into ideological corners that ensure that peace is impossible without ideological surrender of the other side.

Second, the ongoing conflict has resulted in both sides suffering grievous injuries at the hands of their opponents. Peace requires a new way of thinking where these past injustices are forgiven if not forgotten.

Third, because Israel has been victorious in every war, all of Palestine has fallen to the Jewish state. Israel still controls most of the land. Thus far, Israel has not been prepared to take the draconian step of expelling the millions of Palestinians who live there. Peace will require that Israel give up the most to end the conflict.

Fourth, Israel can win the military battles, but without peace, Israel is in danger of losing the demographic war with the Palestinians. In a recent editorial the *New York Times*, citing Israeli sources, stated the following:

> The real argument lies in the demographics which become increasingly clear for a state that seeks to define itself as Jewish. There are 3.2 million Palestinians in the West Bank and Gaza, with an annual growth rate of 4.2 percent.

The editorial later states,

> In Israel itself there are 1.3 million Arabs and 5.4 million Jews liv-
> ing between the Mediterranean Sea and the Jordan River. By 2020,
> Jews will be a minority.[23]

The doomsday scenario is an Israeli evolution into a new South Africa, with a Jewish minority attempting to maintain political control over a majority Palestinian population. Without peace and stability, few Jews on the outside can be expected to move to Israel. The failure to attract American and European Jews to live in Israel could be a demographic time bomb for Israel.

Finally, it will take cooperation between Palestinians and Israelis for either of the two cultures to prosper. Without continued outside aid, neither entity can succeed on its own. There is no place for Palestinians and Israelis to go.

As the Second Intifada grinds to a halt, the same issues that confronted the peacemakers in 2000 remain. The areas of dispute blocking peace are not hard to identify. The first of these issues will be land. How much will be returned to the Palestinians and how much needs to be retained for Israel's military security? A complicating factor is the numerous Israeli settlements that are now part of the Palestinian landscape.

The second issue is water. There is not enough water for everyone. The desert is worthless without water. At present, the Israelis take most of the water for their own use, starving many of those Palestinian farmers who remain in the West Bank.

The third issue is refugees. Almost half a million Palestinians either fled or were forced from their homes in 1948. In every war since that time more Palestinians have gone into exile. Their future status was one of the deal breakers in the 2000 negotiations. It is unreasonable to expect Israel to absorb the millions of Palestinians whose families once lived in what is now Israel. However, to obtain peace, a form of compensation that is fair to those who lost their homes and businesses must be found.

The fourth issue involves the repatriation of Palestinians in Israeli jails. This is an explosive issue that is in part driving the Second Intifada. To the Israelis, many of these people are terrorists. To the Palestinians, the prisoners are freedom fighters working to free their homeland. This issue can be resolved. A prisoner release program has been successful in Northland Ireland and it can be in the Middle East.

Fifth is the issue of Jerusalem. Here religion has become mixed with nationalism on both sides. This makes retreat from the stated demands of Israelis and Palestinians almost impossible. The issue is complicated by the size of the area that is the subject of most of the dispute, the Old City. The walled portion of the Old City is approximately 1,000 by 1,500 meters. Christian, Jewish, and Moslem holy places are literally stacked one on top of the other. No Palestinian or Israeli leader can negotiate away claims to the

Old City. For peace to occur, a way must be found to provide for a Palestinian presence, if only symbolically, in the Old City.

Finally, the creation of a Palestinian state must occur. At present, the territories nominally under Palestinian control are so "Balkanized" that a viable state is impossible. Some solution to the statehood aspirations of the Palestinians must be reached if peace is to be achieved.

The negotiations held in 2000 made a great deal of progress toward a comprehensive peace. It is easy for outsiders to see what needs to be done to achieve a final settlement. However, it will require new thinking by Palestinians and Israelis if the parties are to escape the endless cycle of violence.

At the present time, many Palestinians refuse to pay more than "lip service" to the idea of co-existence with a permanent Israeli state. At the same time, many Israelis cannot let go of the idea that a "greater state" of Israel, including large parts of the West Bank territories, should be created.

The Iron Laws of the Arab–Israeli Conflict

Israelis say that the Palestinians can make peace with the terrorist groups, such as Islamic Jihad and Hamas, or they can make peace with Israel, but they cannot do both.

Palestinians say that Israel can have the occupied Palestinian land, or they can have peace with Palestinians, but they cannot have both.

All conflicts eventually come to an end. Historians tell us that even the Hundred Years War and the Thirty Years War in Europe came to an end. Palestinians and Israelis have two choices. They can continue this seemingly endless conflict of attack and retaliation until both sides are devastated and exhausted or find creative ways to resolve this dispute.

Peace will require short-term beginning compromises from both sides. In the long run, the right to a Palestinian state living in peace side by side with Israel will have to happen. The borders of the two states will largely be the old ones that existed in 1967. Parts of Jerusalem will be shared between the parties. Many Israeli settlements, but not all, will have to be abandoned. Palestinians will have to accept the idea that for most of them, the dream of returning to modern Israel to live is gone in favor of a fair compensation. Finally, Palestinians must truly accept the reality of a permanent Israeli state. One can hope that these conditions for peace are realized sooner than later.

THE PALESTINIANS

The Palestinians are an ancient people who trace their origins to the Philistines in the Bible. After the Arab conquest, their sense of national consciousness remained dormant until World War I, when they began again to speak of a Palestinian people. During the negotiations that preceded the creation of the state of Israel, serious proposals were also made in the United Nations (UN) for the creation of a Palestinian state. The Arab side rejected the UN proposal. Unfortunately, any further hope for the establishment of a state that would parallel the one created in Israel was lost with the Arab defeat in the 1948 war. Since that time, all the parties to the Arab-Israeli dispute attempted to manipulate the aspirations of the Palestinians. The Palestinian Liberation Organization (PLO) claimed to represent the interests of the Palestinian people. When the leadership of the PLO agreed to an autonomy agreement, they took a chance that measurable results could be achieved before the opposition to a limited agreement could grow. Many Palestinians, especially those exiled abroad, believed that the current agreement would never lead to Palestinian sovereignty. Furthermore, they charged that limited autonomy permanently surrendered the lands taken from the Palestinian people in 1948. The slow pace of events since the signing of the accord has strengthened the opposition to a settlement with Israel.

The decline of PLO fortunes after 1993 resulted in the corresponding rise of the Islamic fundamentalist organization Hamas. Unlike the PLO, Hamas was opposed to any peace talks with Israel. By active participation in the Intifada, Hamas earned the respect of many Palestinians. Hamas was a "home grown" organization rising out of the occupied territories. Unlike the PLO, Hamas leaders were not intellectuals imported from the Palestinians living abroad. Furthermore, the Hamas opposition to Israel was clear and uncompromising. To a people forced to live under Israeli military occupation, this hard line struck a responsive chord. Facing Hamas, moderate Palestinians were placed in a no-win position. When they moved to compromise with the Israelis and the West, they weakened their position with the Palestinians they claimed to represent. To the chagrin of both the PLO and the Israeli authorities, Hamas has been raised to the status of a major player in Palestinian politics.

In 2006, Hamas scored an upset win in the Palestinian elections. They were able to win by taking advantage of divisions in the PLO combined with the general perception that the PLO authorities were doing little about Israel while lining their own pockets with money intended for the Palestinian people.

Now that Hamas is in power, there are questions about the ability of a revolutionary Hamas being able to become a legitimate, internationally respected government. Can Hamas get past the rhetorical violence of the past and evolve into a force that can deal with Israel and with the rest of the world? If, like the Irish Catholics and Protestants, Hamas makes this evolution, the lot of the Palestinian people will improve dramatically. If, on the other hand, Hamas cannot make this transition it is likely that their rule will be short. No major power can be expected to deal with Hamas if it attempts to implement the parties stated policies. Political and financial support for Palestine will end. The Palestinian people will be condemned to living in the continuing misery that they find themselves in today. Finally, a militant Hamas takes the pressure off of Israel to make any further concessions to the Paletinians.

For their part, the Palestinians have endured a political and social tragedy that colors their politics. They fear that a grand peace may be negotiated by the great powers at their expense. This concern was raised to a higher level in April 2004. After a meeting between President Bush and Prime Minister Ariel Sharon, the American President announced that if negotiations between the Palestinians and Israel failed he would support an Israeli plan for a unilateral withdrawal from Gaza and the West Bank included the following steps:

- Israel would remove all settlers and troops from the Gaza Strip;
- Israel would dismantle some, but not all, settlements in the West Bank;
- Israel would not have to accept any Palestinians wishing to return to their former homes in Israel.

This move was portrayed by the Americans and the Israelis as an interim step along the "Road Map for Peace." To the Palestinians, American support for this unilateral action would create a Palestinian Ghetto state in an Israeli-dominated land. In 2005, Sharon withdrew Israeli settlers and troops from Gaza and a small part of the West Bank. Israel continued to build what was called a temporary security fence that stretched from one end of the West Bank to the other.

By their often-violent actions, the Palestinians have attempted to ensure that their cause will not be ignored. The result is a Palestinian problem that is influencing issues everywhere in the Middle East.

THE IRAQI DISPUTES

Iran

If it is true, as the old saying goes, that "the bones of the Middle East were buried by the dogs of British imperialism," the Iraq-Iran dispute is a case in point. The British that favored the Ottomans over the Persians created the border as the result of a nineteenth-century mediation. The object of this effort was to keep Russia out of the Persian Gulf by giving control of the Shatt-al-Arab River to the British-backed Ottomans. Although the Persians objected to the location of the border on the east bank of the river instead of the usually accepted main channel, it was not until 1975 that Iraq, the Ottoman's successor, agreed to use the navigable channel as the border. In return, the Shah of Iran agreed to stop aiding the Kurdish rebellion against Iraq. After the Shah's demise, Iraq unsuccessfully attempted to restore the old border by invading Iran in 1980. The result was one of the more terrible wars in modern history. When the fighting ended, the battle lines were in approximately the same location as the prewar border. To free troops for service in Kuwait in 1990, the Iraqi authorities conceded all of their major war gains to Iran.

Kuwait

On August 2, 1990, the Iraqi army invaded Kuwait. This was the latest in a series of disputes between Kuwait and Iraq going back for more than a half-century. These disputes were raised by Iraq as challenges to the historical legitimacy of Kuwait.

Kuwait's history can be traced to the eighteenth century, when the Al-Sabah family gained control. This dynasty has remained in power since that time. During the nineteenth century both the Ottomans and the British attempted to influence the Al-Sabahs. The Iraqi claims rest on the argument that the Al-Sabahs recognized that Kuwait was part of the Ottoman Empire because it was nominally administered from the Iraqi city of Basra. The Iraqis argue that all of the Ottoman Empire that was administered from Basra should be part of Iraq. To them only British intervention during the early years of this century deprived Iraq of Kuwait.[24] During the twentieth century, Kuwait was administered as an independent state under British protection; however, during this period both Saudi Arabia and Iraq claimed parts of its territory.

Although grounded in history, the latest dispute between Iraq and Kuwait was over oil. Because Kuwait controlled the third-largest reserves of crude oil in the world, it was able to influence the world price. The Iraqis charged that Kuwait violated agreements and dumped oil on the world market to harm Iraq. Iraq also disputed the Kuwaiti claims to an oil field on the border of the two countries. Finally, Iraq charged that Kuwait had failed to share its oil wealth with the poor Arab states.[25]

This dispute was complicated by the demographics of Kuwait. With the discovery of oil came thousands of foreign workers. Although denied full citizenship, these workers often prospered, and by August 1990, there were more foreign workers in Kuwait than Kuwaitis. Many of these workers were employed by the state even though they were treated as second-class citizens. The 1990 invasion was welcomed by many of these "guest" workers because Iraq had promised that they would be given full citizenship by the new government.

The allied coalition forces routed the Iraqi army during the 1991 liberation of Kuwait. This victory invalidated most Iraqi claims. In the aftermath of the war, Kuwaiti authorities expelled large numbers of foreign workers. By using these harsh methods, the authorities attempted to reduce the danger that guest workers might again threaten the stability of the regime.[26]

Kuwait is a very rich, small nation located in a region noted for poverty. Arab nationalists charge that it has been used as an outpost of

Western imperialism. Appealing to the poor of the Middle East, the Iraqis charge that the oil wealth of the Persian Gulf has been stolen from the Arab nations by Kuwait. To many, the massive military response mounted by the United States against the Iraqi invasion confirms the charge that Kuwait is still a colony of the West.

The 2003 Invasion of Iraq

After years of UN-imposed sanctions, restrictions on oil sales, and international scrutiny of their every move, the Iraqi authorities remained defiant. The Iraqi authorities gambled that the sustained resistance to United Nations restrictions would eventually force an end to the sanctions followed by a Western withdrawal from the Persian Gulf Region. In the spring of 2003 the Iraqi regime was defeated by the United States, the United Kingdom, and other forces who quickly occupied the entire country. Since the end of the Iraqi War and the capture of Saddam Hussein, the American leadership has been confronted by a series of issues, many of which overwhelmed the British almost a century ago.

- ◆ In Iraq, it is much easier to win a conventional war than establish a secure peace.
- ◆ Iraq is an artificial country where Iraqis hold traditional loyalties to religion, region, tribe, and family in higher regard than the conventional nationalistic loyalties to the state so valued in the West.
- ◆ In 2005–06 America, the coalition allies, and their Iraqi friends face the reality of building a modern state while fighting a clandestine war fueled by both internal and external supporters.

If Iraq is to succeed as a product of the 2003 coalition victory, several issues must be satisfactorily resolved in the Iraqi government.

- ◆ Can Iraqis implement and agree to a constitution that guarantees the status of the majority Shi'ia while protecting the autonomy of the Sunni minority and the Kurds?
- ◆ Are Iraqis willing to secure the established rights of women? If they are unable to follow through with this reform, the leadership of Iraq is likely to lose Western political support.
- ◆ While acknowledging a pivotal role for Islam, the authorities must not move Iraq into a religiously intolerant state if Western political support is to continue.
- ◆ Like other societies, Iraq must devise a scheme where the state's vast oil resources are spent for the greater good of all Iraqis and not for just one sectarian group.

None of these issues are resolved at this time. It is clear that Iraq is at a crossroads. If Iraqis are able to fairly resolve the issues raised above, the present conflict will only be a bump in the road toward a modern, prosperous state in the Middle East. If they fail, the alternative could be civil war followed by the breakup of the present Iraqi state.

STRATEGIC WATERWAYS AND OIL PIPELINES

The Turkish Straits

The Dardanelles and Bosporus are narrow straits, between 1 and 4 miles wide, that dominate the Russian-controlled Black Sea. The straits have been a point of conflict between Russia and Turkey for centuries. The continued Turkish control of the Dardanelles and Bosporus is a source of irritation because it has frustrated repeated Russian attempts to gain easy access to the Mediterranean Sea. At present, Russian access to this area is governed by treaty. Should the Turks again attempt to block access, they will provoke a major international conflict.

The Suez Canal

Opened in 1869, the canal, including the Great Bitter Lake and Lake Timsah, is 101 miles long. It serves as the only direct sea passage from the Mediterranean to the Indian Ocean. Much of the history of the modern Middle East has involved struggles for the control of this strategic waterway. Although the canal is at sea level, requiring no complicated, easily sabotaged system of locks, its location near unstable, hostile neighbors makes its access uncertain at times. For example, in the summer of 1984, an unknown terrorist organization was able to mine parts of the canal and the Red Sea to prevent ships from using the waterway. Because of its importance to Europe, threats to close the Suez Canal always raise the possibility of conflict.

The Persian (or Arab) Gulf

The question over name implies a more serious conflict over control of the single most important waterway in the world. It is through the Persian Gulf (Arab Gulf) that two-thirds of the world's oil is exported. The conflict between Kuwait and Iraq raises the possibility of seizure of the Strait of Hormuz by an unfriendly power bent on shutting off oil shipments to the West. Because the United States is committed to keeping the oil flowing from the Gulf, any closure will immediately provoke a great-power intervention, with all of its dangers.

Oil Pipelines

One of the major problems associated with Middle Eastern oil is getting the product to the consumer. Pipelines are an efficient alternative to ships for the movement of petroleum products from the Persian Gulf and Saudi Arabia to Europe. For many years some pipelines have connected Saudi Arabia with Lebanon and Israel, and others have linked Iraq with the Mediterranean through both Syria and Turkey. The chief problem of relying on pipelines is their vulnerability to sabotage that often occurs in the lands they cross during periods of political instability. For example, the pipeline through Israel has been closed since 1948, and the pipeline from Iraq to the Mediterranean was closed by Syria for the duration of the Iran-Iraq war. Until the political situation in the Middle East changes, the potential of moving oil by pipeline remains an unfulfilled dream.

OPEC AND THE POLITICS OF OIL

Halfway through the first decade of the twenty-first century, the world is facing record prices for oil. Some forecasters fear that as the huge populations of China and India modernize, the demands for oil will explode. Will civilization as we know it come to an end because a shortage of oil is becoming one of the major questions of our time?

Other analysts, such as Professor Mukul Sharma of the Department of Petroleum Engineering at the University of Texas, do not think so. He says, "By and large, articles are written by people who know very little about the oil and gas business. It is largely because the media are dominated by people in New York, so they go to energy experts at Harvard and MIT. What the hell do they know about energy, especially the oil and gas business."[27] A colleague of his, Professor Scott Tinker, Director of the University of Texas Bureau of Economic Geology, points out that today "when the well goes dry by these (current) methods, drillers have only recovered, on average, 30 percent of the oil that is there; it's hardly dry."[28] The Cambridge Energy Research Associates have used a field-by-field analysis to project that global oil production capacity will exceed global demand by 7.5 million barrels a day by the end of the decade.[29]

Should we take seriously the comments of the "experts" at the University of Texas? It is possible that the fossil fuel business will remain, as it always has been, an artificially controlled cartel of both producers and distributors. Even Saudi Arabia, the world's key oil power with over a third of the reserves of the Middle East, predicts that it will double its proved reserves in the near future. As Muhammed Ali Zainy, London Center for Global Energy Studies put it, "Since these OPEC countries are closed, the only information available is available to themselves alone. So they can come up with a new reserves figure and the rest of the world will just have to take it."[30] Could it be just another example of how in the past the cartel has encouraged the idea of future shortages to keep the price of oil artificially inflated?

In 1901, a Western adventurer, William D'Arcy, received a concession to explore for oil in Iran. At almost the same time, an Armenian, C. S. Gulbenkian, obtained a similar concession from the Ottoman Empire. Less than 50 years later, these concessions had grown into a vast oil cartel controlled by seven Western companies: Exxon, Mobil, Standard Oil of California, Texaco, Gulf, British Petroleum, and Shell. Called the Seven Sisters, these companies gained a virtual monopoly on the production, refinement, and distribution of Middle Eastern oil.

Designed to present a united front when negotiating prices with the oil companies, the Organization of Petroleum Exporting Countries (OPEC) was organized in 1960 by Iraq, Saudi Arabia, Iran, Kuwait, and Venezuela. Subsequently, OPEC membership grew to include Qatar, Libya, Indonesia, Algeria, Nigeria, Ecuador, Gabon, and the United Arab Emirates.

The OPEC cartel was only marginally effective until the October 1973 Middle East war. At that time, the sale of petroleum products was linked by the Arab members of OPEC to the support for their cause against Israel. The selective withholding of oil caused an energy crisis in the West. During the next decade, OPEC oil rose from a pre-1973 price of around $3 a barrel to over $30 a barrel. This oil shock was difficult for the developed world, but it destroyed the hopes of many Other World states that were depending on low-cost energy to finance development. Ignoring 50 years of Western oil cartel exploitation, newspapers in Europe and the United States were filled with articles editorializing on the "evils" of OPEC. Today, more than 30 years after the first oil crisis in the 1970s, Western observers admit that although the economic impact of OPEC has been considerable, it is a political force in the Other World far out of proportion to its size.

If high prices cause the developed world to convert to other energy sources, it will have serious implications for every state in the region. Like Haiti with sugar and Brazil with rubber, Middle Eastern oil could become just another surplus commodity that is a victim of production elsewhere.

There is little doubt that the competition for these resources will increase with the industrial rise of China and India. This will tempt producers to keep prices high as long as the OPEC cartel can. However, as the price of oil passes 40 dollars a barrel, brand new methods of recovery once thought too expensive become possible. The developed world has the resources to exploit novel recovery methods for the 70 percent of remaining oil in old wells. At above 40 dollars a barrel, the West has the technology to profitably recover energy from oil shale, which exists in vast quantities in North America. Other exotic fuel sources also become practical at these prices, including methane or natural gas, oil from coal, and liquefied natural gas. Professor Sharma pointed out that the world has enough coal unmined that can be converted to fuel current energy needs for the next two thousand years.[31] All it takes to make these conversions possible today is continued high prices to justify the investment.

Finally, at a recent conference in South Africa, Exxon Mobil's president Rex Tillerson stated that some estimates said there were more than 7 trillion barrels of oil yet to be discovered. He further added that 3 trillion barrels could be recovered from conventional fields, oil sands, and other sources that are "more than twice all the oil recovered up to now in all of human history."[32]

SUMMARY

Geographically, the Middle East and North Africa can be divided into three distinct regions: the plains of North Africa and Arabia, the Fertile Crescent, and the northern tier. The Middle East is an area of contrast, including some of the world's most famous deserts, mountain ranges, and rivers. Oil is the most important natural resource of the region. A scarcity of water limits agricultural development throughout most of the Middle East. The monotheistic religions Judaism, Christianity, and Islam have developed in the Middle East. Today, Islam is the professed religion of 90 percent of the population, and most political activity in this part of the Other World is affected by religion.

Nationalism is a second feature of Middle Eastern politics. Case studies in this chapter describe the various forms of nationalism that have developed in Turkey, Iran, Egypt, Saudi Arabia, and Israel. A brief description of Arab nationalism is also included. These case studies illustrate the directions that nationalists have taken in this part of the Other World.

Review Questions

1. Discuss some of the features of Arab nationalism.
2. List the Five Pillars of Islam.
3. What role does oil play in Middle Eastern politics?
4. Why is Islam called a way of life?
5. Compare the nationalisms of Turkey, Iran, Egypt, and Israel.

Key Terms

- **1798**—The date of the French invasion of Egypt which is considered to be the beginning of the modern European colonial period.
- **Allah**—The name of God in the Arabic language.
- **The Fertile Crescent**—The historic land stretching up the eastern Mediterranean and along the southern border of Turkey to exit through Iraq into the Persian Gulf.
- **Monotheism**—The belief in one God.

- **Mohammed**—Considered by Moslems to be a human being who lived a perfect life and was a prophet of God.
- **The Ottomans**—A tribe that came to what is now Turkey, in the Middle Ages, and established a great empire that lasted from 1453 to 1918.
- **The Rightly Guided Caliphs**—The first four successors to Mohammed: Abu Bakr, Umar, Uthman, and Ali.
- **Shah**—Persian word for king.
- **The Suez Canal**—Opened in 1869, the Canal provides a passage from the Mediterranean Sea to the Red Sea.
- **Zionism**—Founded in 1897, Zionism is a Jewish form of nationalism calling for the establishment and maintenance of a Jewish state in Palestine.

Useful Web Sites

Israel: www.israel.org
Iraq: www.iraqi-mission.org
Turkey: www.turkey.org
Egypt: www.idsc.gov.eg
Lebanon: www.erols.com/lebanon/stat.htm

Notes

1. Madeline Miller, and J. Lane Miller, *Harpers Bible Dictionary* (New York: Harper & Row, 1973), p. 688.
2. Population sources: *CIA World Fact Book*, US Central Intelligence Agency.
3. For more information on the politics of water, see Adam Kelliher, "Thrust for Peace Is on Water," *Times* (London), 3 August 1991, p. 6.
4. Lawrence Ziring, *The Middle East Political Dictionary* (Santa Barbara, Calif.: ABC-CLIO Information Services, 1983), p. 415.
5. Lord Kinross, *The Ottoman Centuries* (New York: Morrow Quill, 1977), p. 85.
6. For more information on the Pentecostal Holiness Church, see Ed Housewright, "Faith on a Deadly Scale," *San.*
7. For an example of a charity accused of aiding terrorism see Mary Beth Sheridan, "U.S. raids Islamic charity in Va; Immigration Charges Filed Against Worker," *The Washington Post*, Washington D.C., July 26, 2005, p Metro BO1.
8. The Ka'bah is a cubelike building located in the courtyard of the Great Mosque in Mecca. According to Moslem tradition, it was the first house of worship built by the prophet Abraham. *Francisco Examiner*, 12 March 1995, p. A8.
9. Sometimes called the Battle of the Nile, British Admiral Nelson defeated the French on August 1, 1798, J. R. Hill, *The Oxford History of the Royal Navy* (Oxford, England: Oxford University Press, 1995), p. 111.
10. For pre-1991 Gulf War petroleum export figures, see Richard Teitelbaum, "Where Do We Go from Here," *Fortune*, September 1990, p. 30.
11. Edward Mortimer, Michael Field, "Nationalism, the Steel of the Arab Soul," *Financial Times* (London), 18/19 August 1990, sec. 11.

12. Alfred B. Prados, *Saudi Arabia: Post Issues and U.S. Relations*, C.R.S. Issue Brief No. 1B93113, Congressional Research Service, The Library of Congress, Washington, D.C., 1996.

13. Likbn Antara, "Terrorism Has No Link With Islam: Saudi Foreign Minister," *Nationwide International News*, Indonesia, taken from Lexis-Nexis, the Academic Universe, April 23, 2005.

14. Douglas Jehl, "To Some Saudi Clerics, It's Infidels vs. Islam: Harsh Anti-Western Opinions Resonate Among Citizens," *The Dallas Morning News*, 6 December 2001, p. 19A.

15. Foreign Minister: Islamic Policies, Lawd, not in Turkish Government's Agenda, comments made on Turkish NTV Television, reported by the *Financial Times Information Service*, London, accessed from Lexis-Nexis, the Academic Universe, March 14, 2005.

16. "Turkey and Europe," *Turkish Daily News*, 16 November 2001. Accessed from Lexis-Nexis, the Academic Universe.

17. "Assembly Makes Changes to Boost Bid to Join EU," *The Dallas Morning News*, 4 October 2001, p. 11A.

18. Although never officially acknowledged by the U.S. Government, there is little doubt about the CIA involvement in this episode. See Kermit Roosevelt, *Countercoup: The Struggle for the Control of Iran* (New York: McGraw-Hill, 1979), Chaps 11, 12, 13; and R. G. Gant, *MI 5, MI 6; Britain's Security and Secret Intelligence Services* (New York: Gallery Books, 1989), pp. 113–114.

19. David Sanger, New York Times correspondent, "Election Advances Iran's Nuclear Future," *The Dallas Morning News*, Dallas, Texas, World Section p. 15A, June 26, 2005.

20. Shortly after World War I, nationalists formed the Egyptian Delegation (Wafd al-Misri) to pressure for independence. This group eventually became Wafd party.

21. Jehl, op. cit.

22. Mortimer and Field, op. cit.

23. "The Middle East Math," *The New York Times*, *Late Edition*, Editorial Desk, Section A, p. 30, Col. 1, Sept. 12, 2003.

24. For an interesting account of how the Ottomans, the British, the French, the Germans, and the Russians became involved in the affairs of Kuwait, see William Facey and Gillian Grant, *Kuwait by the First Photographers*, (London, New York: I. B. Taurus Publishers, 1998), pp. 11–16.

25. This charge is countered by Kuwaiti officials who point out that during the last 20 years general assistance aid exceeded $17 billion, or 6 percent of the GNP of Kuwait. This percentage is many times greater than that of any other nation during this period. See Michael Kramer, "Toward A New Kuwait," *Time* 136, No. 27 (24 December 1990): 26–33.

26. For an account of the British-American Activities during the 1991 Persian Gulf War, see John Witherow and Aidan Sullivan, *The Sunday Times: War in the Gulf* (London: Sidgwick & Jackson, 1991).

27. Avrel Seale, "How Long Do We Have?" *The Alcade*, Vol 93, No 6, Texas Exes, Austin, Texas, July/August 2005, p. 42

28. Avrel Seale, op. cit., p. 43.

29. Sudcep Reddy, "Putting a Cap On Oil Supply Worries," *The Dallas Morning News*, June 22, 2005, Sec D, p 1.

30. Saeed Shah, "Oil Reserves Are Double Previous Estimates Says Saudi," *The Independent Online Edition*, London, September 28, 2005.

31. Avrel Seale, op. cit., p 44.

32. Saeed Shah, op. cit.

For Further Reading

Al-Munajjed, Mona. *Women in Saudi Arabia Today.* New York: Macmillan, 1997.

Chebel, Malek. *Symbols of Islam.* New York: Assouline/St. Martin's Press, 1997.

Clapp, Nicholas. *The Road to Ubar: Finding the Atlantis of the Sands.* Boston: Houghton Mifflin, 1998.

Cleary, Thomas. *The Essential Koran: The Heart of Islam.* San Francisco: Harper, 1993.

Evron, Yair. *Israel's Nuclear Dilemma.* Ithaca, N.Y.: Cornell University Press, 1994.

Fernea, Elizabeth. *Guest of the Sheik: An Ethnography of an Iraqi Village.* Garden City, N.Y.: Anchor Books, 1965.

Fromkin, David. *A Peace to End All Peace: Creating the Modern Middle East 1914–1922.* New York: Henry Holt, 1989.

Goodwin, Jan. *Price of Honor: Moslim Women Lift the Veil of Silence on the Islamic World.* New York: Penguin, 2003.

Hazelton, Fran, ed. *Iraq Since the Gulf War: Prospects for Democracy.* London: Zed Books, 1994.

Hourani, Albert. *A History of the Arab Peoples.* Cambridge, Mass.: Belknap Press, 1991.

Howe, Kathleen Stewart. *Revealing the Holy Land: The Photographic Exploration of Palestine.* Santa Barbara, CA: Santa Barbara Museum of Art.

Kamen, Charles. *Little Common Ground: Arab Agriculture and Jewish Settlement in Palestine 1920–1948.* Pittsburgh: Pennsylvania University Press, 1991.

Lacey, Robert. *The Kingdom: Arabia and the House of Saud.* New York: Avon Books, 1981.

Laqueur, Walter and Rubin, Barry. *The Israel-Arab Reader: A documentary, History* 6th ed. New York: Penquin, 2001.

Lippman, Thomas. *Understanding Islam: An Introduction to the Muslim World,* 2nd ed. New York: Penquin, 1995.

Mahler, Gregory. *Israel: Government and Politics in a Maturing State.* New York: Harcourt Brace Jovanovich, 1990.

Mango, Andrew. *Turkey: The Challenge of a New Role.* New York: Praeger, 1994.

Mansfield, Peter. *A History of the Middle East,* 2nd ed. New York: Penguin, 2004.

Norwich, John Julius. *Byzantium: The Decline and Fall.* New York: Alfred A. Knopf, 1996.

Nutting, Anthony. *The Arabs: A Narrative History from Mohammed to the Present.* New York: Mentor Books, 1964.

Pampanini, Andrea. *Cities from the Arabian Desert: The Building of Jubail and Yanbu in Saudi Arabia.* New York: Praeger, 1997.

Peretz, Don. *Intifada: The Palestinian Uprising.* Boulder, Colo.: Westview Press, 1990.

Rubinstein, Alvin. *The Arab-Israeli Conflict: Perspectives.* 2nd ed. New York: HarperCollins, 1991.

Shalev, Aryeh. *Israel and Syria: Peace and Security on the Golan.* Boulder, Colo.: Westview Press, 1994.

Shehadeh, Raja. *Strangers in the House: Coming of Age in Occupied Palestine.* South Royalton, Vt, 2002.

Sherman, A. J. *Mandate Days: British Lives in Palestine 1918–1948.* UK: Thames and Hudson, 1997.

Singerman, Diane. *Avenues of Participation: Family, Politics, and Networks in Urban Quarters of Cairo.* Princeton: Princeton University Press, 1995.

Smith, Charles. *Palestine and the Arab-Israeli Conflict.* New York: St. Martin's Press, 1992.

Wright, Robin. *In the Name of God: The Khomeini Decade.* New York: Simon & Schuster, 1989.

Yapp, M. *The Near East Since the First World War.* White Plains, N.Y.: Longman, 1991.

Zangeneh, Hamid, ed. *Islam, Iran and World Stability.* New York: St. Martin's Press, 1994.

Central Asia and the Southern Near Abroad

Olga D. Novikova-Carter

We live in a moment of history where change is so speeded up that we begin to see the present only when it is already disappearing.

R. D. LAING

What man calls civilization always results in deserts.

DON MARQUIS

During much of their past, nations of Central Asia and the Southern Near Abroad have received little attention from the outside world. For many, this part of the world is most strongly associated with the remote historical times of Genghis Khan, Tamerlane, or the great Silk Road. For most of its history this region was not a coherent nation but a geographically defined area of independent political entities and tribal groups. This territory has been a target for numerous invasions and massive migrations, which had an impact on the population's composition, language formation, cultural similarities, and distinctions.

The current "war on terrorism," competition between oil companies for control of energy resources, and future strategic pipeline routes of the region has led to an increased interest in the affairs of this region's countries, and has contributed to recognition of the fact that this region occupies a new and increasingly important position in world affairs.

WHAT IS CENTRAL ASIA AND THE SOUTHERN NEAR ABROAD?

One does not argue on terms, they are to be agreed upon.
AN ANCIENT GREEK MAXIM

As mentioned in Chapter 7, the subdivisions of Asia are, to a great extent, subjective, contingent on the purposes of the given discussion, and can be described by employing different terms.

For the purpose of our analysis we included in the definition of Central Asia all former Soviet republics of Central Asia, such as Kazakhstan, Kyrgyzstan, Tajikistan, Turkmenistan, and Uzbekistan, as well as a bordering, landlocked Afghanistan. We use the term the Southern Near Abroad in reference to Armenia, Azerbaijan, and Georgia.[1] Although there may be numerous arguments for suggested subdivisions, you may also find that some countries are referred to as the Caucasus, Transcaucasia, Southeastern Europe, or West Asia. We adhere to an Ancient Greek's saying that "one does not argue on terms, they are to be agreed upon," thus the focus of our attention will be on the substance of issues pertaining to this part of the world, rather than on terminology.

(See Table 9.1 for recent data on the countries that make up Central Asia and the Southern Near Abroad.)

GEOGRAPHY

Where Is Central Asia and the Southern Near Abroad?

Central Asia and the Southern Near Abroad make up a landlocked territory on the interior of the Asian continent stretching for hundreds of miles from the Black Sea to the Caspian Sea in the west, to Chinese borders in the east, and from the southern border of Eastern Russia to the borders with Pakistan and Iran. These territories include the Caucasus Mountains, the Aral-Caspian lowland with its vast deserts of Karakum and Kizilkum, and the basins of two great rivers: Sir-Darya and Amu-Darya, which flow into the Aral Sea.

This region is situated in the geographic center of the Eurasian continent and is full of contrasts: from the perpetually snow-capped mountains, Great Steppe, and sand deserts to impetuous rivers, picturesque lakes, and landlocked seas. Large parts of this region are highly seismic, with frequent earthquakes, whose destructive power has wiped centers of great civilizations from the face of the earth over the centuries.

Most importantly, the diverse geography determines the nation's natural conditions and thereby its economic development and culture. (See Figure 9.1.)

TABLE 9.1 Central Asia and The Southern Near Abroad

Country	Population (millions)	Population Growth Rate %	Infant Mortality Rate (per 1,000 live births)	Population Under 15 Years of Age (%)	Life Expectancy (in years)	Urban Population (%)	Literacy Rate (%)	Arable Land (%)	Per Capita GDP ($US)
Afghanistan	28.513	4.77	166	42	42.9	23.3	36	12	700
Georgia	4.693	−0.35	19.3	19	75.88	51.9	99	9	2500
Armenia	2.991	−0.25	24.2	22.2	71.55	64.4	98.6	17	3900
Azerbaijan	7.868	0.59	82.1	28.3	63.35	50	100	18	3400
Uzbekistan	26.41	1.67	73.1	35.5	64.19	36.6	99.3	9	1700
Kazakhstan	15.143	0.3	62.6	41.1	66.55	39.4	85.1	7	1000
Turkmenistan	4.863	1.81	73.1	37.3	61.39	45.3	100	3	5700
Tajikistan	7.011	2.15	112.1	40.4	64.56	24.7	99.4	6	1000
Kyrgyzstan	5.081	1.29	36.8	34.4	68.16	33.9	97	7	1600
Mongolia	2.751	1.45	55.5	32	64.52	56.7	99	1	1800

SOURCE: Population, Infant Mortality Rate, Population Under 15 Years of Age, Urban Population, Life Expectancy, Literacy Rate, Arable Land, and Per Capita GDP from *The World Almanac and Book of Facts, 2005*. Population Growth Rate and Life Expectancy from *CIA World Factbook, 2005*.

FIGURE 9.1   Political and Physical Characteristics of Central Asia and the Southern Near Abroad

Mountains

More beautiful than mountains
Could be only mountains,
Which you have not seen yet.

VLADIMIR VISOTSKY

The mountains of the region are as unique and diverse in character as the people who live in these areas. It is difficult for an outsider, especially for an urban dweller, to distinguish and appreciate all the shades of beauty of these natural "monuments." Mountains dominate the landscape. Great and Small Caucasus,[2] forming a skeleton of Georgia, Armenia, and Azerbaijan in the west, accounting for almost 60 percent of their territory. These mountain systems are young in geological terms and are still in the process of active formation, which leads to frequent and powerful earthquakes, such as the most recent one in Spitak, Armenia in 1988, which completely razed several cities and cost more than 9,000 human lives; as well as the earthquake in Baku, Azerbaijan in 2000, which measured 5.9–6.3 on the Richter scale.[3]

This area is also sadly known for its mud volcanoes and mud slides. If we start our mountain journey beginning from its northwest part, in Kazakhstan, we would see that its edges are adjoined by the round-topped old geological system of the Southern Ural Mountains, which is connected on the northeast with the Altai Mountains (14,700 feet), both being nature's treasury in terms of deposits of coal, iron ore, manganese, chrome, nickel, cobalt, copper, molybdenum, lead, zinc, bauxite, gold, and uranium.

The eastern and southern borders of the region are ringed by the highest, and one of the youngest, geological mountain formations on the planet. This mountain division is the subject of ongoing discussion and disagreement among members of the geographic scientific community. The most known among those mountain systems are the Pamir Mountains, which are referred to by all neighboring nations of the region as the "Roof of the World." At its westernmost extension of the Tien-Shan (21,000 feet), the Hindukush system, Karakorum, and Himalayas hone their peaks reaching more than 22,960 feet.[4]

There are several stories about the origin of the term *Hindukush* (translated as Hindu Killer). The first one suggests that the mountains memorialize the Indian slaves who perished in the mountains while being transported to the Central Asian slave markets; the second suggests that the name came from a corrupted pre-Islamic name of the mountains *Hindu Koh*, which divided Hindu of the southern

Meat on the Hoof: Cattle hooves being sold for food in the market at Almaty, Kazakstan.
SOURCE: OLGA CARTER

Afghanistan from Hindu in the north; the third one points to the possibility of the name being a posited Avestan appellation meaning "water mountains."

Kyrgyzstan, Tajikistan, Uzbekistan, Turkmenistan, and Afghanistan are privileged and burdened by being mountainous countries. While in Uzbekistan and Turkmenistan mountain areas cover only southern parts of the territory, or approximately 20 percent, in other countries, like Azerbaijan and Afghanistan, mountains occupy a significant part of the land, almost 50 percent of the total, and even higher in Tajikistan where mountains cover 93 percent of the country.[5]

The majestic beauty of the mountains of Central Asia has as its hidden cost unexpected and vicious earthquakes. The history of earthquakes became an integral and often tragic part of the ancient and modern history of nations of this part of the world. The world community will never forget the massive earthquakes in Ashgabat (Turkmenbashi), Turkmenistan in 1948, which destroyed most of the city, and the powerful earthquake in Tashkent, Uzbekistan in 1966.[6]

Mountain terrain is an important determinant of the location and development of industries, agriculture, transportation, and tourism. Numerous high passes that transcend the mountains are forming a strategically important interconnected network for the transit of caravans. The completion of tunnels and roads has decreased travel time between major centers from a few days to a few hours. At the same time "old communication arteries," high passes, are still in use for drug trafficking and smuggling of illegal goods because they are difficult to control.

The growth and formation of these great mountain systems, which separated inland area from the Indian Ocean, contributed to the condition of a dry climate and to the formation of the sand deserts Karakum and Kizilkum in Uzbekistan and Turkmenistan.

The remoteness from the oceans and the impact of mountain barriers to the moisture penetration into the region has significant effects on the climate of Central Asia, as well as on the nature of waterways of the region.

Climate

The climate of the region is typical for arid and semiarid steppe, called "continental," with cold dry winters (January temperatures vary from 28° F to –13° F), and hot summers, with temperatures between 86° and 104° F.

In intermountain plateaus a northerly dry wind, known as the "wind of 120 days," blows during the summer months of June through September. This wind is usually accompanied by intense heat, drought, and sandstorms, bringing rough times to the inhabitants of the desert and steppe land.

Mountain areas represent another distinct climate zone, with the main precipitation in the form of snowfall. Permanent snow covers the highest mountain peaks. Because Armenia is 90 percent mountain country, and Georgia 80 percent, their climate is consistent with the general characteristics of this zone, with a few subtropical "implants" on the coast of the Black Sea.

The climate of the Turkistan Plains represents a transition between mountain and steppe. Aridity increases and temperatures rise with descending altitudes, becoming the highest along the lower Amu Darya and in the western parts of the plains, closer to the Caspian Sea. The climate of Azerbaijan and Georgia varies from subtropical dry in central and eastern Azerbaijan to subtropical and humid in the south, while in Georgia it is subtropical dry.[7]

Water Resources: Rivers, Lakes, and Seas

The common statement that "water is life" has been a nondisputed notion for all times and all nations in this part of the world. Although the vast territory of Central Asia and the Southern Near Abroad possesses many rivers, river basins, and lakes, the demand for water for agricultural, industrial, and urban development has always been greater than its limited supply. The blueprint of river systems has undergone numerous changes over time.

For example, in ancient times the Amu-Darya flowed into the Caspian Sea, and only much later changed its course into the Aral Sea. The Amu-Darya's changing character has impacted life of nations of these basins in Afghanistan and Uzbekistan. Many rivers and streams simply empty into arid portions of the region, spending them through evaporation without replenishing; others flow only seasonally. Eight large rivers flow down from the Caucasus mountain ranges into the central Kura-Aras lowland, alluvial flatlands, and delta areas along the seacoast.

The beauty of mountain-surrounded lakes has been an inspiration to the greatest poets of all time. Among those inspirational "eyes of the earth" well known all over the world are the Armenian Lake Sevan, Lake Balkhash, and Issikkol in Kazakhstan. A special place in the water resource system of Central Asia and the Southern Near Abroad should be devoted to two uniquely similar yet distinctly different large, salt-water natural reservoirs: the Caspian and Aral seas. Although these landlocked geological formations look like big lakes, they meet some of the characteristics and criteria of a sea.

CASPIAN SEA REGION

> *Weep not that the world changes—did it keep a stable,*
> *changeless state, 'twere cause indeed to weep.*
> WILLIAM CULLEN BRYANT

Oil and Gas in the Caspian Sea

The Caspian Sea region, which includes the sea and littoral states, is an important player in the world energy markets. It has the potential to become one of the major oil and natural gas exporters over the next decade, if not for a number of complications, such as a lack of adequate export infrastructure, disagreement over new export routes, and border disputes.

The Caspian Sea region is defined to include Azerbaijan, Kazakhstan, Turkmenistan, as well as parts of Russia, Iran, and also Uzbekistan, which, although not a littoral state, is the region's largest natural gas producer.

The Caspian region of the 1990s was like an old, once wealthy city neighborhood gone to seed and then suddenly rediscovered and made fashionable again by a new generation; it was a time of high expectation and change caused by oil.

Oil is not a new phenomenon here; its abundance was noted by Marco Polo 700 years ago. What is new is the politics of the Caspian region. Three new littoral states, Azerbaijan, Kazakhstan, and Turkmenistan, have emerged from the ruins of the Soviet Union and opened the door to the world energy community to share in what was once a Russian monopoly.

It is not clear how much oil is left in the Caspian basin. Some estimates suggest there are nearly 200 billion barrels, approximately as much as the proven reserves of Iran and Iraq combined. Other sources suggest considering proven oil reserves of this region at a range between 17 and 33 billion barrels, which is comparable to OPEC member Qatar on the low end and the United States on the high end.[8]

In 2003, regional oil production reached between 1.5 and 1.7 million barrels per day, comparable to annual production from South America's second-largest oil producer, Brazil.

By the year 2010 the countries of the region are forecast to produce between 2.4 and 5.9 million barrels per day, which exceeds annual production of South America's largest oil producer, Venezuela, in 2003.

Actual production in the region at the moment is far more modest—about 1.1 million barrels a day or 1.9 percent of the world's total.[9] This is due mainly to a difficult economic and political transition period, associated with the collapse of regional trade and cooperation after the break up of the Soviet Union. The power struggle among internal political structures makes this process even less manageable. Measured in dollars of 1995 (the year chosen as a basis of comparison for prices), the region's GDP (gross domestic product) remains below 1992 levels in Azerbaijan, Kazakhstan, and Turkmenistan. It has had a detrimental effect on the standard of living of the population of the region: 49 percent of Azerbaijan citizens and 26 percent of Kazakhstan citizens (two major oil-producing states) were estimated to be living below the poverty level in 2001. The most realistic way of improving the situation is through the successful development of the region's oil and natural gas potentials.

One of the first steps on the way to this goal is achieving a multilateral agreement between the five littoral states on division of the Caspian Sea's resources. At this point in time only a trilateral agreement has been signed by Azerbaijan, Kazakhstan, and Russia regarding subsurface boundaries and collective administration of the sea's waters. According to this agreement, these countries have divided the northern 64 percent of the Caspian Sea into three unequal parts, giving Kazakhstan 27 percent, Russia 19 percent, and Azerbaijan 18 percent.

Delegations from Iran and Turkmenistan refused to sign on, which is expected to make their offshore development even less attractive for foreign investors. In the northern Caspian state of Azerbaijan, oil production is up 70 percent

Black Gold: The Bibi Oil Field in Azerbaijan is the oldest in the world. Out of 11,000 wells only half are producing. Over 200,000 tons of oil have been spilled on the ground causing an environmental disaster area. SOURCE: OLGA CARTER

since 1992. Here there are major oil development projects at Azeri, Chirag, and deepwater Gunashli. In Kazakhstan there is a project at Tengiz. This "Second Caspian oil rush" has contributed to an increase in foreign investment activity in these regions.

The Caspian Sea region has even more growth potential in the natural gas arena. According to some experts, estimates of regional proven reserve of natural gas are around 232 trillion cubic feet (Tcf)—comparable to those in Saudi Arabia. In 2003 natural gas production in the Caspian Sea region was approximately 4.5 Tcf, comparable to the production of South America, Central America, and Mexico combined.

Although the exploration, development, and operation (including construction of an export infrastructure) of a natural gas industry is more capital intensive, this industry has a fast-growing pace due to an increased demand for its product, considered to be one of the most effective energy sources.

Russian oil company, LUKoil, has reported the launch of a drilling program for 2004–2010, with production expected to start in 2005. In July 2003 two Russian oil and gas giants, LUKoil and Gazprom (Russian State natural gas monopoly), formed a joint venture with Kazakstan's state oil company, KazMunaiGaz to develop a promising hydrocarbon structure located on the border of the Russian and Kazakhstani offshore sectors with estimated recoverable reserves of 20 Tcf of natural gas.

Turkmenistan's natural gas production and export has been affected by the competition with Gazprom since the pipeline system connecting the region to the world markets is owned by Gazprom and routed through Russia.

Uzbekistan—one of the world's top ten natural gas-producing countries—has chosen an alternative export strategy: concentrating on domestic consumption and neighboring natural gas markets and avoiding Russia's pipeline systems.

Although the region has exceptional potential for economic development and growth, it will need considerable investment in its infrastructure to realize them in full.

If we take a closer look at the Caspian oil- and gas-producing countries' export routes we note several changes in the region's energy flow:

First of all, there is a shift to an East–West axis towards Europe and away from an existing South–North axis toward Russia. One of the main complicating factors slowing production is the development of the largest part of the new pipeline system.[10] Can the Bosporus Straits, already a major checkpoint for oil tankers, manage additional tanker traffic in an environmentally safe manner? There are two alternative pipeline projects, one for oil, running from Azerbaijan through Georgia to Ceyhan, Turkey, and parallel to it a natural gas line from Azerbaijan through Georgia to Erzurum, Turkey. Although designed to bypass the Bosporus Straits, this development has raised concerns for the archeological treasures of the region. There are doubts concerning its feasibility due to the high cost of construction and operation in rugged terrain.

Extremely fast growth of the demand for oil and natural gas in China brought up a strong support for the consideration of an Eastward axis for oil and natural gas flow. It is based upon the analysis of the market demand for oil and natural gas: in Europe oil demand over the next 10–15 years is expected to grow by approximately 1 million barrels a day, while in Asia it is expected to be around 10 million barrels a day over the same period of time.

There is also a proposal for the development of a Southern axis through either Afghanistan or Iran to supply oil and natural gas to Asian markets. After the Taliban's removal from power in Afghanistan in December 2001, proposals to build a Trans-Afghan natural gas pipeline and the Central Asian Oil Pipeline have reemerged. In 1997 Turkmenistan and Iran completed the $190 million pipeline, connecting those two countries and allowing them to be engaged in low-volume "swap" deals. Under this arrangement oil in tankers is delivered to refineries in Iran's northern regions in exchange for similar volumes of crude oil located in Iranian ports in the Persian Gulf.

Regional Conflicts in the Caspian Region

Regional conflicts in the Caspian region and surrounding countries are by far the most serious consideration in determining export pipeline routes. For the sake of time we will discuss only the most complicated conflicts.

1. Afghanistan is still in the category of a war zone unsuitable for substantial investments, despite the change in central power.
2. The Azerbaijan–Armenian 15-year war over the Armenian-populated Nagorno-Karabakh enclave in Azerbaijan has not yet been resolved, prohibiting development.
3. Separatist conflicts in Abkhazia and Ocetia, Georgia's autonomous republics.
4. Russia's war in Chechnya.

This information is a key to an accurate interpretation of the political climate of this geopolitical area. For example, a sharp criticism of Turkmenistan's policies by Russian experts and politicians was believed to be partially heated up by the Turkmen-Russian pricing and export issue disputes in the past. "Follow the oil (natural gas)," is viewed by analysts as one of the useful principles for a safe navigation in the ocean of political problems of the region.

RELIGION

Islam

> We might as well give up the fiction that we can argue any view.
> For what in me is pure conviction, is simple prejudice in you.
> PHYLLIS MCGINLEY

The conventional view of Central Asia as a Moslem territory requires some clarification. During the last two millennia this region was under the influence of several political and religious doctrines. Islam is the latest religion to arrive and be assimi-lated by Central Asia. It was brought to the region by Arabs in the seventh century and introduced by the force of arms and gifts. Since that time, Islam has become an integral part of the cultural makeup of nations of the region.

The indigenous belief systems of Tengri and Shamanism, which co-existed with Zoroastrianism and Buddhism, not only "broke the equation that Arab equals Moslem," but has altered the character of Islam there. In the eyes of the na-tive population religion and culture are tied together.[11] However, because of the religious oppression of the Soviet system, the vast majority of people have never read the Koran or been to a mosque. People do not practice strict orthodox Islam as practiced by the Arabs in the Middle East. Instead in most of Kazakhstan, Kyrgyzstan, Tajikistan, and other countries people practice Folk Islam. They mix superstition with Moslem practices.[12] They fear the evil eye, which is perceived to be a destructive force resulting from people's envy and ill will. They are wary of spirits which may cause physical or mental illness. Kazaks, for instance, will visit the graves of Moslem saints to try to gain blessing or favor. In many cultures it is common for Moslems to wear *tumars,* which are charms with a Koranic scripture written on them, to try to protect themselves from evil. Appealing to fortunetellers and faith healers when ill is still a common practice. Folk Islam also played an important role in the survival of Islam among the urban population.

Soviet Influence

Islam has been "paganized" by native cultural practices similar to Christianity in new mission fields and by the political realities of the Soviet era. The Soviet au-thorities did not prohibit Islam entirely but oppressed its practices in overt and covert manners.[13] In doing so they achieved various levels of secularization of Islam in most Central Asian countries. They tried to use religious traditions to placate a population, by creating and approving a Moslem Board of Central Asia that acted as a governing agency of the Moslem faith with headquarters in Tashkent, Uzbekistan. The grand mufti, who headed the board, had extensive in-ternational contacts with other countries, but the very nature of all his activities and leadership were carefully screened for political reliability. All Islamic move-ments or networks outside of the control of the state were severely suppressed. The Soviet efforts led to the widening of the gap of understanding between Moslems and others, and contributed to the emergence of competing Islamic ide-ologies among the Central Asians themselves.

During the first years of independence, newly emerged states of Central Asia have been experiencing the resurgence of a more secular form of Islam. This form of Islam relates to the population more in traditional and cultural terms than in re-ligious ones. Many support a revival of religion's status only as an element of na-tional revival. They do not attend mosque services, even occasionally, but adhere to popular Islamic traditions, such as life-cycle events which include births, wed-dings, and funerals. At the same time governments are making a calculated effort to recapture their national history and culture by supporting a growing interest in

Islamic teachings and an open, state-sanctioned observance of religious holidays and practices. Since 1991 hundreds of mosques and religious schools have been built or restored and reopened. It is not the impact of Islam on Central Asian culture that is a growing concern of the world, but the rapid politicization of Islam. History demonstrated that political involvement of religious establishment (as in Afghanistan during and following the Soviet invasion) moved Islam from the position of being a total way of life to the condition of no distinction between religion and state.

The vast majority of Uzbeks, Kyrgyz, Turkmens, Tajiks, and Kazakhs, like their kin in Afghanistan, are Sunni Moslems. There are fewer Shia Moslems, the other main branch of Islam, and the Shia religious practices of Azerbaijan and Kurdish minorities are not politicized. Such a situation is consistent with the proportion of each branch among the world's Moslems.

The historical division of Islam into Sunni, or orthodox Islam, and the Shia was a result of political disagreement over successors rather than doctrinal differences. Sunni communities have no clerical hierarchy: Each individual stands in a personal relationship to God needing no intermediary. Any adult versed in the form of prayer is entitled to lead prayers. Shia, on the other hand, have a highly structured hierarchy of divinely inspired religio-political leaders.

Christianity

The next largest religious community in the region is Christianity. The leading position has been occupied by the Russian Orthodox Church, the historic faith of many Russians and Ukrainians, followed by Roman Catholics. Most Catholics were Germans, relocated into exile during World War II from European territories of the USSR. Baptists and Seventh Day Adventists also live in the region. Other religious groups include small numbers of Jews.

In Azerbaijan the most significant religious minority group is represented by the Zoroastrian religion, which is a legacy of the early Persian influence.[14] Known mostly as a cult of fire, the various rites of this religion center on the eternal flame in the Temple of Fire. Later forms of the Zoroastrian religion teach that through good deeds the righteous person earns an everlasting reward, namely integrity and immortality, as well as resurrection of the dead as a way of the renewal of the world.

The religious composition of Armenia, Azerbaijan, and Georgia has been influenced greatly by their location as a meeting point of southeastern Europe with the western border of Asia. Azerbaijan's population is predominantly Shia Moslem. Only 4.8 percent of the population is Christian, and a small percentage is Jewish. The dominance of Christianity in two other countries of the Caucasus region is overwhelming. Ninety-nine percent of the population in Armenia and 83 percent of the population in Georgia is Christian.[15] These countries accepted Christianity in the early fourth century. The millennium-long history, as well as the history of repression during the Soviet period, encouraged the incorporation of a Christian religious identity into a national identity.

Oriental Carpets: Variety of colors and designs of handmade carpets sold in old part of Baku reflects the cultural history of the Azeri people. SOURCE: OLGA CARTER

PEOPLE

Oh the times! Oh, the customs! (O tempora! O mores!)
CICERO

When you visit a foreign country the most interesting things are not its nature or architecture. The most interesting thing is people.
NIKOLAY GOGOL

The cultural diversity and complexity of the people of the Southern Near Abroad could be compared with the multicolor carpets, which are famous for their designs all over the world, whether they are made in Turkmenistan, Uzbekistan, Afghanistan, or elsewhere in the region. Although cultures of the region are not homogeneous, there are some commonalities:

1. A search for the historical past of each nation, which is currently a subject of reassessment
2. A reinforcement of a sense of national identity and national pride
3. A declining position of Russian language as a second language and a means of intercultural communication

4. Kinship and tribal relations retain a strong influence over the social and political structure of each country
5. A shift from open hostility to a cautious official sanctioning of religion in the social life of each society
6. Cultural values that emphasize honor, solidarity, hospitality, mutual support, shame, and revenge, which determine social order and individual responsibility
7. The respect for elders is great in rural and urban areas
8. The marriage celebration, as well as other life-cycle events, possesses great importance and is arranged according to old customs
9. The role of women in most of the region's societies has never conformed to Western stereotypes about Moslem women. With the exception of Afghanistan, the division of labor remains very strict. Women usually are not visible actors in political affairs outside the home. They never wear the veil or practice strict seclusion.

LANGUAGE

After all, when you come right down to it, how many people speak the same language even when they speak the same language?
RUSSELL HOBAN

The dominance of the Turkic language group is one of the most visible features of the region.[16] The spoken languages of Kazakhstan, Uzbekistan, Turkmenistan, Kyrgyzstan, and Azerbaijan belong to different branches of Turkic language that have been influenced by a diverse history of nations. Language still remains the foundation of cultural interconnectedness. A high degree of language loyalty was reflected in the populations' claims of native language. For instance, 99.4 percent of Turkmen in Turkmenistan claimed the Turkmen language as their native language in a 1989 census. Among the group, represented for the most part by educated urban dwellers, 28 percent claim Russian as their second language. Only 3 percent of Russians in this republic spoke Turkmen. This language distribution is consistent throughout the region.

During the Soviet period, written forms of many languages of the region underwent several reforms, being changed from Arabic script to the Latin alphabet to Cyrillic script. The independent language policy has been marked by a determination to establish native language as the official language and to remove the heritage of a Russian-dominated past. In some countries, specifically in Turkmenistan and Azerbaijan, where the Cyrillic-based alphabet was officially replaced by the Latin-based script, English has been moved ahead of Russian as the "second state language." Nevertheless, Russian does remain a key language in government and other spheres. In the past, Russian language policies created a barrier and a discriminatory factor for nonnative speakers, especially middle-aged professionals, in terms of social status and position, job retention, promotion, social acceptance, and prestige.

The Tajik language *Farsi*, which traditionally had been called *Persian*, belongs to the Iranian language group. Many Persian language writers were called *Tajiks*. Based on instructions of the Soviet central political leadership, they had been identified in that way, although they had not lived in Central Asia.

There are several eastern Iranian peoples of the Pamir Mountain area in Tajikistan. Due to their geographic isolation they have not been assimilated by their Persian or Turkic-speaking neighbors, and have managed to preserve their distinct identities. Only at the end of the Soviet era did the central government allow some form of education and media sources to operate in native Pamiri languages.

The Armenian and Georgian languages grew in different directions. Armenian developed from a combination of Indo-European and non-Indo-European language stock with an alphabet based on the Greek. Georgian, unrelated to any major world languages, uses a Greek-based alphabet that is different from Armenian.

The Afghan language mosaic is the most colorful in the region. It is home to a multiplicity of ethnic and linguistic groups, with a considerable degree of cultural homogeneity, as a result of cultural assimilation. The largest ethnic group, Pushtun, speaks several mutually intelligible dialects of Pushtu. Some also speak Dari. Both of the languages belong to the Iranian branch of the Indo-European language family. Among other language and ethnic groups in Afghanistan the most prominent positions are occupied by Tajik, Uzbek, Turkmen, and Hazara.

HISTORY

A thousand years scarce serve to form a state:
an hour may lay it in the dust.
LORD BYRON

The Southern Near Abroad's location at the meeting point of southeastern Europe with the eastern border of Asia greatly influenced the histories of the people forming its present-day republics. Their people were subject to invasion and control by the Ottoman, Persian, Mongol, and Russian empires. The starting points and the outside influences that formed cultures of the region were quite different.

A legacy of the early Persian influence in the Southern Near Abroad countries as well as a later conquest and centuries of occupation by the Ottoman Empire has added Turkic influence on different aspects of secular culture, most notably in language and art.[17] The diverse people of Central Asia underwent different degrees of displacement and, at different times, experienced growth and decline. The times of independence enabled civilizations to flourish and to individualize their forms of art and literature.

Archeologists working in the deserts of Turkmenistan have discovered evidence of an ancient, literate civilization that existed in Central Asia more than

4,000 years ago.[18] According to experts, traces of lost civilizations suggest that the ancient people of Central Asia were not as isolated as previously thought, but rather had continent-wide connections. New excavation sites are a real goldmine for archeologists. The baked-clay statue found in southern Turkmenistan was similar to a Bactrian one found in Northern Afghanistan and Mesopotamia, which led experts to suggest that a high-level civilization was prospering approximately 3,000 years ago, and was a direct heir to Mesopotamian civilization.

Between 700 B.C. and A.D. 250 Central Asia witnessed the emergence of the Achaemenid Empire, the invasion of Alexander the Great (who set up at least eight cities in the region between 334 and 323 B.C.), and the rise and fall of nomadic and sedentary[19] civilizations, of which the most flourishing were the Bactrian Kingdom and the Kushan Empire. Their high level of social and cultural organization gave rise to a rich and prosperous trade through the Silk Road linking China to the West. The route took its name from silk, the commodity most in demand in Europe.

The period of A.D. 250–750 has been referred to as a crossroad of civilizations. It witnessed complex political events due to the arrival of warring dynasties and ethnic movements, as well as far-reaching social, economic, and cultural upheavals. This was the time of nomadic migrations and the constitution of steppe empires that swept over these sedentary populations and left their imprint not only on social and political life, but also added a new ethnic component to the population. These multicultural societies had assimilated to a various degree great religious traditions of Buddhism, Zoroastrianism, Christianity, and Shamanism. The arrival of Islam at the end of this period brought fundamental changes to all aspects of life.

During the eight centuries of A.D. 750–1500, the new faith of Islam gradually spread, affecting much of Central Asia; many mosques and madrassas were built in the Uzbekistan cities of Samarqand, Bukhara, and Khiva. These were the centuries in which nomadic and military empires arose in the heart of Asia, impinging on the history of adjacent cultures to an unparalleled extent. The most destructive period was the invasion of Genghis Khan in 1220. This left most of the cities in ruins. His descendant Timur, also known as Tamerlane, resurrected once famous cities by using the labor of slaves and artists captured during successful crusades. The formation of the Turco-Mongol Golden Horde had a major, enduring influence on the course of the region's history.

The history of Central Asian civilizations from ca. 1500 to ca. 1850 was a period that witnessed the last phase of nomadism as a viable system of social organization. The shift of the main lines of international trade from the Great Silk Route to the oceanic routes reflected the early impact of colonialism, notably British and Russian.

Beginning in the eighteenth century, the Russian Empire constantly probed this region for possible expansion toward the Black Sea, the Caspian Sea, and India. These efforts involved Russia in a series of wars with the Persian and Ottoman empires, both of which were decaying from within.

The Colonial Experience

To be ignorant of what occurred before you were born is to remain always a child. For what is the worth of human life, unless it is woven into the life of our ancestors by the records of history?

CICERO

Borders are scratched across the hearts of men by strangers with a calm, judicial pen.

MARIA MANNES

The Russians lacked colonies, but there was a world to win on their southeastern frontier. Internal colonialism as an annexation of adjacent territories was the most practical way for Russia to extend its territory and influence, and then change the balance of powers in this area. As soon as the Russian conquest of the Caucasus was completed in the late 1850s, an intensive incorporation of Central Asian states into Russia began. It took different forms, from fairly peaceful colonization, as in case of Kazakhstan with the assembly of Kazakh's elders supporting the decision to join Russia in 1731, to a military conquest in the case of Turkistan in 1873. There the Turkmen put up the stiffest resistance against Russian expansion. By 1876, the territory known today as Uzbekistan either had fallen under direct Russian control or had become a protectorate of Russia.[20] According to the treaty signed by the Khanate of Bukhoro with Russia, khanates retained control over internal affairs, while Russia controlled foreign relations of these states. This form of colonialism gave Russian merchants significant concessions in foreign trade.[21]

A few years later the Russians signed an agreement with the Persians and established what is essentially the current border between Turkmenistan and Iran. In 1897 an agreement was signed between the Russians and the Afghans.

It should be noted that in the second half of the nineteenth century a new type of border had been formed in Central Asia. These borders were different from the European meaning of the term "border." Distinctive sociohistorical environments predetermine the type of geopolitical or state border. In this context, we need to distinguish between two types of borders: European or Western types and Asian and Eastern borders. Even in the middle of the nineteenth century two types of borders existed. There were constant borders of a sedentary population, and flexible, constantly changing borders with the nomadic tribes. The constant borders were the internal borders of the permanent agricultural oases. The flexible borders, similar to the notion of frontiers, reflected the lifestyle of the nomadic populations.[22]

The importance of colonization of the area was based not only on the value of this territory to Russia, as a main source of cotton at the time, but also on its position in the formation of new political realities in the world. Turkistan has been swallowed by Russia unnoticeably, while India was perceived as a real colonial goal. Although India has been separated from the Russian Central Asian periphery by Afghanistan, it is just a perception; the reality is that, in strategic terms, Afghanistan played the role of the border zone between Russia and Great Britain.

During the first period of Russian presence in the area, daily life for Central Asian people did not change much. The Russians did not mix with the indigenous people beyond the needed interaction for cotton production. This Russian separateness led to a nonprejudicial, but rather patronizing relationship between Russian numeric minority and local majority groups that was similar to the position of the British in India.

The most significant social and economic changes produced by the era of Russian rule can be summarized as follows:

1. Moscow absorbed the greatest part of the wealth of Central Asia with an increased emphasis on cotton cultivation.
2. In order to operate successfully in remote colonial places the development of the infrastructure was crucial, including the construction of railroads, communication links, smelting plants, and cotton-ginning machinery.
3. Military hospitals and schools were built to provide adequate training and services to the labor force.
4. There was an expansion of economic relations with Russia.
5. A barter system was created.
6. There was an introduction of a Russian system of administration in the territories.
7. Military-supported bases were created on the borders.
8. There was an agrarian policy, which brought about a gradual shift in the proportion of nomads to a more settled population.
9. Industrial capitalism has been accompanied by a pronounced social differentiation between Russians and the native population.

The reasons for Russian expansion toward Transcaucasian states were slightly different. From 1773 Georgian rulers began efforts to gain Russian protection from the Turks of the Ottoman Empire. The Russian occupation of parts of Georgia turned the country into an arena of Russian-Turkish rivalry for decades. The impact of the colonization of this area can be seen in the following social processes:

1. Russian education and ranks of nobility were introduced.
2. Russianization intensified as time passed.
3. The Georgian Orthodox Church lost its independent status in 1811.
4. A rebellion against intensified Russianization became more pronounced.

From the moment of a seemingly easy conquest of Central Asia, Russia's image was transformed from being an Asia in Europe to becoming a Europe in Asia.

The Sovietization Process

Sporadic antitsarist revolts occurred during the years immediately preceding the 1917 Russian Revolution. This unrest swept through the whole region and was later transformed into an armed resistance to Soviet rule known as the Basmachi Rebellion.[23] Its impact was the strongest in small towns throughout the region between 1920 and 1930.

In the process of creating the new republics of Soviet Russia in the 1920s, the central political leadership arbitrarily defined national identities and national borders which, until that time, had little political importance. These nonetheless became a stumbling block and a source of national armed conflicts. One example is the conflict between Armenia and Azerbaijan.

In 1924 Central Asia was divided into distinct political entities. The process of the establishment of Russian control over these states was a lengthy and costly one. In order to maintain control, the Bolsheviks employed rhetoric appealing to the people of the area, decolonization and national sovereignty was pledged to non-Russians.[24]

Efforts of the Soviet state to undermine the traditional way of life resulted in significant changes in family structure and political relationships, observances of religious holidays, economic activities, and the migration of a rural population into industrial centers.

The massive collectivization of the 1920s and '30s are remembered in the history of Soviet nations as the largest man-made social disaster. The essence of this policy was to introduce the advantages of the collective cooperative agricultural units that were opposed by individual operations. The process of collectivization was supposed to be voluntary and gradual. But neither of these ideals was realized. Stalin's central government required a fast collectivization and suppression of all resistance. Creation of collective farms and agricultural entities was marked as the bloody period of genocide. Individual property was confiscated, owners were imprisoned in concentration camps for decades, and many were killed. Their families were expelled from the traditional lands and had a mark of the "enemy of the nation" for life. They were discriminated against in all areas of life, such as access to higher education, desirable jobs, and social recognition.

Local intelligentsia that was openly critical to such policies was labeled as "bourgeois nationalist" and shared the fate of other persecuted categories. National intellectuals were purged for being nationalists. This was a loosely defined offense that could be applied to any form of opposition to central government policies.

It is important to mention that Stalin and Lavrenti Beria, his chief of secret police from 1938 to 1953, were both Georgians. However, Stalin's oppressions were as severe toward Georgian intellectual opposition, as toward any other group. The best-known manifestation of this was the execution of 5,000 nobles in 1924 and the purge of Georgian intellectuals and artists in 1936–1937.

This was the darkest page in the Soviet history of the region. As much as the rest of the Soviet era has been marked by the same political realities, the intensity of social control and oppression never reached the same magnitude. During the later part of the Soviet period there was a strict control of religious freedoms, entrepreneurship activities, the strict censorship of press, and individual correspondence. Loyalty to regime and Russianization were the prerequisites to obtain any position on the social ladder.

Russianization is one of the social phenomena that requires an objective analysis. As a successor of the tsarist policy of Russianization, the Soviet era added a number of new dimensions.

1. A significant number of Russians and other Slavic and non-Slavic peoples were relocated to the region as part of the state policy of industrialization.
2. An urban concentration of immigrants predetermined the role of the Russian language as the major language of communication.
3. Russian was the language of the state and all official documentation was maintained in Russian. Local officials who participated in the regime did so on Russian terms.
4. In the majority of public schools in urban settings, the educational process was conducted in Russian.
5. Some native language schools existed as a display for the international community. In reality they were only exotic oases of native culture.
6. Because the majority of native speakers lived in rural areas, native languages had been relegated to the position of peasant languages, second-class languages. Every family that had desires for their children to advance in social structure made enormous efforts to provide Russian language instruction for their children as a key to their futures.
7. The funding of native arts and folklore was based on a "leftover" approach, meaning the budget would be provided from local budgets after all other social programs were fulfilled.
8. Russian officials occupied key leadership positions in all spheres of social, political, and economic life. One of the hypocritical realities of that time was the practice for a leader of any entity to be a native, with a Russian national deputy as a must for close control on the issue of loyalty.

An independent observer may ask whether there were other positive and/or negative aspects of the impact of the Sovietization process on the Central Asian region. To be fair in our assessment of the sociopolitical development, we should mention some other social changes occurring during that time.

1. There was intensive industrialization, which contributed to the development of the industrial establishment and energy sectors in each of these countries. However, this policy resulted in a degree of dependency on central decision-making.
2. There was the intensive exploration of natural resources, such as oil, coal, iron ore, and underground water resources in Kazakhstan; natural gas and salt in Uzbekistan and Turkmenistan; and gold and silver in Kyrgyzstan.
3. There was a centrally planned migration of the labor force as a mandatory requirement for all higher education professionals. The required timeframe of such job assignments after graduation from the university was set at three years. For most young people, this is the time of building relationships and starting families, which was a key factor causing them to stay in

Central Asia for life. That's why such a large segment of the Russian-speaking population exists in all former republics of the Soviet Union. This is also why they find themselves unprepared to operate in native languages and now experience severe job and social discrimination.

4. There was an ongoing ethnic integration; intermarriages were at the highest level in industrial centers, such as Alma-Ata, Tashkent, Bukhara, Ashghabad, and Dushanbe.

5. There was a restructuring of the agricultural production in favor of monocultural specialization, with cotton dominance at the expense of sufficient food production by local agricultural state enterprises.

6. There was the development of a highly politicized standardized system of education, with high academic standards.

7. There was an enormous improvement of the healthcare system with the mandatory immunization of the whole population and eradication of epidemics that had killed hundreds of thousands of people in the past.

8. There was the development of a social welfare system providing inexpensive and high quality daycare facilities, free school uniforms, books, lunches for children from big families, free medical services, 12 weeks of paid maternity leave and one year unpaid with a guaranteed workplace, retirement for women at the age of 55 and for men at the age of 60, 25 working days of paid vacation per year, free higher education, inexpensive summer camps for children, resort vouchers for adults, and numerous privileges for families with more than four children.

9. Scientific research institutions were created.

10. State governments depended on funding coming from the center in Moscow, which contributed to the tension between the center and the periphery.

The Aftermath of Soviet Rule

In view of the 70-year period of the oppressive Russianization and central dominance, it should not be surprising to learn that the "pendulum of the grandfather's clock" moved not only to the point of reconstruction of national identities, but even further to an extreme position, giving rise to an open nationalism and discrimination against Russian-speaking minorities.

The economic logic of continued ties to Russia during the post-Soviet period, with the predominant dependency of newly independent states on primary products, raw materials, such as oil, gas, and cotton, with prices set by Russian monopolies below world prices, created a resistance against participation in new treaties, political unions, and integration blocks where Russia was a dominant member. It is a common understanding among the native professionals of every state that such economic cooperation would preserve Central Asia's de facto colonial position vis-à-vis Russian industry.

That's why some of the countries of the region, including Uzbekistan, rejected an offer to be a part of the Commonwealth of Independent States (CIS), an organization of independent states of the former Soviet Union. They are working on the integration of their nations into a broader context of the world economic and political communities. The latest summit of the Shanghai's Organization for Cooperation in May 2003, in Moscow, Russia, emphasized the strong commitment of all members to fight terrorism and drug trafficking, and to contribute to the development of favorable conditions for regional trade and stabilization in the region.[25]

GOVERNMENT

> *A leader is best when people barely know that he exists,*
> *Not so good when people obey and acclaim him,*
> *worst when they despise him.*
>
> LAO-TZU

Any state that emerged from the ruins of the USSR would have proclaimed its intent to create an open society and to build a democratic secular state according to the Western model. Nevertheless, in almost all of the former Soviet Republics of the region the established order could be best described as an "authoritarian political model," based on the power of the individual at the top. This is fully applicable to the countries of Central Asia and the Southern Near Abroad. Presidents of these countries awarded themselves with the functions and powers typical of the former secretaries of the Communist Party of the Soviet era, adding some of the characteristics of Asian rulers from feudal times. This could be seen in the proposition to restore the Halifat, an Islamic medieval feudal state structure in Uzbekistan.

The president of Turkmenistan, Saparmurad Niazov, was awarded the lifelong position of president and the official title of "The Head of the Turkmen."[26] In 1991 the president of Kyrgyzstan, Askar Akayev, was awarded the title of "The Supreme Khan of the Kyrgyz."[27] As much as it may sound unusual for a democratic state, such symbolism played a stabilizing role during times of political crisis, following the failed coup d'etat in Moscow in 1991.

Today all countries in the region claim to have a multiparty system, freedom of press, and other features of developing democracies. At the same time the following characteristics can be found in each of them.

1. Political power has been monopolized by presidents and their allies.
2. Newspapers of the political opposition have been closed.
3. Corruption has affected all areas of life.
4. The use of antidemocratic ways to make amendments to the constitution, especially during election campaigns.

What are the reasons for the "authoritarian transformation" of the political regimes in the region? First, it is the result of a painful transition process from the authoritarian communist model to a Western model; it is a disease of "growth."

Campaigning Soviet Style: Huge pictures of the president of Turkmenistan can still be seen everywhere in Ashghabad, Turkmenistan. SOURCE: OLGA CARTER

Second, the local traditional cultural environment is tearing away foreign elements of the liberal democratic institutions from the West. Third, it is a combination, or synthesis, of two systems. The process of integration of these opposing components could be best illustrated through the analysis of one of the countries of the region.

CASE STUDY

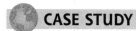

KYRGYZSTAN

Every generation needs a new revolution
THOMAS JEFFERSON.

Several colorfully named revolutions have succeeded over the last few years in the region: the Rose Revolution in Georgia in 2003, the Orange Revolution in Ukraine in 2004, and the Tulip Revolution in Kyrgyzstan in 2005. Was it a "revolutionary bug" that came to Kyrgyzstan or had the local environment generated objective conditions for the protest movement to grow and to erupt in the form of revolution?

In order to understand what had happened and the challenges Kyrgyzstan is yet to face in rebuilding economy and democracy, it is necessary to take a look back, into the recent past of this country.

The territory of Kyrgyzstan is approximately 200,000 square km. Its population is slightly above 4.5 million people. Eighty-eight percent of the population lives below the poverty line, according to the official statistics.[28] Foreign debt is now approaching $1 billion.[29] It has valuable natural resources: gold, silver, other rare metals, and oil. In addition, this small country has the third-largest gold mining industry after Russia and Uzbekistan. Its annual production of gold is more than 20 tons; 40 percent of gold export is done by the Kyrgyz-Canadian joint venture.

During the Soviet period, Kyrgyzia held the largest amount of livestock. Today out of what was once 11 million sheep, only 4 million remain. Unemployment has skyrocketed because 70 percent of the industrial enterprises are closed. The rate of migration to Russia and other countries is worrisome.[30] The average official monthly salary of a doctor is 450 Som, which is about $10 U.S., and a monthly pension is about 400 Som, the equivalent of $9 U.S.

The World Bank has labeled Kyrgyzstan among one of the three most corrupt post-Soviet countries. Corruption takes many forms. Land redistribution based on favoritism and privatization—selling state property for pennies to former state and communist party leaders who became businessmen overnight—runs rampant. "One morning they woke up being millionaires," as one analyst stated. It is alleged that more than 3,800 enterprises were sold dirt-cheap. Another form of corruption encompasses manipulation with government contracts, licenses for energy resources, and brokerage service.[31]

Among numerous examples of corruptive practices by the government were scandals around the license issued to a Canadian Gold Mining Company, Kameko, as well as the fraudulent gasoline transaction of the U.S.-Kyrgyz joint venture "Vostok." Redistribution and misappropriation of international economic aid became one of the new forms of corruption. Due to its claimed democratic image, over the last 10 years Kyrgyzstan received international funds three times higher per capita than any post-communist country in Central Asia. From 1992 to 1998 Kyrgyzstan was awarded foreign loans totaling $1.3 billion by various international organizations and donor countries. In most cases these were 30 year loans with 2 percent interest, the cheapest money ever; however, due to its corruptive practices, providing financial support was like pouring water through a sieve, as it did not make the people better off.[32]

During the last 15 years, the political climate of Kyrgyzstan has been under the influence of two forces, an old state party *nomenklatura*[33] and a new elite that emerged as a result of Mikhail Gorbachev's "perestroika." This contradiction between old and new elite is just the tip of the iceberg. Its base is determined by a historic conflict between the aristocracy of Northern Kyrgyzstan, which had a strong tribal structure, and the nonaristocratic South, with family groups as its power base. During the Soviet period the party leaders were recruited from the South. Northerners were more urbanized, more secularized, and Russianized. Under the strong influence of Uzbekistan, Southerners were representing agrarian regions where traditions of Islam were the strongest.[34]

The most indicative case of the victory of the tribal political groups and clans has been achieved by the former president of Kyrgyzstan, Askar Akayev. He belonged to the largest and most powerful Northern tribe, Sari-Bagysh, and, through his wife, was supported by the most aristocratic clan, the Djegetins.

In this culture where every person knows seven generations of his predecessors, clan-family relationships play a crucial role. As it was admitted by the former president's press secretary, Kamil Bayalinov, "It is not a secret that, in general, high officials of the government are coming from one clan or another."[35] This is reality. "In our small republic, wherever you turn, everybody is somebody's man."[36]

In the 1990s, the essence of the transition of political power in this country was not so much the transition from the communist to the democratic regime, but in reality it reflected the redistribution of power among the ethnic elite and regional political centers. One form of this process was incorporation of traditional institutions into a modern social system. Perhaps the most highly criticized by the International Human rights Organization was the Kyrgyz government decision to grant legitimate status to Aksakal Courts. They were allowed to make decisions related to local issues, and this provision resulted in some unexpected consequences as some of the Aksakal Courts made death penalty decisions which were carried out immediately.

The traditional norm of tribal solidarity prohibits rank and file members of society from contesting their own tribal leadership, but to offer them maximum support in their struggle with other tribal leaders. The logic of this practice is simple: The larger the gain of the tribal elite, the larger the share that will trickle down in the form of investments, subsidies, jobs, and government projects.

Political power allowed members of tribal elite to control the majority of the Kyrgyz energy complex, transportation, communication, production of alcohol products, commercial aviation, as well as the cotton and sugar cane industries. From the Western perspective, such an informal relationship of political power and ownership interests is called corruption.

Not many experts predicted that protest against corruption and dynastic succession of Ascar Akaev, motivated by two rounds of flawed parliamentary elections could take the form of uprising. Unlike peaceful events in Ukraine, the president of Kyrgyzstan broke the pledge of nonviolence. Although the police force was fewer in numbers, it behaved brutally enough to enrage protesters, many of whom were women and teenagers, who had come from the nearby villages. For two nights after the uprising the looters targeted businesses they thought belonged to the Akaev family.[37] Some of the desperate business owners put up signs saying, "We are with people." Despite the fact that the president himself fled to Russia and eventually agreed to sign a letter of resignation, there were practically no anti-Russian sentiments or looting against ethnic Russian businesses (although Turkish and Chinese businesses were damaged).

The revolt in March 2005 left Kyrgyzstan with two parliaments, both of which initially sat in the same building. The Supreme Court of the country favored the old parliament, which had nominated the former prime minister, Kurmanbeck Bakiev, as acting president. He and the other opposition figures did skillful maneuvering for the July 2005 presidential elections. Most observers believed the election was fair for the most part, and as first results were announced, it was clear that the favorite, Kurmanbeck Bakiev, had won a resounding victory.

In this regionally divided country in which the south is separated by a mountain range and culturally by its large Uzbek minority with a devout adherence to Islam, voter turnout was between 82 and 89 percent. On the other hand, the turnout in the north was only between 57 and 67 percent.[38] It was the south that became the scene of the largest demonstrations; these eventually snowballed into a mass movement called the Tulip Revolution that resulted in ousting the former president.

The Organization for Security and Cooperation in Europe, OSCE, of which Kyrgyzstan is one of the easternmost members, reported "a tangible progress toward meeting . . . international communities for democratic elections." The optimism was shared by observers from a very different security grouping, the Shanghai Cooperation Organization, with Russia, China, and four Central Asian countries as its members. They described the vote as "free, open, transparent and legitimate."[39]

But the true revolution is not about throwing out one ruler and replacing him with another; rather the goal of democratic revolutions is to support democratic institutions, market reforms in society, and to fight corruption. Would Kyrgyzstan be able to rise to such a challenge?

◆ FLASHPOINTS ◆

DOMINO EFFECT AND THE CLASH OF INTERESTS

The "ghost of revolution" is rambling throughout the vast fields of Central Asia and the Southern Near Abroad. Georgia, Ukraine, and Kyrgyzstan are just the beginning of the march of democratic forces in the area that Russia once considered to be its political playground. The sequence of revolutions may create a domino effect among other corrupt post-Soviet political regimes; therefore, some of them today have to make the tough decision between two evils: to accept Russian "help" and become politically manipulated by Moscow in order to strengthen their rotten autocratic structures or to maintain an independent course and be crashed by a growing democratic opposition force. During the last 15 years these old post-Soviet powers have tried to balance the United States, the West, and Russia; they now recognize that the only way to prolong their existence is to accept help on Moscow's terms.

After September 11, 2001, a U.S. Air base was established near the capital of Kyrgyzstan Bishkek, in order to support operations in Afghanistan; this has been a proverbial "thorn in Russia's side."

Kyrgyzstan offered coalition forces unrestricted overflight rights to aircraft flying for combat, humanitarian purposes, and search-and-rescue missions for a period of one year, with the possibility of extension during the antiterrorism campaign. According to a June 2005 report, the tents at Manas Air Base (later renamed Ganci Air Base after Chief Peter J. Ganci Jr., chief of the New York City Fire Department, who gave his life on September 11, 2001, during the terrorist attack on the World Trade Center) were being replaced by more permanent structures. It was estimated that there were about 2,000 American and European troops there.[40] Not only was the U.S. Army in Kyrgyzstan building airfield facilities to support Operation Enduring Freedom, it was also constructing bridges of understanding and friendship with local people by helping them to rebuild local hospitals and restructuring the roof of a rural school. In addition, they gave a gift of four computers, and provided training to teachers on how to use them. The U.S. air base has been welcomed by the Kyrgyz people because it has generated jobs for local construction workers, translators, doctors, and security officers, and has contributed to the improvement of living conditions of the common people. This has led to a better understanding of the American people in uniform.

In response to the U.S. and coalition forces air base, Russia created its own air base in Kant, near the capital city, Bishkek. In order to emphasize its strategic importance, Russian President Vladimir Putin arrived in Kyrgyzstan in October 2003 to attend its official opening. According to some in Moscow, Kyrgyzstan was another blow to Russia in the competition for influence in the former Soviet Union after Georgia and Ukraine.

In Moscow's view there are two principal geopolitical challenges to Russia: the expansion of NATO influence in the region and the drift away from Moscow. These challenges are seen as interrelated as the expansion of NATO influence encourages the drift away from Moscow, and the drift facilitates NATO expansion. An area of interest in this regard is the Caucasus state of the Caspian area, Azerbaijan.

Azerbaijan

Azerbaijan's strategic position in the center of the Caspian, its key role in the realization of projects of exploration, and transportation of Caspian energy resources, determines its increasing significance as a major player in the region. The capital of Azerbaijan, Baku, with a population of 2.1 million, is one of the oldest oil fields in the world. The clear line in the establishment of an alliance with Turkey and the West makes Azerbaijan an attractive candidate as leader in the Caucasus region. It is viewed as a possible base for the strengthening of the American influence in the region. Azerbaijan is extremely interested in developing close ties with NATO. There has been much official discussion in Azerbaijan about the possibility of either the U.S. or Turkey acquiring military bases in Azerbaijan. Every taxi driver in the city enthusiastically speculates that Baku might request the closure of the Russian early warning station at Gabalinskaya. The main justification for Azerbaijan wanting NATO bases has been seen in the existence of close political and military relations between Russia and Armenia. Also the presence of Russian military bases in Armenia, particularly as the Nagornyy Karabakh conflict between Armenia and Azerbaijan remains unresolved.[41]

The Russian-Armenian close political, military, and economic partnership in some way counters the decline of Russian influence in the region. It is therefore a mistake to regard Russia as irrelevant to the region. Russia has the power to influence the region's policies in the foreseeable future. The skills and art of the regional political players will be seen in their ability to pursue policies that will enhance the independence of the newly independent states under the balanced relationship with both the West and Russia.

While Russia is loosing its strategic dominance in the region, and the opposition to the post-Soviet regimes are getting stronger in their quest for democratic changes, the chances of a new wave of popular revolutions are higher than ever. In preparation for the November 2005 parliamentary election in Azerbaijan, western observers speculated that Azerbaijan could possibly be the next stop for a colorful revolution. The foremost question reeling in the minds of most people is: Where will the next colorful revolution be—will it be marching through the post-Soviet region, through Kazakhstan, or through Mongolia? Only time will tell.

THE ARAL SEA: AN ENVIRONMENTAL DISASTER

Civilization is being poisoned by its own waste products.
WILLIAM RALPH INGE

In many instances one of the contributing factors to many so-called "natural" disasters is the consequence of inadequate development of policies and practices.

The shrinking Aral Sea, located on the border of Kazakhstan and Uzbekistan, has become a dual symbol, first of the destructive power of the Soviet central planning system in the area of water management, and secondly, the Central Asian government's inability to cooperate on a crucial regional issue. According to UN experts, if left untouched, this symbol will likely no longer exist by 2020.

Specialists estimate the Aral Sea's surface is now only 25 percent of the surface that existed before Soviet central planners implemented in 1970, a poorly researched and ill-calculated project of diverting the flow of the sea's two main rivers, the Amu Darya and the Syr Darya to agricultural irrigation schemes, in order to turn Central Asia into the Soviet Union's primary cotton region. The Aral Sea has actually divided into three parts: the Northern Aral Sea (NAS) and the Southern Aral Sea (SAS), which consists of two sections along the north-south axis. Thousands of tons of salt and sand from the dried up seabed are being scattered by winds across a 300-mile radius. The president of Kazakhstan, Nursultan Nazarbaev, called the sea's shrinkage a "global disaster," noting that salt and sand from the sea affected the environment as far as the Arctic Ocean.[42]

With the help of the World Bank, Kazakhstan is trying to secure the survival of the northern segment of the Aral Sea by constructing a closure dyke and stimulating additional flow of water into this part of the sea. The complex set of measures targeting the improvement of ecological and environmental conditions of the delta area would result in a higher volume of water channeled into the NAS.

After the construction of the dyke, the surface area of the NAS would increase by between 20 and 25 percent. However, this will not solve the whole problem.

The preservation of the Aral Sea is not just a matter of general improvements to the landscape of the region. UN experts are urging the Kazakhstani government to "stop spending money on restoration of the Aral Sea and direct the main part of the immediate spending on evacuating people from an ecological disaster area."[43]

The Aral Sea basin contains some 35 million people, with .5 million of them living in the disaster zone, which encompasses most of the two regions of Uzbekistan, the Northern regions of Turkmenistan, and the south-central Kazakh province of Kyzyl-Orda. Public attention was drawn to this tragic situation for the first time during Gorbachev's perestroika and glasnost period. The analysis of experts at that time emphasized the dramatic effect of the disappearance of the Aral Sea on the health of the people in the region. Disease, malnutrition, and birth defects caused by the spread of salts containing high concentrations of pesticides and residues of chemical fertilizers are at deadly levels.[44]

Experts and practitioners are unanimous in their opinion that rehabilitating the depleted sea would be practically impossible without the international community's support. This critical situation has led to regional cooperation and to the search for practical, cost-effective solutions for more efficient water management strategies.

The rising impact of disasters is becoming a commonly cited indicator of unsustainable development. However, these risks can be managed and people can be made less vulnerable to natural phenomena.

SOVIET NUCLEAR TESTING SITE IN KAZAKHSTAN

The Nation that destroys its soil destroys itself.
FRANKLIN D. ROOSEVELT

The means by which we live have outdistanced the ends for which we live. Our scientific power has outrun our spiritual power. We have guided missiles and misguided men.
MARTIN LUTHER KING, JR.

The second of the two gravest environmental threats to Kazakhstan is radiation contamination in Semipalatinsk, where the Soviet Union tested almost 500 nuclear weapons.

Experts' estimates suggest that more than 1.5 million people in Kazakhstan today, almost every tenth citizen, have been affected by the nuclear tests. The radiation continues to adversely affect the health of the local population. There is now a reported seven-degree difference between the temperature of the soil in Semipalatinsk and in neighboring areas.[45] According to the Semipalatinsk prenatal center, only 10 percent of pregnant women in some rural areas nearby are healthy, the rest have problems due to weakened immune systems. Some members of the opposition to the government environmental policy are raising the issue of compensation to the huge number of civilians, who were harmed by nuclear testing during the Soviet era.

The issue of compensation is a sensitive one, since the former officials of the Soviet KGB and the Interior Ministry are receiving additional compensation, while common people receive nothing.[46]

Kazakhstan's experts suggest that it would require more than $1 billion to clean up nuclear contamination; resources that could not be found easily even with an international support. There was an alternative proposal to generate resources through the development of a highly profitable project for the establishment of nuclear waste depository facilities for imported nuclear waste. The criticism of this proposal was so sharp that for a while it was taken off the discussion table. But for how long?

THE STATUS OF WOMEN IN CENTRAL ASIA

The level of development of society can be determined by the role and position of women in it.
FREDERICK ENGELS

What is a woman? I assure you, I don't know . . . do not believe that anybody can know until she has expressed herself in all the arts and professions open to human skill.
VIRGINIA WOOLF

Only the educated are free.
EPICTETUS

The members of the Central Asian family, as well as members of the Caucasus family, occupy carefully graded positions according to age and sex. As in many other traditional cultures, it was commonly understood by all that the daughter would leave the family when she married. However, it was perceived as a loss of productive labor; therefore, this transfer to the family of her husband should be compensated. So the training of daughters in obedience to men and in household activities began early. Emphasis on a traditional extended family provided encouragement for having a large number of children. The current Central Asian proverb, "A home with children is like a bazaar,[47] and a childless home is like a tomb (nazar)" demonstrates this cultural value. Attitudes and practices concerning marriage, family planning, and women's roles are part of the larger issue of family.

Bride Price

As part of its campaign to emancipate the women of Central Asia, the Soviet Government bitterly fought, by law and propaganda, the old customs and traditions related to the role and position of women within the family and society. One of the customs that was prohibited by law was the custom of paying the bride price, *kalim*. Article 196 of the Criminal Code stated that paying kalim "entails correctional labor for a period up to one year" for both the donor and the recipient. The basis for Soviet opposition to the custom was the Russian misconception of the role of the bride price in Central Asian marriage. It was a lack of understanding of the nature of the marriage agreement in Central Asia, which in fact bypasses not only the bride but the groom as well. From the point of view of European Russians and other Slavic cultures, the payment of bride price meant that the woman was being sold as a *chattel*, or slave, to the family of the groom. This practice, as well as other traditional customs of Central Asia, was considered among the "feudal survivals of old customs degrading to women."

To the Central Asian, the bride price is not only a payment to the bride's family for having raised the girl, but also a protection for a woman in case she returns home because of mistreatment by her husband. Bride price is still paid today, but in many instances it is little more than a symbolic payment.

Education and Equality

Soviet family policy in Central Asia was aimed at bringing the family closer to a contemporary Russian model. Despite the official suppression of old traditions, the Central Asian family has not changed as rapidly or as markedly as the Western family. The Soviet regime was aware that the fastest and surest way to change traditional societies in Central Asia and the Caucasus was by getting women out of the family and into schools and other outside activities. To this end, the constitutions of each of these republics contained a paragraph dealing with women's rights, including the caution that ". . . the drawing of women into study, into agricultural or industrial production, into the governing of the state or into social or political activities is punishable by law."[48]

In all fairness to the Soviet system, it should be noted that the process of the elimination of illiteracy among the women of Central Asia was an enormous success story. Families were accountable for sending school-aged kids to get free public education at all levels, including high school. It was not an easy process for those parents in rural areas, who did not object in principle, but whose livelihood depended on children's labor in small private gardens and on collective farms. The whole tobacco, cotton, and rice industries rested on women and children. So, the quality of education was significantly lower in rural areas than in cities.

The practice of marrying off girls at the traditional marriage age, which was fourteen and up, was prohibited by law. Nevertheless the practice existed sporadically and was a reality of life in remote areas. There was also a category of parents in some places who kept girls out of school at an early age in order to get a higher bride price from the groom's family. It was a nonspoken rule that an uneducated wife-to-be would be at a high demand, because she would be more dependant and submissive, and would keep traditional cultural norms unchanged.

The regime was encouraging women to participate in different public activities. But even after many years of official pressure, the residues of traditional behavioral patterns and basic customs were seen in rural areas, among working class groups, and at some meetings, plays, and movies. Women often sat separately from men in public. There were even women's sections in some local government offices.

The Soviet socialist ideology emphasized equality of women. The Soviets created a variety of social programs to encourage women to participate in industrial and social development. They opened up wide-ranging educational and job opportunities for women. Though the number of women in all professions and at all educational levels was the highest in Soviet Asia compared to other Asian and African countries, there was still a notable lack of Central Asian women in public life. Since the collapse of the Soviet Union in 1991, women in all countries of the Southern Near Abroad region have experienced a drastic decline of living standards, along with the drastic shrinkage of career opportunities. Since the declaration of independence by each of these countries, political leaders have promoted a state-managed revival of Islamic and traditional cultural values. They view such policies as a crucial component of a broader strategy of establishing distinct national identities. As a result, some of the gains made by women during the Soviet era have eroded during the past decade. For example, literacy rates have slid from above 90 percent to around 60 percent.

Due to the breakage of the connections with the other countries of the former Soviet Union and the reduction of government funding and social programs, industrial and agricultural production has shrunk by as much as 60 percent. The skyrocketing unemployment rate, combined with corruption, instability, and little respect for human rights, hit women hard. Women were the first to lose their jobs and to face discrimination, harassment, and violence. Because an independent existence has become almost impossible, women are under enormous pressure to get married.

Drug Trafficking and Human Trafficking

When up to 80 percent of the population of the region lives below the poverty line, and families are caught in a hand-to-mouth existence, women become scapegoats. There is evidence that girls' education is being curtailed, and domestic abuse of women has emerged as a serious problem. In such a desperate economic climate, a growing number of women have resorted to illicit activities, including prostitution and drug smuggling, in order to subsist. Large numbers of drug traffickers in Tajikistan, for example, have used women as couriers, assuming they would attract less scrutiny at border checkpoints. There is much anecdotal evidence that some women involved in drug trafficking are not even paid in cash, but instead get paid with flour or other essential goods that they need to feed and care for their families, as reported by representatives of the International Harm Reduction Development Program, a nongovernmental project that works on addiction-related issues. Drug addiction among women in Tajikistan has exploded. Addiction among women was virtually unheard of prior to 1991. But recent data compiled by the same agency indicates that women now make up to 3.2 percent of the total number of registered addicts in the Tajik capital of Dushanbe. Their incarceration creates even more problems, contributing to a growing number of abandoned and homeless children and exploitation of children.[49]

But drug trafficking is only one facet of the larger picture; human trafficking is on a steady rise. Comparing the trafficking problem among the countries of Central Asia, we can see similar circumstances in all of them, such as high rates of unemployment, corruption, and poverty. But while in Tajikistan, the issue of labor exploitation in trafficking is more of a problem, in Uzbekistan and Kazakhstan it is more of an issue of trafficking for sexual exploitation. There is a different context, but the scope of the problem is pretty much the same.[50]

HIV/AIDS

International organizations report a frightening increase of women contracting HIV/AIDS. Of those that contract HIV/AIDS in the Kyrgyz Republic, 55 percent are thought to be female, although the majority of those officially registered with the disease are males. In about 80 percent of cases of female HIV/AIDS in Kyrgyzstan, husbands infected their own wives. There are several reasons for such a picture. The most typical, according to experts, are lack of sex education, low awareness of sexually transmitted diseases, revival of old traditions of kidnapping future wives, unofficial polygamy, and increased extramarital sex, often with prostitutes.[51]

To combat HIV/AIDS and other health-related problems, such as high maternal and infant mortality rates, society needs to address the larger issues of gender equality, power reduction, and social protection. At this point the effort of the international community is to engage women in addressing these problems through women-operated nongovernmental organizations.

One of the positive developments in this direction can be seen in Kazakhstan, where women take an active role in almost 40 percent of small- and medium-sized businesses. The Kazakh legislature was the first to address and implement a government supported program for small and medium-sized women's businesses. In 2004, 150 million KGS—Kyrgyzstani som (equivalent to $3.5 million US)—were allocated for the development of these types of businesses; in 2005 the sum was doubled.[52] It is projected to remain in the same range for 2006. Though this is a sign of progress in Central Asian women's rights and conditions, there is a long way to go. The hope comes from the fact that despite women's unequal treatment in Central Asia, they have demonstrated great strength, flexibility, and openness to change in the post-Soviet transition.

AFGHANISTAN

> *It is your concern when the wall next door is on fire.*
> HORACE

> *Let the word go forth from this time and place, to friends and foe alike,*
> *that the torch has been passed to a new generation.*
> JOHN F. KENNEDY

The lands that currently make up Afghanistan have been at a crossroads since ancient times. It was here historic figures, including Alexander the Great, Cyrus and Darius the Great, Ghengis Khan, and Tamerlane all fought for control of this important crossroads of Asia. The region has been important because it was an area surrounded by contending states rather than having value itself. As a buffer area, Afghanistan has always had strategic importance.

During the nineteenth century, both the Russians and the British were repeatedly involved in Afghan intrigues called the "Great Game." Frederick Hartmann emphasized the buffer status of nineteenth-century Afghanistan this way:

Afghanistan has played such a role ever since British power was expanded up to its southern borders in India and the Russians established a common frontier with the Afghans on the north. There is an old Afghan saying that defines the role of mountainous Afghanistan: "this goat separating the lion from the bear."[53]

Rouhollah Ramazani has made a similar comment:

Russia's direct agreements (usually after territorial conquest) with the Northern Tier states in the nineteenth century largely provided the basis for her present long boundaries with these states. Furthermore, her direct negotiations with Great Britain as in the case of Afghanistan, and her collaboration with Great Britain as in the case of Iran and Turkey, were influential in defining the boundaries of these latter states with each other.[54]

This nineteenth-century competition between Russia and Britain in Central Asia was called "the Great Game." During the twentieth century, Britain, Russia, Germany, Iran, China, Pakistan, India, and the United States all played their parts in the destabilization of Afghanistan.

Afghanistan maintained the status of a buffer state during the cold war. Both the United States and the Soviet Union vied for influence by extending aid to the Afghans. In 1973, King Zahir Shah was overthrown by the Afghan military. A military government, headed by General Mohammad Daud Khan, ruled until 1978. In 1978, a coup d'etat brought a Marxist government to power in Afghanistan. Splits within the Afghan Communist Party over both Islam and socialist reforms soon threatened the very survival of the Marxist revolution. It was this volatile situation that caused the Soviets to intervene on the night of December 24, 1979. The Afghan prime minister was killed, and in his place the Soviets installed Babrak Karmal. Soviet forces eventually swelled to around 120,000 before their withdrawal in 1989.

The Soviet intervention provoked open civil war. A number of loosely organized resistance fighters calling themselves the *mujahedeen* (holy warriors) were able to tie down the Soviet military for a decade. Soviet policy throughout much of the Other World was subjected to harsh criticism until the "new thinking" of Mikhail Gorbachev brought a Soviet withdrawal, coupled with military and economic support for the last Soviet-installed government, led by former Afghan Secret Police Chief Najibullah. Tainted by its association with the Soviets, that government failed to establish legitimacy either at home or abroad. More than 5 million refugees fled Afghanistan, most settling in Pakistan near the Afghanistan border.

A stalemate that characterized the final years of Soviet intervention continued for a time after the Soviet withdrawal; however, the combatants looked for support from outside states, including the former Soviet Union, China, the United States, Pakistan, Saudi Arabia, and Iran. Given the drastic changes that occurred in the international environment, such support soon

Lunch: Soviet special forces looking for Mujahedeen commanders among prisoners during food distribution. SOURCE: OLGA CARTER

diminished as other priorities emerged. In April 1992, the Najibullah government collapsed and several *mujahedeen* rebel groups entered Kabul, the capital. In the months and years that followed, the nine *mujahedeen* factions that waged war against the old Soviet-installed governments increasingly turned their weapons on one another.

A tenth faction appeared in early 1995. The new faction, known as the Taliban, or "Seekers," was originally made up of students of Islam from the southeastern city of Kandahar. Its avowed aim was to end Afghanistan's internal conflicts and lawlessness and to institute an Islamic government in that state. With covert support from Pakistan, the Taliban gained control of eight of Afghanistan's twenty-eight provinces within a few months. Within the next few years they extended their control to Kabul and most of the remainder of Afghanistan. In an effort to reform society to conform with their version of Islamic law, they proceeded to ban all music except for religious songs and eventually banned movies, television, and videocassettes. Severe restrictions were also placed on women's clothing and activities. Meanwhile, armed resistance continued in the countryside.

Although unrest and a fitful civil war continued for years after the Taliban gained control of most of the country, it was the September 11, 2001 terrorist attacks in the United States that propelled Afghanistan from the shadows to the "center stage" of world events. Western analysts deduced that the attack on the United States was either mounted or supported by the wealthy Saudi Arabian, Osama bin Laden's Al-Qaeda terrorist organization. Al Qaeda and bin Laden received sanctuary from the Afghan Taliban. In the aftermath of the attacks, U.S. President George W. Bush was unequivocal in stating to the states of the world, "We have found our mission and our moment," then declaring, "Either you are with us or you are with the terrorists."[55]

When the Taliban government refused to meet the American demands to turn over bin Laden and the Al-Qaeda leadership, along with several Americans and Europeans being held for allegedly preaching Christianity, U.S. and British forces aided opposition forces in a military campaign in Afghanistan. This campaign resulted in a total Taliban defeat in December 2001. Even before the Taliban government collapsed, there were moves to end more than 20 years of civil war with the establishment of an interim council that would serve until more permanent political arrangements could be made. Meeting in Bonn, Germany under the sponsorship of the United Nations, most of the rival Afghanistan factions agreed to take steps that, if successfully implemented, could lead the country toward a peaceful future.

The Bonn agreement provided for a series of steps intended to result in an acceptable post-Taliban government. Most of them have been implemented over the years. A general and open democratic election was successfully held for the first time in the history of the country. A crucial step towards the future unification of the conflicting groups in the society was the fact that a majority Pashtun leader, Hamid Karzai, became the first ever democratically elected president. The process leading to this historic election has not been easy. But the government of President Karzai and the people of Afghanistan have not been deterred. Despite security challenges, threats of violence by terrorists, and freezing weather, more than 84 percent of the registered voters—both men and women—enthusiastically formed long queues at the polling stations to cast their ballots on October 9, 2004.[56] Afghans voted for peace and democratic change and for the rebuilding of their war-torn country with opposition against extremists of all kinds. The world community applauded the historic victory of President Karzai and congratulated the Afghan people for their courage and determination in laying this foundation for the future of their society.

Equally important was the signing of a new constitution by President Karzai into law in January 2004, which determines the new strategic vision for the Afghanistan development. Article 43 of the Constitution, for example, states that education is the right of all Afghan citizens and it is provided free of charge by the state covering up to the level of a bachelor's degree.

The End of an Empire: Soviet special forces leaving Afghanistan. SOURCE: OLGA CARTER

Such strong emphasis on the importance of equal and accessible education reflects government-wide understanding of the role of education in the development of a stable and self-sufficient society.

Rebuilding Afghanistan requires assistance not only in the educational area but also in every sector of its society, including rehabilitation of agriculture, improving health care, creating jobs, rebuilding the infrastructure, and empowering women.

The past internal conflicts among different ethnic groups and warlords will not disappear overnight; in fact, they manifest themselves in armed conflicts from time to time, but most of all in growing corruption. Current problems in building a unified democratic society in Afghanistan stem, to some extent, from the artificial historic nature of the Afghan state.

Although Afghanistan has had a form of independence since Ahmad Shah unified the tribes in 1747, the current borders are largely the result of the nineteenth-century rivalries of Russia and Britain. Again, author Rouhollah Ramazani addresses this point:

> In the case of Afghanistan and Iran, Great Britain assisted through arbitration in providing a basis for their present boundary. And in the case of Afghanistan and the part of India that is now Pakistan, Great Britain established the controversial Durand Line, which cuts between ethnically related tribal groups.[57]

Afghanistan is surrounded on all sides by neighbors that are hostile to each other. In the past, all of these states have attempted to exploit the tribal and religious differences that already existed because of the arbitrary way that Afghanistan was shaped in the first place. It can be said that "the Great Game" in Central Asia still continues, only with different players.

In the immediate aftermath of the Taliban fall, the effort of the international community was concentrated on two main issues: security and reconstruction. Much has been accomplished. In the capital of Afghanistan, Kabul, and some areas of the north of the country, Afghan businesses and markets are thriving. Women are increasingly confident that they can walk down the streets without heavy cloth, or *bhurkas*.[58] One million refugees have returned to rebuild their homes and lives and many roads are being repaired, yet much work remains. Security and reconstruction are still huge challenges. Today Taliban fighters are not the same people who fought during the U.S.-led bombing campaign in 2001. They are new recruits, drawn from the poor *madrassahs* (Islamic religious schools) of neighboring Pakistan. These groups receive support from influential religious fundamentalists in Pakistan and other countries. One such fighter said that he was paid $55 in U.S. dollars in Pakistan to come and fight the holy war against the Americans and their Afghan surrogates. The Taliban is using the media to manage its image, to be viewed as freedom fighters. An increase of attacks linked to Taliban fighters on newly opened schools for girls and government and humanitarian agencies, the refusal of warlords to disarm and relinquish territory, and an increase in opium production and drug trafficking to the world markets, won't stop plans to complete a constitution, hold elections, and rebuild the country. International effort is focused on working with local partners to provide water and healthcare services to millions of people. In some areas of Afghanistan, these agencies are engaged in community-based education, large-scale agricultural projects, sanitation, and health education.

The State Department's Afghanistan coordinator, William B. Taylor, Jr., acknowledged that though the gains are tenuous, failure is not an option in Afghanistan. In the "New Great Game," currently called the War on Terror, the participants are Russia, China, the United States, the United Kingdom, India, Pakistan, Iran, and the former Soviet States of Central Asia. How long it will take for these outside parties to unite the internal forces to build a terrorist-free, peaceful Afghanistan remains to be seen. Many others have tried and failed to bring stability to this part of the world. One should not forget the warning that Rudyard Kipling issued 100 years ago to outsiders who ventured into this part of the world:

> One sword-knot stolen from the camp will pay for all the school expenses of any Kurrum Valley scamp who knows no word of moods and tenses. But, being blessed with perfect sight picks off our mess-mates left and right.[59]

SUMMARY

More than any other time in the region's history, Central Asia and the Southern Near Abroad face a crossroads. One path leads to the development of the social and political institutions of these countries compatible with the Western system. The other leads to the restoration of national identities through revitalization of traditional social norms. There is a hope that the wisdom of generations of these nations will help to constructively integrate the two.

Deeply woven into the fabric of Central Asian and world economic cooperation, the region is becoming an important component of peace stabilization in the area. The war in Afghanistan, lasting for the last three decades, and the impact of the U.S.-military presence in the region, predetermine a serious interest in the analysis of the recent developments and different aspects of life in the nations of this part of the world. It indicates that the new century is indeed becoming an Asian one.

Review Questions

1. What are the main oil- and natural gas-producing countries of the region?
2. What factors contributed to the environmental disasters of the Central Asian region?
3. Describe the commonalities and differences in social changes in Central Asian countries under Russian rule and Soviet rule?
4. What are the specific characteristics of the process of transition to a democratic society and market economy in countries of the region?
5. What was the essence of the Soviet policy of Russianization in Central Asia and the Southern Near Abroad countries?
6. What was the goal of the Soviet policy regarding the role of women in society in Central Asia and in what way was it affected since the disintegration of the former USSR?
7. Why can Afghanistan be called an artificial country? What are its crucial problems at the present time?
8. What are the causes and consequences of increased drug trafficking in Central Asian countries?

Key Terms

* **Annexation**—The process of permanent incorporation of an adjacent territory with the national domain.
* **Authoritarian political model**—An order based on an absolute and unlimited power of the individual at the top of the political pyramid; common for all Central Asian countries in the past. Current political models in these countries have strong resemblance with those in the past.
* **Collectivization**—The process of a forceful merger of private farms into large agricultural enterprises in the former USSR in the 1930s, accompanied by the

massive confiscations of private land, livestock, and property of those who declined to join such units voluntarily. Massive persecutions, imprisonment in concentration camps for farmers, combined with the ineffective management of the confiscated property, led to a significant decline in agricultural production in the country.

- **Communist political model**—An order based on the absolute power of the ruling, working class, called *proletariat*. The goal of this model was to establish the dictatorship of the proletariat and for the Communist Party to be the Central decision-making body in all areas of life.
- **Confiscation**—A transfer of ownership by the government, which does not involve compensation to the owner.
- **Feudalism**—A social and economic system in which social position was based on land ownership. In Central Asia feudalism created a form of personal dependency of peasants on their landlords in all areas of life.
- **Intelligentsia**—A group of people with a substantial level of education and ability to think critically, interested in improvements of learning and cultural values of society. This term originated in the Russian revolution to differentiate the intellectual classes from the bourgeoisie and proletariat.
- **Perestroika**—Perestroika translates from Russian as "reconstruction," a new ideology introduced by the leader of the Soviet Union, Mikhail Gorbachev in 1986. According to this innovative set of views and new regulations, more decision-making power was delegated by the central government to the local governing agencies and elements of a market economy were encouraged. People of the Soviet Union were allowed to create small, private business enterprises, more foreign visitors were allowed to visit the country, and more Soviet people were allowed to travel abroad. Freedom of the press was the leading force to a new openness in society.
- **Privatization**—The transfer of ownership from the government to private companies and individuals, including foreign investors.
- **Russianization**—The process of forceful implantation of Russian language as the language of official communication and education, suppression of local traditions, and implementation of Russian cultural elements.
- **Urbanization**—The process of the growth of cities and development of a specific lifestyle, associated with accumulation of wealth and power in big cities.

Useful Web Sites

Central Asia: www.centralasiadaily.com
One World.net: www.oneworld.net
EurasiaNet: www.eurasianet.org
GlobalSecurity.org: www.globalsecurity.org
Caspian World news: news.caspianworld.com
Central Asia and the Caucasus: www.ca-c.org
Business Information Service for the Newly Independent States: www.bisnis.doc.gov
Afghanistan: www.afghan-web.com

Armenia: www.cia.gov
Azerbaijan: www.azer.com
Georgia: casww.iatp.org.ge
Kazakhstan: casww.freenet.kz
Kyrgyzstan: casww.freenet.kg
Turkmenistan: casww.iatp.edu.tm
Turkmenistan: turkmenistan.ru
Uzbekistan: www.mfa.uz OR www.uzreport.com

Notes

1. The spelling of the name of each country is as officially registered by the government at the United Nations.
2. The term *Caucasian Racial Group* (used almost exclusively in North America to refer collectively to the people of European, Middle Eastern, South Asian, and North African ancestry) was first proposed by the German scientist Johann Frederich Blumenbach (1752–1840). His studies based the classification of the Caucasian race primarily on skull features, which he claimed were optimized by the Georgians, a people living in the Southern Caucasus. The name *Caucasian* stems from the Caucasus mountains, the region imagined to be the location where, according to Biblical legend, Noah's Ark eventually landed after the Deluge. From this area, known as Mount Ararat, Noah's son Japheth, traditional Biblical ancestor of the Europeans, established his tribe prior to its supposed migration into Europe. Even though the mountain is located in Turkey (approximately 18 miles south of Armenia) Ararat is the national symbol of Armenia.
3. D. Giardini and S. Balassanian, *Historical and Prehistorical Earthquakes in the Caucasus* (Netherlands: Kluwer Academic Publishers, 1977); *The Catalogue of Strong Earthquakes of Armenia and Adjacent Territories*, M 6.0 (Lat 38.0–42.0 N; Lon 43.0–47.0 E); S. A. Pirousyan, S. Balassanian, A. Avanessyan, A. Arakelyan, and H. H. Harutunyan, *National Survey for Seismic Protection of RA*, Davidashen IV massiv, 375054, (Yerevan, Republic of Armenia).
4. For more information on the mountain systems of Asia see: www.globalgeografia.com/asia_eug/asia_mountains.htm.
5. For more information on the territories covered by mountains in each country of the region see: Library of Congress Country Studies at: lcweb2.loc.gov.
6. "Seismic Activity of the Turkmenistan in 1992." *Seismology. Report of Turkmenistan.* (Ilim, 1994)-N 2. pp. 83–92.
7. These are technical terms that the ordinary reader may not know: The *steppe* refers to a vast plain devoid of forest and is one of the largest plains in Russia and Kazakhstan. A *continental climate* is typical for an interior of a large landmass, such as Central Asia. Such regions usually experience hot summers and cold winters, being far away from the moderating influence of the ocean. A *climate zone* refers to a region characterized by a certain average temperature, rainfall, and dryness. A *subtropical climate* is typically a middle-temperature region with moderately dry summers and very wet, overcast winters.
8. For more information about oil reserves in the region see: Country Analysis Brief: Caspian Sea Region at www.eia.doe.gov.
9. Bernard A. Geg, CRS Report for Congress, April 9, 2002, Caspian Oil and Gas: Production and Prospects.

10. The Caspian Pipeline Consortium project (CPC), connects Kazakhstan's Caspian Sea area oil production fields with Russia's Black Sea oil tankers port of Novorossiysk, and then by tankers with the world markets.

11. R. N. Frye, "Zoroastrier in der islamischen Zeit" *Der Islam* (Berlin 1965) p. 41; idem, "The History of Ancient Iran" (1958); idem, *The Heritage of Persia* (1963).

12. Gavin Hambly, ed., *Central Asia* (London, 1969). First English Edition.

13. Gelene Carre d'Encaussee, *Decline of an Empire: The Soviet Socialist Republics in Revolt* (NY, 1979); Paul B. Henze, "Marx on Russians and Muslims," *Central Asian Survey* Vol. 6, No. 4, 1987.

14. Mary Boyce, "Zoroastrians: Their Religious Beliefs and Practices" (1984); idem, *A History of Zoroastrianism* (1975–1991): 3 Vols. (Vol. 3 with Franz Grenet).

15. For more information on the religious composition of the countries in the region see: Library of Congress Country Studies at lcweb2.loc.gov.

16. Kasgarli Mahmuc, Kitab Diwan Lugat at Turk. Completed ca. A.D. 1074/1077. Editio Princeps by Kilisli Rifat (3 Vols.) (Istanbul, 1917–19). English translation by R. Dankoff with J. Kelly as Compendium of Turkic Dialects (3 Vols.) (Cambridge, MA, 1982–84).

17. Beatrice Forbes Manz, *The Rise and Rule of Tamerlane* (Cambridge University Press, 1989).

18. *Tourism* No.1 (2, 2001) pp. 26–27.

19. An unsettled lifestyle of a tribe or nation is known as *nomadism*; this term implies a constant movement from one territory to another. Without a domestication technology, people must follow their food supply. Such a lifestyle is in direct contrast with a *sedentary lifestyle* where people are living in permanent or semi permanent settlements. People within this lifestyle commonly have well-developed agricultural technology.

20. "Z. V. Togan: On the Origins of the Kazakhs and the Ozbeks," H. B. Paksoy, ed. *Central Asia Reader* (New York: M. E. Sharpe, 1994).

21. George J. Demko, "The Russian Colonization of Kazakhstan 1896–1916," *University Uralic-Altaic Series Vol. 99* (Bloomington, Indiana 1969). Soviets also made land demands on other nationalities, and took land by military force, including in the Baltic region.

22. A. Lamb. *The Sino-Indian and Sino-Russian Borders: Some Comparisons and Contrasts/ Studies in the Social History of China and South-East Asia* (Cambridge, 1970) pp. 135–152; Wieczynski, J. L. "The Russian Frontier," *The impact of borderlands upon the course of early Russian history.* (Charlottesville: Univ. Press of Virginia, 1976).

23. "The Basmachi (Turkistan National Liberation Movement)," *Modern Encyclopedia of Religions in Russia and Soviet Union,* Vol. IV (Academic International Press, 1991), pp. 5–20; Idem; "Zeki Belidi Togan's Account: The Basmachi Movement from Within," H. B. Paksoy, ed.; *Central Asia Reader* (New York: M. E. Sharpe, 1994). The term *Basmachi* was used as a derogatory reference toward the Turkestan national liberation movement against Soviet annexation of Central Asia between 1920 and 1930.

24. R. L. Cansfield, "Soviet Gambit in Central Asia," *Journal of South Asian and Middle Eastern Studies* Vol. 5, No. 1.

25. Anvar Boboev, "Dobrije Namerenia Dadut Dobrie Vskhodi" newspaper "Delovoj Partner Uzbekistana," June 5, 2003, No. 24, p. 481.

26. R. Grankin, "Saparmurad Niyazov (Turkmenbashi)," Secretniye Materiali 20 Veka, No. 12 (114), June 2003, International newspaper.

27. The *khan* title, which refers to the supreme leader, has been used throughout history in traditional Kyrgyz society.

28. Fred J. Hill and Andrew Wad. "Kyrgyzstan," *Nations of the World: A Political, Economic and Business Handbook,* 4th ed. (Grey House Publishing, September 2003) p. 812.

29. Idinov Narynber, "Kyrgyzstan: Politicians Wrangle Over Gold Production," RFE/RL 6-02-1998.

30. James Critchlow, "Corruption, Nationalism and the Native Elites in Soviet Central Asia," *The Journal of Communist Studies*, (Vol. 4, No. 2, 1988).

31. A. Turchinov, "Tenevaya Economika i Tenevaya Politika," *Demoni Mira I Bogi Voini.* Cotsialnije konflikti v Postkommunisticheskom Mire, (Kiev, Politichna Dumka, 1997).

32. Timirbayev Viacheslav, *"Sprut po Imeni Korruptsija,"* (Vecherniy Bishkek, 11.19.1999); Grigory Shulgin "Akayev," Secretnye Versii, No. 7, July 2003, pg. 11, Kyiv, Ukraine.

33. The term *nomenclatura* refers to a system of relationships in the former Soviet Union under which appointees of the high level of the government or Communist party were rotated within the highest level of the system. It is a reflection of the corrupted form of bureaucracy of the former USSR.

34. James Critchlow, "Corruption, Nationalism and the Native Elites in Soviet Central Asia," *The Journal of Communist Studies*, (Vol. 4, No. 2, 1988).

35. A kinship group whose members are believed to be descended from a common ancestor far enough in the past that they cannot trace their specific genealogical ties to one another is known as a *clan.* Clan members can usually trace their ancestry up to seven generations down.

36. V. E. Hanyn. "Conflicts in Kyrgyzstan." *The Word of Kyrgyzstan* (Bishkek), July 15, 1995.

37. "Order Sought in Kyrgyzstan," *The Dallas Morning News*, 26 March 2005.

38. "Landscape win for New Kyrgyz Leader," *Institute for War and Peace Reporting*, 26 August 2005. Accessed from www.iwpr.net.

39. Ibid.

40. "Manas International Airport, Ganci Airbase, Bishkek, Kyrgyzstan," 8 June 2004. Accessed from www.globalsecurity.org.

41. R. Orudzhev, "Armiane Oskorbliaut Genseka Soveta Evropi," *Ekho Plus*, 23 July 2005.

42. Elina Karakulova, "Prirodoohrannie NPO v Kazahstane Okazivaut Vsio Bolshee Vlijanie na Politileu, vcura sianez," *Kazakhstan Daily Digest*, 20 August 2003. www.eurasianet.org.

43. Ibid.

44. "Kazahkstan: Dyke project to save part of the Aral Sea," IRINews Asia, 20 August 2003. www.centralasiadaily.com.

45. "The Caspian Sea Level Changes and Its Influence on the Seismicity of the Western Turkmenia," *Inducing of Earthquakes by Underground Nuclear Explosions: Environmental and Ecological Problems.* (Russia, Moscow, 1994) p. 69; "A possibility of seismic activity induction by technogenic processes in Kara Bogas-Gol gulf," "Earthquakes Induced by Underground Nuclear Explosions," *Environmental and Ecological Problems, NATO ASI Series.* (Spring, 1995) pp. 383–390.

46. Ina Lankulova. "Kazakn Senator Seeks Compensation for Nuclear-Test Victims," *Kazakhstan Daily Digest*, 20 August 2003. www.eurasianet.org.

47. A traditional type of an open market in Asian societies is called a *bazaar.* It is known for its art of bargaining; it is very noisy and highly entertaining.

48. Nuria R. Ismagilova "Women in Mind: Educational Needs of Women in Central Asia General Rocorn-Ureudations and Strategies for Development, Khujand, Tajikistan," 1 February 2001. Accessed from www.mtnforum.org.

49. Press Release: Justin Burke, "Women Likely to Suffer Most in Central Asia's Turmoil." *Women's News*, 7 October 2003. Accessed from Lexis-Nexis Academic database.

50. Central Asia: 10M welcomes U.S. counter-trafficking assistance. 7 December 2003, UN Office for the Coordination of Humanitarian Affairs. Accessed from www. IRINnews.org.

51. "HIV/AIDS rates among women," 16 September 2003, Bishkek-accessed from OCHA IRIN database.

52. Aitkul Sawakova, "Women's Role in the Central Asia"-International Conference, Almaty, 2 September 2003. Accessed from news.caspianworld.com.

53. Frederick H. Hartmann, *The Relations of Nations*, 5th ed. (New York: Macmillan Publishing Company, 1978) p. 331.

54. Rouhollah Ramazani, *The Northern Tier: Afghanistan, Iran, and Turkey* (New York: D. Van Nostrand Co., Inc., 1966) p. 50.

55. "Seeing the World Anew," *The Economist* (London), 27 October 2001, U.S. Edition Special Report Section.

56. Press Release: Embassy of Afghanistan, "Embassy Hosts Afghanistan: Open for Business," 26 May 2004. Accessed from www.embassyofafghanistan.org.

57. Ramazani, op. cit., p. 50.

58. *Bhurkas* are the traditional dress style of women in some Islamic countries; it covers women's faces completely with a mesh fabric at the eye level for visibility and air circulation.

59. Quoted by Valerie Pakenham, *Out in the Noonday Sun: Edwardians in the Tropics*, (New York: Random House, 1985) p. 194.

For Further Reading

Bransten, Jeremy. "Kyrgyzstan: A Democracy Only for the Rich." RFE/RL, 14-10-1997.

Brydon, Diana. "Commonwealth or Common Poverty?" *Kunapipi: Special Issue on Post-Colonial Criticism*: 11-1 (1989).

Hovoself, Erlend. "Tribalism and Modernity in Kirgizia," Sabour and Biktor (eds.) *Ethnic Encounter and Culture Change* (Bergen London: 1997) p. 100.

Huskey, Eugene. "Between Democracy and Authoritarianism: Askar Akayev." Paper, Presented at the ASN 4th Annual Convention. (Columbia University, 1999). 15–17 April.

Idinov, Narynber. "*Kyrgyzstan: Politicians Wrangle over Gold Production.*" RFE/RL, 6-02-1998.

Johnson-Odim, Cheryl. "Common Themes, Different Contexts: Third World Women and Feminism," *Third World Women and the Politics of Feminism*, Bloomington and Indianapolis: Indiana University Press, 1991.

Kostyukova, Irina. "The Towns of Kyrgyzstan Change Their Faces: Rural-Urban Migrante in Bishkek," *Central Asian Survey* V. 13 No. 3 (September, 1994) p. 428.

Mederoy, Sultan. "Analyses of Privatization in Kyrgyz Republic, Its Main Result and Further Strategies," *Journal of Economic Cooperation Among Islamic Countries* V. 18 No. 1–2 (1997) p. 35.

Murzalin, Ahanbolat. "Central Asia: Are There Limits to Authoritarian Development?" *The Times of Central Asia*. V. 2 No. 23(66). 8-06-2000.

Osmanalieva, Raya. "Tribalism in Kyrgys Society," *Central Asia Moniter* (1999) No. 5, p. 10–11.

Pryde, Iam. "Kyrgyzstan: Secularism vs. Islam," *The World Today* V. 48 No.11 (November 1992) p. 208.

Sangari, Kumkum. "The Politics of the Possible," *The Nature and Context of Minority Discourse*. Abdul Jan Mohammed and David Lloyd. New York: Oxford UP, 1990.

The Times of Central Asia Thursday, 23-03-2000.

Conclusion
WHAT WE HAVE TRIED TO TELL IN THIS EDITION

Dianne Long and Joseph Weatherby

The Other World is a place of dynamic change. Change is multifaceted: it can be simple or complex, positive or negative, of short- or long-term consequences. Change is welcomed by some, opposed by others, can be anticipated or unforeseen, or be a combination of all of these factors.

Political geographers argue that the international system will soon undergo the most profound change since the modern state system was created. The number of recognized states may even double within the next quarter century. These changes will be the result of trends that are already observable in the Other World. New states are being created as the last colonies become independent. Others are being established as nations break away from already existing states to form additional entities. Finally, new states are also evolving out of the turmoil resulting from both the collapse of the Soviet Union and the end of the cold war. Geographer George Demko succinctly described this process when he observed, that the changes in the political and economic geography of the world today are as significant as what the world went through after the Treaty of Westphalia.

Twentieth-century conflicts were largely fought by nation states over ideologies. Many analysts believe that disputes in the early twenty-first century will focus on the struggles for clean air, water, and energy. These struggles will become part of more fundamental clashes of civilizations. As early as in 1993, Samuel Huntington identified this process by pointing out that civilization identity will be increasingly important in the future, and that the world will be shaped in large measure by the interactions among seven or eight major civilizations. In comments made in 2004 to the National Center for Policy Analysis, Her Majesty Queen Noor of Jordan described this conflict in a different way. She pointed out that rather than a clash of civilizations the real problem was for the moderates in each culture to defend these civilizations against the growth of extremism and fanaticism. Regardless of which point of view is correct, it is likely that the most important conflicts of the future will occur along the cultural fault lines separating these civilizations from one another. Geographically, most cultural/religious fault lines will involve parts of the Other World.

This textbook focuses on the process of change in the Other World. As used here, the term *Other World* has a broader meaning than the more commonly used expression *Third World*. The Other World includes both underdeveloped and developed states that because of geography, history, or culture have similar interests and perceptions.

Poverty is a breeding ground for extremism and conflict regardless of geographic location. Poverty is an everyday issue for one-fifth of the world's people. They live with no more than a dollar a day on average, little food, or clean water.

Disease is easily spread through contaminated water and open sewers. For many, plumbing and irrigation do not exist. Diet is poor and agriculture inefficient. Good schooling, which could make long term improvements, is often nonexistent. HIV/AIDS is raging in many poor areas. One can trace the spread of this disease by following the trucking routes that extend out from the cities of the Other World.

War, ethnic conflict, government corruption, and pollution cut short the lives of many. Of every 10 people in the Other World, eight have substandard housing, seven are illiterate, and five suffer malnutrition. Governments fail to provide even the most basic services for residents. All too often scarce revenues are spent supporting the elites of these societies and their instruments of power. The gap between the rich and poor continues to widen.

Political instability and economic stability are linked. Ethnic and regional conflicts go hand-in-hand with clan strife and banditry. Refugees flee their homes in search of safe havens in the cities, which increases the pressure on what are already inadequate resources there. The result is that these refugees often end up in refugee camps which are the flashpoints of unrest. Unable to compete successfully for jobs, many descend into degradation, prostitution, and crime. They prove ready recruits for extremist elements in the Other World.

Many of today's struggles are rooted in who will control precious resources such as land, water, and minerals. Peacemaking is difficult as old grudges and injustices leave their scars. Individual states continue to intervene in the Other World to settle disagreements. Old institutions created to resolve these problems are evolving as new members from the Other World demand to be heard. In order to reach an acceptable level of security, new policies need to be developed to address new problems such as the proliferation of weapons of mass destruction, along with the old problems of poverty, hunger, and disease.

Finally, the reader should recognize that all people make assessments of others that are based on their own cultural biases. For example, we know that a person's color is not a behavioral or cultural characteristic. Nevertheless, because most of the people in the Other World have dark skin and problems of poverty, hunger, and disease, and most of the people in the developed world have white skin, cultural and behavioral stereotypes are common. People in the developed world often assume that darker skin is a symbol of backwardness. At the same time, the colonial experience has caused people in the Other World to view white skin as the representation of evil exploitation. If we are to make any headway in understanding others, we must attempt to avoid such stereotypes.

It is not necessary to be Western in order to be modern. For over a hundred years, Western cultural imperialism has conditioned us to assume that westernization and modernization are the same, however, they are not, as any person on the streets of Jeddah, Hong Kong, or Seoul can point out. To understand the process of change that is taking place in the Other World, the reader must accept this fundamental fact.

The breadth of subjects covered in these chapters has required us to make generalizations, although we have attempted to be specific where possible. At the same time, we hope that we have provided the reader with a useful introduction to the major issues facing the peoples of the Other World.

Index